# The Byzantine Apocalyptic Tradition

# The Byzantine Apocalyptic Tradition

Paul J. Alexander
EDITED WITH AN INTRODUCTION BY
DOROTHY deF. ABRAHAMSE

UNIVERSITY OF CALIFORNIA PRESS
Berkeley • Los Angeles • London

University of California Press
Berkeley and Los Angeles, California
University of California Press, Ltd.
London, England
© 1985 by
The Regents of the University of California

1 2 3 4 5 6 7 8 9

Library of Congress Cataloging in Publication Data

Alexander, Paul Julius, 1910–1977
   The Byzantine apocalyptic tradition.

   Includes bibliographical references.
   1. Apocalyptic literature.  2. Christian literature,
Byzantine.  I. Abrahamse, Dorothy deF.  II. Title.
BS646.A43 1984     270.3     82-23816
ISBN 0-520-04998-5

# Contents

List of Abbreviations     vii
Introduction by Dorothy deF. Abrahamse     1

PART ONE. TEXTS

I. The Syriac Apocalypse of Pseudo-Methodius     13
    Appendix 1: Three Lists of Regions (Peoples) Overrun by the Arabs in the Syriac Text of Pseudo-Methodius     34
    Appendix 2: Translation of the Syriac Text of Pseudo-Methodius from Cod. Vat. Syr. 58     36

II. The First Greek Redaction of Pseudo-Methodius     52

III. The *Visions of Daniel*: Extant Texts     61
    1. The *Slavonic Daniel*     62
       Appendix: English Translation of *Slavonic Daniel*     65
    2. Pseudo-Chrysostom     72
    3. *Daniel Καὶ ἔσται*     77

IV. *Visions of Daniel* Summarized by Liudprand of Cremona     96

V. Three Conglomerate Texts     123
    1. The *Apocalypse of St. Andrew the Fool*     123
    2. The *Cento of the True Emperor* ("Anonymous Paraphrase of the *Oracles of Leo*")     130

3. Pseudo-Ephraem     136
    Appendix: Syriac Original of Pseudo-Ephraem     142

PART TWO. THEMES

I. The Last Roman Emperor     151
II. Gog and Magog     185
III. The Legend of the Antichrist     193

Index     227

# List of Abbreviations

BHG         F. Halkin, *Bibliotheca Hagiographica Graeca.* 3 vols. 3rd ed. Subsidia Hagiographica, 8a–c. Brussels, 1957.
BZ          *Byzantinische Zeitschrift.* Leipzig, 1892–.
CMH         *Cambridge Medieval History.* Cambridge, England, 1913–. Vol. IV, 1966.
CSHB        *Corpus Scriptorum Historiae Byzantinae.* Bonn, 1828–97.
GCS         *Die griechischen christlichen Schriftsteller der ersten drei Jahrhunderte.* Leipzig, 1897–.
MGH         *Monumenta Germaniae Historica.* Hanover and Berlin, 1826–.
PG          J. P. Migne, *Patrologiae Cursus Completus: Series Graeco-Latina.* Paris, 1857–66.
*Thesaurus Syriacus*   R. Payne Smith, *Thesaurus Syriacus.* London, 1901.

# Introduction
by Dorothy deF. Abrahamse

Throughout Christian history, apocalyptic visions of the approaching end of time have provided a persistent and enigmatic theme for history and prophecy. The world of early Christianity and late Judaism, as recent scholars have emphasized, was permeated with the expectation of an imminent Messianic drama; the Old and New Testaments, as well as numerous extra-canonical works, testify to the pervasive belief that God was about to end the known political order.[1] Through prophetic visions the believer might be prepared to recognize the signs of the impending eschatological drama in wars, famines, invasions, and other extraordinary political events. And although the immediacy of Messianic expectation receded, it left its mark in a tradition of prophetic writing that has surfaced again and again in times of tension and adversity.

By medieval times the belief in an imminent apocalypse had officially been relegated to the role of symbolic theory by the Church; as early as the fourth century, Augustine had declared that the Revelation of John was to be interpreted symbolically rather than literally, and for most of the Middle Ages Church councils and theologians considered only abstract eschatology to be acceptable speculation.[2] Since the nineteenth century, however, historians have recognized that literal apocalypses did continue to circulate in the medieval world and that they played a fundamental role in the creation of important strains of thought and leg-

---

1. For a survey of recent work, see *Journal for Theology and the Church*, vol. 6, "Apocalypticism," ed. Robert W. Funk, (1969); *Interpretation* 25, 4 (1972) (special issue devoted to apocalyptic); and Bernard McGinn, "Apocalypticism in the Middle Ages; An Historiographical Sketch," *Medieval Studies* 37 (1975), pp. 252–86.
2. Paul Alexander, "The Medieval Legend of the Last Roman Emperor and Its Messianic Origin," *Journal of the Warburg and Courtauld Institutes*, 41 (1978), p. 13.

end. German historians discovered in apocalyptic literature the source for legends of the Antichrist, Gog and Magog, and (of particular interest for their times) the legend of a Roman Empire that would last to the end of time.[3] More recently, scholars have seen in chiliasm the impetus for popular religious and political movements of the Middle Ages, and the existence of a strain of prophetic thought in the works of Joachim of Fiore and his circle has received new understanding and appreciation.[4] There can now be no doubt of the continuing importance of the eschatological tradition in medieval life and thought.

One important contribution of early studies of the legends of the Last Roman Emperor was the discovery that the idea was neither developed from general oral tradition nor taken directly from biblical themes, but came to the West from pseudonymous prophecies circulating in the Byzantine world. As early as 1877, Gerhard von Zezschwitz announced that the earliest Western treatise on the end of time containing the figure of the Last Roman Emperor (the tenth-century Burgundian abbot Adso's *Libellus de ortu et tempore Antichristi*) was based on a Byzantine apocalypse.[5] In a continuing debate over the contemporary significance of medieval emperor legends, other scholars at the end of the last century established the outlines of a medieval apocalyptic literary genre derived from ancient texts and lasting to the late Middle Ages, with versions surviving in many of the languages of Christendom. From the editions produced by German and Russian scholars it became clear that a body of Byzantine prophetic literature, created and revised within the confines of a strict form, had served as a continual bridge between ancient eschatology and the medieval Western world.[6]

The basis of the tradition, as shown in the important studies of Ernst Sackur, Wilhelm Bousset, and V. M. Istrin, was a group of prophecies written pseudonymously in the name of Church Fathers or biblical fig-

---

3. Paul Alexander, "Byzantium and the Migration of Literary Works and Motifs: The Legend of the Last Roman Emperor," *Medievalia et Humanistica* n.s. 2 (Cleveland/London, 1971), pp. 47–68. Pages 49–54 describe the growth of German historical interest in the legend.

4. Norman Cohn, *Pursuit of the Millennium* (London, 1959), and review by M. Reeves in *Medium Aevum* 28 (1959), pp. 225–29; Cohn, "Medieval Millenarism: Its Bearing on the Comparative Study of Millenarian Movements," in *Millennial Dreams in Action*, ed. S. L. Thrupp (The Hague, 1962), pp. 31–43. Marjorie Reeves has produced a standard new account of Joachim of Fiore and his influence: see *The Influence of Prophecy in the Later Middle Ages: A Study in Joachism* (Oxford, 1969). A cooperative volume in honor of Marjorie Reeves, entitled *Prophecy and Millenarianism*, (London, 1980) includes an article by Professor Alexander on "The Diffusion of Medieval Apocalypses in the West and the Beginnings of Joachimism," pp. 53–106.

5. Alexander, "Migration," pp. 52–53.

6. Alexander, "Migration," p. 54.

ures, copied and reedited time and again to respond to the urgency of new historical circumstances.[7] Long before the tenth century, the form had developed distinctive themes and characters. Divided into sections of "historical" and "prophetic" events, its composition was marked by the author's use of the technique of *vaticinium ex eventu*—an historical event turned into prophecy. An apocalypse thus typically began with a series of historical facts (the reigns of emperors, dynastic alliances, wars) put into the mouth of a prophet, and continued more vaguely to announce eschatological events at the end of time. The transition from history to prophecy is frequently transparent, and can serve as a guide to the time and place of composition.[8] In the early Middle Ages, prophetic works circulated in several successive guises. Sackur established that a medieval Latin prophecy attributed to the Tiburtine Sibyl was an interpolation of a late Roman text, composed as a Christian formulation of the pagan Sibylline oracle.[9] In 1967, Professor Alexander published an edition of a Greek version of the Tiburtine Sibyl whose composition he was able to place in the reign of Anastasius in the region of Heliopolis-Baalbek in Syria. He proposed that both texts derived from a lost Greek original of the late fourth century; these (and presumably other) versions must have been popular in the empire between the fifth and seventh centuries.[10]

In the seventh century, Sibylline prophecies were eclipsed by a new apocalyptic composition attributed to one Bishop Methodius of Patara in Lycia. Greek and Latin texts of this prophecy were published by Istrin and Sackur, who recognized its importance as a new composition which was to dominate the genre throughout the early Middle Ages, but were unable to agree on its origin.[11] In 1931 a Hungarian Orientalist, Michael Kmosko, argued that the work was originally composed in Syriac, and that a manuscript in the Vatican (Cod. Vat. Syr. 58) represented the earliest text of the work.[12] Sometime in the ninth century the litera-

---

7. Ernst Sackur, *Sibyllinische Texte und Forschungen* (Halle a.d.S., 1898; reprint Torino, 1963). Wilhelm Bousset, *Der Antichrist in der Überlieferung des Judentums, des Neuen Testaments und der alten Kirche: Ein Beitrag zur Auslegung der Apokalypse* (Göttingen, 1895); V. M. Istrin, *Otkrovenie Mefodiia Patarskago i Apokrificheskiia Videniia Daniila v Vizantiiskoi i Slaviano-Russkoi Literaturakh*, in Chteniia v Imperatorskom Obshchestvie Istorii i Drevnostei Rossiiskikh pri Moskovskom Universitete 181 and 183 (Moscow, 1897).

8. Paul Alexander, "Medieval Apocalypses as Historical Sources," *American Historical Review* 73 (1968), pp. 998–1000.

9. Sackur, *Sibyllinische Texte*, p. 162.

10. Paul Alexander, *The Oracle of Baalbek: The Tiburtine Sibyl in Greek Dress*, Dumbarton Oaks Studies 10 (Washington, D.C., 1967), pp. 41–65.

11. Sackur, *Sibyllinische Texte*, pp. 53–55.

12. Michael Kmosko, "Das Rätsel des Pseudo-Methodius," *Byzantion* 6 (1931), pp. 273–96.

ture underwent another, less dramatic change, and abbreviated and interpolated versions of Pseudo-Methodius appeared as *Visions of Daniel*. It was in this form that the apocalypse must have reached Adso in tenth-century Burgundy.[13] Surviving manuscripts of these works testify to a continuous and copious tradition of prophecy, but extant texts do not tell the whole story. Apocalypses were often summarized and incorporated into other sources for various reasons, sometimes in enough detail to provide clear evidence for the development of prophetic themes and ideas. Thus, the tenth-century emissary Liudprand of Cremona's account of his stay in Constantinople includes a detailed discussion of prophetic books shown to him by a Byzantine circle, and among the "edifying subjects" discussed in an encyclopedic saint's life, the *Life of St. Andrew the Fool*, was the approach of the end of time.[14] Finally, disparate writings which have survived as attributions to early authors appear to be pastiches of other pieces of prophecy; for this reason they have been difficult to date or use.

The sum of this evidence is a body of material of crucial importance in the creation and transmission of eschatological ideas for later ages. The figure of the Antichrist, which was to play such an important role in later Western speculation, was already present in the Revelation of John, but in these Byzantine prophecies he acquired an elaborate history and personality. Moreover, his appearance had come to be preceded by a detailed drama peopled by new characters: wars and invasions, in the Byzantine tradition, were to be brought to an end by the rise of a Last Roman Emperor, who would arise from sleep to defeat enemies and initiate an era of peace and rejoicing. In his time, however, the "unclean nations" of Gog and Magog, imprisoned by Alexander the Great behind the Gates of the North, would be loosed to commit abominations on the Christians. Then the Antichrist would be revealed: the Last Emperor would return to Jerusalem to lay his crown on Golgotha, return the empire to God, and so set the stage for the rule of the Antichrist and the return of Christ.[15] The significance of these themes for later Western history has been a subject of such interest that it is surprising to discover that their origins and development in Byzantine literature remain obscure. Where did the vision of a Roman Empire lasting to the end of time, and a Last Roman Emperor who would lay down his crown on Golgotha, come from? How were the nations of Gog and Magog, known in biblical tradition, united with the Alexander legend?

13. See below, Chapter IV, "*Visions of Daniel* Summarized by Liudprand."
14. See below, Chapter V.1, "The *Apocalypse of St. Andrew the Fool*."
15. Alexander, "Migration," pp. 54–55.

Introduction [ 5

How did Byzantine legend develop details of the career of Antichrist—his life history, association with the Jews, ability to change shape, and conflict with Enoch and Elijah, "Sons of Thunder" and "last comforters of mankind"? The explanation for these and the many other puzzling features of the apocalyptic tradition in the East clearly depends on a thorough understanding of the Byzantine textual tradition, its sources, and the way it was transmitted to the West, but in spite of new manuscript discoveries and important advances in all areas of Byzantine studies, prophecy has received no comprehensive treatment since the days of Sackur and Istrin. Thus, the appearance of a new study of Byzantine apocalypses promised to be of major importance for Byzantinists and Western medievalists alike.

For more than fifteen years prior to his death in 1977, Paul Alexander devoted his energies to the elucidation of the origins, development, and diffusion of Byzantine apocalypses between the fourth and eleventh centuries. His work resulted in the publication of numerous preliminary studies on individual texts and their historical significance.[16] Unfortunately, he was not able to complete the major monograph to which they pointed. Many sections of the work had been drafted, and although the author certainly intended to revise them into a unified text, the studies even as they stand represent important contributions to the clarification of an exceptionally difficult tradition. From the outline and preliminary reports completed by Professor Alexander, it is evident that he had intended to divide his work into three sections, tentatively entitled Principal Texts, Events, and Themes. The first portion, on the principal texts, had been completed in draft form. Studies of three ideas had been drafted for the third part: the Last Roman Emperor, Gog and Magog, and the Antichrist. Here, although the author had carried out an analysis of textual similarities and thematic development of the tradition, the treatment of origins remained uncompleted. Professor Alexander's ideas on the relationship between the Byzantine apocalyptic tradition and Late

16. Six of these studies were included in a Variorum collection entitled *Religious and Political History and Thought in the Byzantine Empire* (London, 1978). These articles are: "Psevdo-Mefodii i Etiopiya" (Pseudo-Methodius and Ethiopia), *Antichnaya Drevnost i Srednie Veka*, Sbornik 10 (Sverdlovsk, 1973), pp. 21–27; "Byzantium and the Migration of Literary Works and Motifs: The Legend of the Last Roman Emperor"; "Medieval Apocalypses as Historical Sources"; "Les Débuts des conquêtes arabes en Sicile et la tradition apocalyptique byzantino-slave," *Bollettino del Centro di Studi Filologici e Linguistici Siciliani* 12 (Palermo, 1973), pp. 7–35; "Historiens byzantins et croyances eschatologiques," *Actes du XIIᵉ Congrès International des Etudes Byzantines* 2 (Beograd, 1964), pp. 1–8; "Historical Interpolations in the *Zbornik Popa Dragolia*," *Actes du XIVᵉ Congrès International des Etudes Byzantines, Bucarest, 6–12 September 1971*, 3 (Bucarest, 1976), pp. 23–38. Subsequently two studies, "The Medieval Legend of the Last Roman Emperor," and "The Diffusion of Medieval Apocalypses in the West," have appeared.

Jewish eschatology were still developing; he showed in the section on the Last Roman Emperor included here, as well as in an article which appeared only after his death, how much the theme and description had grown out of Jewish apocalyptic material.[17] In the sections on the Antichrist and Gog and Magog, the question of extra-canonical sources had not yet been fully treated, and it seems clear that the author intended to extend his work in the light of these relationships. The studies as they stand, however, offer an extensive and valuable treatment of the thematic development and variations on apocalyptic ideas through six centuries of Byzantine eschatology.

The final part of the work—the analysis of the historical evidence of Byzantine prophecies—remained unwritten at Professor Alexander's death. In two important articles he had demonstrated the possibilities of the material through a study of the evidence of one of the richest of these works—the *Slavonic Daniel* and its interpolations—for the Arab invasions of Sicily and an eleventh-century Bulgarian rebellion.[18] He had also described the careful methodology that must be applied to apocalyptic texts before they can be used as historical evidence.[19] Here, particularly, we must regret that the project could not be carried to completion, for the exposition of the connection between ideas and historical events was one of the most characteristic and profound features of all of Paul Alexander's work.

One of the author's most important contributions to the clarification of the Byzantine apocalyptic tradition was the establishment of the priority of the Syriac Pseudo-Methodius, as suggested by Kmosko, as the source of the composition, and the explication of its date and provenance. The Syriac text of this work is contained in a single manuscript of the sixteenth century; as a part of the study, Professor Alexander had prepared a transcription of the text and a translation. Because of the unavailability of the text, his translation is included here as an appendix to the study of the Syriac Pseudo-Methodius in Chapter I; it is hoped that the text and translation may eventually be published together.

All of the textual studies presented here are united by a methodology described by the author in his paper on "Medieval Apocalypses as Historical Sources."[20] Using a combination of historical and philological detection, Professor Alexander attempted to establish the time, place,

---

17. "The Medieval Legend of the Last Roman Emperor," pp. 6–9.
18. See "Les Débuts des conquêtes arabes" and "Historical Interpolations in the *Zbornik Popa Dragolia*."
19. "Medieval Apocalypses as Historical Sources."
20. See note 8 above.

and circumstances of composition for each of the major surviving texts. In spite of the problems posed by sources that habitually changed names and dates, deliberately obscured identities, and required revision each time they were copied, these textual studies offer evidence of a surprisingly detailed tradition, which will be outlined here. The author proposes that the Syriac Pseudo-Methodius, which should be considered the starting point of medieval prophecy, was the product of a mid-seventh-century cleric in the region of Singara in northern Mesopotamia, whose writing reflects the immediate impact of the Arab invasions. The work argued that the Byzantine Empire, rather than Ethiopia as "some" thought, would be the eschatological savior for the captive Christians. Sometime before 800, the First Greek Redaction was produced by a cleric who substituted Greek texts for the biblical quotations from the Syriac Pešitta, omitted or deemphasized features of Syrian topography, and removed unflattering references to the clergy. More specific circumstances can be derived from the next version, the *Visions of Daniel*, in which the prophetic sections of Pseudo-Methodius were expanded to reflect the eschatological significance of later invasions. The *Slavonic Daniel* is shown to be a translation from a Greek original, probably composed in Sicily between 821 and 829; a second text, identified here as Pseudo-Chrysostom, is proposed as a response to an Arab attack on Attalia in Pamphylia in 842. Finally, the author argues that a third version, called here *Daniel Καὶ ἔσται*, is an apologetic for Basil I, described as the "New Phinehas" soon after his murder of Michael III. This last version was composed of fragments of eighth- and ninth-century prophecies written in Italy and Sicily. Two other texts—Pseudo-Ephraem and the *Cento (Oracles of Leo the Wise)*—are pastiches of existing works whose composition is of uncertain date.

Finally, these studies examine three tenth-century reports of apocalyptic texts. Liudprand of Cremona's arguments with Byzantine scholars over the meaning of their prophetic books have long been favorite *exempla* for the misunderstanding of East and West. But, Professor Alexander proposes here, Liudprand's description is circumstantial enough that two separate apocalypses can be identified. The first, called a *Vision of Daniel* in the text, was an Eastern prophecy that must have been compiled in the reign of Nicephorus Phocas (963–968). Liudprand recounts in more detail the contents of a second oracle, which he ascribes to "Hippolytus, bishop of Sicily," and which predicted that a Western, rather than Byzantine, ruler would fulfill the apocalyptic role of Last Emperor. In this chapter, the author suggests that a Latin translation of Pseudo-Hippolytus was the source of Adso's eschatological comfort for the Western emperors in a year close to 954. The oracle, in that case, must have been written in Italy. The most likely candidate for the promised emperor, Professor Alexander believes, is the Frankish emperor Louis II (840–875), who led a counteroffensive against the Moslems in southern Italy between 855 and 871 and planned a large-scale liberation of Sicily. The Byzantine adherents of this literature were almost certainly a circle of opponents of the usurper Nicephorus Phocas. The last of the texts analyzed here is a section of the tenth-century *Life of St. Andrew the Fool*, which the author characterizes as part of an encyclopedic work of edification. Although the prophetic portion of the *vita* has many unusual features, its most striking characteristic is the author's deliberate historicism, as he attempted to create a work set in the fifth-century reign of the emperor Leo I.

Even without the synthesis Professor Alexander would have included, a richly detailed tradition emerges from these studies. Byzantine apocalypses were indeed written for consolation in times of trouble, and they reflected the hopes and despairs of contemporaries in very concrete historical events.[21] The localization of these texts shows how often apocalyptic hopes arose in the fringes of Byzantine society, where the threats of invasion were greatest, and in response to events whose importance has long since receded out of historical memory. As they were transmitted from one portion of the empire to another, and translated from language to language, themes developed in response to immediate concerns and localities or out of a simple misunderstanding of the text. With all its unlikely sources, however, perhaps the main impression of the Byzantine apocalyptic tradition, as it is uncovered by the author, is the extent to which it remained a concrete and creative source for the expression of political and religious thought throughout the early medieval world.

It has seemed important to the editor to make Professor Alexander's research available in a form as unaltered from the original as possible. Thus, his work is published here as *The Byzantine Apocalyptic Tradition* with little editorial comment. Where new editions have appeared, or where important works were later noted by the author, additions to his footnotes have been included in brackets. In one or two instances Professor Alexander had changed his mind on the details of some arguments. Here I have noted his explanation for the change and the implications for the subsequent argument in the footnotes.

The editor and Mrs. Alexander gratefully acknowledge the support

21. "Medieval Apocalypses as Historical Sources," pp. 1005–1007.

that enabled Professor Alexander to devote substantial periods of time to his research. In 1970–1971 and again in 1974–1975, while on sabbatical leave, he received fellowship grants from the Humanities Research Committee of the University of California, Berkeley. In 1970–1971 he enjoyed the hospitality of the Institute for Advanced Studies in Princeton. In 1974–1975 he was awarded a Senior Fellowship by the National Endowment for the Humanities.

I would like to thank Leif Eric Trondsen of California State University, Long Beach, Peter Brown of the University of California and John Hayes of UCLA for assistance with the Greek and Syriac texts. My debt to Jane-Ellen Long and Paul Psoinos of the University of California Press goes beyond the customary acknowledgments to an author's editors. This book could not have been finished without the help of Paul Alexander's former students and colleagues at Berkeley. I am particularly grateful to Michael Maas, now of Dartmouth, for his advice on the initial organization of the manuscript, and to Barbara and Robert Rodgers, now at the University of Vermont, who retyped much of the manuscript and transcribed the Syriac references. Above all, it was the advice and encouragement of Robert Brentano and Thomas Bisson of the History Department of the University of California at Berkeley that made the completion of this project possible, and I would like to express my thanks to them here.

PART ONE
# Texts

# I.
# The Syriac Apocalypse of Pseudo-Methodius

The document to be discussed in this chapter was, as will be seen, composed far beyond the frontiers of the Byzantine Empire, in fact, on enemy territory: in Mesopotamia during the first decades of Arab domination. Still, it deserves a detailed discussion, indeed a place of honor, in this study of the Byzantine apocalyptic tradition, and this on two grounds. In the first place, it was, for reasons that will become clear in the second part of this book, translated into Greek soon after its composition, and in its Greek form it became the basis of the most important branch of the Byzantine apocalyptic tradition. The Greek translation was copied frequently and adapted to historical events as they developed. In 1897 the editor of the Greek text, the Russian philologist V. Istrin, distinguished four Greek redactions, of which the last three were based on the first, and used at least fourteen manuscripts.[1] Actually, the number of surviving manuscripts is larger[2] and must have been very considerable in mid- and late-Byzantine times, to judge from texts excerpted, translated, or otherwise derived from codices now lost. In-

---

1. V. Istrin, *Otkrovenie Mefodiia Patarskago*. The first part of this work (vol. 181) is entitled *Izsledovanie* (Investigation) and contains Istrin's philological study of the texts edited in the second part (vol. 183) entitled *Teksty* (Texts). To simplify citation, vol. 181 will henceforth be quoted as Istrin, *Izsledovanie*, with the page number, and vol. 183 as Istrin with the page number. Carl E. Gleye presents an excellent critical summary of Istrin's conclusions in *BZ* 9 (1900), pp. 222–28. [The Greek texts have now appeared in a critical edition prepared by Anastasios Lolos, *Die Apokalypse des Pseudo-Methodios*, Beiträge zur klassischen Philologie, Heft 83 (Meisenheim am Glan, 1975). This text appeared too late for detailed criticism or use by the author, but because of its superiority and greater accessibility, citations and variant readings will be added to the author's notes.]

2. See *BHG* 2036–2036f and *BHG*³ 2036a, 2036c, 2036g. See now also Lolos, pp. 26–40, and his subsequent edition of further versions of the text, *Die dritte u. vierte Redaktion*.

deed, an entire branch of Byzantine apocalyptic literature, the *Visions of Daniel* (many specimens of which will be discussed later), were in fact combinations of Pseudo-Methodian excerpts with materials of more recent origin. The many translations of the Greek texts into other languages (notably into Slavic languages and into Latin) are another measure of the popularity of the work both in the Byzantine Empire and abroad. A second reason for this discussion of the Syriac text is the effect that it had, through its Greek translation, on other branches of Byzantine apocalyptic literature, apart from the Pseudo-Methodian tradition proper. In fact, it is no exaggeration to say that in the development of the Byzantine apocalyptic tradition the translation of the Syriac text of Pseudo-Methodius into Greek marked the end of the era of Antiquity, and the beginning of that of the Middle Ages. None of the apocalyptic writings written after the translation was made fails to show traces of its influence. Moreover, inasmuch as the Syriac text was informed by the spirit of a non-Classical civilization, that of Syriac Christianity, it was natural that the ideas contained in the Syriac work, as translated into Greek, contributed to the Orientalization of Byzantine apocalyptic literature. True, this Near Eastern element had not been absent from apocalyptic literature before Pseudo-Methodius' work was translated into Greek, for the entire genre was of Near Eastern—Hebrew and Aramaic—origin. Yet one need only compare the last major apocalypse antedating the Greek Pseudo-Methodius, the *Oracle of Baalbek*, with this Greek text or with any later apocalypse to realize how thoroughly the genre was infused with Syriac features by the translation of Pseudo-Methodius' Syriac text into Greek.

Until 1930, scholarly discussion of the apocalypse of Pseudo-Methodius was based on the Greek texts and their Latin and Slavic translations. Istrin's study and text editions of 1897 were useful in that he studied and edited (although not in what would now be called critical form) a number of Greek, Slavic, and Latin manuscripts and elucidated their mutual relationships. He failed to discuss, however, the most interesting historical and literary questions raised by these texts: when were they composed? who were the authors—particularly, who was the author of the original text? for what purpose or purposes was the apocalypse written? what were its sources? However, one year after Istrin's Russian publication and in ignorance of it, the German medievalist Ernst Sackur provided a critical edition of the oldest form of the Latin text, based on four manuscripts of the seventh or eighth century.[3]

---

3. Ernst Sackur, *Sibyllinische Texte*.

Unfortunately, he consulted Greek versions only sporadically. However, Sackur provided his excellent edition with an elaborate introduction and explanatory footnotes in which he answered some of the questions set aside by Istrin. The two publications of Istrin and Sackur, therefore, supplement each other in a most fortunate way. Sackur concluded that Pseudo-Methodius wrote his apocalypse in the last quarter of the seventh century, that he was a Syrian Christian, and that the Iranian influences discernible in his work were to be explained by its origin in northern Syria. Sackur even considered the possibility of the work having been written in the Syriac rather than the Greek language—only to reject the hypothesis, primarily on the ground that no Syriac manuscript of the full work was known to him.[4] He realized that Pseudo-Methodius' work had left significant traces in Syriac literature, in particular that long excerpts appeared in Solomon of Basra's thirteenth-century *Book of the Bee*, but he seems to have thought that the Syriac authors either read a Greek original or a Syriac translation.[5]

Not much progress was made in the study of Pseudo-Methodius' apocalypse until 1931. In that year the Hungarian Orientalist Michael Kmosko published an article in which he opened up new vistas on the problems posed by this difficult text.[6] If I understand Kmosko correctly, he considered "the Pseudo-Methodian enigma" to consist in the fact that Pseudo-Methodius sets forth, in the historical part of his apocalypse, a summary of ancient history full of the most extraordinary distortions and misrepresentations, which Kmosko characterized repeatedly as "wild" and "extravagant." Kmosko solved this enigma by establishing four principal points: (1) Pseudo-Methodius composed his apocalypse in the Syriac language; (2) this Syriac original survives in a sixteenth-century manuscript, the Codex Vaticanus Syrus 58; (3) Pseudo-Methodius was a native of Mesopotamia, in other words, of the former Sassanid Kingdom; and (4) Pseudo-Methodius' extravagant and wild historical constructions reflect Iranian traditions. Kmosko

---

4. Sackur, *Sibyllinische Texte*, p. 55: "Dass die Schrift auch von vornherein griechisch geschrieben war, nicht etwa syrisch, worauf die Nationalität des Verfassers führen könnte, geht wohl daraus hervor, dass keine einzige syrische Handschrift bekannt geworden ist."

5. Sackur, *Sibyllinische Texte*, p. 7 nn. 5, 55. The *Book of the Bee* was edited and translated by E. A. W. Budge in *Anecdota Oxoniensia*, Semitic Series, vol. I, part II (Oxford, 1886).

6. Michael Kmosko, "Das Rätsel des Pseudo-Methodius." The text of the article represents a lecture delivered at the Sixth German Orientalists' Day at Vienna on 13 June 1930. Kmosko calls it an excerpt from a longer monograph which he hoped to publish not long after. Unfortunately, the monograph never appeared and Kmosko died in 1931. Some useful supplements based on Kmosko's lecture are found in H. Gerstinger, "Der Sechste Deutsche Orientalistentag in Wien," *Byzantion* 5 (1930), pp. 415–27, esp. 422–24.

thus agreed with Sackur in thinking that Pseudo-Methodius was a Syrian Christian, but differed from him in holding that the original language of the apocalypse was Syriac rather than Greek and that its author lived in Mesopotamia and not in northern Syria. Not all the details of Kmosko's pioneering study will stand critical review, but a discussion of the Syriac text, to which he was the first to draw attention, will show that the four conclusions mentioned above are correct and that he did indeed succeed in solving "the Pseudo-Methodian enigma."[7]

Since the Syriac text was the basis for the entire Greek, Latin, and Slavic tradition and since it is unpublished, it will be advisable to analyze it here in some detail.[8] In the *codex unicus* it is entitled "By the help of God the Lord of the Universe, the discourse was composed by my lord Methodius, bishop of Olympus [added in margin], and martyr, concerning the succession of kings and concerning the end of times."[9] Then follows a brief preamble, according to which Methodius asked God to be informed "concerning the generations and concerning the kingdoms." God thereupon sent to him "one from among his hosts [i.e., an angel] to the mountain of Šenāgar" to show him all the generations.[10]

The text proper is divided into two parts, clearly distinguishable even

---

7. The Syriac manuscript which according to Kmosko contains the original text, Codex Vaticanus Syrus 58, was catalogued in the eighteenth century by St. E. and J. S. Assemani, *Bibliothecae Apostolicae Vaticanae Manuscriptorum Catalogus* II (Rome, 1758), p. 342. It was copied in A.D. 1584 by the monk Johannes of Gargar, in the so-called Nestorian script. The text of Pseudo-Methodius begins on fol. 118 verso (the Assemanis say fol. 126). J. S. Assemani, *Bibliotheca Orientalis Clementino-Vaticana* (Rome, 1775), II, p. 503, and III, part 1, p. 27, published the beginning and end of the piece with a Latin translation. He called the manuscript Syriacus XXIX. The codex was brought to Rome from the Orient between 1718 and 1721 by Andreas Scadar. The present red-leather binding dates from the years 1775–1779. A much earlier manuscript of the same text was once in the library of Ebed Jesu (eleventh century); see J. S. Assemani, *Bibliotheca Orientalis*, III, part 1, p. 27: *Methodii episcopi Liber de successione generationum*. An important aid for the constitution of the Syriac text is the excerpts in Solomon of Basra's *Book of the Bee*, ed. Budge.

8. [The author's translation of the Syriac text of Cod. Vat. Syr. 58 has been included as Appendix II.]

9. The Greek and Latin manuscripts called Methodius bishop of Patara. Solomon of Basra wrote of Methodius bishop of Rome.

10. This preamble, which is of crucial importance for the history of the Syriac text (see p. 27 below), was not included by the Greek translator and is consequently missing in all versions derived from the Greek. It is strange that Kmosko failed to refer to it in his article and especially in his summary of the Syriac text. See his article, pp. 277–82, for an analysis comparable to the one given here, but I felt that a somewhat different summary was necessary. The heading of the Syriac text is patterned, as is much else (see Sackur, *Sibyllinische Texte*, pp. 12–16), after that of the *Cave of Treasures* (see Paul Riessler's German translation in *Altjüdisches Schrifttum ausserhalb der Bibel* [reprint Darmstadt, 1966], p. 942: "Die Schrift über die Ableitung der Stämme"). Just as the author of the *Cave of Treasures* had explained the succession (*iūbalā*) of generations (*šarbē*; Riessler translates as *Stämme*, "tribes"), so Pseudo-Methodius proposed to describe the succession (*iūbalā*) of kings (*malkē*).

in form: the first, cast in the normal tense of Syriac narrative, the perfect, stops just prior to the beginning of the Arab invasions (fol. 127 verso), and the rest, written, after a few transitional sentences, in the Syriac tense of prophecy, the imperfect, begins with these invasions.[11]

The first or historical part of the work begins with Adam and Eve's departure from Paradise and is divided into three-times-two millennia. The first two millennia ended with the story of the Flood, with Noah leaving the Ark, and his sons building a town called Temanōn, after the eight (*temanē*) survivors. The second two millennia began with the birth of a son of Noah called Ionṭon. Later Ionṭon departed for the East, where he resided near a sea called Fire of the Sun (*nūr šemšā*). He received from Nimrod, of the sons of Shem, the first king, both instruction in wisdom, and craftsmen who built for him a city which he called after his own name, Ionṭon. He prophesied that in a war between the two other kingdoms of the day, that of Nimrod and that of Pupiënus (*Pūpīnus*), son of Ḥam, the latter would be defeated. This happened as predicted. The story continues with successive rulers of "the kingdom of the Babylonians" and their wars against Egypt, down to the end of the fourth millennium.

The last two thousand years began with an invasion led by a descendant of Ionṭon, Šamʻiʻsar,[12] king of the East, into the lands from the Euphrates to Adroigan,[13] the three kingdoms of the Ethiopians,[14] and

11. The transition is marked in the manuscript by a marginal gloss written, it seems, by the same hand as the text: "beginning of the sons of Hagar the Egyptian" (fol. 127 verso).
12. The Syriac name, unattested elsewhere, is difficult to explain. Its first part is connected with the verbal root "to hear"; the second part means "ten." It looks as if the name as spelt in the Syriac manuscript is corrupt. Unfortunately, it does not appear in Solomon of Basra's excerpts. The Greek manuscripts offer many variants (p. 12.8 Istrin): Σαμψίας ὁ τοῦ Βάρ, Σαμψισέκαρ, Ἀμψισέκαρ, Σαμψισάνω, Σάμψισαν, Σαψισάβαρ, Σαμψισλήβ (p. 64.14 Lolos), Ἀψισέκαρ (p. 65.12 Lolos). The Latin tradition has (p. 66.16 Sackur): *Samsishaibus, sāsis ahib (haib), sampsisaibus, sampsabus, samisab* (p. 78 Istrin). The first Slavonic translation (p. 86.25 Istrin) has *Sam"raikar'*. The Greek and Latin traditions agree that the first component of the name was *samsi* or something like it, so the Syriac name probably began with *šemšā*, "sun," a term very appropriate for a ruler residing in the East at the Lake of the Fire of the Sun (above) and one which can hardly have been invented by the Greek or Latin tradition. With regard to the second component of the name, too, the Greek and Latin versions come closer to the truth than does the sixteenth-century Syriac manuscript. Several Greek manuscripts have -σεκαρ, which may represent Syriac *sekar*, "to shut," *seqar*, "to envy," *šekar*, "to insult," *šakar*, "to disfigure," or *šeqar*, "to deceive," none of which is plausible. The Latin variant *shaib*, however, deserves respect, for the Pael *šaieb* means "to blight with heat." Perhaps, then, the original form of the name was *šemšašaieb*, "the sun scorches."
13. The above is the spelling of the Syriac manuscript; again, there are a great many variants in the Greek and Latin traditions. See Istrin p. 12.10 (= p. 64.4 Lolos) and Sackur p. 66.18. Sackur, *Sibyllinische Texte*, pp. 66f., n. 4, is undoubtedly right in claiming that Pseudo-Methodius meant Azerbaijan, normally spelt *Adurbigan* in Syriac. Sackur also referred to De Boor's p. 316.1 critical note in his edition of Theophanes.
14. *Hendwaie*, a word that can also mean Cushites or Nubians, but here Ethiopians are meant. See n. 16 below.

the camps of Ismael (i.e., the Arabs). As a result of this Eastern invasion Ismael fled from the desert of Jethrib (Medina) and invaded the land of peace (cultivated earth, inhabited earth). This Ismaelite invasion is then described in considerable detail. They voyaged across the sea "in vessels of wood" and came "as far as the great Rome and as far as Illyricum and Egypt and Āfnasōliōs and the great Lūzā beyond Rome."[15] After sixty years the Ismaelites, whom the author identifies with the Midianites (*medianaiē*), were defeated by the Israelites recently freed from slavery in Egypt. The Ismaelites made peace with the Israelites, and seven of their tribes withdrew to the desert of Jethrib, from which they had come. They will, so says the first of three prophetic passages interrupting the "historical" narrative, erupt once again and rule the world "from Egypt to Cush and from the Euphrates to Ethiopia [*Hendū*][16] and from the Tigris to the sea called Fire of the Sun . . . and from the North to the great sea of Pontus" (fol. 122 verso). After ten weeks of years, i.e., seventy years, however, they will be subdued by the Roman Empire.

After this prophetic passage Pseudo-Methodius returns to his subject, "the succession of kingdoms." He mentions a series of Babylonian and Persian kings, for example, Sasan the Old and Piroz; the series ends with Cyrus. There follow remarks about the "subduing" of certain "kingdoms of the East" by other kingdoms[17]—for example, of Babylon by the Medes, of Medes by Persians, of Hebrews and other kingdoms (Cush, Sheba, Sāba) by Babylonians, of Thracians by Cyrus, of Greeks by Romans. Pseudo-Methodius then concentrates on the four kingdoms of Cush (Ethiopia), Macedonia, the Greeks, and the Romans, and how they were subdued by one another, in fulfillment of Daniel's prophecy (7:2) of the four winds of heaven "making gush forth the great sea."[18] The "subduing" of Cush by Macedonia then prompts the author to tell in great detail the story of Philip of Macedon and of Alexander the Great: Philip married Cusheth, daughter of King Pīl ("the elephant") of Cush, and she gave birth to Alexander. Alexander conquered Persia and

---

15. The last two place-names are obscure. The Greek and Latin translations substitute for them Thessalonica and Sardinia respectively, but that must be a counsel of despair. Could Āfnasōliōs be a corruption of *efesus*, Ephesus? *Lūzā* means "the almond tree" and the *Thesaurus Syriacus* II, p. 1905, mentions several places of that name.

16. In this passage Pseudo-Methodius distinguished between *Kūš* and *Hendū*; elsewhere he calls Ethiopia *Kūš* (cf. n. 14 above). Perhaps in the passage translated in the text, *Kūš* means Nubia. It is not certain whether the words "the great Rome" refer to the city or the empire.

17. The "subduing" (*ḥesan*) of kingdoms is a key theme of the work.

18. The words translated in the text are the text of Daniel 7:2 according to the Pešitta. The Septuagint has ἐνέπεσον or προσέβαλον, for the Syriac *megiḥin*, "making gush forth."

travelled east as far as the Fire of the Sun (the land of Ionṭon). There he encountered "Unclean Nations" and built a gate of bronze to contain them. However—and here is a second prophecy interrupting the narrative—at the end of time, in fulfillment of Ezekiel's prophecy about "Agog and Magog" (Ezekiel 38:1), these twenty-two unclean peoples will erupt from their prison and defile the earth.

After Alexander's death his mother, Cusheth, returned to her father in Cush, and his generals ruled in his stead. The land of Cush was then attacked by the general Germanicus, by order of Byzas, king and founder of Byzantia. Pseudo-Methodius here implies, apparently, that this attack led to the "subduing" of Cush by Byzantium. Byzas then made peace with Pīl and married Cusheth, widow of Philip and mother of Alexander. She bore a daughter, named Byzantia after the newly founded city. The princess Byzantia married Armalāos, king of Rome, who gave her Rome as a bridal gift, much to the dismay of "the chiefs who were at Rome." The couple had three sons: Armalāos (the Younger), Urbanos, and Claudius, and they eventually ruled over Rome, Byzantia, and Alexandria respectively. Thus, so Pseudo-Methodius concludes, the kingdoms of Macedonians, Greeks, and Romans came to be ruled by princes descended from the Cushite princess Cusheth.

This dynasty—and here is the third prophecy within the narrative—will reign for all eternity, for King David predicted in Psalm 68:31 that "the kingdom of the Greeks [*iaunaiē*], which is from the seed of the Cushites, will hand over the hand [or: dominion] to God at the end of times" (fol. 126 recto).[19] But, Pseudo-Methodius continues, "many brethren of the clergy"[20] interpreted the verse of the Psalmist to refer to the kingdom of the Cushites. This, however, was an error, for the kingship of the Greeks from the seed of Cusheth is meant. No other kingdom will be able to subdue the kingdom of the Christians as long as it possesses the Cross set up in the middle of the earth; on the contrary, the kingdom of the Christians will subdue all the kingdoms of the world and thus will be to "hand over the hand [dominion] to God." Pseudo-

---

19. In the Pešitta Psalm 68:31 runs as follows: "Cush will hand over the hand [or: dominion] to God." The Septuagint text is Αἰθιοπία προφθάσει χεῖρα αὐτῆς τῷ θεῷ; see also the New English Bible: "Let Ethiopia stretch out her hand to God." In a note to this translation it is noted that "stretch out" is the probable reading and that the Hebrew text is obscure. This passage, which appears as 68:31 in the Revised Standard and the King James versions, as 68:32 in the Masoretic text, and as 67:32 in Douay, will be cited as 68:31 after the Revised Standard Version throughout.

20. *Sagīā aḥē min bnai ʿedtā*. In the Greek text these words are replaced by the colorless τινες (p. 22.16 Istrin [= p. 88.4 Lolos]; see also p. 77.7 Sackur: *quidam*). The Greek translator obviously was not interested in the internal quarrel among Syriac-speaking Christians; see p. 54 below.

Methodius justifies his view of the permanence of the Roman Empire by a reference to II Thessalonians 2:7, where St. Paul promises that the Lawless One will not be revealed before "that which restrains at present is removed from the middle"[21] and, further, by the explanation that "that something which is in the middle" is the priesthood and the kingdom and the Holy Cross, which, so Pseudo-Methodius implies, will never be removed from the Roman Empire (fol. 126 verso). This empire already subdued the kingdom of the Hebrews at the time of Vespasian and Titus; it has conquered Egypt, Media, Persia, and Armenia. In the end the kingdoms of the barbarians, that is, those of the Turks (*turqiē*) and of the Avars (*abarios*), contended with the Roman Empire.

Thus ends the historical part of Pseudo-Methodius' tract and, with it, the sixth millennium of the world. He goes on to prophesy that now that the kingdom of the Hebrews[22] has fallen, Rome will contend for ten year-weeks (seventy years) with the Ismaelites, whom David called "seed of the South."[23] The wild ass of the desert, Ismael, will set out from the desert of Jethrib. The Ismaelites will assemble at Gaba'ōt the Great, and there will conquer, in fulfillment of Ezekiel 39:17, "the fattened ones of the kingdom of the Greeks" (fol. 128 recto). The terrible destruction that they will perpetrate will be permitted by God not because he loves the Ismaelites but because of the sins of the Christians.

Pseudo-Methodius then describes Christian vice in great detail, with citations from St. Paul. The four leaders of the Ismaelites—Desolation, Despoiler, Ruin, and Destroyer—will cast lots for the conquered lands. Persia, Syria, Sicily, Hellas, the land of the Romans, the islands of the sea, Egypt, Syria, the places of the East, and the Promised Land will fall under their sway.[24] Ismael will inflict terrible suffering on the conquered, and Pseudo-Methodius describes in great detail the economic misdeeds of the Arabs: confiscation of land and movable property, imposition of poll tax (*qespā rīšā*) even on orphans, widows, and holy men—"they will ask one hundred [dinars?] even from the dead." They will chastise (*rdā*) all groups of the population, in fulfillment of St.

---

21. The words cited in the text are a translation of II Thess. 2:7 according to the Syriac text. The Greek text has μόνον ὁ κατέχων ἄρτι ἕως ἐκ μέσου γένηται [only that which restrains it now until it shall be out of the way].

22. The Syriac manuscript reads clearly *de'ebraiē* (of the Hebrews), but one would expect *deparsaiē* (of the Persians). This is indeed the reading of the Greek (p. 26.3 Istrin = p. 94.8 Lolos) and Latin (p. 80.14 Sackur) texts.

23. The manuscript reads clearly *zar'a* (seed). The Septuagint has βραχίονα (arm) and the Pešitta the corresponding *dera'ā*. Confusion of *z* with *d* was easy in Syriac writing, but it is not clear whether the fault lay with a copyist of the Pešitta or with Pseudo-Methodius.

24. For this list of countries, see Appendix 2.

Paul's prediction in II Thessalonians 2:3: "unless this chastisement [*mardūtā*] comes beforehand, and thereupon will be revealed the man of sin, the son of perdition" (fol. 130 recto). They will slaughter priests, sleep with their wives and captured mistresses in the churches, wear on their persons the holy vestments, and defile the tombs of martyrs and saints. Only a small remnant will remain faithful to Christianity, as in the days of Elijah, and without compulsion most members of the clergy "will agree with the unbelievers," i.e., apostacize. There will be rewards for the wicked, the blasphemous, the ignorant, who are "ministers of that one" (*mešamšanē dehau*: of Mohammed? fol. 132 recto). No honor will be rendered to the priests, and the divine liturgy will no longer be celebrated. In the tenth year-week, when Ismaelite power will come to an end, men will be forced to sell their sons and daughters to the Ungodly. Thus the Ismaelites will reach the end of their oppression and destroy Persians, Armenians, Cilicians, Isaurians, Cappadocians, *sīlīqelīē* (Sicilians?), *eladanīē*(?), and the dwellers in the land of the Romans and of the islands of the seas (fol. 133 recto).²⁵ The conquerors will blaspheme, saying: There is no deliverer for the Christians. Then the king of the Greeks will go forth against them from the land of the Cushites, awakened like a man who shakes off his wine (Psalm 78:65), who is considered like a dead man. He will attack and defeat them in the desert of Jethrib, and their servitude will be a hundred times harsher than their yoke. The earth will be at peace, and the Christian remnant will return to their native lands and inheritance: Cappadocians and Armenians and Cilicians and Isaurians and Africans and *eladīē*(?) and Seleucians (fol. 133 verso).²⁶ Egypt, Arabia (*arabā*, reading uncertain), and Hebron (*ḥebrūn*) will be devastated (by the Greeks?) and the isthmus of the sea (*lešon iamā*: Constantinople?) will be at peace.²⁷ The king of the

25. See Appendix 2.
26. See Appendix 2.
27. The Syriac manuscript reads clearly *ḥebrūn*, the city of Hebron in southern Judaea, and this reading is confirmed by Solomon of Basra, *Book of the Bee*, ed. Budge, p. 144 (Syriac pagination). The item is, however, surprising. Of the two preceding items *agibṭos* refers to a region. In the text item the manuscript is not easy to read—both *araqa* and *arabā* are possible, but certainly not *araba* or *arabia*. The last spelling would be normal for Arabia and it is highly probable that this is what Pseudo-Methodius wrote or at least meant. If this is so, then it is disturbing to find the names of two regions followed by that of the town of Hebron. Why should Hebron be singled out in this fashion? In most manuscripts of the Greek version used by Istrin the item is omitted, but two of his manuscripts have it in the form ἡ γῆ τοῦ ἀβρανοῦς ἐρημωθήσεται [the land of Hebron will be made desert]. Here ἀβρανοῦς (Hebron) obviously takes the place of the *ḥebrūn* of the Syriac text. The Latin tradition shows that something like ἀβρανοῦς is as old as the eighth century, for while most Latin manuscripts have *terra Ausaniae cremabitur* (p. 91.3 Sackur), one of them reads *auranie*. This last reading, certainly "more correct" than the *ausaniae* adopted by Sackur, is interesting. Not only does it correspond to the ἀβρανοῦς of two of

Greeks will punish those who denied the (Christian) faith. He will punish the apostates; the world will be at peace and the clergy honored (fol. 134 recto).

Then the Gates of the North will be opened and the Unclean Peoples will commit unspeakable misdeeds. Eventually they will assemble in the Plain of Joppe (*iupē*) and will there within an hour be destroyed by an angel. The king of the Greeks will then take up residence at Jerusalem for a year-week and a half (ten and a half years) and the Son of Perdition (the Antichrist) will be revealed. Immediately after his appearance, the king of the Greeks will ascend Golgotha (*gagūltā*) and will place his diadem (*tāgā*) on top of the Holy Cross. He will stretch (*pešaṭ*) his two hands to heaven, hand over (*mešalem*) his kingship to God the Father, and then die. Cross and crown (*kelīlā*) will then ascend to heaven, because the Cross will precede Christ at his Second Coming. Thus will be fulfilled the prophecy of David (Psalm 68:31): "Cush will hand over the hand [dominion] to God," inasmuch as the descendant of Cusheth, daughter of King Pīl of the Cushites, will hand over the dominion to God. Then the Son of Perdition will be revealed, as was prophesied in Genesis (49:17) about Dan, the horse, and "that which biteth," which Pseudo-Methodius interprets as referring to the Son of Perdition: he will be destroyed by the Lord at his Second Coming.

This analysis of the Syriac text should have brought out that Pseudo-Methodius composed his apocalypse for a polemical purpose. In a pivotal part of his work, where he made the transition from "historical" narrative to eschatological prophecy, he relied heavily on Psalm 68:31. In keeping with the narrative, he interpreted this verse to mean that it would be a Byzantine emperor, as the descendant of the Ethiopian princess Cusheth, who would hand over his empire to God: "the kingdom of Greece, which is from the seed of the Cushites—it will hand over the hand to God at the end of times." But he was aware that members of the same clergy to which Pseudo-Methodius belonged insisted on a literal exegesis of Psalm 68:31 and believed that at the end of time the ruler of contemporary Cush, i.e., the Ethiopian ruler, would fulfill the prophecy contained in this passage.

The historical circumstances under which this controversy over the

---

the Greek manuscripts (where -υ- was corrupted into -β-, as often in Greek manuscripts), but *auranie* clearly refers to the region of Hauran, east of the sea of Galilee and south of Damascus. The Latin tradition makes it very likely that the Syriac original of the Greek version referred to Hauran rather than to Hebron. The normal spelling of this region in Syriac is *ḥauran*; cf. *Thesaurus Syriacus* I, p. 1232. As it is the name of a region rather than that of a city, it is very probably the correct Syriac reading, with *ḥebrūn* a corruption of the Syriac tradition.

interpretation of Psalm 68:31 arose will be of concern in Part Two, Chapter I, below. Here it must suffice to point out its political implications, which Pseudo-Methodius makes quite clear throughout his work. If a Byzantine emperor was to hand over his dominion to God at the end of time, that meant that the Byzantine Empire itself would last to the final consummation and that none of its enemies would ever be able to destroy it. This is a point that Pseudo-Methodius never tires of emphasizing.[28] Inasmuch as this political thesis of the invincibility of the Roman (Byzantine) Empire was based on Psalm 68:31 and consequently presupposed the identification of the Psalmist's Cush with this empire, the entire narrative part of Pseudo-Methodius' work, culminating in the dynastic alliance of Byzantium's mythical founder, King Byzas, with Cushite royalty represented by the eponymous princess Cusheth, has as its primary objective to lay the "historical" foundation for Pseudo-Methodius' interpretation of Psalm 68:31: the Cush mentioned in the Psalm is the Roman (Byzantine) Empire because its ruler is a descendant of Cushite kings. The "enigma" of Pseudo-Methodius is thus solved by the polemic-political purpose pursued by the author.[29]

---

28. For example, fol. 122 verso, in the course of the "first prophetic interruption of the narrative" concerning an Ismaelite invasion at the end of time: "And after ten weeks of years they [the Ismaelites] also will be subdued and subjected by the kingdom of Rome because it subdues all the kingdoms and will not be subdued by any one of them"; fol. 126 recto, following the passage on Psalm 68:31 discussed in the text: "for there is no people or kingdom under heaven which can subdue the kingdom of the Christians . . . ," whereupon Pseudo-Methodius proceeds to justify his thesis of the invincibility of the Roman Empire by a lengthy exegesis of II Thess. 2:7 and a quick survey of world history down to the Avar attack on Constantinople in A.D. 626. Pseudo-Methodius was not the first Christian author to proclaim the invincibility and eternity of the Roman (Byzantine) Empire. For example, about a century before him there appeared in Cosmas Indicopleustes' *Christian Topography* II.74f., ed. W. Wolska-Conus, pp. 388ff.: θαρρῶν γὰρ ἀποφαίνομαι ὅτι, εἰ καὶ διὰ τὰς ἡμετέρας ἁμαρτίας πρὸς παιδείαν ὀλίγον ἐχθροὶ βάρβαροι τῇ Ῥωμανίᾳ ἐπανίστανται, ἀλλὰ τῇ δυνάμει τοῦ διακρατοῦντος ἀήττητος διαμένει ἡ βασιλεία κτλ. [For I declare with confidence that, even if, because of our sins, barbarian enemies should rise up against the Roman Empire for a small chastisement, the empire will remain in the power of its eternal rule.] Yet the bases for Cosmas' belief were quite different from those for Pseudo-Methodius'. The former emphasized, in contrast to Pseudo-Methodius, that the Roman Empire was not a successor to the Macedonian Empire. He cited, not Psalm 68:31 or II Thess. 2, but Dan. 2:44. In general, Cosmas relied primarily on the well-known synchronism of the founding of the Roman Empire by Augustus and the origin of Christianity, as first attested by Meliton of Sardes (Eusebius *Hist. Eccl.* 4:26), a concept foreign to Pseudo-Methodius. Consequently, although Cosmas was heavily indebted to Mesopotamian (Nestorian) Christianity for much of his cosmological speculation (Wanda Wolska, *La Topographie chrétienne de Cosmas Indicopleustès* [Paris, 1962], esp. pp. 63–86), his thesis of the invincibility and eternity of the Roman Empire rested on entirely different foundations from that of Pseudo-Methodius.

29. It was one of Kmosko's achievements in "Rätsel" to have established the connection between Pseudo-Methodius' "historical narrative" and his thesis. Kmosko did not, however, see that this thesis of Pseudo-Methodius' was a polemic against some of his colleagues—"many brethren of the clergy," as he called them. And I cannot follow Kmosko's

When was this apocalypse composed? The Latin manuscript tradition furnishes as *terminus ante quem* the eighth century, for of the four codices used by Sackur in his edition one was copied in the seventh to eighth century and three in the eighth century.[30] A safe *terminus post quem* is the Moslem invasion of the Near East that began A.D. 634, for it is clearly known to the author, and his prophecies concerning it are to a large extent *vaticinia ex eventu*. How much can these limits be narrowed down? When, in the course of what was called above the first prophetic interruption of the historical narrative, Pseudo-Methodius mentioned an earlier Ismaelite (Midianite) conquest of the world, he wrote: "And in vessels of wood they flew over the waves of the sea and they went to the lands of the West and came as far as the great Rome" (fol. 121 verso). It is true that this passage referred to a legendary Ismaelite conquest and that Pseudo-Methodius identified these Ismaelite invaders with the Midianites of the Old Testament. Yet Pseudo-Methodius undoubtedly was so interested in this archetypal invasion precisely because it could be described in terms of the Arab invasion he himself had witnessed. Now, even a shrewd observer of the politico-military situation in the seventh century could not have predicted that the landlocked inhabitants of the Arabian desert would become a seafaring people unless he lived after they had built their first navy. This happened under the khalif ʿUthman (644–656),[31] so Pseudo-Methodius must have written after the accession of that ruler.

The text of Pseudo-Methodius' tract seems to have been composed not long after the beginning of the invasion, for the events of the conquest are remembered rather clearly. Pseudo-Methodius complains bitterly of the invaders' greed. He writes of the Arabs enslaving men, beasts, birds, waters, even waste places, "and the tyrant will record them as his" (fol. 129 verso). This sounds like an Arab equivalent of the *Domesday Book*. He mentions confiscations of natural resources (fish, trees, fruit, land, and crops), merchandise, and precious objects, including votive gifts. The poll tax is collected without mercy; prosperous cities are destroyed and Christian sanctuaries defiled. This tale of woe ob-

---

suggestion (p. 290) that Cusheth (or, as he transcribes the name: Kušath) was an archaizing form of *Kūšītā*, meaning "negress" or "black slave girl," and that Pseudo-Methodius transformed this term, originally implying an insult to the Byzantine emperor, into a foundation for his pro-Byzantine theory of history. In this respect, as in others, Kmosko's thesis seems to be unnecessarily complicated, and he might very probably have revised it had he lived to complete his intended monograph. Cusheth is simply the eponymous ancestress of Byzantium's Cushite dynasty, as Byzas is its eponymous Greek ancestor.

30. Sackur, *Sibyllinische Texte*, p. 57.
31. George Ostrogorsky, *History of the Byzantine State* (rev. ed., New Brunswick, N.J., 1969), p. 116.

viously contains some of the conventional complaints of a conquered population and some of it is probably exaggerated or even untrue, but it reflects a conquest still in progress or at least one that does not belong to the distant past.

There are certain arguments from silence that point in the same direction. Not a word is said in the Syriac text of the outbreak of civil war in the Arab dominions between the supporters of ʿAli and of Muʿāwiya (656–661) or about the battle of Siffin (657); of the peace treaty concluded in 659 by Muʿāwiya with the Byzantine emperor Constans II, in which the prince of Damascus agreed to pay tribute; or, most significantly, of the unsuccessful Arab siege of Constantinople (674–678). Nor is there any allusion to the subsequent peace for thirty years, according to which Damascus undertook to pay an annual tribute of three thousand pounds of gold to the Byzantine Empire. Admittedly, it is dangerous to argue from an author's silences, but this is a somewhat special case. The military superiority of the Byzantine Empire over its enemies is, as we have seen, the principal thesis of Pseudo-Methodius' work, and in one lengthy section he draws up a list of historic Roman (Byzantine) victories over various opponents, ending with the repulsion of the Avar siege of the capital in A.D. 626.[32] A mention of the Arab failure before the walls of Constantinople would therefore have been grist to his mill, and it is difficult to imagine why, had he written after 678, he should have abstained from mentioning this well-known event. The evidence, then, points to a date of the Syriac text after A.D. 644 and prior to 678—probably even earlier than the outbreak of the Arab civil war in 656.[33]

32. On fol. 127 recto, Pseudo-Methodius discusses the Roman victories over the Jews under Vespasian and Titus, over Macedonian Egypt, over Media, Persia, and Armenia. Then follows on fol. 127 verso: "And when the kingdom of the Macedonians . . . was destroyed, the kingdoms of the barbarians contended with the kingdom of Rome, namely those of the Turks and Avars." This sentence leads immediately into the story of the Arab invasion. It is not certain which people Pseudo-Methodius had in mind as the "Turks" (*turqiē*) who in conjunction with the Avars "contended with" the Byzantine Empire. Perhaps he meant the Bulgar tribesmen who joined the Avar hordes: see George of Pisidia *Bellum Avaricum* 17, ed. A. Pertusi (Studia Patristica et Byzantina 7 [Ettal, 1959], p. 176) and the editor's note, p. 210. But the passage may be an allusion to the alliance negotiated at that time by the emperor Heraclius with the Khazars (Ostrogorsky, *History*, p. 103). For a similar pairing of Turks and Avars see Mauricius, *Strategicon*, ed. H. Mihaescu (Bucarest, 1970), esp. pp. 74.17, 268.12ff., a source dating probably from the late sixth or early seventh century (see Gyula Moravcsik, *Byzantino-Turcica* [2nd edition, Berlin, 1958], pp. 417–419).

33. Kmosko, "Rätsel," p. 285, concludes that Pseudo-Methodius wrote "bereits in der ersten Hälfte der Alleinherrschaft des Muâwijah I" and means, I suppose, the sixties of the seventh century. My suggestion is not far different from his, but I hope to have advanced somewhat firmer arguments. All earlier discussions of the chronological problems—e.g., Sackur, *Sibyllinische Texte*, pp. 47–51 (last years of Constantine IV, 668–

Where was Pseudo-Methodius' tract composed? Here certain observations by Sackur are relevant, although they were made long before Kmosko's discovery of the Syriac text and were based largely on the Latin rather than the Greek tradition.[34] Sackur held that the thought of the work, its chronological scheme, and the sources used point to Syriac Christianity as the origin of the work, a conclusion that was enormously strengthened by Kmosko's discovery of the full Syriac text. Specifically, Sackur showed that Pseudo-Methodius had relied heavily on a Syriac work, the *Cave of Treasures*, composed (in Mesopotamia) in the sixth century, and that he used other Syriac sources such as the *Romance of the Emperor Julian*, probably composed in the early sixth century.[35] But Sackur was also aware of Pseudo-Methodius' interest in Babylonia and that his knowledge of Babylonian history and legend was derived from Iranian traditions. To account for both Syriac and Iranian influences on Pseudo-Methodius' work, Sackur concluded that he wrote in northern Syria.

This conclusion was close to the truth, but it could not be maintained in all details after the Syriac text was discovered in 1931. Kmosko agreed with Sackur that the intellectual roots of Pseudo-Methodius lay in Syriac-speaking Christianity, but he demonstrated that the author had lived in Mesopotamia during the last years or decades of Sassanid rule, and he pointed to many Iranian features in Pseudo-Methodius' work.[36] Not all of the features he mentioned are equally cogent,[37] but

---

685)—were superseded by Kmosko's discovery of the Syriac text. As early as 1878, Adolf von Gutschmid, in a very influential review that was reprinted in his *Kleine Schriften* V (Leipzig, 1894), pp. 495–506, had suggested the years 676–678 as the date of composition for the Greek text. He did not give his reasons, but undoubtedly he was thinking of the Arab siege of Constantinople.

34. Sackur, *Sibyllinische Texte*, pp. 53–55.

35. Sackur, *Sibyllinische Texte*, pp. 10–16. The *Cave of Treasures* was edited and translated into German by C. Bezold (Leipzig, 1883–1888) and translated into English by E. A. W. Budge, *The Book of the Cave of Treasures* (London, 1927). There is another German translation in Paul Riessler (n. 10 above). The *Romance of Julian* was edited by J. G. E. Hoffman (Leiden, 1880) and translated into English by Hermann Gollancz (Oxford, 1928).

36. Kmosko, "Rätsel," pp. 287–91.

37. Kmosko pointed out ("Rätsel," p. 287) that, like Pseudo-Methodius, the Persian tradition knew of the city of Temanōn, founded by Noah, and of Ionṭon, a fourth son of Noah, but these features occur already in the *Cave of Treasures* (n. 35 above) and therefore cannot be used to decide whether Pseudo-Methodius wrote in Syria or Mesopotamia. Kmosko also believed that no inhabitant of Syria could have proclaimed, as did Pseudo-Methodius, that all Roman and Byzantine rulers were members of the same dynasty, but that such a concept was altogether compatible with the Persian mentality, which connected all Persian rulers down to the last Sassanid with the mythical dynasty of Pišdādīē. In my opinion, this argument for Mesopotamian origin underestimates the potential of Syrians for mythical thought.

there are additional reasons for believing that Kmosko was right. First of all, there is the passage to which in my summary of Pseudo-Methodius' work I referred as the first prophetic interruption of the historical narrative. There the author predicts the Arab invasion of his own time. The Moslems, he writes, will conquer lands "from Egypt to Cush [Nubia?] and from the Euphrates to Hendū [Ethopia?] and from the Tigris to the sea called Fire of the Sun and the kingdom of Ionṭon, son of Noah, and from the North to the great Rome and the great sea of Pontus" (fol. 122 verso). It is striking that Mesopotamia, the land between the rivers Euphrates and Tigris, is excluded from this "prophecy" of the Moslem conquests. Now it is impossible to believe that an author writing, as we have seen, in the mid seventh century anywhere in the area of Syriac Christianity, and keenly interested in Babylonia and Persia, should not have known that Mesopotamia was conquered by the Arabs between 640 and 642. There is only one way to explain this strange omission: the Moslem conquest of Mesopotamia was so obvious to the author and his prospective readers that it deserved no special mention—because he and they lived in Mesopotamia, with the results of this conquest all around them.

There is a second and, I think, decisive argument in favor of the Mesopotamian origin of the tract. The preamble to the Syriac text, omitted in all other versions, runs as follows:

This blessed man [Methodius] asked of God to know concerning the generations and concerning the kingdoms, how they were handed down from Adam and until today. And the Lord sent to him one from among his hosts to the mountain of Šenāgar and he showed him all the generations. . . .

Although the spelling of the place-name is unusual,[38] Šenāgar and its mountain must refer to the ancient city of Singara and the nearby Ğebel Sinğar, about a hundred kilometers northwest of modern Mosul and southeast of ancient Nisibis. In the second century A.D. the city became an important military base as part of the Roman *limes*, and it remained part of the Roman Empire until it was captured and razed to the ground by the Persian king Sapor II in 360. It then disappeared for about two centuries from the political and military annals. At the beginning of the sixth century the territory of Singara was inhabited by a tribe called Qadišaiē, Καδισηνοι, who were of Kurdish or Arab descent. Later in the same century the emperor Maurice (582–602) recaptured it from the Persians, but it undoubtedly fell once again into Persian hands under

---

38. The *Thesaurus Syriacus* (II, pp. 4137, 4242) lists the city as Sīgar and Sengar.

Phocas (602–610), and it was finally conquered by the Arabs under the command of ʿIyād ibn Gānan.[39]

Mount Singara, the Ğebel Sinğar—"deserted and horrible," as an ancient hagiographer called it[40]—was an ideal location (comparable to Mount Sinai) for a supernatural vision like the one attributed to Methodius in the preamble to the Syriac text. Early hermits and, later, several monasteries had bestowed upon it an aura of sanctity. Yet Mount Singara never became a common sanctuary of all Christendom or even of Syriac Christianity. The only reason the author chose it as the site for the eschatological vision of Methodius can have been that he wrote not far from it and for a public that lived in its vicinity.

Another clue to the personality of the author is provided by the passage about the "many brethren of the clergy," which, as we have seen, reveals the politico-polemical purpose of the author. In the first place, a Pseudo-Methodius who referred to his opponents as "brethren of the clergy" must himself have been a cleric, a priest or a monk or both. But of which church?

Missionaries first came to the area in 536–537. They were not members of the Nestorian Church, to which most Christians in the Sassanid state belonged, but followers of the great Monophysite propagandist John, bishop of Tella. In the following decades the Monophysites made great progress in Persia. Under King Chosroes II (590–628), the court physician Gabriel, a native of Singara and a convert from Nestorianism to Monophysitism, played a highly important role in affairs of state.[41] The first bishop ministering in the territory of Singara had only an itinerant clergy preaching to the tribes residing there. As early as the fourth century there is evidence for hermits on Mount Singara, and by the mid sixth century there are reliable data for a Monophysite monastery and, later in the same century, for several Nestorian monasteries on the mountain.[42] The area remained, however, a Monophysite center.[43] Not long after Heraclius' victories over Persia, four eastern bishops, with the permission of the Monophysite patriarch Athanasius of Antioch, or-

---

39. Friedrich Sarre and Ernst Herzfeld, *Archäologische Reise im Euphrat- und Tigris-Gebiet*, 4 vols. (Berlin, 1911–1920), esp. I, pp. 199ff. Much historical material on Singara was collected by P. Peeters in his article "La Passion arabe de S. Abd al Masih," *Analecta Bollandiana* 44 (1926), pp. 270–341, esp. 278–81. See also M. Plessner, "Sindjar," *Encyclopedia of Islam*, vol. IV (Leiden, 1934), pp. 454f.
40. *Vita Johannis episcopi Tellae auctore Elia*, trans. E. W. Brooks, Corpus Scriptorum Christianorum Orientalium, Ser. 3, vol. 25 (Paris, 1907), pp. 42–44.
41. J. Labourt, *Le Christianisme dans l'empire perse sous la dynastie sassanide* (Paris, 1904), pp. 219f.
42. Peeters, "Abd al Masih," pp. 283–86.
43. Labourt, *Christianisme*, p. 220.

dained at the seat of the patriarch a Great Metropolitan of Tagrit on the Tigris, Mārūtā, and four further bishops for Mesopotamia, including George of Šīgarā. From that time onward Singara remained one of the suffragan sees of the head of the Monophysite Church in Mesopotamia, the *maphrianos* ("Fructifier") at Tagrit.[44]

It is significant that Pseudo-Methodius' "many brethren of the clergy" in seventh-century Mesopotamia had so high an opinion of Ethiopia that they thought and taught that it would be the ruler of Ethiopia who, in fulfillment of Psalm 68:31, would at the end of time "hand over the hand [dominion] to God." In the distant past there had been strong religious ties between Syriac-speaking Christianity and Ethiopia; in particular, Syrian missionaries had played an important role in the Christianization of Ethiopia.[45] Furthermore, for a short period in the first half of the sixth century, Ethiopia had intervened militarily in the affairs of southern Arabia and had even held a place in Mediterranean diplomacy.[46] But in 570 the Persian conquest of Yemen put an end to Ethiopia's role as a military power.[47] Consequently, the reason that in the mid seventh century Pseudo-Methodius' unnamed opponents, his "many brethren of the clergy," were so concerned to find a biblical guarantee for the permanence of the Ethiopian kingdom must only have been that Ethiopia was then the one country in the world where Monyphysitism was the official religion and where the ruler was a Monophysite.[48] This devotion to the only existing Monophysite ruler presupposes that Pseudo-Methodius' opponents and, therefore, Pseudo-Methodius himself, who called them his "brethren," were Monophysites.[49]

---

44. Ernst Honigmann, *Le Convent de Barsauma et le patriarcat Jacobite d'Antioche et de Syrie*, Corpus Scriptorum Christianorum Orientalium, Subsidia 7 (Louvain, 1954), pp. 95–97 (with map II of the Monophysite sees).

45. On Syriac influences on the beginnings of Ethiopian Christianity see C. Conti Rossini, "La Leggenda di Abbā Afsē in Etiopia," *Mélanges Syriens Offerts à M. René Dussaud*, vol. 1 (Paris, 1939), pp. 151–56, esp. 151. On the general history of Ethiopia see the informative article by G. Lanczkowski, "Aethiopia," *Jahrbuch für Antike und Christentum* 1 (1958), pp. 134–52.

46. A. Vasiliev, "Justin I (518–527) and Abyssinia," *BZ* 33 (1933), pp. 67–77; *Justin the First: An Introduction to the Epoch of Justinian the Great*, Dumbarton Oaks Studies 1 (Washington, D.C., 1950), pp. 284–85, 295, 300–302.

47. C. Conti Rossini, *Storia d'Etiopia*, vol. I (Milan, 1928), pp. 196–201.

48. Lanczkowski, "Aethiopia," p. 145.

49. [Alexander later changed his mind about the Monophysite sympathies of Pseudo-Methodius. In a note in his collected articles, he wrote: "I expressed the opinion that Pseudo-Methodius was a Monophysite. The basis for my view was a sentence from the Syriac original which I translated as follows . . . 'However, many brethren of the clergy suppose that the blessed David spoke this word [Psalm 68:31] concerning the kingdom of the Ethiopians.' My reasoning was that in the seventh century when Pseudo-Methodius composed his apocalypse, Ethiopia no longer played a role in the international politics of the Near East, and that the author's political reliance on the Ethiopian ruler was therefore

The erroneous belief that there existed no full Syriac manuscript of Pseudo-Methodius' tract had prevented Sackur from drawing the obvious conclusion from his study of the content of the work and had forced him to adopt the implausible theory that Pseudo-Methodius was a Syrian writing in Greek.[50] Kmosko's rediscovery of Codex Vaticanus Syrus 58 showed that Sackur's conclusion had been unnecessarily complicated.[51] In addition, Kmosko adduced a number of arguments in favor of the view that the original language of the work was Syriac, but reserved a full treatment of the question for a larger study which, unfortunately, never appeared. In what follows I shall summarize those arguments of Kmosko's that seem to me cogent and add others that he would undoubtedly have mentioned in his projected fuller study. A

---

explicable on the ground that Ethiopia was then the only country where Monophysitism was the official religion. However, my translation was inaccurate: the verb rendered above by the present tense ('suppose') appears in the Syriac original in the 'perfect' (*asberu*), the form of the historical narrative. The author, therefore, means not that contemporary members of the Mesopotamian clergy placed their hope on the Ethiopian ruler but that members of the Mesopotamian clergy had done so in the past. This statement is not surprising as ecclesiastical relations between the Syrian churches and Ethiopia had long been close and as in the sixth century Ethiopia had collaborated militarily with Byzantium in the Red Sea region. The sentence mentioned above, in its revised translation ('supposed'), therefore neither requires nor allows any inference as to Pseudo-Methodius' Christological orientation or ecclesiastical affiliation" (*Religious and Political History* XII, pp. 68–68a). This line of argument thus suggests that Pseudo-Methodius saw the Roman Empire not as an alternative to Ethiopia as a source of hope, but as an historically proven successor to such ideas.]

50. Sackur, *Sibyllinische Texte*, p. 55.

51. Kmosko, "Rätsel," pp. 291f., was of the opinion that Pseudo-Methodius, because he was so fanatical an adherent of Byzantine imperial ideology, must also have shared Byzantium's Chalcedonian Christology. Since, however, Kmosko was well aware that the Chalcedonian, i.e., Melkite, Church was not represented in Mesopotamia, he connected Pseudo-Methodius with a pro-Chalcedonian movement initiated in the Nestorian Theological School of Nisibis at the end of the sixth century by its rector, Henānā of Ḥedajab. This entire construction is without foundation, for the text does not afford any interpretation of Pseudo-Methodius' religious sympathies. Kmosko, pp. 293ff., builds on this first hypothesis a further theory according to which Pseudo-Methodius, because of his pro-Byzantine and allegedly pro-Chalcedonian views, was forced to leave his native Mesopotamia and find refuge at the monastery on Mount Sinai. The reason for the last assumption was an observation made by Sackur, *Sibyllinische Texte*, p. 79 nn. 2, 4, 5, that there are literal agreements between the text of Pseudo-Methodius and Anastasius of Sinai's *Disputatio adversus Judaeos*—agreements which, according to Kmosko, were most easily explained by personal acquaintance between the two authors. However, quite apart from the fact that agreements between writers normally mean no more than that there were literary relationships, the verbal agreements observed by Sackur in the Latin text are completely absent from the Syriac version. They were undoubtedly added by the Greek translator, who derived them from Anastasius' work or from Anastasius' source. (In fact, the agreement of Pseudo-Methodius' Greek text, pp. 24–26 Istrin [= pp. 93–94 Lolos], with Anastasius, *PG* 89.1212, is even more striking in the Greek text than in Sackur's Latin version.) Kmosko's inferences with regard to Pseudo-Methodius' religious affiliation and flight from Mesopotamia to Egypt, therefore, are unfounded.

complete demonstration will have to wait for a future editor of the Syriac, Greek, Latin, and Slavic texts.

First, a stylistic observation: in the Greek text of Pseudo-Methodius it occurs frequently that the subject or other noun of a clause is placed at its beginning and later referred to by means of a demonstrative pronoun.[52] This type of construction, unusual in Greek, is normal in Syriac.[53] In addition, there are other Semitisms in the Greek text.[54]

Then there is the fact that Pseudo-Methodius consistently cited the Syriac text of the Bible, the Pešitta, rather than the Greek Septuagint. This is clear in several instances where the biblical quotations were more or less incidental,[55] but also, more importantly, in biblical citations that are pivotal to his argument. Throughout the tract Pseudo-Methodius cited and used Psalm 68:31, a passage notoriously obscure in the Hebrew original. The Syriac Pseudo-Methodius quotes it in the following form: "Cush [Ethiopia] will hand over the hand [dominion] to God."[56] Here the Septuagint reads: "Ethiopia will stretch out her hand to God." Pseudo-Methodius invariably interpreted this verse to re-

---

52. I note the following examples: p. 10.15 Istrin (= p. 60.8–9 Lolos) ἡ βασιλεία τοῦ Ἰάφεθ αὕτη μέλλει κτλ.; p. 22.18 (= p. 88.61 Lolos) ἡ γὰρ ἐκ τοῦ σπέρματος τῆς Αἰθιοπίας συνισταμένη βασιλεία αὕτη κέκτηται κτλ.; p. 26.7 (= p. 96.1–2 Lolos) ἐν γὰρ τῇ ἐσχάτῃ χιλιάδι... ἐν ταύτῃ ἐκριζοῦται ἡ τῶν Περσῶν βασιλεία; p. 46.3 (= p. 132.14 Lolos) ὁ σταυρὸς... αὐτὸς μέλλει φανήσεσθαι κτλ.

53. Th. Nöldeke, *Kurzgefasste Syrische Grammatik* (2nd ed. Leipzig, 1898), pp. 240f.

54. P. 16.13 Istrin, for example: ἡνίκα εἰσῆλθε Σενερὶ τοῦ πολεμῆσαι (Lolos, p. 72.13, has συνῆλθε on the basis of Ms. B [Coll. Bodl. Laud. 27, Saec. XV]; Mss. DGR have εἰσῆλθε.) The verb εἰσέρχομαι followed by the genitive of the infinitive makes no sense in Greek. The Syriac text has *wakad 'al senaḥerīb dene'bed qerabā* [and then Sennacherib began to engage battle] (fol. 123 recto), where the verb *'al* does not have its most basic meaning "to enter" but signifies "to begin." On fol. 130 verso Pseudo-Methodius describes in detail the destruction wrought by the Arabs: "for these cruel barbarians are not human beings but sons of the sword [*ḥarbā*] and upon the sword their faces are set." Here the Greek text has (p. 32.8 Istrin = p. 108.99 Lolos) τέκνα ἐρήμου ἔσονται εἰς ἐρήμωσιν ἥξουσιν. If the Syriac text was original, it is easy to see that the Greek translator misread (or confused) *ḥarbā* (sword) for *ḥurbā* (desert), but the reverse process is difficult to imagine.

55. Kmosko, "Rätsel," p. 285, mentioned the following case. Among the twenty-two "Unclean Peoples" imprisoned by Alexander the Great, the Syriac text mentions the *daifar* or *dīfar* (fol. 124 verso). This name derives from the Syriac Bible, which mentions *dīfar* among the sons of Gomer, but the Septuagint reads, in Gen. 10:3, Ῥιφάθ. Somewhat later, Pseudo-Methodius mentions that the Romans under Vespasian and Titus destroyed the Hebrew state and cites in this connection Dan. 9:26 in the following form (fol. 127 recto): "And after the Anointed is killed, it will destroy the city of holiness." This does not resemble the Greek text—ἐξολοθρευθήσεται χρῖσμα... καὶ τὴν πόλιν καὶ τὸ ἅγιον διαφθερεῖ—very closely, for here there is no mention of the Anointed, only of an anointment, and the καί separates city from holiness. The text of the Pešitta is much closer to the Syriac Pseudo-Methodius: "The Anointed will be killed... and the town of holiness destroyed."

56. Cited in this form on fol. 126 recto and 135 verso, and alluded to several times more: Αἰθιοπία προφθάσει χεῖρα αὐτῆς τῷ θεῷ.

fer to a handing-over of power, a meaning usual for the Syriac word *īdā* but impossible, or at least extremely far-fetched, for the Greek χείρ.[57]

Another case in point is the passage in which the Syriac Pseudo-Methodius describes the defeat of the Roman (Byzantine) army by the invading Arabs. He locates this defeat at a place he calls Gabaʿōt Ramtā ("the High," fol. 127 verso). No such place is mentioned in the Septuagint, but the Syriac Old Testament knew of a locality of that name where Gideon defeated the Midianites (Judg. 7:1): "and so he encamped north of Gabaʿōt Ramtā in the valley." The Septuagint, on the other hand, locates Gideon's camp at Gabaathamōra. Now Kmosko pointed out that according to the Old Testament (Gen. 37:25 and Judg. 8:24) Gideon's enemies, the Midianites, were Arabs and that Pseudo-Methodius specifically identifies the Ismaelites at the time of their legendary first conquest (n. 16 above) with the Midianites (fol. 122 recto). In view of this identification it is fitting to locate the second battle with the Ismaelites-Midianites in the same place as the first, all the more so as the famous historic battle between Byzantines and Arabs, normally named after the river Yarmuk (636), was fought near a town with a name similar to that of the biblical battlefield: Γαβιθᾶς or Gābiia.[58] All this typology would have been impossible on the basis of the Septuagint, where, as observed above, the site of Gideon's victory is called Gabaathamōra.

Kmosko's most powerful, indeed, decisive argument for the priority of the Syriac over the Greek text concerns II Thess. 2:3, a Pauline text basic to most Christian apocalypses and cited and alluded to frequently in Pseudo-Methodius' work. In the Greek text of the New Testament this passage reads μή τις ὑμᾶς ἐξαπατήσῃ κατὰ μηδένα τρόπον. ὅτι

---

57. In one passage (fol. 135 recto) Pseudo-Methodius seems at first sight to combine the Pešitta and Septuagint texts of Psalm 68:31: "he stretches out [*pešaṭ*; cf. προφθάσει] his two hands to heaven and hands over [*mešalem* or *mašlem*; cf. *tašlemi* in Pešitta] the kingdom to God the Father." Yet the mention of "kingdom" and "the Father" shows that Pseudo-Methodius was here combining Psalm 68:31 with I Cor. 15:24: "and then comes the end when he hands over the kingdom to God the Father." The stretching-out of the hands was probably Pseudo-Methodius' own addition, although Kmosko may be right in suggesting that because of the identity of the verb in I Cor. 15:24 and Psalm 68:31 he felt justified, according to the rules of Talmudic exegesis, to use the latter passage ("the hand") for the interpretation of the former.

58. Theophanes, p. 332.10 de Boor (A.M. 6121) uses similar Old Testament typology for this battle: . . . ἀνέστη ὁ ἐρημικώτατος Ἀμαλὴκ . . . καὶ γίνεται πρώτη φοβερὰ πτῶσις τοῦ Ῥωμαϊκοῦ στρατοῦ, ἡ κατὰ τὸν Γαβιθᾶν λέγω καὶ Ἰερμουχὰν [Yarmuk] καὶ τὴν Δάθεσμον αἱμοχυσία. [The desolate Amalek arose . . . and the first fearful fall of the Roman army came about; I mean the blood-letting at Gabitha and Yarmuk and Dathesmos.]

ἐὰν μὴ ἔλθῃ ἡ ἀποστασία πρῶτον καὶ ἀποκαλυφθῇ ὁ ἄνθρωπος τῆς ἀνομίας, ὁ υἱὸς τῆς ἀπωλείας. (Let no one deceive you in any way; for unless first the rebellion comes and the man of lawlessness, the son of perdition, is revealed. . . .) In the Syriac text the word ἀποστασία, "rebellion," is translated by *mardūtā*. This Syriac word derives from the verbal root *merad*, "to rebel," and is therefore an adequate rendering of the Greek ἀποστασία. The Syriac noun is, however, ambiguous: it can also be related to the verbal root *redā*, "to chastise," and then means "chastisement" or "punishment." The Syriac Pseudo-Methodius understood *mardūtā* in the sense of punishment and throughout his tract referred to the Arab invasion as a divine punishment for Christian sins.[59] The Greek translator was puzzled, for his text of II Thess. 2:3 did not contain the notion of punishment, yet he realized that the author of the Syriac apocalypse understood St. Paul to predict a punishment. He therefore cited the biblical text correctly in the Greek form, but surrounded it at its first occurrence with a commentary of his own that interpolated the notion of punishment.[60] This procedure shows clearly that the Syriac and not the Greek text of Pseudo-Methodius was original: the notion of the Arab invasion being a divine punishment for Christian sinfulness could never have been based upon the Greek text of II Thess. 2:3.[61]

---

59. II Thess. 2:3 is first cited on fol. 130 recto; from then on the notion of God punishing the Christians for their sins recurs throughout the tract.

60. P. 31.12 Istrin (= p. 108.1–5 Lolos) ἡ γὰρ ὑπὸ τοῦ ἀποστόλου λεχθεῖσα παιδεία ἤτοι ἀποστασία αὕτη ἐστί [namely, the Arab invasion]. φησὶ γὰρ "ὅτι ἐὰν μὴ ἔλθῃ ἡ ἀποστασία πρῶτον καὶ ἀποκαλυφθῇ ὁ ἄνθρωπος τῆς ἀνομίας, ὁ υἱὸς τῆς ἀπωλείας." ἡ γὰρ ἀποστασία παιδεία ἐστὶ καὶ παιδευθήσονται πάντες οἱ κατοικοῦντες τὴν γῆν. [For the chastisement or rebellion spoken by the apostle is this. For he says, "for unless first the rebellion comes and the man of lawlessness is revealed, the son of perdition." The rebellion is the chastisement, and all the inhabitants of the earth will be punished.] See also the corresponding Latin passage at p. 85.1ff. Sackur.

61. For a long time I thought that an etymological pun was another powerful argument in favor of the priority of the Syriac over the Greek text. On fol. 120 recto of the Syriac text it was said that after leaving the Ark, the sons of Noah built a town and named it "Temanōn because of the names of those eight [*temanē*] souls that remained in the world." The Greek text has here (p. 8.13 Istrin [= p. 56.4 Lolos]) θάμνον ἐπ' ὀνόματι τοῦ ἀριθμοῦ τῶν ἐξελθούσων ὀκτὼ ψυχῶν ἐκ τῆς κιβωτοῦ. The Greek translator seems to have understood that the Syriac author was attempting an etymological explanation (cf. ἐπ' ὀνόματι) but he did not imitate it. The etymology was, however, taken from the *Cave of Treasures* 20.8, p. 965 Riessler "Temanon wegen der acht Menschen, die aus der Arche gegangen waren." It is just another of the many passages and features that Pseudo-Methodius borrowed from this sixth-century work of Mesopotamian origin. As it is conceivable (though unlikely) that a Greek author could have derived it directly from the *Cave of Treasures*, I have abstained from mentioning it in the text among the arguments in favor of the priority of Pseudo-Methodius' Syriac text.

## APPENDIX 1: THREE LISTS OF REGIONS (PEOPLES) OVERRUN BY THE ARABS IN THE SYRIAC TEXT OF PSEUDO-METHODIUS

These lists have been mentioned briefly in the analysis of the text given above (pp. 20–22). The first of them occurs when Pseudo-Methodius prophesies that the four leaders of the Ismaelites—Desolation, Despoiler, Ruin, and Destroyer—will cast lots for the conquered lands. Pseudo-Methodius names for each region the leader to whom it will be allotted and then describes its fate in some detail (fol. 129 recto). The second list is inserted, as it were, retrospectively, where the author describes the height of Moslem power and overconfidence and reviews the nations conquered (fol. 133 recto). A third passage lists the peoples the Christian remnants of which will return to their native lands after the defeat of the Arabs by the Last Emperor (fol. 133 verso). These three lists are presented in tabular form. Names that are beyond doubt are given in the normal English spelling. In doubtful cases the Syriac letters are transcribed. Unfortunately, the lists cannot be controlled by the excerpts of Solomon of Basra (n. 5), because he did not choose to incorporate them.

| *First List,* *fol. 129 recto*[62] | *Second List,* *fol. 133 recto* | *Third List,* *fol. 133 verso* |
|---|---|---|
| 1. Syria | 1. Persians | 1. Cappadocians |
| 2. *sīqīliā* | 2. Armenians | 2. Armenians |
| 3. *eladā* | 3. Cilicians | 3. Cilicians |
| 4. Land of the Romans | 4. Isaurians | 4. Isaurians |
| 5. Islands of the Sea | 5. Cappadocians | 5. *perīqīē* or *ferīqīē* |
| 6. *mezrein* (Egypt) | 6. *sīlīqelīē* | 6. *eladīē* |
| 7. Syria | 7. *eladanīē* | 7. *silūqīē* (Seleucians) |
| 8. Places of the East | 8. Dwellers in Land of Romans | |
| 9. Promised Land | 9. Islands of the Seas | |

62. [Note in Alexander's hand] In the first list, the Greek translation (p. 102.10 Lolos) has Cappadocia in lieu of item 1, Syria. Cappadocia must be correct because Syria reappears as item 7.

This tabulation shows that the first list stands by itself, in form (each item followed by a longish description of its fate; regions rather than peoples), order, and choice of items.

The second and third lists, however, are closely related. Both are bare lists, without commentary. Both enumerate peoples rather than regions. The order of items is partially identical (nos. 2–4). It is probable that in the third list item 5 (*perīqīe*, obviously a mistake for *ifrīqīe*, Africans) is a replacement for (corruption of?) the first item in the second list (Persians). In fact, the two lists are so similar that one feels justified in emending the doubtful names of one with the help of indications in the other. This is certainly appropriate for the impossible item 6 in the second list: *sīlīqelīe*. Here it is easy to see what happened. Every name in the second list is preceded by the preposition *l*, which in the Syriac language marks the determinate object. The only exception is this item, where the scribe erroneously added the *l* at the end rather than at the beginning and changed the -*ū*- into -*ī*-. Thus the entry can be corrected, with the help of the seventh item in the third list, to read: *selūqīe*, "Seleucians."[63] The seventh item in the second list, *eladanīe*, however, is "more correct" than the corresponding entry no. 6 in the third list, *eladīe*. It is true that *eladīe* is unobjectionable in form, and one is at first inclined to emend item 7 in the second list to conform with it. But quite apart from the fact that *eladīā* is attested for "Hellas" but not *eladīō* for "Hellene," it is not easy to see why an author so obviously focusing on the Near East as Pseudo-Methodius is should be interested in Hellas and, particularly, why he should mention Hellenes in addition to "Dwellers in the Land of the Romans" (item 8 in the second list). The problem is resolved by the assumption that here, as in item 6, a copyist inserted the preposition *l*. If these emendations are correct, items 6 and 7 of the second list refer to the Moslem conquest of Seleucia and Adana (*adanīe*) and the third list has these same items in reverse order.[64]

The great advantage of these proposed emendations is that they remove the people of Sicily and Hellas from the second and third lists, in which they disturb the Near Eastern focus. No such controls exist for the first list, but here too one suspects that the second and third items originally referred to Seleucia and Adana rather than to Sicily and

---

63. Note that in the third list this last item is misspelt *sīlūqīe* (in lieu of the normal *selūqīe*). The normal spelling for the city occurs on fol. 123 recto: *selīq*.

64. [Note in Alexander's hand] Were the Seleucians and Adanians originally a gloss on the Cilicians? They were located in Cilicia. Does this explain their corruption, especially the uncertainty as to the proper position of the preposition?

Hellas, though this cannot be proved. If it should be confirmed in the future by new evidence, this would mean that the prophecies of a Moslem conquest of Greece and Sicily, which, as we shall see, gave rise in medieval times to the entire branch of Sicilian apocalyptic literature called the *Visions of Daniel* and in modern times formed a serious difficulty for a correct dating of Pseudo-Methodius' work, were paradoxically due to nothing more serious than early copyists' mistakes in the Syriac tradition.

## APPENDIX 2: TRANSLATION OF THE SYRIAC TEXT OF PSEUDO-METHODIUS FROM COD. VAT. SYR. 58

[118 verso] By the help of God the Lord of the Universe we wrote the discourse composed by my blessed Lord Methodius, bishop [in margin: bishop of Olympus] and martyr, concerning the succession of kings and the end of times.

This blessed man [Methodius] asked of God to know how generations and kingdoms were transmitted from Adam until today. And the Lord sent him one from among his hosts to the mountain of Šenāgar [Singara?]. And he showed him all the generations. [119 recto] He will then also set forth at the beginning of our discourse the kingdoms one by one to distinguished men of learning.

When Adam and Eve departed from Paradise, both of them were virgins. And thirty years after their expulsion from Paradise, Adam knew his wife Eve. She conceived and gave birth to Cain, the first-born of Adam, together with Kelima his sister. And after thirty years she conceived and gave birth ‹to Abel› and Abel's sister Lebuda. And in the hundredth year of Adam's life Cain slew his brother Abel. And Adam made lament over his murder one hundred years. And in the year 230 of the first millennium there was born Seth, a handsome man in the image of Adam. And in the year 500 of that first millennium the women rebelled against their husbands in the camp of the house of Cain and were whores. And without shame the men came in to them and practiced fornication with them publicly. And in the year 800 of the life of Adam wantonness and fornication grew among the daughters of Cain. And Adam died in the year 930 of the first millennium. Immediately the progeny of the house of Seth and his kindred separated from the sons [119 verso] of the slayer. And Seth led away and took with him all his kind, his sons and his grandsons, to the summits of the mountains of

Paradise; and Cain and his kin remained below in the plain where he killed his brother Abel. And in the year 40 of Jared there ended the first millennium, there lived those artificers of sin who were sons of iniquity in the camp of the sons of Cain, Jubal and Tubal-cain, sons of the blind Lamech who killed Cain. And Satan entered and resided in them and they composed and produced all kinds of music, harps and flutes. And in the year 500 of the second millennium men and women ran riot inside the camps of the sons of Cain, and publicly women ran after men and behaved in the pride of mares in a wild herd. Thus the women ran riot in the wantonness of fornication, men as well as women. Satan did battle with the sons of Seth. And at the end of the second millennium there occurred a deluge of waters and the handiwork of 2,000 years was destroyed in one hour. And in the year 312 of Noah's life, in the twelfth generation [120 recto] ‹and› the third millennium, when Noah left the ark, Noah's sons built buildings in this outer region and named the town Temanōn, because of the name of those eight [*temanē*] souls that survived in the world. And in the year 700 of Noah's life and ‹after› 100 years of the third millennium, there was born to Noah a son, a man in stature like his image, and he called his name Ionṭon. And in the year 300 of the third millennium Noah gave gifts to his son Ionṭon and sent him to the East. And after Noah's death in the year 790 of the third millennium, Noah's sons went up from the East and built for themselves a tower in the plain of Babylonian Sin'dor. And there their tongues were confused and they were scattered over the entire earth. And Ionṭon the son of Noah returned to the East and came to the sea called Fire of the Sun, from which the sun rose from the East and where he [Ionṭon] resided. Ionṭon received revelations of wisdom from God and he began first to be familiar with those * * * of the course of the stars. And Nimrod went down to him and he instructed him in all the wisdom. And from him he [Nimrod] received precepts [120 verso] that he would be king, for Nimrod was a man from the sons of Shem. He was the first king over the entire earth. And in the year 799 of the third millennium, in the year 30 of the kingship of Nimrod, he sent men of great power from among the sons of Japheth, wise men and craftsmen skilled in knowledge. And they went down to the East to Ionṭon son of Noah and built for him a beautiful city. And he lived in it and it was called Ionṭon. And there was peace between the kingdom of Ionṭon and the kingdom of Nimrod until the present day. But between the kingdom of Nimrod son of Shem and the kingdom of Pupiënus son of Ham there was not peace, because in the days of Nimrod the sons of Japheth and the sons of Shem waged war against each other. And Ionṭon son of Noah wrote to them ‹saying›: The kingdom of the sons of Japheth will conquer the kingdom of the sons ‹of Ham›. Those two kingships [Japheth and Ham] were in the world from the first, and then occurred the beginning of all the kingships of the nations, and afterward the kingship of Nimrod. When the third millennium was completed, in the year 70 of Aṙu, that is, the year 39 [121 recto] of the fourth millennium, the two kingdoms waged war against each other. And the kingdom of the house of Nimrod conquered the kingdom of Egypt. And the Babylonian kingship was handed down in succession from the seed of mighty Nimrod until the reign of mighty Hormizd. He took himself a wife from the kin of Ham. When Hormizd died, his son 'Azri married his mother and from her there was born to him Hormizd. He assembled many armies, went up to the kingdom of the son of Ham, and captured, destroyed, and burned by fire all the lands of the West. And in the year 2 of the reign of Kodros son of Hormizd there assembled the kingdoms of the Babylonians. In number they were 320,000 foot-soldiers, all of whom were carrying sticks only. And when Kodros heard about them, he laughed and allowed them to come and proceed as far as the Tigris. And against them the powerful king of the Persians sent ‹soldiers› [or: the king sent powerful Persians] as well as mighty warriors riding on elephants. And he went up against them and killed them, and not even one of them survived. And when the fourth millennium was completed, which was the twenty-fifth year of Hormizd, in the first year [121 verso] in which the fifth millennium began, Šam'i'sar, king of the East from the kin of Ionṭon son of Noah, descended and ravaged, from the Euphrates and into Adroigan [Azerbaijan], ninety-seven cities and all their surroundings. And he invaded the three kingdoms of the Ethiopians [Indians] and ravaged and captured and burned with fire, and departed for the desert. And he ravaged and captured the camps of the sons of Ismael son of Hagar the Egyptian handmaid of Sarah wife of Abraham. And he [Ismael] fled from the desert of Jethrib. And they [Ismaelites] invaded the land of peace. And he [Ismael] fought with the kings of the nations and destroyed them. And they [the Ismaelites] laid waste and captured and conquered all the kingdoms of the nations, and the entire land of promise was subject to them, and the earth was full of them and of their camps. And like locusts they walked naked, and they ate meat in vessels of meat and drank the blood of animals. And when the sons of Ismael conquered and subjected the entire earth, they ravaged cities and towns and occupied all the kingdoms of the nations. And in vessels of wood they floated above the waves of the sea and they went to the lands of the West and came as far as the great Rome and as far as [122 recto] Illyricum[?] and

Egypt and Āfnasōliōs[?] and Lūzā the great beyond Rome. And when they had occupied the land for sixty years and had done to it what they wished, after eight weeks and a half [= 60 years], they prevailed over all the kingdoms of the nations and raged and raved in the pride of their haughtiness. And the kings of the Hittites and the kings of the Hivites and the kings of the Amorites and the kings of the Jebusites and the kings of the Girgashites and the kings of the Canaanites and the kings of the Ammonites and the kings of the Philistines were their slaves. And at that time there were four tyrannical leaders, sons of Demunitehta, Oreb and Zeeb and Sbah and Zalmunna. And when he [God] delivered the Israelites by the hands of Moses and Aaron from the oppression of the Egyptians and when they invaded the land of repose[?] and were harnessed under yet another [literally: a double] yoke of slavery for the chastisement of the sons of Ismael, these Midianites boasted. And when God saw the harsh distress distressing them, he delivered them and destroyed them [the Midianites] and their leaders and expelled and drove them out of the cultivated land into the desert of Jethrib. And the survivors made [122 verso] a compact of peace with the sons of Israel. And seven tribes departed for this further desert, but they will come out and ravage the world and bear rule over it. And they will capture places and passes and entrances to the cultivated land from Egypt to Cush and from the Euphrates to India [Ethiopia] and from the Tigris to the sea called Fire of the Sun and the kingdom of Ionṭon son of Noah and from the North to the great Rome and the great sea of Pontus, because their yoke weighs double over the servitude of all nations. And there is no people or kingdom under heaven with whom they [Ismaelites] will fight and not overpower. And after ten weeks of those years they [the Ismaelites] also will be overpowered and subjected by the kingdom of Rome, because it overpowers all the kingdoms and will not be overpowered by any one of them because it possesses truly that unconquerable weapon that conquers all. Henceforward consider closely the successions of the kingships and immediately the truth will be known to you and will show itself to you without disguise and without deception. And until Hadarzaraq, king of the heroes, the ‹house› of the sons of Nimrod [123 recto] held the kingdom of Babylon. And from Hadarzaraq and until Sasan the Old the Persians ruled, and from Sasan and until Piroz, king of kings, ‹and from Seleucia and until Ctesiphon› and from Piroz and until Sennacherib. There was born to him [Sennacherib] from Ainqaṭ, the Corduenian woman, Adramelech [in the margin: these are the royal families] and Šeraṣad ‹and Sarchadom›. And these two sons slew their father. And they fled to the land of the Corduenians. And his son

Sarchadom came to rule in Babylonia in place of his father Sennacherib, and after him Nebuchadnezzar. He [Nebuchadnezzar] was ‹born› from a Lydian father and from the queen of Sheba. And when Sennacherib began to make war on the king of the Indians [Ethiopians], he advanced until Iba [Sheba?] and destroyed many places in it. And his son [Sarchadom] went out with him and he was *Rab Mehaimanē*.[65] And because of his wisdom and manliness there was given to him the kingdom of Babylonia. And he took for wife a woman from Media, Hormazdu the Median, and Darius took for wife Rud the Persian, from whom was born Cyrus the Persian. Listen now how one by one the kingdoms of the East were overpowered. The ‹kingdom of› the Babylonians was overpowered [123 verso] by that of the Medes, and that of the Medes by that of the Persians, and that of the Babylonians overpowered that of the Cushites and of Sheba and of Sāba and the kingdoms of the nations from the sea unto the Euphrates besides the kingdom of the house of David. And the kingdom of Babylonia overpowered the ‹kingdom of› the house of David through Nebuchadnezzar. He overpowered the Hebrews and the Egyptians, and Darius the Mede overpowered the Indians and the Luziē [Lydians?], and Cyrus the Persian overpowered the Thracians and restored the sons of Israel. Listen now how these four kingdoms were overpowered one by the other, that of the Cushites by that of the Macedonians and that of the Macedonians by that of the Greeks, and that of the Greeks by that of the Romans. And these are the four winds of heaven which Daniel saw pouring forth the great sea. Philip, father of the king of kings Alexander, was a Macedonian, and whom did Philip take for wife? Cusheth, daughter of King Pīl of the Cushites. And from her there was born King Alexander of the Macedonians. He built the great Alexandria and ruled in it twelve years. He went down to the East and killed Darius the Mede [124 recto] and conquered many places. And he marched round the earth and descended to the East and went as far as the sea called Fire of the Sun. And he saw there nations filthy and ugly to look at, who were sons of Japheth. And when he saw the abominable deeds which they were doing—they ate the vermin of the earth, mice and dogs and kittens, and they did not enshroud and bury their dead, and the embryos which the women aborted they ate as if it were some delicacy—and when Alexander saw their abominable deeds, he called God to his aid. And he assembled and expelled them and their wives and their sons, and all of their camps he expelled from the East. And he

---

65. [N.B. "leader of the faithful" and "head eunuch" are crossed out as possible translations for the term *Rab Mehaimanē* in Alexander's text.]

placed them and enclosed them from the ends of the North inside the entrance which is the gate of the world from the North, and there is no other entrance nor outlet from the uttermost part of the world from East to West. And King Alexander prayed before God and God hearkened unto him. And God commanded the mountains called Sons of the North, and they drew near each other to a distance of no more than twelve cubits. And he [Alexander] made a gate of brass and anointed it on the inner side with Tāseqtis. [124 verso] If one applies iron in order to open it, one does not affect it. And if one wants to melt it by fire, it quenches the fire brought near to it because the nature of Tāseqtis is not affected by iron, nor by the operation of demons. Also not even fire can destroy ‹it› at all if it is applied to it, for these Unclean Nations who were imprisoned inside used all the wickedness of witchcraft. And through these two mighty things he brought to nought their entire activity so that neither through iron nor through the operation of evil spirits ‹could› it be opened before them and they depart and corrupt men and defile the earth. But at the end of the ages, as was the saying of the prophet Ezekiel which was prophesied concerning them, saying: In the end of times, at the end of the world, the followers of Agog and of Magog will come out upon the land of Israel [Ezek. 38:16]. These are the people whom Alexander imprisoned inside the gates of the North: Ogug and Magog and Joel and Agag and Ashkenazu and Dīpar and Puṭoio and Lydians and Huns and Persians and Daqlaie and Tebelie and Darmetaie and Kaukebaie and Emrataie and Garmidmaie and Men-Eaters who are called Cynocephali [125 recto] and Thracians and Alani and Pīsīlie and Deshie and Salṭraie. These twenty-two kingdoms were imprisoned inside the gates of the North. And when Alexander, the first king of the Greeks, died, because he did not take a wife and had no sons, there ruled after him those generals of his. And Cusheth, mother of Alexander, returned to Cush to the house of her father. And King Byzas, who built Byzantium, the capital surrounded by the sea, sent the general Germanicus to Pīl, king of the Cushites. And he made peace with him and wrote to him concerning his daughter, the mother of Alexander, so that he might take her to wife and might make her queen. And when the king of the Cushites received the letter that was in the hands of Germanicus, commander of Byzas king of the Greeks, ‹and› when he saw the gifts and honors which he sent to him, he rejoiced greatly. And at once Pīl also took with him from the choice produce of the kingdom of the Cushites and also his daughter Cusheth and went up to Byzantium to King Byzas together with thirty thousand Cushites. And he was received hospitably by King Byzas beyond the sea of Chalcedon [125 verso]. And he gave gifts to the hosts that entered inside Byzantium with him, and great honors and gifts according to the bounty of the king he gave to him. And the king of Greece took Cusheth, daughter of King Pīl of the Cushites. And there was born to him from her a daughter, and he named her Byzantia, because of the name of the city that he built. And Armalāos [Romulus], king of the Romans, took to wife Byzantia. And because she was exceedingly beautiful he took her. And because he was an upright [or: simple] man and there was no cunning in him, not even a little, he wrote to Rome and gave her as a gift to Byzantia in Byzantia's marriage settlement. And when this thing was consummated, there arose among the chiefs who were at Rome a great clamor against this thing. And Armalāos begot three times from Byzantia, daughter of Byzas king of Byzantium, and she was the daughter of Cusheth mother of King Alexander: Armalāos and Urbanos and Claudius. And Armalāos [the Younger] reigned in Rome in place of Armalāos [the Elder] and Urbanos reigned in Byzantium the city of his mother, and Claudius reigned in Alexandria, a city in the kingdom of his father. And the offspring of Queen Cusheth, daughter of Pīl king of the Cushites possessed [126 recto] the kingdom of the Macedonians and Romans and Greeks * * * from the offspring of Cusheth daughter of Pīl until eternity because the kingship of Greece which descends from the offspring of the Cushites will hand over the hand to God at the end of times. When the blessed David beheld with far-seeing eye the spirit of God, he saw that from Cusheth daughter of King Pīl of the Cushites it would happen that the kingdom of Greece would be handed down. However, many brethren of the clergy supposed that the blessed David spoke his word concerning the kingdom of the Cushites. And those who thought so erred. For concerning this kingdom of Greece which descends from the offspring of Cusheth and will possess that thing which is placed in the center, which is the Holy Cross, concerning this ‹kingdom›, yea, concerning it, the blessed David said: Cush will hand over the hand [dominion] to God [Ps. 68:31]. For there is no people or kingdom under heaven that can overpower the kingdom of the Christians as long as it possesses a place of refuge in the life-giving Cross, which is set up in the center of the earth and possesses its power over height and depth. Also the bars of Hell which are the tyrants of impiety [or: heathendom] cannot prevail over this kingdom [126 verso] of the Christians. Thus ‹runs› the true saying of Our Savior who spoke to Simon [Matt. 16:187]: Which is the power or kingdom of people below heaven that is mighty and strong in its power and will be able to prevail over the great power of the Holy Cross in which the kingdom of the Greeks, that is of the Romans, possesses a place of refuge? The blessed Paul wrote to the Thessalonians in the second letter when he warned them: Do not be frightened by quick and vain rumors saying: Behold, the day of the Lord Jesus has come [II Thess. 2:2]. As long as this kingdom which possesses an abiding place of refuge is the center, the Son of Perdition will not be revealed, for that something which is in the center is the priesthood and the kingship and the Holy Cross. And this kingship of the Christians overpowers all kingdoms of the earth, and by it all leaders and all authority will be paralyzed and come to nought and all its people will be left destitute, and by it they will be conquered and through it they will come to nought. And in the whole earth there will not be left one leader nor one authority when the Son of Perdition will be revealed, except the kingdom of the Greeks which will hand over the hand to God, as ‹was› the saying of the apostle who said [127 recto]: And he will bring to nought every leader and all authority over all powers, thereupon the son will hand over the kingdom of the Christians to God the Father [I Cor. 15:24]. For the kings of many nations went to battle with the kingdom of the heroes and could not conquer it. Not even the kingdom that overpowered Egypt and slew thirty-one kings of the nations and two lords of the kingdoms of the Amorites, Siphon and Og, and all the tyrants of the Philistines could overpower the kingdom of Babylonia and the kingdom of Rome, which is that of the Greeks. It [the kingdom of Rome] overpowered the kingdom of the Hebrews and destroyed and overthrew it from its foundations and in it has remained not a survivor, not even one trace. And it will sprout again and bring forth fruit—because already it was surrendered into the hands of Vespasian and of his son Titus through whom the kingdom of the Hebrews was destroyed. And immediately their kingdom ravaged the one about which Daniel prophesied: After the Messiah will be killed, it will ravage the holy city [Dan. 9:26]. When the Babylonians overpowered the kingdom of the Hebrews in which were these exalted and most excellent things, priesthood and prophecy and kingship, and when Vespasian plundered and destroyed the holy city [127 verso] there was not found one of these gifts in one of their tribes. Nor ‹could› the kingdom of the Egyptians [resist?], which is that of the Macedonians, which [was overpowered?] by that of the Romans. The kingdom of Media and of Persia and of Armenia was brought to nought. This kingdom [Rome] overthrew all the kingdoms of the earth. After thousands of years the kingdom of the Hebrews was destroyed and ‹that› of the Egyptians after three thousand years. And when the kingdom of the Macedonians which is ‹that› of * * * was destroyed, the kingdom of the barbarians was left destitute by [or: contended with?] the kingdom of Rome, namely, that of the Turks and of the Avars. And when the kingdom of the Hebrews was brought to nought, the sons of Ismael, son of Hagar, contended with Rome in its stead, whom Daniel called seed of the South [in margin: beginning of the sons of Hagar the Egyptian]. And he [Ismael] contended with it [Rome] ten weeks of years because he understands the end and there is no duration in the middle, for ‹it is› in this last millennium, which is the seventh, that is brought to nought the kingdom of the Persians and that the sons of Ismael will depart from the desert of Jethrib and come and assemble, all of them, there at Gabaʻōt the Great. And there will be fulfilled the word of [128 recto] Our Lord who said: ‹We› are like the animals of the field and the birds of heaven, and call them ‹saying›: Assemble and come because today I shall make a great sacrifice for you [Ezek. 39:17]. Eat the flesh of the fattened ‹animals› and drink the blood of the mighty men. For at Gabaʻōt the fattened ‹animals› of the kingdom of the Greeks, who destroyed the kingdom of the Hebrews and of Persia, will be exterminated. And thus they too will be exterminated in Gabaʻōt by Ismael, the wild ass of the desert, who was sent in the wrath of ire against men and against animals and against cattle and against trees and against plants. And it is a punishment in which there is no love. And these four leaders will be sent before them against the entire earth, Ruin and Destroyer and Desolation and Despoiler for every existing city and desolation that destroys everything, for he [God] said through Moses: Not because he loved you did the Lord your God bring you to the land of the nations that you may inherit it, but because of the sins of its inhabitants. Also it was not because God loves these sons of Ismael that he granted to them [128 verso] that they enter the kingdom of the Christians, but because of the iniquity and sin perpetrated by the Christians. The like of it was not perpetrated in any of the preceding generations that men arrayed themselves in licentious clothes of harlots who adorned themselves like virgins and stood publicly in the streets of cities and ran riot in drunkenness and wantonness without hesitation and had intercourse with one another. Also female harlots were standing publicly in the streets, and a man entered and went a-whoring, and he went out and his son came, and with the same woman he polluted himself. And brothers and fathers and sons all polluted themselves with the same woman. And concerning this thing the apostle Paul said: Their males abandoned the use of the nature of women and indulged in lust with one another and males behaved unseemly with males. Again also women abandoned the use of the nature of men and partly held intercourse contrary to nature [Rom. 1:26–27]. Because of this God will deliver them to the defilement of the barbarians.

And heroic men will [first time future tense] be buffeted by the punishment of distress [129 recto] and their women will defile themselves with the sons of uncleanness. But I when I looked and saw these four princes of punishment, Desolation and Despoiler and Ruin and Destroyer, they were casting lots for the land. The land of Persia was given to desolation that it might bring destruction upon it and its inhabitants to captivity and to murder and to desolation. And Syria was given to destruction of desolation and her inhabitants to captivity and to murder. Sicily ‹was given› to ruin and destruction and her inhabited places to captivity and to murder. Hellas ‹was given› to destruction and to desolation and her inhabitants to captivity and to murder. The land of the Romans ‹was given› to desolation and destruction and her inhabited places to flight and to spoiling and to captivity. And the islands of the sea ‹were given› to flight and their inhabitants to captivity of ruin. Egypt and Syria and the places of the East will be harnessed under the yoke of tribute and tax, that is, tribute, in suffering seven times ‹that of› prisoners. And the land of promise will be filled with men from the four winds of heaven like locusts which are assembled by a storm. And there will be in it famine and distress and mortality, and the Despoiler will grow strong. And his horn will be raised and he will adopt [literally: mount, ascend] pride and he will assume ostentation until the time of wrath, and he will seize the entrances of the North and the roads [129 verso] of the East and the straits of the sea. And men and sheep and animals and birds will be harnessed under the yoke of their slavery. And the waters of the seas will be subjected to them, and the waste places, which are deprived of their cultivations, will belong to him, and the tyrants will record them as his. And the fish in the sea and the trees in the forests and the plantings of their fruit and the dust of the earth with its stones and its harvest and the merchandise of the merchants and the cultivation of the husbandmen and the inheritance of the rich and the gifts and holy objects of gold and of silver and of bronze and of iron and clothing and all their utensils of ostentation and the adornments and the foodstuffs and the dainties and all their pleasures and delicacies will be his. And he will be arrogant in his person and in his pride until he will demand one hundred [tribute] from the dead that lie in the dust. And he will take a poll tax from orphans and from widows and from holy men. And they will have no mercy upon the poor and they will not give justice to the oppressed. And they will treat with insolence people of old age and they will sadden the spirit of those that are troubled. And they will take no pity on the sick and will not have mercy on those weak in might, but they will laugh at wise men [130 recto] and will mock at lawgivers and will deride men of learning. And the veil of silence will spread over all men, and all inhabitants of the earth will sit in surprise and in consternation. And the route of their [the Arabs'] advance will be from them [inhabitants] and by them, and what is small will be reckoned like big and mean like noble. And their commands will cut to pieces like that which is in swords [i.e., steel] and nobody will change the assurance of their commands. And their advance will be completed from sea to sea and from the North to the desert of Jethrib and it will be a way to distress. And on it [the way] will journey old men and old women and rich and poor while they are hungry and thirsty and suffer in harsh bondage until they pronounce blessed the dead because this is the visitation of which the apostle said: Unless this punishment cometh beforehand, and thereupon will be revealed that man of sin, the Son of Perdition [II Thess. 2:3]. And this chastisement will not be sent upon men alone but also on everything that is upon the face of the entire earth, upon men and upon women and upon unmarried youths and upon animals and upon cattle and upon birds. And men will suffer [130 verso] in that chastisement, they and their wives and their sons and their daughters and their possessions, and old men weak in power and the weak, together with the powerful and the poor with the [?] rich because God called their father Ismael the wild ass of the desert. And the deer and all the wild and the tame animals inside the cultivated land will be afflicted by them. And men will be pursued and animals and cattle will die and trees of the forest will be cut down and the beauty of the plants in the mountains will be spoiled. And they will destroy prosperous cities and they will capture places without a traveller in them. And the earth will be polluted with blood and the harvests will be taken from it. For these cruel barbarians are not human beings but are sons of desolation and upon desolation their faces are set upon the sword. They are despoilers and for destruction they will be sent. And perdition they are and for the perdition of everything they set out. And polluted they are and pollution they live. And in the time of their eruption from the desert they will tear the infants from the sides of their mothers and like unclean animals they will dash them against the rocks. And they will slaughter those who minister in the sanctuary. And also they will sleep with their wives and with [131 recto] their captured mistresses [literally: daughters of capture] inside the sanctuaries. And they will make liturgical vestments their clothing and that of their sons, and they will bind their beasts of burden inside the coffins of the martyrs and graves of the saints. And they will be cruel and murderers and bloodthirsty and destroyers and a testing furnace for all Christians. For the blessed apostle said: Not all of Israel are Israel [Rom. 9:6]. Also all who are called Christians are not Christians, for seven thousand only were left over from the Israelites in the days of the prophet Elijah. They worshipped the Lord God and all Israel was saved through them. Thus also in the time of the punishment of these tyrants, few from many will be left over who are Christians, as Our Savior showed us in the Holy Gospel and said: When the Son of Man cometh, will he find faith on earth? [Luke 18:8]. Behold also, the spirit of those perfected in portents will grieve in those days of punishment and the multitude of the clergy will deny the true faith [131 verso] of the Christians and the Holy Cross and the mysteries of power. And without compulsion and blows and wounds they will deny Christ and will associate with the unbelievers. And because of this the apostle also proclaimed concerning them: In the last times men will abandon the faith and will go after unclean spirits and after the teachings of demons [I Tim. 4:1] and will be tyrants and slanderers and boastful and haters of virtue and traitors and wild. And all those who are false and weak in the faith will be tried and known in that punishment. They will separate themselves from the congregations of the Christians of their own accord, because that time challenges them to go after its uncleanness. For the humble and the modest[?] and the friendly and the tranquil and the truthful and the freeborn and the wise and the select will not be sought at that time because they will be looked down upon and despised, but instead of them there will be sought the proud and the overbearing and the boastful and the vain and the slanderers and the detractors and the seditious and the unchaste and those who are destitute of love and the robbers and the spoilers and the wild and unskilled and those void of understanding and of the religion of God and those who revile [132 recto] their parents and those who blaspheme concerning the sacred mysteries and deny the Messiah and ignorant men in whom is not the wisdom of God. They will be servants of that one [Mohammed?] and their false words will find credence. And concerning anything that is said to them they will comply. And true men and clerics and wise men and good men will be held in contempt in their eyes and they will be like dung, for they will be ‹subjected› to the punishment of the Ismaelites. And they will be distressed until they abandon hope for their lives. And honor will be lifted from the priests, and the divine liturgy and living sacrifice will cease from the Church. And at that time priests will be like the people, and their corpses will be thrown like mud upon the roads without burial. And throughout those days blows of wrath will be sent upon men, two and three in one day. And a man will go to sleep in the evening and will wake up in the morning and will find outside [132 verso] his door two and three oppressors and they will ask tribute and money. And all thought of things given and of gain will disappear from earth. And at that time men will sell their brasses and their weapons of war. And in that tenth week, when everything ends, they will give their sons and their daughters to the heathens for money. For what reason does God avert his countenance from the aid of the faithful who will endure this distress? So that they be tried and the believers be separated from the unbelievers and the tares and those rejected from the select grains of wheat, because that time is indeed a testing furnace. For God will be patient [grant a respite?] when the worshippers are persecuted who by the punishment will be known as sons, as the apostle proclaimed to us before: Yea, we are without punishment, we are strangers and not sons [Hebr. 12:7]. Also Our Savior ordered and said to us: Blessed are you when they insult you and persecute you and say about you every wicked word because of me lyingly. Thereupon rejoice and jubilate that your reward is great in heaven, for thus they persecuted the prophets who were before you [Matt. 5:12] [133 recto] and: He who hopes until the end will rest [Matt. 10:22]. And after these calamities and punishments of the sons of Israel, at the completion of that week when men lie prostrate in danger of punishment, are completed and there is no hope that they may be saved from that harsh servitude, when they are persecuted and oppressed and beaten and hungry and thirsty and tortured by the harsh punishment, those fierce tyrants too will delight themselves with food and drink and repose and will glory in their victories, they who slew and destroyed the Persians and Armenians and Cilicians and Isaurians and Cappadocians and Seleucians[?] and Hellenes [inhabitants of Adana?] and the settlers of the land of the Romans and all their islands of the seas. And they will be dressed like bridegrooms and will be adorned like brides. And they will blaspheme and say: There is no deliverer for the Christians. Then suddenly there will be awakened perdition and calamity as ‹those› of a woman in travail, and a king of the Greeks will go forth against them in great wrath, and he will be aroused against them like a man who shakes off his wine, and who plots[?] against them as if they were dead men. He will go forth against them from the sea of the Cushites and will lay desolation and ruin [133 verso] in the desert of Jethrib and in the habitation of their fathers. And the sons [allies?] of the king of Greece will seize the places of the desert and will destroy with the sword the remnant that is left of them in the land of promise. And fear of all those around them will fall upon them. They and their wives and their sons and their leaders and all their camps and the entire land of the desert of their fathers will be given into the hands of the kings of the Greeks, and will be surrendered to desolation and destruction and to captivity and murder. And their servitude will be one hundred times more severe than their yoke ‹had been›. And they will be in harsh distress from hunger and from torture. And they will be slaves, they and their wives and their sons, and will minister as slaves to those that had been ministering to them, and their servitude will be a hundred times more bitter than that of theirs [their former slaves]. And the earth will be at peace, which was desolated of its inhabitants, and the remnant that is left will return, everyone to his land and to the inheritance of his fathers, Cappadocians and Armenians and Cilicians and Isaurians and Africans and Hellenes and Seleucians[?]. And the entire remnant [134 recto] of the captives that remained and which was in servitude because of the captivity will return, every man to his country and to the house of his father. And men will multiply like locusts on the earth which has been devastated. And Egypt will be laid waste and Arabia will be burned and the land of Hebron [Hauran?] will be laid waste and the tongue of the sea will be at peace. And all the wrath of the ire of the king of the Greeks will be completed upon those who denied. And there will be peace on earth the like of which had never existed, because it is the last peace of the perfection of the world. And there will be joy upon the entire earth, and men will sit down in great peace and the churches will arise nearby, and cities will be built and priests will be freed from the tax, and priests and men will rest at that time from labor and tiredness and torture, because that is the peace of which He said in His gospel: There will be great peace the like of which never existed, and men will sit down in repose and will eat and drink and rejoice in the joy of their heart, and men will take wives and wives will be given to men [Matt. 24:38]. And they will build edifices and will plant vineyards. And when they eat and drink and rejoice and are merry, there is no wickedness and no thought of wickedness and no fear and trembling [134 verso] in their hearts. During that ‹period of› peace the Gates of the North will be opened and those hosts of nations will come forth who were imprisoned there, and the earth will shake before them. And men will be frightened, and they will flee and will hide in mountains and in caves and in tombs, and they will die from fear and from hunger, and there is none to bury them. And they will be devoured before their fathers when they see them because these nations that will come forth from the North eat the flesh of men and drink the blood of animals and eat the creeping things of the earth and mice and snakes and scorpions and all the unclean reptiles that creep on earth and the bodies of unclean animals and the abortions of sheep. And they slaughter children and will give ‹their flesh› to their mothers and force them to eat the bodies of their sons. And they eat dead dogs and kittens and every ‹kind of› uncleanness and they ravage the earth and there is none who can stand before them. And after one week of calamities all of them will assemble in the plain of Joppe because in that place all these nations will assemble, both they and their wives [135 recto] and their sons. And to that place God will send against them one of the captains of the hosts of the angels, and he destroys them in one hour. And then the king of the Greeks descends and settles in Jerusalem for one week and a half week, in numbers ten years and a half. And then the Son of Perdition will be revealed, the false Christ: He will be conceived in Chorazin and will be born in Ṣaidan and will rule in Capernaum. And Chorazin will glory in him that he was born there, and Beth-saida that he was raised there and Capernaum that he ruled there. And because of this Our Lord pronounced the *Woes* over the three of them in his gospel when he said: Woe to thee, Chorazin, and woe to thee, Beth-saida, and thou, Capernaum, that hast exalted thyself unto heaven, thou wilt descend to Hell [Matt. 11:20–24]. And immediately when the Son of Perdition is revealed, then the king of the Greeks will go up and will stand on Golgotha and the Holy Cross will be set [laid] in that place in which it [the Cross] was set up when it carried the Christ. And the king of the Greeks will place his diadem on top of the Holy Cross, and will stretch out his two hands to heaven and will hand over [135 verso] the kingship to God the Father. And the Holy Cross on which Christ was crucified will be raised to heaven and the crown of kingship with it, because the Holy Cross on which Christ who was crucified for the salvation of all men who believe in him crucified[?] is a sign which will be seen prior to the coming of Our Lord so that it will put to shame the Jews and there will be fulfilled the saying of the blessed David which he prophesied concerning the end of times and said: Cush will hand over the hand to God [Ps. 68:31], because it is the son of Cusheth, daughter of King Pīl of the Cushites, who will hand over the hand to God. And immediately the Holy Cross will be raised to heaven, and the king of the Greeks will give up his soul to his creator. And immediately every leader and every authority and all powers will cease. And immediately the Son of Perdition will be revealed, who is from the tribe of Dan, as is prophesied and said in the prophecy of Jacob: "Dan will be a basilisk that lies on the path [Gen. 49:17–18]" that leads to the kingdom of heaven. Then "that which biteth the horse" are the words in the form of justice. Then "that which throws the rider [136 recto] backward of himself" are the saints who turn aside to his error. "The heel" is the completion of the ages and the end of years declared to us and those holy men who live at that time, and those who ride on the word of holiness who are humble and cast down by labors of justice. "He biteth" them through signs of fantasy of his acts of deception which he performed, and they run after the impostor when they see the lepers cleansed and the blind made to see and the paralytics made to walk and the demons go forth and the sun darken [and it darkens] and the moon being changed to blood on his orders and the trees producing fruit from their branches and the earth bringing forth roots and the springs of water failing[?]. And through these signs of fantasy he will lead astray the saints. Because of this he said: "It biteth the horse in its heel." Indeed for every wound inflicted upon a live body by an iron ‹weapon› or the bites ‹of an animal›, some scar will appear on it. So also for every sin inflicted upon a soul, eternal fire and torment are reserved for it, for "backward" signifies the sinners [literally: side of the left]. And when the blessed Jacob gazed with the eye of the spirit and saw the calamity which was at that time, he spoke thus: Your salvation I wait for, O Lord. And again Our Lord said: If possible Satan will also lead astray the Elect, for this Son of Perdition will enter Jerusalem and will sit in the Temple of God and will pretend to be like God, for he is a man of sin clothed in a body from the seed of a man, and he will be born from a married woman from the tribe of Dan. This child of perdition, through the bitterness of his disposition, will lead astray everyone if possible, because he was made a habitation of all the demons and all their activity will be completed in him. And at the coming of Our Lord from heaven he will be delivered to Hell-fire and to outer darkness. And there he will be in weeping and gnashing of teeth together with all those who believed in him. Us, however, Our Lord Jesus Christ will consider worthy of his heavenly kingdom together with all those servants of his will, and we shall offer up praise and honor and veneration and exaltation now and at all times for ever and ever. Amen.

# II.
# The First Greek Redaction of Pseudo-Methodius

Not long after it was composed, the Syriac text of Pseudo-Methodius was translated into Greek. The Greek text thus is part of that literary current that brought works of Oriental literature to the attention of readers speaking and reading Greek. This important Oriental-Byzantine, East-West direction of literary borrowings is often neglected as compared with the better-known translation of Byzantine works into Syriac, Arabic, Armenian, Georgian, and Coptic, yet it has been studied, particularly for the field of hagiography.[1]

Here the Syriac text of Pseudo-Methodius will be compared with the First Greek Redaction. Emphasis will be placed on the differences, because they may be expected to throw light on the circumstances and mentality of the translator. It should be noted, however, that not all the differences between the two texts were due to the translator. In the first place, there exists as yet no critical edition of the Greek text; it is therefore not always easy to ascertain the reading of the Greek archetype, and even where the reading of the archetype is beyond doubt, changes may have occurred between the time of the translation and the archetype. Furthermore, there are several instances of mistakes in the Codex Vaticanus Syrus 58 where it is the Greek text that preserves the correct reading.[2] Finally, in at least one case, the prophecy of the duration of

---

1. P. Peeters, *Orient et Byzance: Le Tréfonds oriental de l'hagiographie byzantine*, Subsidia Hagiographica 26 (Brussels, 1950). Another seventh-century writer whose ascetical treatises were translated from Syriac into Greek was Isaac of Nineveh: see A. Baumstark, *Geschichte der Syrischen Literatur* (Bonn, 1922), pp. 223–25 and A. J. Wensinck, "Mystic Treatises by Isaac of Nineveh," *Verhandelingen der Koniklijke Akademie van Wetenschappen* (Amsterdam, 1923).

2. On fol. 131 recto of the Syriac text one finds, for example, "And at that time priests will be like the people and their corpses will be thrown like mud upon the roads without

Arab rule, there is evidence of a deliberate textual change in the Syriac tradition while the Greek version preserves what must have been the original Syriac text.[3] In the following discussion the attempt will be made to single out those variants in the Greek text that seem to be due to the author of the First Greek Redaction, but it goes without saying that this procedure entails a series of subjective judgments.

The manuscript tradition of the First Greek Redaction of Pseudo-Methodius has been studied and the text edited by V. Istrin.[4] Here the supposed author, Methodius, is called bishop "of Patara," rather than "of Olympus," as in the Syriac text. In the title the translator also characterizes the content as "the kingship of the nations and the last times," rather than "the succession of kings and the last times," as in the Syriac original.[5] By specifying that the tract deals with the βασιλεία τῶν ἐθνῶν the translator undoubtedly wishes to warn his Byzantine audience to expect a discussion of Median, Persian, Babylonian, Ethiopian, Greek, and pagan Roman rulers, not (or only indirectly) a treatise on the Christian rulers of Byzantium.[6]

The translator rendered into Greek the entire Syriac tract, but some

---

burial." In the corresponding passage of the Greek text it is said (p. 35.8 Istrin = p. 116.6 Lolos): καὶ ἔσονται οἱ ἱερεῖς ὡς ὁ λαός· καὶ ἐν τῷ καιρῷ ἐκείνῳ ἤτοι τῷ ἑβδοματικῷ ἑβδόμῳ χρόνῳ, ἡνίκα πληροῦται ὁ ἀριθμὸς τοῦ χρόνου τῆς δυναστείας αὐτῶν ἧς κατεκράτησαν τῆς γῆς, πληθυνθήσεται ἡ θλίψις ἐπὶ τοὺς ἀνθρώπους καὶ ἐπὶ τὰ κτήνη καὶ ἔσται λοιμὸς καὶ λιμός. καὶ φθαρήσονται οἱ ἄνθρωποι καὶ ῥιφήσονται ἐπὶ τῆς γῆς ὥσπερ χοῦς κτλ. [And the priests will be like the people. And in that time—the seventh age of the world, when the time of their rule over the entire earth shall be fulfilled—oppression over people and beasts will be multiplied and there will be plague and famine. And people will be destroyed and thrown on the ground like mud, etc.] Here the words καὶ ἐν τῷ καιρῷ . . . λιμός are clearly necessary to the context, as they explain the presence of corpses: they must therefore have been part of the Syriac text.

3. See Chapter I, n. 25 above. The Syriac original, fol. 122 verso, has Arab domination lasting ten year-weeks; the Greek versions, edited by Lolos, have, alternately, seven and seventeen year-weeks (p. 66.22 Lolos). [For this as a piece of chronological adjustment to account for the apparent non-fulfillment of the prophecy, see remarks in "Medieval Apocalypses as Historical Sources," p. 1001.]

4. BHG 2036, ed. Istrin, pp. 1–49, discussion in Izsledovanie, pp. 25–69. It should be noted that the Greek text printed by Istrin is not a critical edition, but represents the text of Codex Vaticanus Reg. Pii II 11, saec. XVI. In the critical apparatus Istrin notes the variants of seven further manuscripts, none of them earlier than the fifteenth century. Of the Latin translation of the Greek text much earlier manuscripts are extant, one from the seventh to eighth century and three from the eighth: see Sackur, Sibyllinische Texte, p. 57. [See now pp. 24–36 Lolos for a discussion of earlier editions. This text offers the first critical edition of the Greek text.]

5. Title in Cod. Vat. Reg. Pii II 11 Τοῦ ἐν ἁγίοις πατρὸς ἡμῶν Μεθοδίου ἐπισκόπου Πατάρων περὶ τῆς βασιλείας τῶν ἐθνῶν καὶ εἰς τοὺς ἐσχάτους καιροὺς ἀκριβὴς ἀπόδειξις.

6. Cf. pp. 16.21–17.5 Istrin (= pp. 74.1–10, 76.1–5 Lolos) Ἄκουε τοίνυν πῶς συνήφθησαν ἀλλήλοις οὗτοι οἱ τῆς Βαβυλωνίας μὲν τοῖς Μήδοις καὶ περικρατεῖς γεγόνασιν οἱ ἐκ Βαβυλῶνος τῆς τε Αἰθιοπίας καὶ Σαβὰ καὶ τῶν βασιλέων τῶν ἐθνῶν, and p. 17.11 Ἄκουε τοίνυν . . . πῶς αἱ τέσσαρες βασιλεῖαι ἀλλήλαις συνήφθησαν Αἰθίοπες Μακεδόσι καὶ οἱ Ῥωμαῖοι Ἕλλησιν κτλ.

major omissions are noteworthy. He neglected to translate the brief preamble in which the Syriac author represents Methodius as asking God "concerning the generations and concerning the kingdoms" and receiving an answer from one of the angels on "the mountain of Šenāgar."[7] One cannot be certain why the translator omitted this passage, but it is probable that he was not familiar with Ğebel Sinğar, or thought that his readers did not know it, or both. He also replaced the revealing reference to "many brethren of the clergy" by the neutral "some" ($\tau\iota\nu\varepsilon\varsigma$) where the Syriac text discusses conflicting interpretations of Psalm 68:31.[8] Again, it is probable that the Greek translator had little interest, and could presuppose little interest on the part of his Byzantine readers, in the internal disagreements of eastern Syrian churchmen. Moreover, there are in the Greek translation other instances (to be discussed presently) of the translator suppressing or toning down remarks unfavorable to the clergy, and he may have felt that this reference to priestly disagreements belonged in that category.[9]

While there are thus a number of significant omissions in the First Greek Redaction of Pseudo-Methodius, the additions of the Greek translator are few, short, and unimportant, except for certain expansions of the scriptural evidence which will be discussed later. On the whole the translation is faithful—at points literal, in other passages reflecting fairly accurately the intent of the Syriac text. There is, however, one passage where the Greek text differs radically from the Syriac original. It occurs where the Syriac Pseudo-Methodius discusses the past victories of Rome over Hebrews, Macedonians, Medes, Persians, and Armenians. This entire section is replaced in the First Greek Redaction by a very different development that also stresses the invincibility of the Roman Empire but is limited to the history of the Jewish people and its

---

7. Chapter I, n. 10 above.
8. Chapter I, n. 20 above.
9. Other omissions of the Greek translator are more difficult to explain. On fol. 122 recto the Syriac text mentions a series of kings of pre-Israelite tribes of Canaan enslaved by the Midianites, comparable to that in Josh. 3:10, but in the Greek text (p. 14.2 Istrin [= p. 66.68 Lolos]) this list is suppressed. On fol. 129 recto the Syriac text describes in visionary language how the countries conquered by the Arabs were each allotted to one of "these four princes of punishment, Desolation and Despoiler and Ruin and Destroyer," but this lively and plastic vision of an allotment to personified principles of destruction is so obscured in the Greek text (pp. 28.16ff. Istrin [= pp. 100.9ff. Lolos]) that it is almost impossible to recognize. On fol. 134 recto the Syriac writer describes in rather crass colors the prosperity of Christians after the defeat of the Arabs by the Last Emperor ("they eat and drink and rejoice and are merry"), but these words are omitted by the Greek translator (p. 44.1 Istrin [= p. 128.95–100 Lolos]) perhaps precisely because of their crassness. Possibly for the same reason the Greek translator left out some of the more lurid elements in the description of cannibalistic practices of the Unclean Peoples (cf. fol. 134 verso of the Syriac with pp. 43.13ff. Istrin [= pp. 128.90–95 Lolos]).

relations to Rome.[10] Ernst Sackur pointed out as early as 1898 that the Greek passage, which he considered in Latin translation, agreed, partly verbatim, with the text of Anastasius of Sinai's *Disputatio adversus Judaeos*.[11] However, in view of the serious doubts over the authenticity of this work it would be imprudent to rely on this agreement in defining the time of the translation.[12]

The omission of the preamble with its reference to Ǧebel Singar makes one wonder whether the Greek translator may have obliterated

10. Compare Syriac Pseudo-Methodius, fol. 127 recto: "For the kings of many nations went to battle with the kingdom of the heroes and could not conquer it. Not even that kingdom which overpowered Egypt and killed thirty-one kings of the nations, and two lords of the kingdom of the Amorites, Sehon and Og, and all the tyrants of the Philistines could overpower the kingdom of Babylonia and the kingdom of Rome, which is that of the Greeks. It overpowered the kingdom of the Hebrews and destroyed and overthrew it from its foundations, and in it has remained no survivor, not even a trace. And it will change and put forth fruit because already it has been handed over into the hands of Vespasian and his son Titus, through whom the kingdom of the Hebrews was destroyed. And their kingdom ravaged immediately the one about which Daniel prophesied: After the Messiah will be killed, it will ravage the city of sanctity. When the Babylonians overpowered the kingdom of the Hebrews in which are these exalted and most excellent things, priesthood and prophecy and kingship, and when Vespasian plundered and destroyed the city of sanctity, there was not found one of these gifts in one of their tribes. Nor [could] the kingdom of the Egyptians [resist?], which is that of the Macedonians, which existed because of that of the Romans. The kingdom of Media and of Persia and of Armenia was brought to nought. This kingdom [Rome] overthrew all the kingdoms of the earth" with pp. 24.15–25.10 Istrin (= p.92.7–14 Lolos) ποῦ γὰρ ἔστιν ἢ ἔσται βασιλεία ἢ ἑτέρα δυναστεία ταύτης ὑπερηφανεστέρα. Εἰ δὲ βούλει σκοπῆσαι τὸ ἀκριβές, λάβε μοι τὸν Μωσέα λαὸν τὸν τοσούτοις σημείοις καὶ τέρασι καὶ βυθῷ θαλάσσης τοὺς Αἰγυπτίους ἐκτείλαντα. ἴδε μοι Ἰησοῦν τοῦ Ναυῆ, ὑφ' οὗ καὶ ὁ ἥλιος κατὰ Γαβαὼν ἵσταται καὶ ἡ σελήνη κατὰ φάρυγγα Ἐλώμ, καὶ ἄλλα τινὰ ἐξαίσια θαύματα γεγονότα καὶ ἁπλῶς ἅπαν τὸ τῶν Ἑβραίων ἐννόησον κράτος, πῶς ὑπὸ τῆς τῶν Ῥωμαίων βασιλείας ἐξήλειπται. οὐ Τίτος καὶ Οὐεσπασιανὸς κατέκοψαν ἅπαντας; οὐκ ἀρότρῳ τὸν ναὸν ἐκπορθήσας Ἀδριανὸς ἠρωτρίασεν; τίς οὖν ἄρα γέγονεν ἢ γενήσεται κατ' αὐτὴν ἑτέρα βασιλεία; ἀλλ' οὐδεμία(ν) εὑρήσομεν εἴπερ τῆς ἀληθείας φροντίσομεν. οὐ χίλια ἔτη ἐβασίλευσαν οἱ Ἑβραῖοι καὶ ἐξεκόπη ἡ βασιλεία αὐτῶν; [Where is there or will there be a kingdom or any other power surpassing this? If you wish to examine the accuracy of the statement, take the people of Moses, who put the Egyptians to flight with so many signs and wonders, even in the depths of the sea. Consider Joshua son of Nun, for whom the sun stood still on Gabaon and the moon at the mouth of Elom and various other extraordinary miracles took place, and, to put it clearly, the whole power of the Hebrews understood that it would be eclipsed by the empire of the Romans. Did not Titus and Vespasian destroy all? Did not Hadrian, having pillaged the church, plough it under? What other kingdom came or will come against it? We will find no other if we care for the truth. Did not the Hebrews rule a thousand years, and yet their kingdom was destroyed?] The next two sentences, while not identical in the Syriac and Greek versions, are so closely related that it is difficult to say whether the translator here returned to the Syriac text of Pseudo-Methodius or continued to rely on the source he had used in the section immediately preceding.

11. Sackur, *Sibyllinische Texte*, pp. 40, 79, and cf. PG 89.1212 and Kmosko, "Rätsel," pp. 293–95.

12. The authenticity of *Disputatio adversus Judaeos* and its date are a matter of doubt, but it is noteworthy that independently of each other Charles H. Haskins, "Pascalis Romanus, Petrus Chrysolorus," *Byzantion* 2 (1925), pp. 231–36, esp. 231f., and Kmosko, "Rätsel," p. 294, have given reasons for assuming that the original version of the work was composed in the seventh century.

or obscured other allusions to the Mesopotamian background of the Syriac work and perhaps replaced them by features more familiar to a Greek-reading public. The treatment of Alexander the Great is interesting in this respect. On fol. 123 verso the Syriac Pseudo-Methodius calls Alexander "king of kings" and a few words later "king of the Macedonians," but in the Greek text the first title is omitted altogether and the second replaced by the surprising term Ἑλλήνων (or: Ἕλλην) τύραννος γεγονώς.[13] How are these changes to be explained? Presumably the translator considered the Babylonian title "king of kings" too unusual for his audience, so he applied instead to Alexander the designation "tyrant of the Greeks," introduced into Greek literature by the author of IV Maccabees for a successor of Alexander, Antiochus IV Epiphanes.[14]

Frequently, the Syriac Pseudo-Methodius refers to the Byzantine Empire and its emperor as "the kingdom of the Greeks" (*malkūtō deiaunoiē*) and "king of the Greeks" (*malkō deiaunoiē*).[15] In these passages the Greek translator has replaced the words "of the Greeks" by "of the Romans" or has added the latter expression.[16] Here the translator wishes to make it absolutely clear that Pseudo-Methodius' prophecies referred to the Roman (Byzantine) Empire. Twice the Syriac author refers to three talismans: to priesthood, prophecy, and kingship in the case of the Jewish state, and to priesthood, kingship, and the Holy Cross for the "kingdom of the Christians."[17] Both passages have disappeared in the Greek translation—although the Byzantine Empire could certainly claim the last three items—perhaps because the Syriac author's belief in royal talismans did not appeal to the taste of the translator or his readers.

The translator was also concerned lest anything unfavorable be said about the clergy. It has already been mentioned that where the Syriac

---

13. P. 17.15–17 Istrin (= p. 76.6–8 Lolos).

14. IV Macc. 18:20: ὁ πικρὸς Ἑλλήνων τύραννος. I owe this solution to a suggestion of Professor Frank Gilliam of the Institute for Advanced Study, Princeton.

15. Fols. 123 recto and 128 recto: kingdom of the Greeks. Fols. 133 recto, 134 recto, 135 recto (three times): king of the Greeks.

16. Replacement: pp. 22.15, 42.12, 45.1, 45.11, 45.14 Istrin (= pp. 88.35, 126.80, 130.112, 132.7–8, 132.10 Lolos). Addition: p. 27.1 (= p. 96.9 Lolos) οἱ δυνάσται τῶν Ἑλλήνων, τουτέστι τῶν Ῥωμαίων.

17. Fol. 127 recto: "When the Babylonians overpowered the kingdom of the Hebrews in which were those exalted and most excellent things, priesthood and prophecy and kingship, and when Vespasian plundered and destroyed the city of sanctity [Jerusalem], there was not found one of those gifts in any of their tribes." Fol. 126 verso: "As long as [?] this kingdom which possesses an abiding place of refuge in the center [exists?], the Son of Perdition will not be revealed, for that which is in the center [II Thess. 2:7] is the priesthood and the kingship and the Holy Cross."

author alludes to disagreements among the clergy concerning the interpretation of Psalm 68:31, the translator eliminates the reference to the clergy. And in his "prophecy of the Arab Invasion" Pseudo-Methodius predicts that "the multitude of the clergy will deny the true faith of the Christians and the Holy Cross and the sacraments," but the translator simply attributes this apostasy to πολλοί, without specifying the clergy.[18]

Underlying the Syriac Pseudo-Methodius' thesis of the duration of the Roman (Byzantine) Empire to the end of time, as the heir of Ethiopian royalty, is the conviction that the prerogatives of a kingdom were inherited by its conqueror. That is why the notion of the "overpowering" of one kingdom by another is a key concept throughout the Syriac tract. The Greek translator normally renders this notion satisfactorily by verbs such as κατακρατεῖν (prevail over) and κατακυριεύειν (gain dominion over).[19] A few lines before and after these accurate translations, however, he replaced, at least partially, the Syriac author's remark that the Medes overpowered Babylonia, the Macedonians overpowered Ethiopia, the Greeks the Macedonians, and the Romans the Greeks by the very different concept that the aforementioned realms were joined together (συνήφθησαν).[20] This tendency is so marked that Sackur, who knew the Latin and (to a lesser extent) Greek texts only, thought that the principle underlying Pseudo-Methodius' narrative and thesis was that of dynastic marriages.[21] This principle is indeed implied by the Syriac original, as is evidenced in the many stories of princesses of one house marrying princes of another and thereby passing on to their husbands some of their families' possessions and prerogatives (e.g., Hormazdu the Median marrying Sennacherib, king of Babylonia; Cusheth of Cush marrying Philip of Macedon and, later, Byzas of Byzantium; Byzantia of Byzantium marrying Armalāos of Rome), but it is the Greek translator who by his use of the word συνάπτειν makes this implication explicit. It is probably for the same reason that he transforms the generals who, according to the Syriac Pseudo-Methodius, succeeded Alexan-

---

18. Compare fol. 131 recto of the Syriac text with p. 33.12 Istrin (= p. 112.10 Lolos).
19. E.g., p. 17.6 and 7 Istrin (= p. 74.12 Lolos).
20. For the Syriac text see fol. 123 recto: "Listen now how one by one the kingdoms of the East were overpowered" [eṯḥesen] and fol. 123 verso: "Listen now concerning these four kingdoms how they were overpowered [eṯḥesen] one by the other, that of the Cushites by that of the Macedonians and that of the Macedonians by that of the Greeks and that of the Greeks by that of the Romans." Compare p. 16.21 and 17.11 Istrin (= pp. 74.5–6, 76.1–2 Lolos) (n. 6 above).
21. Sackur, *Sibyllinische Texte*, p. 20: "Da bemerkt man denn sehr bald, dass der Geschichtserzählung ein bestimmtes Prinzip zu Grunde liegt. Der Autor, der die Abfolge und Vereinigung der verschiedenen Reiche darlegen will, lässt dies durch Heiraten geschehen." See also ibid., p. 33.

der into Alexander's sons, in spite of the statement of the Syriac author (omitted by the translator) that Alexander had no sons.[22]

Very strange also is the translator's attitude toward Byzantium and Rome. The Syriac text tells how King Armalāos of Rome gave the city to his bride, the princess Byzantia of Byzantium. He characterizes the bridegroom as *pešiṭ*, which can mean either "upright" or "simple," and states that he was a man without a trace of cunning (fol. 125 verso). The translator, on the other hand, renders this by calling Armalāos ἄγαν ἁπλοῦς καὶ μεγαλόψυχος (very simple and generous [romantic?]) (variant: μεγαλόδωρος, munificent). He thus chose to translate the Syriac adjective *pešiṭ* in its pejorative sense and even strengthened this meaning by the addition of the word ἄγαν. The second Greek adjective, μεγαλόψυχος, if this is the correct reading, supposedly is meant by the translator as an equivalent for the absence of cunning noted by the Syriac author, but it is difficult to know whether he is using it in the positive sense of "generous" or the negative meaning of "romantic" or "quixotic."

The net effect of the translator's characterization of King Armalāos and of his gift of the city of Rome to his Byzantine bride seems to be thoroughly critical, but nothing indicates that he had any Roman affiliations or anti-Byzantine prejudices—rather the contrary. The translator's objection to the gift must therefore have been aimed not against the particular gift, the city of Rome, but against the act of donation as such. Roman law had from early times known the institution of the dowry (*dos*) given by the father of the bride to the bridegroom. On the other hand, early Roman law had been extremely hesitant toward gifts made by the bridegroom or husband to his bride or wife. Until the time of Justinian I, such gifts had to be agreed upon prior to the marriage. The institution of *donatio propter nuptias* permitted by Justinian found its way into later Roman law from various Eastern legal systems such as that of Syria and perhaps of Greece.[23] It has been pointed out above that the translator makes explicit the principle, implied in the Syriac original, that by marriage a husband acquires the possessions and claims of his wife. It is therefore not surprising that the translator should have

---

22. Compare fol. 125 recto of the Syriac text, "And when Alexander, the first king of the Greeks, died, because he did not take a wife and had no sons, there ruled after him those generals of his," with p. 20.17 Istrin (= p. 84.1–2 Lolos) τελευτήσαντος τοιγαροῦν τοῦ ᾿Αλεξάνδρου ἐβασίλευσαν ἀντ' αὐτοῦ οἱ τέσσαρες παῖδες αὐτοῦ· οὐ γὰρ ἔγημε πώποτε. [And then when Alexander died there ruled after him his four sons. For he never married at all.]

23. On the *donatio propter nuptias* in post-classical Roman law and its Eastern origins see Max Kaser, *Das römische Privatrecht*, Handbuch der Altertumswissenschaft, zehnte Abteilung, dritter Band, zweiter Abschnitt (Munich, 1959), pp. 134–36.

disapproved of a husband like Armalāos divesting himself—by donation to his bride—of his claim to the city of Rome. Such a procedure presented no difficulty for the Syriac Pseudo-Methodius, because the *donatio propter nuptias* was an ancient feature of Syrian law; but from the translator's point of view, Armalāos in his excessive simplicity had allowed himself to be taken advantage of by his beautiful Byzantine wife. The translator's attitude toward Armalāos is, therefore, another instance of abandoning a feature of the Syriac background and substituting for it an attitude based on Roman (Byzantine) tradition.

The Greek translator's treatment of biblical quotations deserves a few words. It has been shown above that he normally translates the Pešitta text found in the Syriac original of Pseudo-Methodius. But it has also been mentioned that where differences between the Pešitta and Septuagint texts were relevant to the Syriac writer's thesis or argument, he adopts a compromise. Furthermore, in one major passage the wording of the Greek translation differs radically from the Syriac original, yet the meaning is fairly similar. On fols. 135 verso to 136 recto the Syriac text cites word by word Gen. 49:17, each word being followed by an interpretation. In the Pešitta the biblical passage reads as follows: "Dan will be the snake on the path and the serpent on the ways that bites the horse in its heel and throws its rider behind it. I wait for thy salvation, O Lord." The Syriac and the Greek texts agree that the words are a prophecy of the Antichrist because he will be descended from Dan. The Syriac text of Pseudo-Methodius interprets the "path" to be the way to heaven, and "that which biteth the horse" to be the "words in the form of justice," i.e., the Christian faith; the "rider" stands for "holy men," and the "biting" is the apparent miracles performed by the Antichrist. All these interpretations occur in different terms in the First Greek Redaction, where the entire biblical passage is cited consecutively. It is noteworthy that in this case the translator cites the biblical verse from the Septuagint ("Dan will be the snake in the way sitting on the path that bites the heels of the horse, and the rider will fall to the rear awaiting the salvation of the Lord"); he has ἐγκαθήμενος (sitting), for which there is no counterpart in the Syriac Bible, πεσεῖται ὁ ἱππεύς (the rider will fall) where the Pešitta has "he throws its rider" and περιμένων (awaiting) in lieu of "I wait for." He proceeds in similar fashion with II Thess. 2:1–8.[24] Again, the translator supplies a longer excerpt from Rom. 1:26f. than the Syriac Pseudo-Methodius; moreover, he corrects

---

24. II Thess. 2:1–8 is cited with one omission from the Greek New Testament on p. 23.14–24.8 Istrin (= p. 90.3–13 Lolos), while the Syriac Pseudo-Methodius cited from this long passage only verse 2 of the Syriac Bible and that in a very free and abbreviated way.

the order in which the passage was cited in his Syriac original.²⁵ Finally, he provides two longish excerpts from the Greek text of I Tim. 4:1–2 and II Tim. 3:1–5, while the Syriac Pseudo-Methodius contains only a brief fragment of the first quotation and nothing of the second.²⁶ It seems, then, that wherever the translator felt impelled to supply a biblical quotation on his own authority, he derived it from the Greek rather than the Syriac Bible.

This internal analysis of the First Greek Redaction has thrown some light on the attitudes and mentality of the translator but has determined nothing definite as to his time and place. He lived in the Byzantine Empire, as is shown by his sharp distinction between it and the "kingdoms of the nations" and by his use of the Greek Bible whenever he cited on his own authority. Perhaps he was a refugee from areas occupied by the Arabs, which would explain his knowledge of the Syriac language. Because he lived in the Byzantine Empire and wrote for a Byzantine public he deemphasized, adapted, or omitted several features of the Syriac background. In addition to quoting from the Greek Bible, he borrowed a lengthy passage from Anastasius of Sinai's *Disputatio adversus Judaeos* and wrote of Alexander the Great in unflattering terms borrowed from the author of IV Maccabees' designation of Antiochus IV. The fact that he omitted several unfavorable references to the Christian clergy makes it probable that he himself was a priest or a monk. The translation must have been made after the middle of the seventh century, when the Syriac original was composed, and before A.D. 800, the latest possible date for the earliest manuscript of the Latin translation,²⁷ which was derived from the Greek text.

25. The Syriac text of Rom. 1:26f. runs: "Because of this did God hand them over to the pains of dishonor, for their women changed the use of their nature and had intercourse in some way contrary to nature. And again also their men in the same way abandoned the use of nature of women and had intercourse in lust one with the other." The Syriac Pseudo-Methodius quotes this text fairly literally (fol. 128 verso) but cites the phrase about men before that on women. The Greek translator took the quotation from the Greek New Testament, beginning with the statement on women and mentioning the men second. He also expanded the citation by adding to the part quoted by the Syriac Pseudo-Methodius the beginning of verse 26 and the end of verse 27 (p. 28.8–13 Istrin [= p. 100.3 Lolos]).

26. Compare fol. 131 verso of the Syriac text with p. 34.5–10 and 16–21 Istrin (p. 114.1–5 and 11–16 Lolos).

27. Sackur, *Sibyllinische Texte*, p. 57.

# III.
# The *Visions of Daniel*: Extant Texts

The translation of the Syriac apocalypse of Pseudo-Methodius into Greek marked the beginning of a new era in the history of Byzantine eschatology. Most, if not all, of the apocalypses composed after the appearance of this translation show its impact to a greater or lesser extent. In later centuries, the first Greek translation underwent repeated editorial revisions to which are due the later Greek redactions and the Latin and Slavic translations.

In addition to the later Greek redactions placed by the editors under the name of Methodius, there are other reworkings of Pseudo-Methodius' apocalypse where the name of Methodius has disappeared and which are attributed to a prophet and apocalyptist of the Old Testament: the *Visions of Daniel*. Istrin has shown that the pieces that go under this title are truncated and interpolated redactions of the Greek Pseudo-Methodius.[1] Normally they abbreviated, or even omitted altogether, those parts of Pseudo-Methodius' work that dealt with ancient history—thereby obliterating the author's principal thesis of the permanence of the Byzantine Empire, or at least depriving it of its pseudo-historical underpinning. Presumably, the authors of the *Visions of Daniel* were interested less in Pseudo-Methodius' speculations about early history, which to a public even vaguely familiar with the Classical tradition must have appeared as preposterous as they do to us moderns, than in his descriptions, couched in prophetic language, of the Arab invasions and his predictions about victories over the Arabs. In turn, certain sections of Pseudo-Methodius' apocalypse dealing with the Arabs

---

1. Istrin, *Izsledovanie*, passim, esp. pp. 253ff., 325f.

offered the authors of the *Visions of Daniel* opportunities for interpolating new materials based on historical experiences that had accumulated after the time of Pseudo-Methodius or that they themselves were witnessing.

Four texts entitled *Visions of Daniel* are preserved in full.[2] The original text of the first of them is lost, but a Slavonic translation survives. To facilitate reference, I shall call it the *Slavonic Daniel*.[3] A second text was attributed erroneously to St. John Chrysostom, and I shall cite it as Pseudo-Chrysostom.[4] To a further Greek *Vision of Daniel* I shall refer, for lack of a better designation, by its first words: *Daniel* Καὶ ἔσται.[5] Finally, there is a piece called *The Last Vision of Daniel*, here cited as the *Last Daniel*.[6]

## 1. THE *SLAVONIC DANIEL*

An annotated English translation of this text will be found in the Appendix.

The title of this piece, in the only manuscript that preserves it, is *Vi-*

---

2. [Alexander was not able to include two recently published texts related to the *Visions of Daniel*: *L'Apocalisse Apocrifa di Leone di Constantinopoli*, ed. Riccardo Maisano (Naples, 1975) (composed, according to the editor, in the early decades of the ninth century), and a Syriac apocalypse of uncertain date, Hans Schmoldt, "Die Schrift 'von Jungen Daniel' und 'Daniels Letzte Vision,' Herausgabe u. Interpretation zweier apokalyptischer Texte," Diss. Hamburg, 1972.]

3. Edited three times: by P. S. Srechkovic, "*Zbornik Popa Dragolia*," Srpska Kralievska Akademija, *Spomenik* 5 (1890), pp. 10f., from a manuscript, now lost, once no. 466 [632] of the Belgrade National Library, thirteenth century; then by Istrin, pp. 156–58, from Codex Athos Chilandar 24, twelfth or thirteenth century; finally, by P. A. Lavrov, *Apokrificheskie Teksty*, Sbornik Otdeleniia Russkago Iazyka i Slovesnosti Imperatorstago Akademia Nauk 67, no. 13 (St. Petersburg, 1899), pp. 1–5, from the Chilandar manuscript, with the variants from the Belgrade codex. Unfortunately, Lavrov failed to reprint from the Belgrade codex the *incipit* missing in the Chilandar manuscript. Normally, I mean by the term *Slavonic Daniel* both the lost original and the Slavonic translation. Whenever I want to distinguish between the two, I have noted this. The *Slavonic Daniel* is discussed by Istrin, *Izsledovanie*, pp. 260–68, and by Wilhelm Bousset, "Beiträge zur Geschichte der Eschatologie," *Zeitschrift für Kirchengeschichte* 20 (1900), pp. 103–31, 261–90, esp. pp. 262–81.

4. *BHG* 1871, ed. A. Vasiliev, *Anecdota Graeco-Byzantina* (Moscow, 1893), pp. 33–38. On this text, see the philological analysis by Istrin, *Izsledovanie*, pp. 256–59; Bousset, "Beiträge," pp. 103–131, 261–90. Bousset called the piece M II and paid much greater attention to its historical interpretation than did Istrin.

5. *BHG* 1872, ed. Vasiliev, *Anecdota*, pp. 38–43. See Istrin, *Izsledovanie*, pp. 260–68 (discussed in conjunction with the *Slavonic Daniel*); Bousset, "Beiträge," called it D I. I regret the inelegant designation proposed in the text but was unable to find another that would not anticipate my conclusions as to times and places of composition.

6. *BHG* 1874, ed. Vasiliev, *Anecdota*, pp. 43–47; see Istrin, *Izsledovanie*, pp. 268–87; Bousset, "Beiträge," referred to this text as B V. [Alexander had not completed an analysis of this text, and since he did not refer to it in any articles or later sections of the work, it is not clear whether he intended a separate treatment of this version.]

*sion of the Prophet Daniel on the Emperors and the Last Days and on the End of the World.*

The text begins with a short preamble (1) in which the angel Gabriel places the prophet Daniel on a high mountain and predicts the future of the human race. The prophecy itself then starts with a lengthy series of rulers (2) in which it is easy to recognize, one by one, the Byzantine emperors, referred to as animals, horns, or scepters, beginning with Leo III "the Isaurian" (717–741) and ending with Michael II (820–829) and his son and co-emperor Theophilus (co-emperor since 821, alone 829–842). There follows a brief traditional piece (3) concerning a cruel ruler, then a tetrarchy and an emperor from Heliopolis. Without any kind of transition it is then prophesied (4) that he (the emperor from Heliopolis?) will send messengers to the Western regions and that various internal disorders will culminate in an Ismaelite (Arab) invasion of an island. Several place-names (Akrodunion, Mariana, Enna) are mentioned in this section. There follows a short excerpt from the First Greek Redaction of Pseudo-Methodius which includes that author's list of countries ravaged by the Arabs, ending with Sicily (5). To this the *Slavonic Daniel* appended a section on the anointment of a divinely revealed emperor at Akrodunion and on his victory at Perton over the Arabs (6).

It is then predicted that the victorious emperor will tame the Blond Beards (Peoples?), will expel the Arabs, and will thus fulfill a prophecy: "Dog and whelp together will pursue the field." The emperor will proceed to Rome via "Longobardia" (7). From there he will march to the City of the Seven Hills (Constantinople), destroy several rivals, and enter the city. He will rule peacefully for thirty-two years; his reign is described in language borrowed from Pseudo-Methodius (9). Under the following ruler an eruption of the Unclean Peoples is described, again in the terms of Pseudo-Methodius. They will finally be exterminated by an archangel (10). The Last Emperor then takes up residence at Jerusalem and deposits his crown on Mount Golgotha on the Cross. The text ends with the Son of Perdition (the Antichrist) slaying Enoch and Elijah (11).

The original text of this work was certainly written in Greek, as is shown, for example, by several words that make no sense in Slavonic and reveal themselves as erroneous translations from Greek.[7] It is also clear that the author borrowed heavily from the First Greek Redaction of Pseudo-Methodius—namely, most of (5) describing the effects of the Moslem invasions on the Christian churches and the geographic extent

---

7. See Appendix below, nn. 16, 25, 27, 31, 35.

of these invasions; the picture of the Christian churches after their future liberation by a Messianic king (9); the prophecy of the invasion of Unclean Peoples (10); and that of the Antichrist and of a Last Roman Emperor surrendering his empire unto God (11).[8]

With regard to the date of the *Slavonic Daniel* it is of interest that the list of emperors (2) ends with Michael II and his son and co-emperor Theophilus and that it is there predicted that Michael II will be led to the Κυνήγιον, i.e., executed.[9] In fact, Michael II died from a disease of the kidneys;[10] the list must therefore have been completed after the designation of Theophilus as co-emperor (12 May 821) but prior to his father's death (October 829).[11] This interval can be narrowed down further by a consideration of (4). As I have shown elsewhere, the author was here describing the rebellion of Euphemius and the beginnings of the Arab occupation of Sicily in the summer of 827.[12] It is surely noteworthy that both the list of emperors (2) and the Sicilian paragraph (6) can be dated to the reign of Michael II. Since these are the only historical parts of Pseudo-Chrysostom's apocalypse, it is clear that the work must have been written in Sicily between 827 and 829.[13]

---

8. Cf. Istrin, *Izsledovanie*, pp. 257, 263f., and the Appendix below, nn. 41, 43, 45, 56–58.
9. See Appendix below, n. 25.
10. J. B. Bury, *A History of the Eastern Roman Empire* (London, 1912), pp. 118f.
11. Bury, *Eastern Roman Empire*, pp. 80, 119.
12. See below, Appendix, p. 68 and n. 34, and my paper referred to there. It is difficult to know whether the author knew of the Arab siege of Syracuse (827–828). Section (4) ended without referring to it and (5) was derived from Pseudo-Methodius. It seems, however, that the mention of Sicily by Pseudo-Methodius prompted the author to return in (6) to events in Sicily, for both the Rebel City and Akrodunion, mentioned in (4), recur here. At one time (4) and (6) may have formed a whole.
13. I imagine the process of composition as follows. A Sicilian living at the time of the Arab invasion of the island in 827–828 was struck by the mention of Sicily in the First Greek Redaction of Pseudo-Methodius and by his description of the difficulties experienced by the Christian clergy in the occupied areas, which he considered applicable to the historical situation of Sicily under the Arabs. This Sicilian therefore retained of Pseudo-Methodius' work (5) and (9)–(11). He then grouped around (5), where the Greek Pseudo-Methodius had prophesied the Arab conquest of Sicily, an historical section explaining how that conquest of Sicily had come about (4) and a formulation of his hopes for miraculous Greek victories over the Arabs, (6) through (8). To round off his composition he added a preamble (1) on the circumstances of the Vision, a list of historical emperors (2) to establish his prophetic credentials, and some traditional material (3). In remarks that I found difficult to follow in detail but are nevertheless valuable, Istrin, *Izsledovanie*, pp. 256–59, shows that three specific borrowings from Pseudo-Methodius in the *Slavonic Daniel* were due neither to the Slavonic translator nor to the author of the (lost) Greek original, but were already part of a (lost) source of this Greek original, for the same borrowings are found in Pseudo-Chrysostom. If Istrin is right in his philological analysis, my remarks at the beginning of this footnote apply to the source of the *Slavonic Daniel*'s Greek original as postulated by Istrin, rather than to the Greek model of the *Slavonic Daniel*.

## APPENDIX: ENGLISH TRANSLATION OF *SLAVONIC DANIEL*[14]

### Vision of the Prophet Daniel on the Emperors and the Last Days and on the End of the World

[1] The angel Gabriel came to the prophet Daniel and spoke as follows: Daniel, beloved man, I have been sent to you to announce and show you the last days. Do place them in your heart and listen to what is going to happen to the human race because of the sins of those who will live in them [i.e., the last days]. The angel took me and placed me on a high mountain where there was no trace of a human being. And the angel said to me: Place this in your heart and listen! Behold four large beasts coming out of the sea. They are the four winds.[15] And I said to the angel: My lord, what are these beasts that have come out of the sea?

[2] And the angel said to me: These are the great empires in the last days. The first beast, whose shape is like a lion, is the Isaurian Empire. It will rise up against the altar and destroy it. It will hold its empire strongly and forcefully for twenty-two years. And at the end of it, it will blaspheme with shameless face and attention against the Highest God. It will drive a priest from his throne. And because of his blasphemy there will rise up ‹against him one› from his race and from his empire. He will drive him from his throne for three years. And this emperor will return and slay him, and all his princes will be afraid.[16] And another scepter will arise from the root of his throne and his name will be bestial, which is called by the name of a wild animal. And it will take a wife from a Helladic place.[17] And there will arise another scepter[18] from his

---

14. This translation is based on Lavrov's edition of the text, which gives the text from the Chilandar codex. Since the beginning is missing in this manuscript, I have translated this part from Srechkovic's edition of the (lost) *Zbornik Popa Dragolia*. In cases of variants, I translated what I considered the correct reading. Only significant variants are noted in the notes to the translation.

15. Dan. 7:2–3.

16. The Byzantine emperors Leo III, the "Isaurian" (717–741), and Constantine V (741–775). Both were Iconoclasts. In 730 Leo deposed the patriarch Germanos. At the beginning of his sole reign Constantine was faced with the rebellion of his brother-in-law Artavasdos (742–743) and temporarily lost the capital to him; eventually the rebel was blinded. Cf. Ostrogorsky, *History of the Byzantine State*, pp. 165f. The use of the Slavonic noun *česarstvo* in the sense of "dynasty," here and later, is interesting. Normally, it means "kingdom" or "empire" rather than "dynasty." The author was translating Greek βασιλεία—which can mean either "empire" and "dynasty"—and erroneously chose to render the first meaning. This is the first of many passages showing that the Slavonic text is translated from a Greek original.

17. The emperor Leo IV (775–780), son of Constantine V and husband of Irene of Athens.

18. With this word the Chilandar manuscript begins.

loins. Its name is written in Hellenic script with the first letter of the alphabet, but in the Roman script it begins with the eighth letter. And it will rule with its mother the empress and with her it brings about revivals [from the dead?]. And while he will rule together ‹with her›, his mother will fraudulently lay hands upon him.[19] So I, Daniel, said to the angel: My lord and prince of the angels, and the horns which I saw? ‹The angel replied:› They are the Roman empires. They will rise up in the last days. The first ‹horn› will lay hands upon its son. Afterward it rules five years. Woe to thee, Babylon of the Seven Hills, because in thee the woman with the one breast rules.[20] Another horn will arise, an emperor from the race of Gopsin, which has the number * * * and his rule is firm and strong. In his days a powerful nation will set out and wage war against him. And this nation will flee before him. And afterward this people will return and fight, then it weakens. Later this emperor will give up his weak soul miserably.[21] Then another horn will

19. For most of 780–797, Constantine VI, son of Leo IV and Irene, ruled jointly with his mother. The apocalyptist's remark about the initial letter of the emperor's name is mysterious. It seems to indicate that it began with an *alpha* in Greek and the letter "H" in Latin. Is Hadrian or a similar name meant? This kind of semi-learned camouflage of a name is old apocalyptic practice: see the *Oracle of Baalbek*, line 157 (pp. 18f., ed. Alexander) concerning the name Zeno: ἔστι δὲ τὸ ὄνομα αὐτοῦ ἐν γράμμασι Ῥωμαϊκοῖς εἰς τὸ τέλος τοῦ ἀλφαβήτου, γραφόμενον δὲ Γραικῶς ἀπὸ τοῦ ἑβδόμου γράμματος; [His name stands in Roman letters at the end of the alphabet but is written in Greek letters beginning with the seventh letter]; also line 164 about Anastasius Silentiarius (with my note *ad locum*, p. 37). Constantine VI, however, never had another name, so there must be some confusion. His mother had him blinded in 797. The Slavonic word translated above by "empress" is *vasilija*, where the Chilandar manuscript reads *mr'tv*, "dead." This variant is probably connected with the enigmatic item on "revivals." Istrin, *Izsledovanie*, p. 262, suggests plausibly that there is here a confusion of ἀνάστασις and ἀποστασία.

20. Reference to the sole rule of Irene, 797–802, after the blinding of her son. ἡ ἑπτάλοφος is a standard designation of Constantinople. Irene is here thought of as an Amazon.

21. The emperor Nicephorus I (802–811). The *Zbornik Popa Dragolia* reads *Gotin* for *Gopsin*. The numeral is hopelessly corrupt in both manuscripts; did it express the sum of the numerical values of the letters making up the name of Nicephorus or of Gopsin? The nation against which Nicephorus went to war were the Bulgars. He was defeated and slain by them in 811 (Ostrogorsky, *History*, p. 196). Very interesting is the remark about the descent of the emperor Nicephorus from the house of Gopsin. The Arab historian Tabarî reported that according to Roman sources the emperor Nicephorus "was a descendant of Gafna of Ghassān" (E. W. Brooks, "Byzantines and Arabs in the Time of the Early Abbassids," *English Historical Review* 15 [1900], pp. 728–747, esp. 743.) The above passage in the text shows that Tabarî was right and that the tradition of Nicephorus' Arab descent was indeed Byzantine. Here it appears for the first time, in a Byzantine source composed less than two decades after the emperor's death. The Syriac chronicler Michael the Syrian (†1199) offered a fuller version of this tradition according to which an ancestor of Nicephorus, Djabalā, settled in Cappodocia (French translation of this chronicle by J. B. Chabot, III [Paris, 1905], p. 15, and, derived from it, the *Chronography* of Bar Hebraeus, vol. I [London, 1932], pp. 120f.). On the dynasty of Gafna see Th. Nöldeke, "Die Ghassânischen Fürsten aus dem Hause Gafna's," *Abhandlungen der Kgl. Akademie der Wissenschaften zu Berlin* (1887), and on Djabalā ben al-Ayham in particular, ibid., p. 45 (Nöldeke dated him ca. A.D. 635); also Irfan Shahîd, "Ghassan," *Encyclopedia of Islam* I² (Leiden, 1965), pp. 1020f., and "Djabala b. al-Ayham," ibid., pp. 354f.

arise from his seed, briefer than all ‹the others›.²² Another horn will arise, with an angelic name, and take its throne.²³ A fifth horn will arise and seven years will go by.²⁴ And afterward there will arise another horn beginning with the first imperial letter. And while it occupies the throne, ‹there is› another horn and they will begin to utter blasphemy against the Highest. And because of its blasphemy it will perish miserably and they will lead him to the Hunter.²⁵

[3] And afterward another horn will arise, which has a name adding up to 5,631[?].²⁶ And it holds its throne as a cruel beginning of the entire world in the land of his empire.²⁷ In his days there will arise four emperors, two from the East, two from the West, as you saw the four winds coming out and stirring up the sea.²⁸ They are those and they will wage fierce war and destroy each other like the grass of the field. And there will be much disorder on earth. And there will arise an emperor from the City of the Sun and he will destroy them. And he will win a great victory and enter the City of the Seven Hills and bring peace to the people. After that ‹there will be› a massacre[?]. And blessed is he who rests in the faith.²⁹

---

22. Stauracius, son of Nicephorus, in a battle against the Bulgarians (26 July 811) received a wound that was to prove fatal; he was proclaimed emperor, but abdicated on his deathbed in October 811 (Ostrogorsky, *History*, pp. 196f.).

23. The emperor Michael I Rangabē (811–813), proclaimed to replace the dying Stauracius.

24. The emperor Leo V (813–820). It is surprising that the author, who condemns Leo III and Constantine V so strongly for their Iconoclasm, fails to praise Irene for her restoration of image worship or to censure Leo V for his renewal of the fight against religious images.

25. The emperor Michael II (820–829), founder of the new Amorian dynasty, and his son and co-emperor (since 821) Theophilus are meant. Both were Iconoclasts. The word *lovic* signifies "hunter," which makes no sense. It is clearly a literal translation either of Greek Κυνηγός, which was the name of one of the quarters of Constantinople situated on the Golden Horn, or, better, of Κυνήγιον on the Seraglio Point near the Palace of Mangana (R. Janin, *Constantinople byzantine*, 2nd ed. [Paris, 1964], pp. 376f.). In the latter quarter executions frequently took place. The apocalyptist, therefore, predicts that Michael II will be executed like a common criminal. This prediction proved wrong, for Michael II died from a kidney disease (Bury, *Eastern Roman Empire*, pp. 118f.). The passage was therefore written while Michael II was still alive. It is also important because the word *lovic*, meaningless in this context, proves that the Slavonic text was translated in an excessively literal fashion from a (lost) Greek original.

26. The words "which . . . 5,631" have dropped out in the Chilandar manuscript because of a repetition of the participle *imy*. The meaning of the numeral is obscure.

27. The words *načelo liuto* ("cruel beginning") are meaningless. All is well, however, if one assumes (cf. n. 25 above) that *načelo* is a mistranslation of ἀρχή, which can mean both "beginning" and "rule."

28. Dan. 7:2.

29. The preceding paragraph (3) contains traditional material. In particular, the tetrarchs and the emperor from Heliopolis (City of the Sun) are ancient apocalyptic motifs. For the emperor from Heliopolis see, for example, my edition of the *Oracle of Baalbek*, line 205. A tetrarchy of two kings from the East and two from Syria is mentioned ibid., line 180. The notion of a king from the City of the Sun is much older, for it

[4] And he will send trustworthy envoys also to the Western regions. And[30] when they reach the Western regions, the inhabitants of the city called Tyrannis will rebel, sally forth, and begin to commit acts of injustice.[31] And afterward those who are in that place will rise up and destroy ‹each other› by the sword. And they will arise against each other and fight battles with each other. And two rebels[32] will arise, the first from the East of that city and the other from the West.[33] And they will meet each other in a place called Akrodunion.[34] And they will destroy each other so that the sea will be mingled with their blood. And a pregnant woman will arrive from the territory of that city where there stood in those days a sign.[35] And when she sees her brother lying dead, she will beat her breast and give birth to her child.[36] And grief[37] will overcome her for a long time. And the Ismaelites will enter the extremity of that island[38] and take much booty. And so they will come to a place called Mariana.[39] And the rebel[40] will establish them in that place. And he will

---

occurs already in the *Apocalypse of Elijah* 30.2 (transl. Paul Riessler, *Altjüdischer Schrifttum ausserhalb der Bibel* [reprint Darmstadt, 1966], p. 118), and in *Oracula Sibyllina* 13.151 ἡλιοπέμπτος ἐκ Συρίης [sun-sent from Syria]. Bousset, "Beiträge," pp. 106f., thought that Odaenathus of Palmyra was meant.

30. The words "also. . . . And" are omitted in the *Zbornik Popa Dragolia*, clearly because of the twofold mention of the "Western regions."

31. In the Chilandar manuscript the city is called Tyinaris, and in the *Zbornik Popa Dragolia* it is Turinis. The latter manuscript adds after this word: "of the city of Serdica" (= Sofia), the first of a series of interpolations to be discussed separately. The verbal form translated in the text by the verb "to rebel" is *mučeše(i)*, from *močiti*, "to torture." Now the noun *mučitel'* (n. 32 below) is used in Slavonic to render the Greek τύραννος; see the First Church Slavonic Redaction of Pseudo-Methodius, p. 87. 16 Istrin. The verb *močiti* is a fairly adequate translation of Greek τυραννεῖν in the sense of "to behave like a tyrant." Here, however, it must be used to render τυραννεῖν with the meaning of "to rebel," another example of a faulty, because excessively literal, translation from the Greek. [The historical interpolations were discussed by Alexander, "Historical Interpolations in the *Zbornik Popa Dragolia*."]

32. *Mučitele*, lit. "torturers."

33. After "West" *Zbornik Popa Dragolia* adds (cf. n. 31 above): "from Glavinica."

34. *Zbornik Popa Dragolia*: "Krodunium." I have investigated the historical events referred to in (4) in "Les Débuts des conquêtes arabes en Sicile et la tradition apocalyptique byzantino-slave" (see "Introduction," n. 16, above), and shown that they refer to the Arab campaign in Sicily A.D. 827. "Akrodunion" is Achradina, suburb of Syracuse.

35. *Znameniiem*, "sign." This must be another mistranslation from Greek σῆμα or σημεῖον, which can mean "sign" and also "tomb." This clause about the "sign" or "tomb" is, incidentally, the only one with the verb in the aorist tense; everywhere else the writer uses the present. The *Zbornik Popa Dragolia* interpolates after the word *znameniiem*: "at Pernik."

36. The Chilandar manuscript: "And she sees her brother lying dead and beats her breasts and her child." The *Zbornik Popa Dragolia*: "She sees her brother, being a mother, beats her breast and gives birth to her child." Neither of the manuscripts seems to be altogether correct.

37. *Zbornik Popa Dragolia*: "sleep."

38. *Zbornik Popa Dragolia* adds: "of the Danube."

39. *Zbornik Popa Dragolia* adds: "and to Mraka."

40. *Mučitel'*; cf. n. 31 above.

come as far as a place called Enna.⁴¹ And people will come to its aid and they [the Ismaelites] will not occupy it.

[5] And Daniel said to the angel: Tell me, my lord, why do these afflictions befall the entire world? And the angel said to me: Because the Lord God does not⁴² love Ismael will he give him strength to encompass the land of Rome, but because of the sins of those residing in it. The honor of the priests will be cancelled and the sacrifice disappear from the churches. And the priests will be like people.⁴³ At that time in the seventh age⁴⁴ when the number of the Ismaelites will be full and when they already hold their power, they will plunder Persia and Romania [the Roman Empire] and the other islands of those[?] who reside near Jerusalem, and Calabria⁴⁵ and Sicily. And they will blaspheme and say: The Romans will escape from our hands.⁴⁶

[6] And without announcing it they will set forth secretly from this city called Rebel ‹City›⁴⁷ and find there someone by divine revelation in the midst of it carrying two coins in order to receive crumbs. And they will seize him, whose name is in the thirtieth chapter, and lead him to Akrodunion. And there they will anoint him forthwith emperor, whom people considered like a dead man. He will set out against the Ismaelites with great ire and a multitude of men. He will meet the Ismaelites in a place called Perton⁴⁸ and will fight[?] a fierce battle. And there is in that

41. *Zbornik Popa Dragolia* adds: "Vel'blud [modern Küstendil]."
42. Omitted in *Zbornik Popa Dragolia*. The angel's reply in this paragraph is derived, with many mistakes, from Pseudo-Methodius, e.g., pp. 27, 35 Istrin (= pp. 96, 116 Lolos). In this reply, the text is altogether different from the corresponding passage in the First Slavonic Redaction of Pseudo-Methodius, p. 97 Istrin—another proof that the *Slavonic Daniel* is an independent translation from a lost Greek original. The entire passage from the beginning of (5) to the end of (8) reappears verbatim in Pseudo-Chrysostom, p. 36.3–37.13 Vasiliev. These parallel Greek texts can be used to correct mistakes in the *Slavonic Daniel*. Here Pseudo-Methodius, p. 27.12 Istrin (= p. 98.4 Lolos) and Pseudo-Chrysostom, p. 36.15 Vasiliev, show that in the Chilandar manuscript the negative stands in the wrong place and that the passage should run "Not because the Lord God loves Ismael," etc.
43. Pseudo-Methodius, p. 35.7 Istrin (= p. 116.4 Lolos) οἱ ἱερεῖς ὡς ὁ λαός [the priests like the people]; Pseudo-Chrysostom, p. 36.10 Vasiliev ἱερεῖς ὡς ὁ κοινὸς λαός [priests like the common people].
44. Mistranslation of τῷ ἑβδοματικῷ χρόνῳ [in the seventh year-week]; cf. Pseudo-Chrysostom, p. 36.11 Vasiliev.
45. Chilandar: "Ilavria"; *Zbornik Popa Dragolia*: "Lavria." Cf. Pseudo-Chrysostom, p. 36.14 Vasiliev Ῥωμανίαν τε καὶ Πισιδίαν καὶ τὰς λοιπὰς νήσους εὑρισκομένους πλησίον Ῥώμης, Καλαβρίαν τε καὶ Σικελίαν.
46. Cf. Pseudo-Methodius, p. 39.4 Istrin (= p. 120.4 Lolos) οὐκ ἔχουσιν ἀνάρρυσιν οἱ Χριστιανοὶ ἐκ τῶν χειρῶν ἡμῶν [the Christians will have no escape from our hands]; Pseudo-Chrysostom, p. 36.16 Vasiliev οὐκ ἔχουσιν ἀνάρρυσιν ἐκ τῶν χειρῶν ἡμῶν οἱ Ῥωμαῖοι [The Romans will have no escape from our hands]. These parallels show that a negative has been omitted in the Slavic text.
47. *Zbornik Popa Dragolia* adds: "of Serdica [Sofia]."
48. After this name *Zbornik Popa Dragolia* adds: "There are two hills on one side of Serdica [Sofia]."

place a well with two mouths so that the blood of Romans and Ismaelites will be mingled. And the Lord God will surrender the Ismaelites into the hands of the emperor.

[7] And afterward he will send ‹envoys› to all his ‹lands› and build naval armaments. And he will send his forces into the inner Roman lands and they will tame the Blond[?] Beards.⁴⁹ Both will drive away ⁵⁰ Ismael. And then there will be fulfilled the saying that dog and whelp together will pursue the field.⁵¹ And when the emperor journeys to Rome, he will come to a place called Longobardia⁵² and those who are in that place offer resistance. And he will accept [them?]⁵³ and enter Rome. And he will come to a place where a vessel is hidden. And he will knock with his whip against the bronze idol in which the vessel is hidden. By divine command it will open and he will make gifts to the people from this gold.

[8] And he will leave Rome with a multitude of people and journey on land to the City of the Seven Hills by this dry road. And none will oppose him because the Lord God is with him. And the fear of the emperor, whose name is in three hundred, meaning ‹it begins with the letter› *tau*, will be heard everywhere. And when the two hundredth ‹number›, meaning ‹it begins with the letter› *sigma*, hears of his cruelty, it will flee from the City of the Seven Hills into the inner regions of the Eastern land and will perish miserably. And there will arise the tenth horn which lasts less than one year. And it will fight with the Ethiopian emperor and many of his princes will flee to him. And the tenth horn will be destroyed by the Ethiopian emperor.⁵⁴ And he will enter the ‹City

---

49. Pseudo-Chrysostom, p. 36.32 Vasiliev, reads ξανθὰ ἔθνη. Clearly either the Greek original had corrupted γένη into γένεια or the translator had confused the two words. ξανθὰ ἔθνη "the Blond Peoples," is the standard Byzantine designation of the Western peoples: see Mauricius *Strategicon*, ed. Mihaescu, pp. 106.25, 140.1, 274.18.
50. Chilandar: *oba ko proženet*; *Zbornik Popa Dragolia*: *i tako proženet*; Pseudo-Chrysostom, p. 36.32 Vasiliev καὶ ὁμοῦ διώξουσιν [and they will pursue together].
51. Cf. Pseudo-Chrysostom, p. 36.34 Vasiliev . . . κύων καὶ σκύμνος διώξουσιν ἀγρόν [the dog and the whelp will pursue the field]; *Daniel* Καὶ ἔσται, p. 39.33 Vasiliev λέων καὶ σκύμνος ὁμοῦ διώξουσιν [the lion and the whelp will pursue together]; Pseudo-Hippolytus, as cited by Liudprand of Cremona *Legatio* 40, p. 196 Becker (see p. 101 below) λέων καὶ σκίμνος ὁμοδιώξουσιν ὄναγρον [the lion and the whelp will pursue the ass together]. Undoubtedly, Liudprand comes closest to the original wording of the prophecy, but the Pseudo-Chrysostom proves that the Slavonic translator was rendering it in a highly corrupt form (λέων changed to κύων, ὄναγρον to ἀγρόν).
52. Chilandar: "Vardiia"; *Zbornik Popa Dragolia*: "Ibardiia." Both manuscripts add *Longi-* after the next word. See Pseudo-Chrysostom, p. 37.1 Vasiliev εἰς τόπον λεγόμενον Λωγγιβαρδίας [to the place called Longobardia].
53. Chilandar: *prějeet*; *Zbornik Popa Dragolia*: *prějem*; Pseudo-Chrysostom παρακαλέσας. Was the correct reading *priz"vli*, from *priz"vati*?
54. *Zbornik Popa Dragolia* adds: "The first day of the coming month of August passes after Michael has taken the empire. And the mountains begin to divide [and] the fish to die in the streams and the Lord will be with him forever."

of ‹the› Seven Hills[55] from the West and hold his empire with all ‹his› might. And he will humble his enemies under his foot.

[9] And ‹his› scepter[56] rules thirty-two years. And all his wrath will be ‹directed› against both his ire and[57] against those who have turned away from the Lord. And the entire earth will be at peace and there will be great rejoicing on earth such as neither existed nor will exist. And princes will be like emperors and paupers like rich men. And he will send ‹envoys› to the four corners of the entire world. And they will assemble pious men who fear God and seek retaliation for innocent blood and for the scoffing of the Church. And there will be talking among the many ‹people› assembled. And the emperor will sit with them and they will discuss together. And the churches of the saints will be restored even in their images. And they will build the destroyed altars. And there will be none in those times to do or suffer injustice. And the scepter will end in peace and the Lord God will grant it rest.

[10] Afterward another scepter will arise. In his times twelve emperors will arise from the Gates of the Snakes.[58] And the earth will shake before their face and people will be afraid and flee to the mountains and to the caves. And many will perish, and there will be none to bury the bodies. Indeed, those Unclean Peoples will depart from the mountains and begin to eat human flesh and to drink the blood of wild beasts. And these Unclean ‹Peoples› will eat the bodies of the dead. And the earth will be defiled by them. And none will be able to stand against them until the time that is ordered for them. And after their time is completed, the Lord will send one of his archangels and destroy them.

[11] And afterward there will arise a Roman Emperor. And he will take up residence at Jerusalem for twelve years. And afterward there will appear the Son of Perdition. Thus he will be born in the village of Chuza[59] and be raised in Vit'saida and rule in Kaper'nauma [Capernaum]. Woe to thee, Chuzina [Chorazin], for he will be born in thee, and to thee, Vit'saida [Beth-saida], because he will be raised in thee and

---

55. *Zbornik Popa Dragolia* substitutes "Thessalonica."
56. *Zbornik Popa Dragolia* adds "at Thessalonica" and has "thirty-three" instead of "thirty-two."
57. The words "against both his ire and" seem superfluous. The passage from "all his wrath" to ‹will exist› is derived from Pseudo-Methodius, p. 42.12–43.3 Istrin (= p. 126.10–12 Lolos), where "both his ire" is missing. Istrin, *Izsledovanie*, p. 264, points out that the form in which paragraph (9) appears in the *Slavonic Daniel* is closely related to the *Daniel Καὶ ἔσται*, p. 41.10–24 Istrin, and explains this relationship by the fact that both passages are based on the same source derived from Pseudo-Methodius.
58. *Aspidov' vrat'*. Are the Caspian Gates meant? The rest of paragraph (10) is derived from Pseudo-Methodius, p. 44.3–16 Istrin (= p. 128.11–130.11 Lolos).
59. *Zbornik Popa Dragolia* adds "at Strumica."

to thee, Kaper'nauma, because he will rule in thee.[60] And when the Son of Perdition will appear the Roman Emperor will ascend the Place of Skulls. And the Emperor will place his crown on the Cross and pray to the Lord God. And he will lift his hands to heaven and hand over the Christian Empire to the God and Father. And after that the Son of Perdition will begin to do signs and wonders. And the springs will dry up and the Egyptian sun be turned into blood. And two men will appear who have not tasted death, Enoch and Elijah. And the Son of Perdition will fight with them and slay them on the Cross ‹on which› was crucified Our God Jesus; and he will receive their soul from their mouth. Glory to Our God forever and ever.

## 2. PSEUDO-CHRYSOSTOM

In the manuscripts this short piece is attributed to St. John Chrysostom, but in fact it was composed in a much later age. It is made up largely of fragments from earlier apocalypses, notably from Pseudo-Methodius' *Revelation*, so much so that it could be called an abbreviated version of that work. It consists of four parts. It begins with Pseudo-Methodius' narrative concerning the Ethiopian princess Cusheth, her daughter from King Byzas, Byzantia, the latter's marriage to Romulus, and the interpretation of Psalm 68:31 according to which the Christian Empire is to last to the end of time.[1] There follows, as a second part, a piece not found elsewhere, in which it is said that God, because of the sinfulness of Christians, will call in the Ismaelites, who then will enter the City of the Seven Hills (Constantinople) with arms and horses, shed much blood, carry off large amounts of booty, and advance ἕως ’Ατταλῶν.[2] The third part reproduces, again almost literally, certain parts of the (lost) Greek original of the *Slavonic Daniel*. In section (5) of that work, where the angel speaks of the devastation by the Arabs of certain countries, Pseudo-Chrysostom inserts after the mention of Sicily the words: "the so-called Rebel City" and then continues with the *Slavonic Daniel's* prediction of a divinely revealed emperor

---

60. Matt. 11:20. Much of (11) is derived from Pseudo-Methodius, pp. 45f. Istrin (= pp. 130f. Lolos).

1. Compare pp. 33–35.28 Vasiliev with Pseudo-Methodius, p. 17.11–24.16 Istrin (= p. 84.4–90.3 Lolos). The borrowing is almost literal, with some omissions and abbreviations.

2. Pp. 35.28–36.3 Vasiliev: [The Ismaelites] εἰσελεύσονται ἐν τῇ πόλει τῇ ἑπταλόφῳ ἐν ἅρμασι καὶ ἵπποις καὶ ἕνεκαν τούτων πολλῆς αἱματεκχυσίας [Vasiliev suggests a lacuna], οὐκ ὀλίγον ποιήσαντες δὲ καὶ σκῦλα. τί χρὴ λέγειν; καὶ εἰσῆλθεν ’Ισμαὴλ [τῷ ἀγγέλῳ] ἕως ’Ατταλῶν. I have bracketed the words τῷ ἀγγέλῳ because they recur in, and belong to, the next line.

anointed at Achradina and destined to defeat the Arabs at Petrinon.³ The fourth and final part is again literally taken from Pseudo-Methodius and is strictly eschatological: the coming of the Antichrist, the episode of Enoch and Elijah, and the Second Coming.⁴

This analysis of Pseudo-Chrysostom's *Vision of Daniel* shows that the only part with a claim to originality is the second.⁵ It must, then, be here, if anywhere, that the author reveals his concerns and gives a clue as to the place and date of composition. This brief section presents two striking features, which may facilitate the interpretation of the entire work.

In the first place, the author must have written it after 827–828, for that is, as has been shown above, the date of the *Slavonic Daniel* and it has just been mentioned that in his third part Pseudo-Chrysostom excerpted it. Now, the ninth century was a period when Byzantine warfare against the Arabs took place in Asia Minor, far from the walls of Constantinople; when, except for occasional Arab forays such as the khalif

---

3. Compare pp. 36.3–37.13 Vasiliev with the *Slavonic Daniel*, sections (5) through (8), ending with the words: "and will perish miserably" (Ch. III, sec. 1, above). Pseudo-Chrysostom was obliged to insert, very clumsily, the words τὴν καλουμένην Τυραννίδα πόλιν ["the so-called Rebel City"] because he had omitted the discussion of Syracusan affairs in the *Slavonic Daniel* in section (4) and therefore had to find a way to connect his list of countries devastated with the prophecy that follows. The name of the place of the anointment is corrupt in the printed text of Pseudo-Chrysostom (μέχρι δίνης ["at a whirlpool"] but it can be emended with certainty from the *Slavonic Daniel* (6) into μέχρι Ἀχραδίνης ["at Achradina"]. It is uncertain, however, whether the *Slavonic Daniel* or Pseudo-Chrysostom is closer to the truth in rendering the name of the place where the battle of Syracusans and Arabs is fought: Perton, or Petrinon.

4. Compare p. 37.13–38 Vasiliev with Pseudo-Methodius, p. 46.5 to end, Istrin (= p. 134.21 Lolos).

5. Neither Istrin nor Bousset ("Beiträge," p. 263) was able to adduce any parallel, but of course the possibility cannot be excluded altogether that this section, too, was derived from an apocalypse as yet unknown or overlooked. Unfortunately, it is not possible to find any chronological signposts in the many differences between the text of Pseudo-Chrysostom and those of his sources—see the study of these differences by Istrin, *Izsledovanie*, pp. 257f., 261–63—though these differences frequently permit textual emendations of the texts (see, for example, the preceding note). One might be tempted to derive a *terminus post quem* from the fact that in the list of countries devastated by the Arabs, which the author borrowed from the *Slavonic Daniel*, Pseudo-Chrysostom added Calabria before Sicily (p. 36.15 Vasiliev). The Moslem conquest of Calabria did not begin before the late thirties or early forties of the ninth century (Julius Gay, *L'Italie méridionale et l'empire byzantin [867–1071]* [Paris, 1904], p. 51), so if the mention of Calabria were a clear addition to the Greek original of the *Slavonic Daniel* this would mean that the text was written after 840. The Slavonic text makes it probable, however, that the mention of Calabria originated as a mere palaeographic variant in the Greek tradition of the *Slavonic Daniel*, for as mentioned above (Chapter III.1, n. 45), in the Slavonic text there appeared an "Ilavria" or "Lavria," corresponding to the Ἰσαυρία of Pseudo-Methodius, p. 39.2 Istrin (= p. 120.2 Lolos). The probability, then, is that in the Greek tradition underlying the *Slavonic Daniel* Ἰσαυρία was corrupted into Ἰλαυρία and it was then a natural "emendation" to write Καλαβρία, especially since the region was mentioned in close textual proximity to Sicily. It would therefore be dangerous to draw any chronological inferences from the mention of Calabria in Pseudo-Chrysostom.

al-Muʿtasim's capture of Ancyra and Amorium in 838, the Byzantine-Arab frontier was stabilized at Mount Taurus; and when, in the latter half of the century, the Byzantines began to take the offensive against the Arabs. It is surprising to find a ninth-century apocalyptist predicting a new Arab siege of Constantinople, compared to the ones undertaken by the Umayyad khalifs in 674–678 and again in 717–718, and even an Arab entry (εἰσελεύσονται) into the Byzantine capital. Such an entry never took place, an observation that makes it clear that this is a case of a genuine, though unfulfilled, prophecy.

A second puzzling feature of the second part is Pseudo-Chrysostom's statement that the Arabs would advance ἕως 'Ατταλῶν. Most probably, the author means the port of Attalia in Pamphylia, in the Cibyrrhaeot theme. At first sight it seems an anticlimax that the author should follow up his prediction of a Moslem entry into Constantinople with a second prophecy that the Arabs would reach the harbor town of Attalia so close to the frontier and separated from the capital by the entire width of Asia Minor. The suspicion arises that the Arab advance to Attalia was an historical event which the apocalyptist interpreted to imply a threat to the capital.

In fact, in the ninth century several Abbasid khalifs revived the designs of their Umayyad predecessors upon the Byzantine Empire and its capital. In the last quarter of the ninth century the Arab historian Yaʿqūbī quoted the khalif al-Maʾmūn (813–833) as saying in 833–834, at the beginning of an abortive campaign against Amorium: "I shall fetch the Arabs [Bedouins], I shall bring them from their deserts and install them in all the towns that I shall conquer, until I attack Constantinople."[6] Al-Maʾmūn captured some Byzantine fortresses but died before he was able to make much progress on his grand design. Under his successor, al-Muʿtasim (833–842), there was no fighting between Arabs and Byzantines until 837, for until that year the Byzantine emperor Theophilus (829–842) concentrated all his military efforts on the defense of Sicily, and the khalif was busy suppressing the dangerous revolt of Bābek. In 837, however, Theophilus, under the prodding of Bābek, reopened hostilities and captured the important cities of Zapetra, Arsamosata, and Melitene near the Upper Euphrates. Later in the same year Bābek fell into the khalif's hands and suffered death by torture. Al-Muʿtasim, feeling that his hands had been freed, decided to carry out al-Maʾmūn's plans against Amorium. In 838 his armies cap-

---

6. Translated in A. A. Vasiliev, *Byzance et les Arabes*, vol. I: *La Dynastie d'Amorium* (Brussels, 1935), p. 274.

tured Ancyra and Amorium, the latter being the place of origin of the reigning Byzantine dynasty and the second most important fortress of the empire.[7]

Like his predecessor, al-Muʿtasim considered Amorium a stepping-stone on the way to an advance upon Constantinople.[8] It was clear to him, from the record of the Umayyad expeditions against the Byzantine capital, that Constantinople could not be taken without considerable naval power. The khalif therefore gave orders for the construction of an armada and, after several years of preparation, a squadron of 400 warships set sail in 842 from Syrian ports against Constantinople, under the command of an admiral whom the Byzantine sources call Apodinar; Arab sources fail to mention the expedition, presumably because it ended in failure. It was a formidable undertaking. It is true that for the siege of Constantinople by Maslama (717–718) the Syriac chronicler Michael mentions 5,000 ships and the Greek chroniclers 1,800—even the lower figure is probably an exaggeration[9]—but in 825 Crete was captured by 40 vessels, and two years later the qadi Asad invaded Sicily with either 70 or 100 ships.[10] But Apodinar's squadron was destroyed at the Cibyrrhaeot Promontory, near the Chelidonian Isles south of Attalia, a dangerous spot for navigation since ancient times. Only seven ships returned to Syria.[11] Nothing is said as to whether an Arab land

---

7. On these events see ibid., pp. 124–27, 137–43, 144–74; Bury, *Eastern Roman Empire*, pp. 252–56, 259–72.
8. Bury, *Eastern Roman Empire*, p. 262.
9. Michael the Syrian, transl. J. B. Chabot, II, p. 484; Theophanes, p. 393.25 de Boor; Nicephorus, p. 53 de Boor.
10. Bury, *Eastern Roman Empire*, p. 298.
11. *Vita Theodorae Imperatricis* (*BHG* 1731), ed. W. Regel, *Anecdota Byzantino-Russica* (St. Petersburg, 1891), p. 11: ἐν τῇ οὖν αὐτοκρατορίᾳ Μιχαὴλ, Ἀποδινάρ, ὁ τῶν ... Ἀγαρηνῶν φύλαρχος, ἐκ πολλῶν χρόνων παρασκευαζόμενος ἐν δυνάμει μεγάλῃ καὶ βαρείᾳ σφόδρα μετὰ πλοίων φοβερῶν τετρακοσίων καταπλήκτων ἤρχετο κατὰ τῆς θεοφρουρήτου Κωνσταντινουπόλεως, ἀλλὰ τοῦτον ἡ ... τριὰς ... εἰς τέλος ἠφάνισε τὸν ἀλάστορα καὶ διόλεσεν, πάντων τῶν φοβερῶν καὶ καταπλήκτων ἐκείνων πλοίων αὐτάνδρων συντριβέντων ἐν ἀκρωτηρίῳ τῶν Κιβαιρυωτῶν εἰς τὰ λεγόμενα Χελιδόνια, ἑπτὰ καὶ μόνον διασωθέντων ἐν Συρίᾳ καὶ ἀπαγγειλάντων τὴν τῶν Ῥωμαίων νίκην τε καὶ σωτηρίαν καὶ τὴν ἑαυτῶν ἧττάν τε καὶ πανολεθρίαν. [In the reign of Michael, Apodinar, the Arab general, who for many years had been preparing a large and very strong force of 400 fearful ships, came against the divinely fortified Constantinople, but the third day destroyed the wretch completely; all those dreaded and astonishing ships were shattered with all their men at the Cibyrrhaeot promontory at Chelidonia, and only seven returned safely to Syria to announce the victory and safety of the Romans and their own loss and destruction.] Except for the last phrase (καὶ ἀπαγγειλάντων κτλ.) the passage was copied almost verbatim by George the Monk *Chronicon*, 2.801 de Boor. Cf. Vasiliev, *Byzance et les Arabes*, I, p. 192, and Bury, *Eastern Roman Empire*, p. 274. Vasiliev, I, pp. 406f., considered the possibility that the leader of the Arab squadron, Apodinar, may be identical with an Aḥmad ibn Dīnār ibn ʿAbd-Allāh celebrated in a poem by Buḥturī (820–897) as the admiral commanding an expedition in which his sailors won a naval victory over "the sons of Caesar" by means of the Greek Fire. If this identification is

army was cooperating with Apodinar's naval force, but it is difficult to imagine that al-Muʿtasim should have repeated Muʿāwiya's disastrous mistake of 674–680 and have relied primarily on a naval force to capture Constantinople.

It must have been the expedition of al-Muʿtasim against Constantinople that prompted Pseudo-Chrysostom to write his apocalypse. Nothing is known, it is true, about the route followed by Apodinar's naval squadron or by the (hypothetical) land army cooperating with it, but the Byzantine sources state that the armada sailed from Syria and was destroyed at the Chelidonian Isles. It is plausible that it should have entered ($εἰσῆλθεν$) Attalia, for in the ninth century Attalia was the naval base of the elite units of the thematic fleets, the Mardaites, and it would have been foolhardy for the Arab navy to have bypassed this formidable stronghold. Eighteen years later, in 860, the port was captured by a much smaller Arab squadron of twenty ships.[12] The Arab historian Masʿūdī (†956/7) told that already after his conquest of Amorium (838) al-Muʿtasim had wanted to march upon Constantinople and attempt to capture the city by land and by sea.[13] He had been delayed in carrying out his plans by internal problems and by the building of the fleet. Small wonder that when in 842 Apodinar's squadron captured Attalia, an anonymous Byzantine apocalyptist, Pseudo-Chrysostom, should have seen in this event a threat to the capital itself.

Like many other apocalypses, Pseudo-Chrysostom's thus illuminates a brief moment in history. The author knew of the capture of Attalia in 842 by Apodinar's Arab fleet or by the cooperating land army or by both, but nothing yet of the fleet's destruction off the Chelidonian Isles a short time later. It is inconceivable that he should have written after he learned of the disaster that had overtaken the enemy, for there was no reason to fear a Moslem siege of and entry into the capital soon after so egregious a setback for the Arabs. As to the place of composition, it is impossible to arrive at certainties, yet it is probable that an author so

---

correct, it would mean that a naval engagement took place between the Byzantine and Arab fleets. It should be noted that neither the author of the saint's life nor the chronicler states explicitly that Apodinar's fleet was destroyed by a storm, although this seems to be implied by the references to the Trinity and to divine justice. Yet it is striking that the hagiographer wrote of a Roman victory and an Arab defeat! Perhaps a battle was indeed fought, and Buḥturī's hero is identical with the Apodinar of the Byzantine sources.

12. Vasiliev, *Byzance et les Arabes*, I, p. 246. On the naval importance of Attalia in the ninth century see H. Ahrweiler, *Byzance et la Mer* (Paris, 1966), p. 108.

13. As translated in Vasiliev, *Byzance et les Arabes*, I, p. 332: "Muʿtasim livra la ville [Amorium] au pillage et à l'incendie. . . . Il voulut ensuite marcher sur Constantinople, en occuper le canal (Bosphore) et aviser aux moyens de prendre cette capitale par terre et par mer."

concerned with the fate of the capital wrote in or near Constantinople. While he still thought that an Arab armada of 400 warships was sailing from Attalia around Asia Minor to Constantinople, he wrote his apocalypse to warn his readers that their sinfulness was bringing divine retribution upon the Christian Empire as well as a repetition of the terrible dangers that Constantinople had faced in the days of Muʿāwiya and Maslama.

## 3. *DANIEL* Καὶ ἔσται

This text, preserved anonymously in one manuscript only, is entitled *Vision of Daniel Concerning the Last Time and Concerning the End of the World*. Unfortunately, it is corrupt in many places. It is divided into two parts of unequal length: a very brief historical part, and a lengthy eschatological section.[1] Both components are made up of a large variety of very short fragments so that, to a much greater extent than the apocalypse of Pseudo-Chrysostom, this piece gives the impression of a mosaic built from often minute pebbles.

The first, historical part of the piece is composed of five fragments.

1. In the first fragment it is predicted that an Arab youth will on "wooden arks" set forth against all the lands and islands of the Roman Empire, work great slaughter, and humble princes and destroy men of power. He will set his countenance against the gateways (προπύλαια) of Peter and Paul, will obtain St. Peter's keys, and will humble Rome. The reason for these disasters will be the fact that kings and potentates summoned him (the Arab youth) in the temples and altars of idols (ἐν τοῖς ναοῖς εἰδώλων καὶ βωμοῖς), defiled the smoke of the sacrifices, and harmed the saints.[2]

While not all the details of this passage are clear, it must refer to the Arab naval attack on Rome in 846. By that time, the Arabs in Sicily, later reinforced from Africa and Crete and called into southern Italy by Neapolitans and warring Lombard factions, had seized Tarentum and Bari, established a colony at Beneventum, and were threatening the Papal State. On 23 August 846 a fleet of seventy-three ships assembled by the emir of Palermo, Abū al-Aghlab Ibrāhīm (835–851), appeared at the mouth of the Tiber. It is unlikely that it was commanded by the emir in person, as he could hardly have been called a youth in 846 and as he

---

1. The historical part extends from the beginning to p. 39.15 Vasiliev. The rest of the piece is eschatological prophecy.
2. Pp. 38.22–39.1 Vasiliev. I emend ἐλυμήνατο on p. 38.31 to ἐλυμήναντο.

conducted all his warfare through his lieutenants.³ The Arab armada sacked the Church of St. Peter, built by the emperor Constantine the Great, and the Church of St. Paul, both situated on the right bank of the river outside the Aurelian Walls of the city. The armada was unable to capture the city itself. It is interesting, however, to find here a reference to the keys of St. Peter captured by the Arabs. In the early Middle Ages these keys to the *confessio* of Old St. Peter were considered to possess miraculous healing powers because of their physical contact with the tomb of the apostle, and were frequently sent by popes to high dignitaries whom they wished to honor. Their capture by the Moslems in 846 must therefore have been felt to be a humiliation for the Christian faith.⁴ In other ways, too, the indications given by the apocalyptist agree with what is known about Old St. Peter and the Moslem sack of 846. The Church indeed had a gateway.⁵ It is also true that "kings and potentates" had summoned the Arabs, for they first appeared in southern Italy as allies of Neapolitan and Lombard rulers. These "kings and potentates" did in fact "harm the saints," for in order to pay their Saracen allies they plundered churches and monasteries.⁶ It is, however, surprising that they should have summoned the Arabs "in the temples and altars of idols."⁷

2. There follows a second fragment mentioning the devastation of

3. Michele Amari, *Storia dei Musulmani di Sicilia*, 3 vols. (2nd ed. Catania, 1933–1939), p. 455.

4. Amari, *Storia*, I, pp. 492–506; Gay, *Italie Méridionale*, pp. 49–56; Ludo M. Hartmann, *Geschichte Italiens im Mittelalter*, III, part 1 (Gotha, 1908), pp. 194–214. On the keys of St. Peter in particular see Schüller-Piroli, *2000 Jahre Sankt Peter* (Olten, 1960), p. 230: "Noch heute befindet sich an der Innenseite der Fenestella ein grosser Haken. An diesem wurden in Alt-St. Peter verschiedene Gegenstände, insbesondere Tüchlein, an Schnüren befestigt, um so mehrere Stunden in grösstmöglicher Nähe der Grabreliquie hängen zu können. . . . Man schrieb den 'brandae' genanreten Tüchlein wundertätige Kräfte zu. Noch mehr galt dies von den 'claves,' den goldenen Schlüsseln zu den Gittertoren der Konfessio, die aber nur die höchsten Würdenträger von den Päpsten zum Geschenk erhielten. Sie waren oft als Reliquiare gearbeitet, innen hohl und enthielten Eisenfeilen von den Ketten Petri." On these keys see also Heinrich Fichtenau, "Zum Reliquienwesen im früheren Mittelalter," *Mitteilungen des Instituts für Österreichische Geschichtsforschung* 60 (1952), pp. 60–89, esp. 85f., and Percy E. Schramm, "Die Anerkennung Karls des Grossen als Kaiser," *Kaiser Könige und Päpste* I (Stuttgart, 1968), p. 240.

5. Reconstruction of Constantinian basilica in Schüller-Piroli, *2000 Jahre*, pp. 82, 163; Richard Krautheimer, *Early Christian and Byzantine Architecture* (Baltimore, 1965), p. 34. On the entrance gate see Schüller-Piroli, pp. 84, 178; Krautheimer, p. 36.

6. Gay, *Italie Méridionale*, pp. 52f.

7. In the ninth century there were of course no idol-worshippers left in Italy, and it is unlikely that in 846 there should have been Iconoclasts in Italy. Could the remark be a reference to mosques built by the Arab conquerors in southern Italy? If so, it would be a serious misunderstanding of Islam to talk of the mosques as ναοὶ εἰδώλων. Or is this remark a trace of an ancient source used by the apocalyptist for this part?

Σπανία and Ἀρβενία.[8] Σπανία is obviously the Iberian Peninsula; by Ἀρβενία the author must mean the land of the Ἀρβερνοί or Ἀρουερνοί, who had resided in Aquitaine and given their name to all of southwestern Gaul, including the Auvergne of the present day.[9] The apocalyptist was here referring to the Moslem conquest of Spain (711–715) and to their advance through Aquitaine to the Loire, where they were stopped in the battle of Tours (732) by Charles Martel. Since the preceding and following sections deal with events of the ninth century, one wonders why the apocalyptist inserted this item on the eighth century.

3. He next "predicts" wars everywhere, and especially disturbances in Λογγιβαρδία. In Byzantine terminology, this could mean either the Lombard duchy of Beneventum, southern Italy in general, or Italy as a whole.[10] Inasmuch as the passage occurs in a context concerning the Arab invasion of Western Europe, it must refer to the internecine quarrels among the south Italian principalities during the fourth and fifth decades of the ninth century, in the course of which the Moslems from Sicily and elsewhere began to colonize southern Italy.[11]

4. The following section is particularly important. The text is corrupt in several places, but the drift of the argument seems sufficiently clear. Here it is said that a ῥῆξ will be set up in an iron city and will read Latin letters in the place of Rhegion. The next phrase is seriously disfigured by corruptions; the section ends with the people of the ῥῆξ (or of Rhegion) saying: Behold the sojourner in our midst.[12] It is not difficult to see what is wrong in the corrupt sentence. The meaningless συνομάστη may be gently emended to σειρομάστης or σιρομάστης in the sense of "barbed lance." Furthermore, a lacuna must be postulated—probably after the word αὐτοῦ and caused by a homoioteleuton—containing at least the verb and possibly in addition a direct object. The sentence thus would say that the spear held in the hand of the ῥῆξ will do something to Rhegion (or its inhabitants).

In interpreting the passage one is inclined at first sight to think of

8. P. 39.1 Vasiliev.
9. See Pape-Benseler, *Wörterbuch der griechischen Eigennamen*, 2 vols. (3rd ed. Berlin, 1884), s.v. Ἀρβερνοί. (I owe this identification to a suggestion of Dr. John P. C. Kent of the British Museum.) Ἀρβενία should be emended to read Ἀρβερνία although even this form is not attested.
10. Gay, *Italie Méridionale*, pp. 169f.
11. Gay, *Italie Méridionale*, pp. 49–53. "Longobardia" was used in the sense of southern Italy also in the *Slavonic Daniel* (7) and in Pseudo-Chrysostom, p. 37.1 Vasiliev.
12. P. 39.2–5 Vasiliev . . . καὶ σταθήσεται ῥῆξ ἐν πόλει σιδηρᾷ καὶ ἀναγνῶ γράμματα λατίνα ἐν τόπῳ Ῥηγίου καὶ ὁ συνομάστη [sic] ὁ ἐν τῇ χειρὶ αὐτοῦ τοῦ τόπου. καὶ λέγει ὁ λαὸς αὐτοῦ· ἰδοὺ ἡ παροικία ἡμῶν.

Rhegium (Reggio) in Calabria, on the mainland side of the Straits of Messina, particularly as it is preceded by a reference to Λογγιβαρδία in the sense of southern Italy. The difficulty is, however, that a city called Iron City (ἐν πόλει σιδηρᾷ), the other topographical clue of the passage, did not exist, to the best of my knowledge, anywhere in the Byzantine Empire, certainly not in Sicily or Italy. It is of course conceivable that the author is not attempting here to reproduce the city's name but to allude in metaphorical language to its location or to its natural resources or to the moral character of its inhabitants, but if so, an allusion of this type must have appeared as obscure to his contemporaries as it is to the modern reader. A slight emendation will permit us to construe the entire passage as referring to Constantinople. If the reading πόρτῃ or, better, πύλῃ is substituted for πόλει, one finds here a topographical feature frequently mentioned in Byzantine texts. In fact, students of Constantinopolitan topography know no fewer than three Iron Gates in the capital: one led to the Brazen House and thence to the Imperial Palace of Daphne; a second stood near the Port of Julian or of Sophia on the Propontis; and a third was near the Golden Horn.[13] It is not immediately clear which of these three Iron Gates was meant in this context, but a consideration of the identity of the ῥῆξ "set up" at one of them may now prove helpful.

The Byzantines normally used the word ῥῆξ, a transliteration of Latin rex, to designate a barbarian king, particularly a Western ruler.[14] In this case, however, a barbarian prince can hardly be meant, as it is said that he will be "set up"—that is, presumably, proclaimed or lodged —at one of the Iron Gates of Constantinople. A Byzantine ruler must therefore be meant. Now there was, in the long history of the Byzantine Empire, only one Byzantine emperor who for a very short time had the title ῥῆξ. When, on 26 May 866, Michael III appointed the Macedonian Basil his co-ruler, he bestowed on him this title. This is proved by two well-known bronze coins struck by the mint of Constantinople: on the obverse there is a portrait of Michael III with the legend MIHAEL IMPERATOR, and on the reverse the effigy of Basil inscribed BASILIUS REX, with the legends implying the superiority of Michael both over the Western emperor Louis II recognized by Byzantium in 867 and over his Byzantine colleague Basil.[15] These coins must have been struck prior to

---

13. Janin, *Constantinople byzantine*, pp. 423f.
14. See, for example, the list of addresses in Constantine Porphyrogenitus *Book of Ceremonies* 2.48, pp. 686–92 CSHB, and Werner Ohnsorge's remarks on the concept of ῥῆξ at Byzantium in *Abendland und Byzanz* (Weimar, 1958), pp. 241–54.
15. W. Wroth, *Catalogue of Imperial Byzantine Coins in the British Museum* II (London, 1908), p. 432 and pl. I.2. On the interpretation see Ernst Stein, "Post-consulat et

23 September 867, when a group of conspirators led by Basil murdered Michael and when Basil became sole ruler. The ῥῆξ "set up" at the Iron Gate must, therefore, be Basil I in his capacity as co-emperor of Michael III.

From the narrative sources we know that there did exist a connection between Basil and one of the Iron Gates at Constantinople. According to the chroniclers, on one occasion Michael III became annoyed that nobody in his entourage was able to tame a fiery horse brought to him by the *strategos* of the Bucellarian theme. At that point, Theophilitzes, a relative of the emperor, remarked that he had in his service a young man experienced and courageous with horses—Basil. An imperial chamberlain was therefore dispatched to fetch him, and he found Basil at the Iron Gate.[16] Janin was of the opinion that the Iron Gate at the entrance to the Brazen House was meant; in that case, Theophilitzes would have brought Basil to the entrance to the palace.[17] But it is also possible that the chroniclers are here referring to one of the two other Iron Gates, the one on the Propontis or that near the Golden Horn, and that either Basil himself or his master Theophilitzes resided in the vicinity of one of them. However that may be, the episode establishes a connection between Basil and one of the Iron Gates at Constantinople. The interpretation proposed here seems therefore to be pointing in the right direction and in particular the emendation of ἐν σιδηρᾷ πόλει to read ἐν Σιδηρᾷ Πύλῃ seems justified.

This conclusion further suggests that the τόπος 'Ρηγίου can hardly be Reggio di Calabria but must itself be in or near Constantinople. Modern students of the topography of Constantinople frequently mention a gate in the Theodosian Land Walls of the capital alternatively known as the Gate of Rhesion or Rhegion or Polyandros. It stood near the middle of the wall, the *Mesoteichion*, and is identified with the Gate now called Yenimevlevihanekapi. What makes this Gate particularly tempting for

---

AYTOKPATOPIA," *Annuaire de l'Institute de Philologie et d'Histoire Orientales* 2 (1933–1934), pp. 867–912, esp. 902f. (= *Opera Minora Selecta* [Amsterdam, 1968], pp. 348f.).

16. Leo Grammaticus, p. 230 *CSHB*; Georgius Continuatus, p. 817 *CSHB*; cf. G. Moravcsik, "Sagen und Legenden über Kaiser Basileios," *Dumbarton Oaks Papers* 15 (1961), pp. 61–126, esp. 99f., 115 (= *Studia Byzantina* [Amsterdam, 1967], pp. 188, 204). Pseudo-Symeon, p. 654 *CSHB* (after Theophanes Continuatus) dates the event in the tenth year of Michael III; Moravcsik mentions the tenth year of Theodora or 853. But Pseudo-Symeon wrote specifically of the tenth year of Michael and may therefore have meant the tenth year of Michael's sole rule, 866/7.

17. Janin, *Constantinople byzantine*, p. 423. Cf. also Cyril Mango, *The Brazen House*, K. Danske Videnskabernes Selskab, Arkaeologisk-kunsthistoriske Meddelelser 4, no. 4 (Copenhagen, 1959), pp. 85–87.

our purposes is the fact that on the left console on the west side of the entrance gate there can be read even today a Latin inscription commemorating the building of the walls by the praetorian prefect of the East Constantine in 447.[18] There are, however, difficulties. In the first place, medieval sources never refer to Yenimevlevihanekapi as the Gate of Rhegion, as modern scholars often do, but speak instead of the πόρτα τοῦ ʼΡησίου or τόπος ʼΡήσιος.[19] Second, if the apocalyptist "predicts" that Basil "will read Latin letters" in a certain place, he must mean that they conveyed to him a prophecy of his career, but it is difficult to see how Basil could have discovered in the Latin inscription at Yenimevlevihanekapi, however understood or misunderstood, a reference to himself.

It will, therefore, be necessary to search elsewhere for the τόπος ʼΡηγίου where Basil supposedly read Latin letters—i.e., presumably, a Latin inscription. Now at Büyük Çekmece, about eighteen kilometers west of the Theodosian Walls and inside the Long Walls attributed to the emperor Anastasius, at the site of the ancient and medieval town of Rhegium, there came to light a few decades ago the impressive ruins of a large imperial palace of the fifth or sixth century.[20] The excavators found no epigraphical texts, but Latin inscriptions must have existed in this early Byzantine palace. It is known that at some time in his career Basil rebuilt at Rhegium a church of St. Peter,[21] and it is therefore plausible that he should have discovered there, in 866 or 867, a Latin inscription that seemed to convey a prophecy relevant to his own fate—or at least that the apocalyptist could claim that he had done so or would do it.

What about the corrupt passage concerning a σιρομάστης? The word is rare and the lexica quote as the principal source the Septuagint. In Numbers 25 it is reported that during a plague the Israelites whored with foreign women and in particular that Zimri, son of Salu, had an affair with a Midianite woman. Thereupon Phinehas, son of Eleazar, son of Aaron, arose in the congregation, took a barbed lance in his

---

18. Janin, *Constantinople byzantine*, pp. 277–80. Text of the inscription in B. Meyer-Plath and A. M. Schneider, *Die Landmauer von Konstantinopel*, Denkmäler Antiker Architektur 8 (Berlin, 1943), p. 133: *Theodosii iussis gemino nec mense peracto / Constantinus ovans haec moenia firma locavit / tam cito tam stabilem Pallas vix conderet arcem.* See also Hans Lietzmann, "Die Landmauer von Konstantinopel," *Abhandlungen der Preussischen Akademie der Wissenschaften* no. 2 (1929), esp. pl. IX and figs. 11 and 12.

19. Meyer-Plath and Schneider, *Landmauer*, p. 66.

20. A. M. Mansel, "Les Fouilles de Rhégion près d'Istanbul," *Actes du VI' Congrès International d'Etudes Byzantines* II (Paris, 1951), pp. 256–60. The name of this palace is unknown and I do not find it registered in Janin's *Constantinople byzantine*. On the Long Walls see now R. M. Harrison, "The Long Wall in Thrace," *Archaeologia Aeliana* 4th ser., 47 (1969), pp. 33–38.

21. Theophanes Continuatus, p. 340.10 *CSHB*.

hand, and slew both Zimri and his Midianite concubine.[22] Clearly Phinehas acted here as a representative of a priestly family concerned lest the sacred congregation of Israel be contaminated by foreign alliances. If the apocalyptist represented Basil with a barbed lance, a σιρομάστης, in his hand, he must have done so in order to draw a parallel with Phinehas. Just as Zimri threatened to defile the sacred house of Israel by his foreign alliance, so Michael III threatened to bring down God's wrath on the Byzantine Empire by his buffooneries, drunkenness, and other failings so copiously described by later propaganda favorable to the founder of the Macedonian dynasty. And just as Phinehas had deserved well of the congregation of Israel by piercing Zimri and his Midianite with his barbed lance, so Basil and his co-conspirators had done a good deed in dispatching the wicked Michael III. Thus the mention of a σιρομάστης in Basil's hand makes it virtually certain that in this passage the apocalyptist attempted to justify the darkest moment in Basil's career, the murder of his benefactor Michael: Basil of Macedon acted as the zealous Phinehas had acted, for the honor of God and of the true religion and in the best interests of his people. "Basil the New Phinehas" must, then, be the sense of the passage.[23] It must have been written after 23 September 867, the date of Michael's death at the hands of the conspirators.

5. This passage is followed by another patterned after Pseudo-Methodius' description of the sufferings of the Christian churches. However, the apocalyptist introduces a number of changes, of which the most important is the mention of an earthquake caused by God in his anger over the sins of the Ismaelites. It will be most convenient to translate the fragment together with the next sentences, as the two parts are connected by the double mention of an earthquake:

---

22. Numbers 25:7: καὶ ἰδὼν Φεινεὲς υἱὸς Ἐλεαζὰρ υἱὸς Ἀαρὼν τοῦ ἱερέως ἐξανέστη ἐκ μέσου τῆς συναγωγῆς, καὶ λαβὼν σειρομάστην ἐν τῇ χειρὶ εἰσῆλθεν ὀπίσω τοῦ ἀνθρώπου τοῦ Ἰσραηλείτου (i.e., Zimri) εἰς τὴν κάμινον καὶ ἀπεκέντησεν ἀμφοτέρους (i.e., Zimri and the Midianite woman). [Note in Alexander's hand: A reference to Phinehas and the Midianite is included in Leo *Tactica* XX 148 (*PG* 107.1052D ff.).]

23. The rest of the passage is too corrupt to permit interpretation. In particular, it is not clear what verb and object went with the σειρομάστης, except that τοῦ τόπου makes it likely that the σειρομάστης was somehow related to the τόπος 'Ρηγίου mentioned before. Nor can I explain the next sentence (καὶ λέγει ὁ λαὸς αὐτοῦ· ἰδοὺ ἡ παροικία ἡμῶν). Dr. John P. C. Kent, who kindly discussed the passage with me, suggested emending παροικία to παροιμία, which then might refer back to the γράμματα λατίνα that encouraged Basil in his enterprise. The suggestion is attractive, but difficult to prove. [Note in Alexander's hand: A lance (λογχή) plays a role in the estrangement of Michael III and Basil, according to Theophanes Continuatus IV (Michael III), p. 209 *CSHB*. He reports that Michael wants Basil killed and tells one of his shield-bearers in Kynegion to throw a lance, purportedly to kill an animal but in reality to kill Basil.]

In those days the sacrifice will cease in the churches and the divine [being] will be despised. And priests will be like the laity and the laity like demons, until the sins of the Ismaelites will be full. And the earth will quake from God's anger and the earth will raise its loud groan toward the Lord. And when half of the week is full, the Lord will look upon the earth and will make it quake. And afterward the sons of Ismael will be afraid and will cry out loud while fleeing to Mariana. And afterward the sons of Ismael will once again attack the land of Helinia being appealed to [summoned by the inhabitants]; others will attack the City of the Rebel without appeal.[24]

If this passage is compared with its ultimate source, Pseudo-Methodius, it becomes clear that there are three major differences. In the first place, the two sentences about the "sons of Ismael" are an addition and refer to a specific historical situation. Second, the later apocalyptist transforms Pseudo-Methodius' eschatological prophecy concerning the seventh and last year-week of Moslem triumphs into a *vaticinium ex eventu* of a specific historical defeat of the Moslems.[25] Finally, the apocalyptist twice mentions an earthquake; this, too, is an addition to the text of Pseudo-Methodius.

What was the historical situation envisaged in these changes? The additional passage refers to Arab warfare in Sicily. This is clear from the mention of Mariana, a place that occurred already in the *Slavonic Daniel* (4) (p. 68 above) within an unquestionably Sicilian context. The City of the Rebel is familiar from the same Slavonic text; it is therefore probable that here, too, Syracuse is meant. There remains the puzzling reference to an Arab attack on "the land of Helinia" (εἰς τὴν γῆν τῆς Ἐλινίας). Now it will be remembered that in the *Slavonic Daniel* (4) Mariana appeared in conjunction with Enna and thus it is possible to emend Ἐλινίας to read Ἔννας.[26] The historical situation is thus clear: Enna and Syracuse are still in Greek hands; Mariana is a Moslem stronghold. That means that the author envisaged Sicily between 827, the date of the rebellion of Euphemius, and 859, when Enna fell. The

---

24. P. 39.5–15 Vasiliev. Cf. Pseudo-Methodius, p. 35.6–10 Istrin (= p. 16.3–7 Lolos), also *Slavonic Daniel #5*, Pseudo-Chrysostom, p. 36.8–11 Vasiliev.

25. Pseudo-Methodius, p. 35.9 Istrin (= p. 16.5–6 Lolos) . . . τῷ ἑβδόμῳ χρόνῳ, ἡνίκα πληροῦται ὁ ἀριθμὸς τοῦ χρόνου τῆς δυναστείας αὐτῶν [in the seventh year-week, when the number of year-weeks of their rule is filled], a passage that should be understood in the light of his earlier prophecy (p. 15.6 Istrin = p. 70.8 Lolos) that the Moslems will rule seven year-weeks (according to other manuscripts: seventeen year-weeks). *Daniel* Καὶ ἔσται replaced this date by ἐν τῷ πληρωθῆναι τὸ ἥμισυ τῆς ἑβδομάδος ["in fulfilling the half of the week"] (p. 39.10 Vasiliev).

26. The editor, Vasiliev, suggested the reading Ἑλληνίας, but one expects a specific site, to parallel Μαριανά and the πόλις Τυράννου. A corruption of Ἔννας into Ἐλινίας is very easy to explain in uncial script: N corrupted into ΛΙ. (I first proposed this emendation in "Medieval Apocalypses as Historical Sources," p. 1003.)

Moslems evidently had been ravaging the territory of Enna and perhaps also attacking Syracuse, had been driven back to their base in Mariana by an earthquake, and were now once again ($\pi\acute{\alpha}\lambda\iota\nu$) attacking these two cities.

The earthquake mentioned in the passage, just prior to the Arab flight to Mariana, can be identified. The Greek version of the anonymous Siculo-Arab Chronicle of Cambridge contained in Codex Vaticanus Graecus 1912 of the eleventh century, mentioned under the year 6061 (,$\varsigma\xi\alpha'$), indiction one, "a great earthquake." The item is inserted between an entry on the Arab capture of Rametta (οἱ 'Ρογοί) in 6356 and that of Butera (ἐβοϑήρ) in 6362. It is therefore obvious that the date of the earthquake must be emended to read ,$\varsigma\tau\xi\alpha'$ = 6361. This is, indeed, the tacit assumption of the editor of the text.[27] The "great earthquake" in Sicily therefore occurred between 1 September 852 and 31 August 853.

By that time the Arabs had established a quasi-autonomous emirate at Palermo (831), had conquered many cities in the western part of the island (839–840), and had taken Messina (843), Modica (845), Leontini (846–847), and Ragusa (848). The two greatest fortresses, Enna and Syracuse, had been attacked a number of times. In 852 and 853 the Arab armies commanded by Abbās ibn al-Faḍl, emir of Palermo, operated in the eastern part of Sicily around Enna, Catana, Syracuse, Noto, and Ragusa.[28] It was during these operations that there occurred the "great earthquake" mentioned in the Cambridge Chronicle and in *Daniel* Καὶ ἔσται. It seems, from this second document, that under the impact of this terrifying event the Moslems interrupted their activities in the vicinity of Enna and Syracuse and retired to their base at Mariana, to return (ἐπελεύσονται πάλιν) shortly thereafter, in the case of Enna upon the invitation (κλητοί) of a local faction.

There are clear indications in the Sicilian passage that it was not com-

---

27. G. Cozza-Luzi, "La Cronaca Siculo-Saracena di Cambridge con doppio testo greco scoperto in codici contemporanei delle Bibliotheca Vaticana e Parigina" *Documenti per Servire alla Storia di Sicilia, Pubblicati e Cura della Società Siciliana per la Storia Patria* Quarta Serie II (Palermo, 1890) (with photograph of the Vatican manuscript): ἔτους ,$\varsigma\xi\alpha'$ ἐγένετο σεισμὸς μέγας ἰνδ. A. Reprinted by Vasiliev, *Byzance et les Arabes*, I, p. 345. The passage on the great earthquake occurs neither in the other Greek manuscript of the Cambridge Chronicle, Codex Parisinus Graecus 920 of the tenth century, nor in the parallel Arab text. The *annus mundi*, as emended, and the number of the indiction agree.

28. Ibn al-Atīr, p. 231, transl. Amari, I, p. 378: "Uscito (al-Abbās) di nuovo l'anno dugento trentotto (23 giugno 852–11 giugno 853), egli corse infino a Castrogiovanni con grandi forze, depredando e guastando. Si avanzò poscia fino a Catania, Siracusa, Noto, Ragusa; nei (contadi delle) quali città fece prede, guastò ed arse." Al-Bayān records the same events under A.H. 239 = 12 June 853–1 June 854 (II 10). Cf. Amari, *Storia*, I, p. 458; Vasiliev, *Byzance et les Arabes*, I, p. 208.

posed for the present text of *Daniel* Καὶ ἔσται. In the first place, it is noteworthy that an earthquake is mentioned twice.²⁹ In addition, the author speaks of a *second* attack (ἐπελεύσονται πάλιν) upon Enna, but no attack has been mentioned before. It is therefore certain that the Sicilian passage was excerpted by the author of *Daniel* Καὶ ἔσται from a lost text, probably also a *Vision of Daniel*, in which an earlier onslaught on Enna had been "predicted." This "prediction" must also have included the second mention of an earthquake (ὁ θεὸς . . . ποιήσει αὐτὴν τρομάξαι), for without it the fear and flight of the Ismaelites would be unmotivated. It must also have specified what was meant by "the week" in the midst of which (τὸ ἥμισυ τῆς ἑβδομάδος) the earthquake occurred.³⁰ So far as the earlier reference to an earthquake is concerned (τρομάξεται ἡ γῆ ἀπὸ τῆς ὀργῆς τοῦ θεοῦ), two interpretations are possible. The apocalyptist may have inserted it into the Pseudo-Methodian context merely to connect it with the following fragment from a different source referring to events in Sicily, in which the Sicilian earthquake of 852/3 is mentioned. In this case this first reference would be no more than an extremely clumsy stylistic device and only the second reference would correspond to an actual earthquake. A more satisfactory explanation would be that the two references refer to different earthquakes, the second to the Sicilian earthquake of 852/3 and the first to the terrible earthquake that struck Constantinople in January/February 869.³¹ However that may be, it is clear that the "prophecy" concerning Basil must have been composed in 867 or 869, for it knows nothing concerning Basil's reign except its beginning. The "prediction" on the Sicilian events, on the other hand, was excerpted from a lost source

29. P. 39.9 Vasiliev καὶ τρομάξεται ἡ γῆ ἀπὸ τῆς ὀργῆς τοῦ θεοῦ . . . καὶ ἐν τῷ πληρωθῆναι τὸ ἥμισυ τῆς ἑβδομάδος ἐπιβλέψει Κύριος ὁ θεὸς ἐπὶ τὴν γῆν καὶ ποιήσει αὐτὴν τρομάξαι. [and the earth will quake from the anger of God . . . and as half the week is completed God will look down on the earth and make it quake].

30. A year-week (seven years) may have been meant, as happens often in apocalyptic literature. But it seems more likely that the author thought here of a week of seven days and merely wished to "predict" the earthquake for a specific day of the week (Wednesday or Thursday). At any rate the lost source must have given some indication as to the initial date from which the week was supposed to be reckoned. As the date stands in the preserved text, i.e., without indication of an initial date, it is meaningless.

31. Cf. G. Downey, "Earthquakes at Constantinople and Vicinity," *Speculum* 30 (1955), pp. 596–600, esp. 599; Venance Grumel, *La Chronologie*, Traité d'études byzantines, I (Paris, 1958), p. 479. The second explanation is more satisfactory, because it relates the first reference to an earthquake to what precedes, namely, the "prophecy" concerning Basil I (p. 39.3–5), and at the same time makes it understandable why the apocalyptist should have continued with the Sicilian fragment: he seems to have been under the mistaken impression that the earthquake mentioned in the Sicilian text was identical with the Constantinopolitan earthquake of 869.

composed in or shortly after 852/3, for all in *Daniel* Καὶ ἔσται that follows the second attack on Enna and Syracuse is eschatological.

The historical part of this piece thus consists of five smaller and larger fragments of different times and provenance: a section on the Moslem sack of Rome in 846 composed very probably, because of the many accurate details on Italian events, in Rome or its vicinity; a very brief reference to the Moslem conquest of the Iberian Peninsula and southwestern France in the early eighth century; a fleeting reference to conflicts among the Lombard princes of southern Italy in the 830s and 840s; a somewhat longer "prediction" concerning the murder of the Byzantine emperor Michael III by Basil the Macedonian, the "New Phinehas," in 867, and possibly the earthquake at Constantinople in 869; and, finally, the *vaticinium* concerning Sicilian events in 852/3 probably written, because of the many details on Arab-Sicilian warfare, on the island. Of all the fragments, the one referring to Basil I is the latest, and if any part of the text can claim originality it must be this section. Since it is well informed as to Constantinopolitan topography—the Iron Gate, the τόπος 'Ρηγίου with its "Latin letters"—it was probably composed in Constantinople or its suburbs. The references to earlier events in various parts of the Mediterranean world were joined with it to authenticate the author's prophetic qualifications. It must have received its final shape in 867 or 869, for if the author had known the events of Basil's reign, notably his warfare against the Arabs, he would undoubtedly have added appropriate *vaticinia*.[32]

The second (eschatological) part of the apocalypse, like the first (historical) part, is made up of separate fragments of different periods and provenance; it will therefore be convenient to number its components consecutively after those of the first part.

6. The first section predicts that the inhabitants of the Rebel City will discover, by divine revelation, a man whose name begins with the letter *lambda*, and they will anoint him emperor. He will then defeat the Arabs at Partēnē and again at the Well of Jacob and finally pursue them to Akra.[33] The passage is closely related to a fragment in Pseudo-Chrysostom and for long stretches agrees with it literally,[34] but there are also significant differences. Most interesting are a number of additions.

32. If, as suggested in the preceding note, the author refers to the Constantinopolitan earthquake of 869, this would mean that the piece was written in that year or a little later.
33. Pp. 39.15–40.16 Vasiliev.
34. Compare pp. 39.15–40.16 with p. 36.17–34 Vasiliev.

Unlike Pseudo-Chrysostom, *Daniel Καὶ ἔσται* provides a description of the victorious emperor, resembling in a general way the descriptions of the Antichrist found in many sources: a tattoo on the finger, a pleasant manner of speaking, a crooked nose, a short stature.[35] This text also records not one but two battles of the victorious emperor against the Arabs, the first at Partēnē (unidentified), the second at the Well of Jacob, as well as a pursuit to Akra. In addition, it contains passages allegedly quoted from Scripture and short monologues imitating the language of the Septuagint but not actually found in the Bible.[36]

7. Then follows a second section describing the actions of three emperors. The first of them, perhaps to be identified with the conqueror of the Arabs of the preceding paragraph, will destroy a bronze idol at Rome and will then subdue barbarian peoples. A second emperor will shed the blood of the saints, perform other acts of wickedness, and finally be liquidated by an angel. A third emperor of the Romans will enter Byzantium, adorn the city like a bride, and predict that it will be drowned in the sea.[37] Here, too, there obtains a very close relationship with Pseudo-Chrysostom and the correspondence is frequently literal, but again there are many features in *Daniel Καὶ ἔσται* without parallels in Pseudo-Chrysostom.[38] The former text knew of a spirit, released by the emperor's shattering of the bronze idol at Rome, which fled to the "wing of the Capitoline Hill, beheld the city of Romanos[!] and said to her: your daughter Byza was an adulteress." The distribution of gifts by the emperor was made not from a treasure found in the bronze idol but from gold offered by ten thousand ἄρχοντες. Furthermore, the second and third emperors have no counterpart in Pseudo-Chrysostom.

8. A third section describes the prosperous and beneficial rule of a

---

35. For descriptions of the Antichrist, see Bousset, *Antichrist*, pp. 101f. (*Antichrist* will always be cited in the German original rather than the English translation [*The Antichrist Legend: A Chapter in Christian and Jewish Folklore*, trans. A. H. Keene (London, 1896)], which is often incomprehensible and deficient in the annotation.) Useful synthesis: Jean-Marc Rosenstiehl, "Le Portrait de l'Antichrist," in Marc Philonenko and others, *Pseudépigraphes de l'Ancien Testament et manuscrits de la Mer morte*, Cahiers de la Revue d'histoire et de philosophie religieuses no. 41 (Paris, 1967), pp. 45–60. In detail, there is no agreement between the descriptions of the Antichrist and the portrait of the victorious emperor in *Daniel Καὶ ἔσται*.

36. P. 39.29 Vasiliev . . . τὸ ῥηθὲν ὑπὸ τοῦ προφήτου· παραδώσει τὸν ἁμάρτωλον εἰς χεῖρας ἀσεβῶν καὶ στραφεὶς πάλιν ἐκζητήσει τὸ αἷμα αὐτῶν p. 39.33 . . . πληρωθήσεται ὅτι λέων καὶ σκύμνος ὁμοῦ διώξουσιν [. . . the saying of the prophet: He will give the sinner over into the hands of the ungodly and turning again he will demand an account of their blood; p. 39.33 . . . it will be fulfilled, that the lion and the whelp together will pursue]; p. 40.11 . . . λόγος πρὸς τὸν βασιλέα 'Ρωμαίων· υἱὲ ἀνθρώπου, κάλεσαι τὰ πετεινὰ τοῦ οὐρανοῦ κτλ. [. . . saying to the Roman emperor: Son of Man, call the birds of heaven, etc.]

37. Pp. 40.16–41.10 Vasiliev.

38. Cf. pp. 36.34–37.13 Vasiliev.

The *Visions of Daniel*: Extant Texts [ 89

good emperor who ruled for thirty-two years. This description agrees almost verbatim with a passage in the *Slavonic Daniel*.[39] The only significant difference is that where the Slavonic text stresses the emperor's willingness to discuss matters, obviously ecclesiastical, with "pious men," the Greek text mentions that the emperor will bring prosperity to the (common?) people but will sell ἄρχοντες for two pieces of silver.[40]

9. Another paragraph then prophesies that human vice will provoke God's anger. He will charge an angel with the task of inflicting "the baldness of shame" upon the sons of men and of slaying six hundred thousand of them by the sword. The angel will then open the Apyopylai—undoubtedly a corruption for the Caspian Gates, behind which Alexander the Great had imprisoned the Unclean Peoples. The angel then will strike with his sword at Byzantium and the Unclean Peoples begin their work of destruction, but in the end God will relent and the angel will destroy their encampment like chaff.[41] There existed, to the best of my knowledge, no literary model or close parallel for this section, but the content does not differ significantly from other descriptions, based on Pseudo-Methodius, of the last eruption of the Unclean Peoples and their ultimate destruction.[42]

10. Finally, there is a prophecy concerning a Last Roman Emperor surrendering his empire to God the Father, and concerning the destruction of the Antichrist.[43] The ultimate source of this passage is again Pseudo-Methodius, but in its last sentences it agrees almost literally with Pseudo-Chrysostom.[44]

The eschatological part of *Daniel* Καὶ ἔσται thus presents itself, as did the historical section, as a conglomerate of five components, which often have literal parallels in the *Revelation* of Pseudo-Methodius, the *Slavonic Daniel*, and Pseudo-Chrysostom. It is not possible to identify the immediate sources used by the author for all the sections of this second part, but in the case of the first section (item 6 above) internal analysis makes it possible to trace the tradition that lies behind it.

39. Compare p. 41.10–24 Vasiliev with *Slavonic Daniel* #9.
40. Cf. p. 41.13–20 Vasiliev καὶ προσθήσει ἡ γῆ τοὺς καρποὺς αὐτῆς καὶ φάγονται οἱ ἄνθρωποι τῶν μελῶν (μηλῶν) τῆς γῆς καὶ ἐροῦσιν· ἰδού, ἐπειδὲν τὸν λαὸν αὐτοῦ ... πιπράσει δὲ ἄρχοντα ἐν δυσὶν ἀργυρίοις ["and the earth will add its fruits and mankind will eat the limbs (apples) of the earth and say: behold, he watched over his people ... but he will sell a magistrate for two pieces of silver."] with *Slavonic Daniel* #9 "And they will assemble pious men.... And there will be talking among the many [people] assembled. And the emperor will sit with them and they will discuss together."
41. Pp. 41.24–42.22 Vasiliev.
42. Cf. Pseudo-Methodius, p. 44.1–16 Istrin (= pp. 128.96–130.112 Lolos).
43. P. 42.22 to end, Vasiliev.
44. Cf. Pseudo-Methodius, pp. 45–50 Istrin (pp. 130–140 Lolos) and Pseudo-Chrysostom, p. 38.3 to end Vasiliev.

It is clear, first of all, that the events described here are not historical but, rather, express the author's hopes and expectations. This is clear from the topographic indications. Three places are mentioned: Partēnē called "pool of blood" (λάκκος αἵματος); the Well of Jacob (τὸ φρέαρ τοῦ 'Ιακώβ); and Akra (εἰς "Ακραν). The second of these is easiest to identify. The Well of Jacob was not mentioned in Genesis or, indeed, elsewhere in the Old Testament, but the Gospel of John (4:5) mentions a discussion between Jesus and a Samaritan woman at the Spring of Jacob (πηγὴ τοῦ 'Ιακώβ), later (4:12) referred to as a well (φρέαρ). The well was located south of Shechem in Palestine and its existence is fairly continuously attested since New Testament times; indeed, it is still there today. The site was marked on the sixth-century mosaic map of Madaba and in the late seventh, eighth, and ninth centuries various pilgrims visited the cruciform baptistery or church that had been erected over the well by Theodosius the Great and reconstructed by Justinian.[45]

The third place-name mentioned by the apocalyptist, Akra, was a quarter of the city of Jerusalem. Its exact site is a matter of controversy, but it probably lay to the south of the citadel.[46] The quarter had been fortified and garrisoned by King Antiochus IV Epiphanes in 167 B.C. and from then until its destruction in 142 B.C. it remained the principal stronghold of Seleucid power against the Maccabees and the Jewish armies.[47] It had once lain on high ground—hence its name—but was levelled by the victorious Jews. In spite of this it retained its name, known, for example, to Gregory of Nyssa in the fourth century.[48]

The first place-name mentioned by the apocalyptist, Partēnē, cannot be identified and is almost certainly corrupt.[49] One wonders, naturally, whether some toponymic related to Parthia (Παρϑυηνή?) is meant. However that may be, it seems highly probable that a geographic name

---

45. F. M. Abel, "Le Puits de Jacob et l'église Saint Sauveur," *Revue Biblique* 42 (1933), pp. 384–402 (with map of Shechem area and reproduction of map of Madaba); also his *Géographie de la Palestine*, 2 vols. (Paris, 1933), esp. I, pp. 447f.

46. Kathleen M. Kenyon, *Jerusalem—Excavating 3000 Years of History* (New York, 1967), p. 113 and fig. 14, p. 145 (site L). The *Atlas of Israel* published by the Israel Surveys Department of Jerusalem and Amsterdam (1970), map IX.7B ("Jerusalem in the Period of the Second Temple"), places Akra southwest of the Temple Mount, with the Tyropoeon Valley between them. For some time I had been considering whether the Palestinian city of Accho (Akka, Ptolemais), north of modern Haifa, in Phoenicia, could be meant, for since the First Crusade it appeared under the name of Acre. But the spelling Acre is unattested before the time of the First Crusade.

47. Josephus *Bellum Judaicum* 1.39, 5.138, etc., and the excursus in the edition of O. Michel and Otto Bauernfeind (Hamburg, 1960), I, p. 404.

48. Gregory of Nyssa, *In Ecclesiasten* 7, ed. Werner Jaeger, vol. V (Leiden, 1962), p. 398.11 and my note in the *Testimonia*.

49. The following word, οἰα, is also corrupt in the only manuscript and has been emended by the editor into οἶος, probably correctly. (See Chapter III.2, n. 3).

referring to a region on or east of the Upper Euphrates is intended, for the ending *-ēnē* was characteristic for the lands of that part of the world (e.g., Commagene, Osroene, Gordyene).

The apocalyptist thus predicts that a ruler will defeat the Arabs a first time on or east of the Upper Euphrates, will then drive them southward into Palestine and conquer them in a second battle at Jacob's Well in Samaria, and finally force them to take refuge still farther to the south in the quarter of Jerusalem, Akra, where once Antiochus IV's fortress had stood. This section of the apocalypse must have been written after the Arab conquest of Palestine (636–640), for the author is envisaging a war of liberation from Arab rule, and before 869, when, as has been shown (p. 87 above), the historical part was composed. No Byzantine ruler in that interval ever conducted a campaign of this kind; the passage represents, therefore, not an historical fact but the author's hopes for the future.

The apocalyptist prophesies that the Liberator's name will begin with the letter *lambda*.[50] From this Bousset had inferred long ago that Leo III (717–741) is meant and he was probably correct, although Leo IV (774–780) and Leo V (813–820) cannot be excluded altogether.[51] It follows that the author of *Daniel Καὶ ἔσται* incorporated into his apocalypse a passage describing a campaign of liberation against the Arabs, most probably written under Leo III in the early eighth century, and certainly no later than the early ninth century.

The prophecy contains a number of surprising features. Bousset observed long ago that Leo III had been *strategos* of the Anatolikon theme before his accession to the throne and therefore was hardly an unknown figure who had to be "discovered" by divine revelation.[52] It is also not clear how the prophecy of Pseudo-Methodius to the effect that men considered him as if dead and worthless could be applied to Leo III.[53] And it is strange that the apocalyptist should have imagined Leo III as fighting a battle against the Arabs on or even east of the Euphrates, for during Leo's lifetime the principal problem was still to eject the Mos-

---

50. P. 39.20 Vasiliev τὸ δὲ ὄνομα αὐτοῦ ἔσται τὸ τριακοστὸν στοιχεῖον [his name will be the thirtieth letter]; cf. *Slavonic Daniel* #6: "in the thirtieth chapter" (= κεφάλαιον); Pseudo-Chrysostom, p. 36.23 Vasiliev εἰς τὸ τριακοστὸν κεφάλαιον [in the thirtieth chapter].

51. Bousset, "Beiträge," pp. 266f. See also his remarks on pp. 269f. concerning the notion of an alliance between Byzantium and the West (τὰ ξανθὰ γένη), which had been in the air since the Moslems entered Spain.

52. Bousset, "Beiträge," p. 267.

53. Cf. p. 39.21 Vasiliev ὃν ἐδόκουν οἱ ἄνθρωποι ὡς νεκρὸν εἶναι καὶ ὡς οὐδὲν χρησιμεύειν with Pseudo-Methodius, p. 40.3 Istrin (= p. 122.14 Lolos) ὃν ἐλογίζοντο οἱ ἄνθρωποι ὡς νεκρὸν καὶ εἰς οὐδὲν χρησιμεύοντα.

lems from Asia Minor and the principal battle was fought, in the very last year of his reign (741), at Akroinon in Phrygia, far to the northwest of the Euphrates River. It is of course conceivable that the apocalyptist hoped that Leo would succeed in carrying the war deep into the enemy's own territory, but in that case one would have expected him to make that point more explicit, as he did in fact for the period *after* the battle of Partēnē.[54] Strangest of all is the author's prophecy that the inhabitants of the city where the victorious emperor will be discovered will make him mount a chariot.[55] Chariots are known in the Byzantine ceremonial of triumphs, but not of coronations.

These three features, so surprising in the case of Leo III, are easily explained if one thinks of a much earlier emperor who had long played a key role in apocalyptic tradition—Nero. The legend that this Roman emperor had not died in A.D. 68 but had migrated to the East and would return at the end of time is amply documented, for example, in the *Oracula Sibyllina*. The fourth book, composed prior to A.D. 80, represents Nero after the murder of his mother as fleeing "beyond the ford of the Euphrates" and "beyond the Parthian land" and thence returning to "Syria," where he burns down the Temple at Jerusalem.[56] The eighth book, which received its final form early in the third century, speaks of a return of the matricide Nero "from the ends of the earth."[57] The Neronian legend thus explains the military operations of the victorious emperor on the Upper Euphrates or farther east, the need for a divinely inspired discovery of the emperor (because Nero had lived unrecognized after his supposed death) and the reference to Pseudo-Methodius' prophecy about an emperor "considered as if dead." Above all, the Nero legend illuminates the indication that the inhabitants of the city where the emperor will be discovered will "make him mount upon a chariot" (ἀναβιβάσαντες δὲ αὐτὸν ἐν ἅρματι): the eighth book of the *Oracula Sibyllina* speaks of a *Nero redivivus*, returning with fiery passion from Asia, mounting a Trojan chariot, because the historical Nero had been a fanatical participant in the *lusus Troiae*.[58] This is not to say, of course, that the eschatological part of *Daniel Καὶ*

---

54. P. 39.32 Vasiliev διώξουσιν τὸν Ἰσμαὴλ εἰς τὰς χώρας αὐτῶν.
55. P. 39.20 Vasiliev ἀναβιβάσαντες δὲ αὐτὸν ἅρματι.
56. *Oracula Sibyllina*, 4.115–127 Geffcken. See J. Geffcken, "Studien für älteren Nerosage," *Nachrichten von der Kgl. Gesellschaft der Wissenschaften zu Göttingen* (Göttingen, 1899), pp. 441–62, esp. 446f., and Adolf Kurfess, ed., *Sibyllinische Weissagungen* (Heimeran, 1951), pp. 302f.
57. *Oracula Sibyllina*, 8.72 Geffcken. On the date, see Geffcken, "Studien," pp. 443f.
58. *Oracula Sibyllina*, 8.153–55 Geffcken κώμαξ᾽, εἰ βούλει σύ, τὸν ἐν κρυφίαισι λοχείαις· Ἀσίδος ἐκ γαίης ἐπὶ Τρωικὸν ἅρμ᾽ ἐπιβάντα / θυμὰν ἔχοντ᾽ αἴθωνος. See Geffcken, "Studien," p. 445.

ἔσται had as its direct or ultimate source the *Oracula Sibyllina*, but merely that its author presented a prophecy concerning the emperor Leo III in colors borrowed from the legend about a *Nero redivivus*.

But this is not all, for neither the personality of Leo III nor the Neronian legend is adequate to explain all the features of the later apocalypse. Neither emperor had ever waged war in Palestine, at Jacob's Well or at the Akra, nor could he reasonably be expected to do that. Moreover, the apocalyptist evidently envisaged the Akra at Jerusalem as a place of refuge for the Arabs, for the relevant section of the apocalypse ends with the Arabs driven by the victorious ruler εἰς Ἄκραν.[59] But the Ἄκρα had lost its character as a fortress at the end of the Maccabean wars in 143 B.C., when the victorious Jews had razed the hated Seleucid stronghold to the ground. Even stranger is the apocalyptist's notion that the ruler discovered by divine inspiration would be "anointed."[60] The anointment of rulers was unknown in the Byzantine Empire before the Crusades, and while it was normal in Western Europe, there is no basis in the text for assuming that Western customs are being referred to. There had been, however, one people in the Near East, well known to the Byzantines, who had been in the habit of anointing their kings—the Jews. This clue may serve as a reminder that behind the legend of Nero there stood the figure of the Seleucid king Antiochus IV Epiphanes and his conflict with the Jews.[61] If the apocalyptist knew of the Neronian legend in a form that still preserved features of Nero's prototype, Antiochus, it becomes entirely intelligible that this form could have circulated among Jews during the Maccabean wars. They would have imagined a restoration of the monarchy with its ritual of anointment and the emergence of a Jewish king who would defeat the troops of Antiochus in a battle at Jacob's Well and drive them back to their principal stronghold, the Akra at Jerusalem. This hypothesis would also explain the curious fact that while elsewhere in the eschatological section the author writes of a conflict between Arabs and Romans, the battle at Jacob's Well is presented as one between Hellenes and Ismaelites.[62]

---

59. P. 40.16 Vasiliev: Καὶ ἐκδιώξεται ὁ βασιλεὺς τῶν Ῥωμαίων τὸν Ἰσμαὴλ εἰς Ἄκραν.
60. P. 39.21 Vasiliev καὶ χρίσονται αὐτὸν βασιλέα.
61. Geffcken, "Studien," pp. 442f.
62. Contrast p. 39.25 Vasiliev (battle of Partēnē) ὥστε ἐκ τῶν αἱμάτων τῶν Ἰσμαηλιτῶν καὶ τῶν Ῥωμαίων ἵππον ἐπιβατούμενον ἀποθανεῖν, and p. 40.15 Vasiliev καὶ ἐκδιώξεται ὁ βασιλεὺς τῶν Ῥωμαίων τὸν Ἰσμαὴλ εἰς Ἄκραν on the one hand with p. 40.4 Vasiliev (battle at Jacob's Well) on the other: ἐκεῖ πεσοῦνται οἱ δυνάσται τῶν Ἑλλήνων καὶ κράξονται υἱοὶ Ἰσμαὴλ κτλ. The prophecy about a battle at Jacob's Well had originally referred to the Seleucid war against the Jews, and later apocalyptists had not succeeded in obliterating all traces of its origins.

I conclude, therefore, that the part of the apocalypse here under consideration (pp. 39.18–40.16 Vasiliev) was composed probably under the Byzantine emperor Leo III (717–741), certainly at the latest in the early ninth century, by an apocalyptist envisaging a series of miraculous victories over the Arabs patterned after earlier expectations of Nero returning from the East, which themselves were influenced by Jewish dreams of the Maccabean period concerning a restoration of the Hebrew kingship and a great victory over the forces of the occupying Hellenistic power.[63] Since the study of the historical part of the apocalypse has shown that the apocalyptist lived in the second half of the ninth century, it follows that in his eschatological speculations he relied on an ancient tradition that had been applied to the Byzantine emperor Leo III more than a century before his time. It is likely that the prophecy concerning Leo III had itself been a *Vision of Daniel* and that the surprising reference to the eighth-century Moslem invasion of Spain and Auvergne (p. 79 above), interrupting as it does the *vaticinia* of ninth-century events in the historical past, is a fragment of the same document. While its sources concerning Antiochus and Nero were undoubtedly of Jewish provenance, it is likely that the eighth-century document itself was written by a Christian, for given the general separation of Jews and Christians after the Arab invasions, it is unlikely that a Jewish document could have reached a Christian apocalyptist in the eighth century.[64]

As a result of this analysis it should be clear how *Daniel* Καὶ ἔσται came into being. The author wrote at Constantinople, under the impact of Basil's recent murder of his benefactor and colleague Michael III (867) and probably of the terrible earthquake of 869, which in some quarters may have been considered a divine punishment for the crime committed in the imperial palace. Against this view the apocalyptist at-

---

63. It is not difficult to see why and how old prophecies of Nero's victories over the Parthians and of Jewish victories over the Seleucid armies could be reinterpreted to refer to Byzantine victories over the Arabs; in all three cases it was a question of defeating the great national enemy. It is puzzling, however, that in the eighth century the portrait of the liberating emperor should have been influenced by the activities of such an essentially wicked and anti-Christian figure as Nero. One must assume that the later apocalyptist saw in *Nero redivivus* more the conqueror over the Parthian enemies than the Antichrist, either because the form in which he knew the Neronian legend emphasized the former feature or because he was no longer able to understand the anti-Christian aspects of the legend.

64. Note, however, that a Hebrew poem from the period of the Arab conquests predicted a battle of Edom (Rome) and Ismael "in the plain of Acre / Till the horses sink in the blood." These two lines are very similar to *Daniel* Καὶ ἔσται p. 39.27 Vasiliev. I owe my acquaintance with this text to Bernard Lewis, "An Apocalyptic View of Islamic History," (University of London) *Bulletin of the School of Oriental and African Studies* 13 (1949), pp. 308–338, esp. 336.

tempted to represent Basil as the "New Phinehas," and he performed his apologetic task in the form of an apocalypse. He derived his *vaticinia ex eventu*, quite indiscriminately, from a *Vision of Daniel* composed more than a century before his time under Leo III (item 2) and from other documents composed during the forties or fifties of his own century—i.e., the ninth—in Italy and Sicily (items 1, 3, 5). For the eschatological part he used (item 6) more heavily the same eighth-century *Vision of Daniel* on which he had already relied for a *vaticinium ex eventu*, and he added other traditional materials from Pseudo-Methodius (items 9 and 10) and from a *Vision of Daniel* now lost (item 8).

# IV.
# *Visions of Daniel* Summarized by Liudprand of Cremona

In addition to those *Visions of Daniel* that survive in the Greek original or in a Slavonic translation, there are two lost documents of this type of which fairly detailed paraphrases are given by Liudprand, bishop of Cremona, in his account of his embassy to Constantinople in 968.[1] When recording the Byzantine emperor Nicephorus Phocas' (963–969) departure for his campaign against the Arabs, which was to lead to the capture of Antioch in the following year, Liudprand announces that he will discuss the reasons for the emperor's campaign.[2] One of these reasons, he writes, was certain books that permitted the Byzantines to take an optimistic view of their military prospects. According to Liudprand, these books were in the hands of both Arabs and Byzantines and were called ὁράσεις (Liudprand here reproduces the Greek word) of Daniel. These books, so Liudprand tells, contained indications as to the length of each emperor's life, whether during his reign there would be peace or war with the Saracens, and whether the Saracens would prosper or fail.[3] It was also said in these books, still according to Liudprand, that "at the time of this Nicephorus the Assyrians would be unable to resist the Greeks and that he would live no longer than seven years." After his death an "emperor much worse and much less war-

---

1. Joseph Becker, ed., *Die Werke Liudprands von Cremona* (Hannover and Leipzig, 1915), *Legatio* chs. 39–43, pp. 195–98. English translation by F. A. Wright, *The Works of Liutprand of Cremona* (London, 1930), pp. 257–61.

2. Liudprand *Legatio* ch. 39, p. 195 Becker: *Sed cur exercitum nunc in Assyrios duxerit, quaeso advertite.*

3. Ibid.: *Habent Greci et Saraceni libros, quos* ὁράσεις *sive visiones Danielis vocant, ego autem Sibyllanos, in quibus scriptum reperitur, quot annis imperator quisque vivat, quae sint futura eo imperitante tempora, pax an simultas, secundae Saracenorum res an adversae.*

like than he" would take over. During his reign the Assyrians would gain the upper hand and would occupy all the lands as far as the territory of Chalcedon.[4]

Liudprand's paraphrase is sufficiently detailed and precise to make it possible, on the basis of it and of the surviving specimens of *Visions of Daniel* considered previously, to form a fairly satisfactory idea of the document that the Italian bishop saw at Constantinople during the summer of 968. It was entitled Ὅρασις τοῦ Δανιήλ, as, for example, the Greek text *BHG*[3] 1871. Its author called the enemy *Assyrii*, a designation that can hardly be due to Liudprand, especially as it is a term for the enemy traditional among apocalyptists at least since the days of the *Oracula Sibyllina*.[5] The context in Liudprand leaves no doubt that he and his Byzantine informants understood it to refer to the contemporary Arabs. It is clear, furthermore, that the last item of Liudprand's paraphrase, the prophecy that under a wicked and unwarlike (Roman or Byzantine) emperor the Assyrians would occupy all the land as far as the territory of Chalcedon, is also part of traditional eschatology and long antedated the emergence of Islam, for it occurs verbatim around A.D. 500 in the *Oracle of Baalbek*.[6]

Liudprand also tells that this prophecy was preceded by a reference to his contemporary, Emperor Nicephorus (II Phocas, 963–969, *huius Nicephori*). One wonders whether this identification may not be an inference drawn by Liudprand or by his Byzantine informants. In the first place, as is clear from the discussion of other apocalypses, apocalyptists normally do not name rulers but, rather, paraphrase their names in more or less transparent fashion; moreover, the lifespan of the emperor—seven years—looks traditional (one year-week) rather than historical; and finally, in Byzantine apocalypses the most wicked and least warlike figure is normally the Antichrist, and he is usually preceded by an eschatological ruler whose principal function it is to vanquish the enemy.[7] Now Liudprand informs us that the text (or texts) that he is summarizing contained a list of emperors, with an indication of the number of their years. It must therefore have looked very much like the

---

4. Ibid., pp. 195f.: *Legitur itaque huius Nicephori temporibus Assyrios Grecis non posse resistere nuncque septennio tantum vivere; post cuius obitum imperatorem isto deteriorem . . . et magis imbellem debere surgere, cuius temporibus praevalere debent adeo Assyrii, ut in Chalcedoniam usque . . . potestative cuncta debeant obtinere.*

5. See my *Oracle of Baalbek*, pp. 107n. 16 and 111f.n. 48.

6. See my edition, line 181: ἔσονται οἱ Ἀσσύριοι ὡς ἡ ἄμμος τῆς θαλάσσης ἀναρίθμητοι καὶ παραλάβωσι πολλὰς χώρας τῆς Ἀνατολῆς ἕως Χαλκηδονίας.

7. The Antichrist is, of course, wicked by definition. He wins his converts by guile rather than by force, especially by performing apparent miracles (Bousset, *Antichrist*, pp. 115ff.).

"prophecy of the emperors" in the (lost) Greek original of the Slavonic text discussed above (Ch. III, Sec. 1, *Slavonic Daniel* [2]–[3]). It is possible to guess who the last historical emperor mentioned in that list referred to by Liudprand must have been. Liudprand tells that it culminated in the ruler whom he, or perhaps his Byzantine informants, identified with their contemporary, Nicephorus Phocas. If this identification had the slightest plausibility, the last historical ruler recognizable must have been Romanos II (959–963), just as the "prophecy of the emperors" in the Slavonic text ended with Michael II (Ch. III, Sec. 1, n. 25). For if this list seen by Liudprand had ended with any earlier emperor, say with Constantine VII Porphyrogenitus (†959), an identification of the victorious emperor with Nicephorus Phocas would have met with the natural and fatal objection that the victorious emperor had, in the nature of things, to be the successor of Constantine VII, i.e., Romanos II. I am thus led to the conclusion that, although in the text shown to Liudprand, the victorious emperor is unlikely to have been named, Liudprand's informants were indeed correct in thinking that the author had meant Nicephorus Phocas. Probably he had spoken, *more apocalyptico*, of a victorious emperor (βασιλεὺς νικηφόρος).

This conclusion, in turn, implies that the *Vision of Daniel* seen by Liudprand had been composed no earlier than the reign of Nicephorus Phocas—in other words, between 963 and 968. It seems to have differed from all other *Visions of Daniel* considered so far by the fact that it did not contain any reference to Sicily; at least nothing in Liudprand's summary would lead one to believe that the text was concerned with that island. In fact, the survival of the item on the Moslem advance *in Chalcedoniam usque* makes it highly probable that it was composed in the East, as had been, more than four hundred years earlier, the *Oracle of Baalbek*, which contains the same phrase. Thus we find that in the time that had elapsed between the earlier *Visions of Daniel* and the one seen by Liudprand in 968 at Constantinople, the practice of composing apocalypses of this sort had travelled eastward across the Mediterranean Sea and there, naturally, centered around warfare against the eastern rather than western Arabs.

Liudprand introduces us to a second document of a similar character. Its author, according to the bishop of Cremona, was "a certain Hippolytus, a [or: the] Sicilian bishop."[8] It must have contained prophecies about the Ottonian Empire and a Western people whom Liudprand

---

8. Liudprand *Legatio* ch. 40, p. 196.11 Becker: *Sed Hippolytus quidam Siciliensis episcopus eadem scripsit et de imperio vestro et gente nostra—nostram nunc dico omnem, quae sub vestro* [i.e., the Ottos'] *imperio est, gentem—; atque utinam verum sit, quod de praesentibus scripsit iste temporibus.*

calls, with somewhat labored reservations, *gens nostra*. These prophecies must have predicted something highly favorable to the Saxon rulers, for Liudprand expresses the fervent wish that they may come true. Inasmuch as, according to Liudprand, Hippolytus "wrote the same things" (*eadem scripsit*) about the Ottonian Empire—meaning, presumably, the same things as the *Vision of Daniel* discussed by Liudprand in his preceding chapter—it follows that Hippolytus must have predicted that the Ottos would defeat the Arabs. All the rest of the prophecies (*cetera ut scripsit*), so Liudprand informs us on the authority of his Byzantine informants, have already been fulfilled—that is, presumably it contained a series of *vaticinia post eventum*, as do all apocalypses. One prophecy, however, that apparently is still awaiting its fulfillment, Liudprand cites in Greek: "Lion and whelp together will pursue a wild ass."[9] Much of what follows in the *Legatio* deals with conflicting interpretations given to this prophecy by Liudprand's Byzantine associates on the one hand and by Liudprand himself on the other, rather than with the content of Hippolytus' work. Liudprand does, however, revert once more to it and quotes a highly ambiguous phrase: *Grecos non debere Saracenos, sed Francos conterere*.[10]

This prediction is so ambiguous because it is not clear at first glance what is the subject and what the object of this prophecy. Grammatically, either *Grecos* or *Saracenos* or *Francos* could be the subject. However, it seems clear from the discussion of the earlier parts of Hippolytus' prophecy that he predicted a Western victory over the Arabs. To bring this last citation into harmony with the general intent of Hippolytus' work, one must assume that *Saracenos* is object and *Grecos* and *Francos* alternative subjects. Hippolytus' prophecy should therefore be translated: "Not the Greeks but the Franks will crush the Saracens."[11] This interpretation is in complete agreement with what follows in Liudprand, for he tells us that, inspired by this prophecy, the Saracens had three years earlier defeated an expeditionary force under the magister Manuel Phocas and the eunuch Nicetas in the Straits of Messina and, not much later, the forces of "Exakonta."[12]

9. Ibid., p. 196.15: *Cetera ut scripsit, sunt usque huc completa, quemadmodum per ipsos, qui horum librorum scientiam habent, audivi. Et ex multis eius* [i.e., Hippolytus'] *dictis unum id proferamus in medium. Ait enim nunc completum iri scripturam, quae dicit:* λέων καὶ σκίμνος [sic] ὁμοδιώξουσιν [sic] ὄναγρον. This *scriptura* does not occur in the Bible.

10. Ibid. ch. 43, p. 198.15: *Scribit etiam praefatus Hippolytus Grecos non debere Saracenos, sed Francos conterere.*

11. Wright, *Liutprand*, p. 261.

12. On the expedition of 964 (rather than 965) commanded by the patrician Manuel Phocas and the eunuch Nicetas, see Amari, *Storia*, II, pp. 299–313; Gay, *Italie Méridionale*, pp. 290f.; M. Canard, *Cambridge Medieval History*, vol. IV, part I, (Cambridge,

Liudprand's precise yet lean summary of Hippolytus' work raises many questions. In the first place, who was "Hippolytus"?[13] His designation as "Sicilian bishop" is strange, for bishops are normally designated by the name of their see rather than by that of the region (Sicily) in which that see was situated.[14] It is therefore unlikely that Liudprand's phrase (*Hippolytus quidam Siciliensis episcopus*) derives from the heading of the work as it occurred in the manuscript shown to Liudprand in Constantinople. The simplest explanation of the ascription is that the text was a pseudepigraphon, as are most apocalypses, from the canonical book of Daniel down to and beyond the *Revelation* of Pseudo-Methodius and the *Vision of Daniel* attributed to John Chrysostom (*BHG*³ 1871).[15] Hippolytus of Rome was an ideal candidate for the authorship of an apocalypse, because he published a celebrated commentary on Daniel and a treatise on the Antichrist. The designation of Pseudo-Hippolytus—so it will be proper to refer henceforth to the author of the work paraphrased by Liudprand in chs. 40ff. of the *Legatio*—as *episcopus Siciliensis*, in turn, must be an inference drawn by a copyist of the work or by a reader, perhaps even by Liudprand or his informants, from the Sicilian content of the piece. An inference of this kind was undoubtedly prompted by the occurrence of Sicilian place-names in Pseudo-Hippolytus' tract, as, for example, in Pseudo-Chrysostom's *Vision of Daniel* (*BHG*³ 1871) and the Slavonic text. Indeed, as we have seen, many *Visions of Daniel* were composed in Sicily. The text at-

---

1966), p. 731. I have been unable to identify the expedition under the magister "Exakonta" (cf. Amari, *Storia*, II, p. 311 and n. 4). A Nicephorus Hexakionites was an early supporter of Nicephorus Phocas and played a role in his coup d'état: cf. Leo Diaconus, p. 431 Bonn.

13. Joseph Becker, in his edition of Liudprand (p. 196n.2) suggests that Liudprand is referring to the famous Church Father Hippolytus of Rome (†235) and his *De Antichristo*, chs. 6–18, but there is nothing in that patristic text that resembles Liudprand's summary.

14. In the Arabic text of the Siculo-Arab Chronicle of Cambridge (cf. Chapter III, Sec. 3, n. 27 above), there is a mention of "Leo bishop of Sicily" among the hostages taken by the Arabs at Oria, Apulia, in 925: cf. Amari, *Biblioteca arabo-sicula*, Versione Italiana (Rome, Turin, 1880–81, 1889) I, p. 283; Vasiliev, *Byzance et les Arabes*, II, part 2, p. 104. Already Amari (*Storia*, II, pp. 249f.) compared this passage in the Chronicle with Liudprand's *Legatio* and spoke of "cotesta strana appellazione di vescovo di Sicilia." He explained it by the assumption that by the tenth century only one bishopric continued to exist in Sicily. I shall propose a somewhat different explanation, at least for the passage in Liudprand. Even today, ecclesiastical sees are not abolished even though their bishops are prevented from discharging their functions.

15. Hippolytus does not elsewhere appear as a given name in the mid-Byzantine period. I have consulted various indexes of personal names, such as those in Amari's *Storia*, in de Boor's edition of Theophanes, and in Rodolphe Guilland's *Recherches sur les institutions byzantines*, Berliner Byzantinistischen Arbeiten, v. 35, (Amsterdam, 1967). The only exception is Hippolytus of Thebes, probably of the eighth century; cf. F. Diekamp, *Hippolytus von Theben* (Münster, 1898).

tributed by Liudprand to Hippolytus must have been another *Vision of Daniel* composed in Sicily.

This conclusion also explains other features of Liudprand's summary—first, why he wrote in ch. 39 of *Visiones Danielis*, in the plural. The reason was that the piece attributed to Hippolytus in chs. 40ff. was a second specimen of the genre, just as was the piece paraphrased in ch. 39. It further explains why Pseudo-Hippolytus' work contained the Lion-Whelp prophecy, a feature that occurs only in *Visions of Daniel*.[16] Above all, the conclusion that the work attributed to Hippolytus was a *Vision of Daniel* composed in Sicily explains the most noteworthy feature of the lost text: it prophesied a Frankish rather than a Byzantine victory over the Arabs (*Grecos non debere Saracenos, sed Francos conterere*). In this respect the work of Pseudo-Hippolytus differed from all the other *Visions of Daniel*, including the one paraphrased by Liudprand in ch. 39, in which it was prophesied that a Byzantine ruler would defeat the Arabs. This dramatic break with the entire previous tradition of the *Visions of Daniel* was conceivable only in Sicily, or possibly in southern Italy, for nowhere else were the alternatives envisaged by Pseudo-Hippolytus, of a Byzantine or a Western conflict with Islam, plausible.

The mention of the Franks in Liudprand's summary should prove helpful in solving, at least partially, another question raised by it: what had been the terms of Pseudo-Hippolytus' prophecy that Liudprand rendered as *imperium vestrum et gens nostra*? We have seen that Liudprand's words *eadem scripsit* included the prophecy of a Western victory over Islam. Certainly Pseudo-Hippolytus had not named Otto; such a procedure would have been out of keeping with apocalyptic practice. The application of the prophecy to Otto was clearly an inference by Liudprand (or his informants), which may or may not have coincided with Pseudo-Hippolytus' intent. Yet Liudprand records not the slightest hesitation on anybody's part, his own or his Byzantine informants', as to the identification of the ruler, a fact especially noteworthy as he later mentions a bitter controversy as to the interpretation of

---

16. In fact, Liudprand's summary helps to establish the correct text of that prophecy, although here, too, it appears in an inaccurate form: λέων καὶ σκίμνος ὁμοδιώξουσιν ὄναγρον. In the Slavonic text (above, Chapter III, Sec. 1, n. 51) it runs "dog and whelp together pursue the field," or, translated back into the Greek, κύων καὶ σκύμνος ὁμοῦ διώξουσιν τὸν ἀγρόν. Here κύων and τὸν ἀγρὸν are palaeographical corruptions of λέων and ὄναγρον respectively. In BHG³ 1871 the prophecy appears in the form (p. 30.34, Vasiliev) κύων καὶ σκύμνος διώξουσιν ἀγρόν; here ὁμοῦ is omitted and ὄναγρον again corrupted into ἀγρόν. In BHG³ 1872 it runs λέων καὶ σκύμνος ὁμοῦ διώξουσιν—in other words, the object is left out altogether. The correct text of the oracle may be reconstructed as λέων καὶ σκύμνος ὁμοῦ διώξουσιν ὄναγρον.

the Lion-Whelp oracle. I conclude, therefore, that Pseudo-Hippolytus' text must have made it very clear that a Western rather than an Eastern ruler was meant. (I shall return to this feature later.) On the other hand, Liudprand's somewhat labored comment on *gente nostra*: *nostram nunc dico omnem, quae sub vestro imperio est, gentem* indicates that, taken literally, the prophecy did not fit either the Saxon Otto or the Lombard Liudprand. Pseudo-Hippolytus must, therefore, have named a people other than Saxons or Lombards. If it is now remembered that elsewhere in his tract Pseudo-Hippolytus, according to Liudprand's testimony, mentioned the Franks (*Grecos non debere Saracenos, sed Francos conterere*), it becomes highly probable that with the words *gente nostra* Liudprand was paraphrasing another reference to the Frankish people (τὸ ἔθνος τῶν Φράγγων) by Pseudo-Hippolytus.[17]

It is not easy to understand, at first glance, what role the Lion-Whelp oracle can have played in Pseudo-Hippolytus' *Vision of Daniel*. How exactly that oracle fit into the context is difficult to say; in fact, this context must have been fairly ambiguous, to allow for the divergent interpretations discussed by Liudprand in chs. 40 and 41. In the preserved *Visions of Daniel* it invariably occurs immediately following the great battle in which a Byzantine emperor defeats the Arabs. After this battle, the emperor forces the Western ("Blond") peoples to become his allies, and then Byzantines and Westerners together pursue the Arabs into their own country, thus fulfilling the Lion-Whelp prophecy. Inasmuch, however, as we know from Liudprand that Pseudo-Hippolytus assigned to a Western ruler rather than to the Byzantine βασιλεύς the task of defeating the Arabs, it was inevitable that he also reversed the function of the Byzantine emperor, assigning to him the secondary role of compulsory ally to the Western emperor: the Arabs would be pursued into their own country by a Western ruler assisted by a Byzantine emperor. It is difficult to see what other meaning the Lion-Whelp prophecy can have had within the new political context created by Pseudo-Hippolytus, yet this meaning must have been sufficiently ambiguous to permit not only Liudprand's interpretation of the oracle (Otto I and Otto II) but also the Greek interpretation (Nicephorus Phocas and Otto I).

What else did Pseudo-Hippolytus' prophecy contain, in addition to a Frankish victory over the Arabs and the Lion-Whelp oracle? There must have been, as we have seen, some historical material, especially place-

---

17. Elsewhere in the *Legatio*, too, Liudprand refers to himself as a Frank—e.g., ch. 19, p. 186.6 Becker, where a Byzantine official refers to him as *episcopus. . . Francorum*; ch. 53, p. 203.25 Becker, where he imagines the two Ottos praising him, Liudprand, in the terms *solus es ex Francis, quem nunc diligemus*.

names, referring to Sicily, to account for the designation of the author as an *episcopus Siciliensis,* but it is lost beyond hope. In all probability Pseudo-Hippolytus also prophesied, as did all other *Visions of Daniel,* that the victorious ruler, after his Sicilian victory and after forcing the Byzantine emperor into an alliance, would enter the city of Rome. Did he also predict, as do the other texts, that the Western conqueror would capture Constantinople? That seems unlikely, for, as we stated above, he is represented as the ally of the Byzantine emperor. But what of another feature that forms a regular part of the tradition, the journey of the ruler victorious over the Arabs (so the *Revelation* of Pseudo-Methodius) or of one of his successors (so *BHG*³ 1872 and the *Slavonic Daniel*) to Jerusalem, and the surrender of his power to God? This element of the tradition was the culmination of the emperor's victories over Christianity's principal enemy, Islam. If Pseudo-Hippolytus transferred these victories from the Byzantine emperor to a Western ruler, then the logic of the tradition required that the journey to Jerusalem and the abdication be shifted in a similar way. It is highly probable, if not certain, therefore, that Pseudo-Hippolytus represented the Western ruler who, with the help of his Byzantine ally, defeated and pursued the Arabs, or one of his successors, as journeying to Jerusalem and there surrendering his power to God.

This was indeed a drastic change the political and literary importance of which can hardly be exaggerated. As will be seen repeatedly in this book, the apocalyptic genre is extremely conservative and the preservation of traditional features is its lifeblood. Changes in the tradition are made exclusively for the purpose of safeguarding the prophetic virtues of an earlier representation of the tradition or, to put it differently, only under the compelling force of events prompting a later writer to adjust an earlier prophecy to the actual course of history. Thus numerals are occasionally tampered with to allow more time for a prophecy to be fulfilled, references to geographical features adapted, or, more generally, a vague prediction reformulated in more precise terms so that the reader will understand it to have been fulfilled by a particular historical event. On occasion, such adjustments of the tradition were made in polemical form. Thus we have seen that in the *Revelation* of Pseudo-Methodius the author argued against an interpretation of Psalm 68:31 that considered Ethiopia rather than Byzantium the best hope for liberation from Arab domination. Something similar seems to have happened in the case of Pseudo-Hippolytus. He, too, undertook to combat an older tradition and substituted for the Byzantine emperor, as the liberator from Moslem oppression, a Western ruler. Undoubtedly, even the polemical form in which this substitution appears in Liudprand's paraphrase *Grecos non debere Saracenos, sed Francos conterere* is the rendering of a Greek phrase couched in similarly polemical language.

Given the conservative nature of the apocalyptic tradition, then, Pseudo-Hippolytus must have been prompted by two weighty considerations for breaking with previous *Visions of Daniel* and shifting the principal task of defeating the Moslems from a Byzantine to a Western ruler. In the first place, while to us moderns this appears as a momentous political break, Pseudo-Hippolytus himself must have felt that he was doing no more than proposing a reinterpretation of old prophecies better adapted to the international situation than the old wording had been. To put it differently, he must have considered that he was suggesting not a break with tradition but merely an improved understanding. Second, the international situation at the time of his writing must have facilitated, or even necessitated, this reinterpretation of earlier prophecy. Clearly it must have been based on two convictions on the part of Pseudo-Hippolytus: first, that the Byzantine emperor could no longer be expected to bear the principal responsibility for expelling the Arabs from Sicily—which, as we have seen, was the center of Pseudo-Hippolytus' interest; and second, that a Western ruler could be relied upon to discharge this task. At what point in history could the international situation be presumed to have fostered these two convictions in the mind of a Greek writer about Sicily? A convincing answer to this question will provide a date for Pseudo-Hippolytus.

One's first suspicion is that, as in the *Vision of Daniel* summarized in ch. 39 of the *Legatio*, here too Liudprand may be paraphrasing a tract of very recent origin composed under the impact of Otto I's meteoric rise on the European scene, his defeat of his German rivals, his victory over the Magyars (955), his imperial coronation at Rome (962), and his several powerful interventions in the affairs of the Italian Peninsula. The Byzantine emperors were then absorbed in their warfare against the eastern Arabs and could hardly have been expected to take more than a half-hearted interest in Western affairs. As we have seen, the expeditionary force sent by Nicephorus Phocas to Sicily in 964 to relieve Rametta, commanded by Manuel Phocas and Nicetas, had failed ignominiously, and in 965 the Arabs had entered Rametta. Even the Byzantine naval forces had been annihilated in an engagement in the Straits of Messina.[18] Late in 966 or in 967 Nicephorus Phocas had even made peace with the Fāṭimid khalif of North Africa, al-Muʿizz. There were two rea-

18. Amari, *Storia*, II, pp. 310–313; Gay, *Italie Méridionale*, pp. 290f., 295.

sons for this rapprochement of the Christian emperor and the Moslem khalif. First, the Fāṭimid and Byzantine rulers were united in their enmity to the Ikhshīdid masters of Syria and Egypt: Nicephorus Phocas coveted their Syrian possessions, while al-Muʿizz was making plans for the conquest of Egypt. Second, both rulers were alarmed by Otto I's claims upon southern Italy; they directly threatened Byzantine possessions in southern Italy, and potentially even the Fāṭimid control of Sicily.[19] Here, then—with the Saxon emperor Otto I emerging as the greatest power in Europe and the arbiter of Italy, and the Byzantine emperor Nicephorus Phocas absorbed in the campaigns against his Eastern enemies and now even the ally of the Moslem ruler of North Africa against Otto's design upon the Byzantine themes of Longobardia and Calabria—seems to be just the political constellation that was postulated above as prompting Pseudo-Hippolytus' momentous decision to prophesy a liberation of Sicily from Moslem rule by a Western ruler.

Yet while the years between Nicephorus Phocas' failure in Sicily (965) and Liudprand's stay in Constantinople (968) would be a plausible period to which to date Pseudo-Hippolytus' tract, there exists incontrovertible evidence that the key feature of this work—the shift of the defeat of the Arabs from a Byzantine to a Western ruler—antedated Otto I's imperial coronation (962) and perhaps even his first campaign to Italy (951). This evidence consists of a passage, often cited and discussed, in a letter by the monk Adso (ca. 920–992), who in 967 became abbot of Montier-en-Der in the diocese of Chalons-sur-Marne: *De ortu et tempore Antichristi*, supposedly composed in compliance with a request from, and addressed to, Queen Gerberga, sister of Otto I and wife of the Carolingian king Louis IV d'Outremer of France (936–954).[20] The letter was composed no later than 954, for Adso declares that he includes in his prayers not only the queen but also her husband, King Louis IV (†954), and probably no earlier than 948, for in that year the couple's second son was born, and the text speaks of their "sons," in the

---

19. Amari, *Storia*, II, pp. 314–19.
20. Ed. Sackur, *Sibyllinische Texte*, pp. 97–113. On the author see Max Manitius, *Geschichte der lateinischen Literatur des Mittelalters* (Munich, 1923), II, pp. 432–44; Gaston Zeller, "Les Rois de France candidats à l'Empire," *Revue Historique* 59 (1934), pp. 273–311, 497–534, esp. 277f.; Carl Erdmann, "Das ottonische Reich als Imperium Romanum," *Deutsches Archiv für Geschichte des Mittelalters* 6 (1943), pp. 412–441, esp. 426ff.; Kassius Hallinger, *Gorze-Kluny: Studien zu den monastischen Lebensformen und Gegensätzen im Hochmittelalter* (Rome, 1950), pp. 61f. On the commissioning of Adso's letter by Queen Gerberga, cf. p. 105 Sackur: *sicut mihi servo vestro dignata estis praecipere*. [See also now Robert Konrad, *De ortu et tempore Antichristi. Antichristvorstellung und Geschichtsbild der Abtes Adso von Montieren*, Münchener historische Studien, Abt. Mittelalterliche Geschichte, vol. 1 (Munich, 1964)].

plural.²¹ King Louis's authority was challenged, throughout his reign, by the great dukes of the Western Frankish realm, and Adso seems to reflect the insecurity of Louis's throne in various passages of his letter. He prays that God may preserve for the royal family the *culmen imperii* and assures them that he would like nothing better than to obtain from God for them their entire kingdom, but confesses sadly that he is unable to do so.²² The same tendency to comfort Queen Gerberga and her royal husband concerning the political turbulence of the times underlies a later passage of the letter. Here Adso discusses the Pauline passage II Thess. 2:3, which figures prominently in all discussions of the Antichrist, and interprets it in the traditional way—that the Antichrist will not come until all the kingdoms have fallen away from the Roman Empire.²³ This time, so Adso assures the queen, has not yet arrived even though the kingdom of the Romans is largely destroyed, because, since kings of the Franks are destined to govern the Roman Empire, the dignity of Roman kingship will not perish wholly: it will remain with its kings.²⁴ In these lines Adso visualizes clearly the precariousness of royal power in the Western Frankish kingdom of Louis IV, but he holds out the hope that the *reges Francorum* are destined to continue to govern the Roman Empire. The great dukes of France, so he seems to say, may rebel against the royal power, but in the end the Roman Empire will be restored by a Frankish king.

Adso conveys this idea more clearly immediately following the passage just cited. It is surely remarkable that Adso, who throughout his letter relied on a commentary on II Thessalonians ascribed to Haimo of Halberstadt (†853) as his source, cites in the following words of comfort to his queen a source to which he refers as "certain of our learned

---

21. P. 104 Sackur: *pro vobis et pro seniore vestro domino rege et pro filiorum vestrorum incolumitate Dei nostri misericordiam exoro.* The oldest son of the royal couple, Lothar, was born in 941; the second, Louis, in 948 (he died in 954, the same year as his father; see P. Lauer, *Le Règne de Louis IV d'Outremer* [Paris, 1900], p. 230). A son from Gerberga's first husband, Gilbert of Lorraine, Henry, died in 944 (Lauer, p. 49n.8). Twins, Charles and Henry, were born in 953; the latter died immediately after baptism (Lauer, p. 225).

22. P. 104 Sackur: *ut vobis et culmen imperii in hac vita dignatur conservare.* P. 105: *si potuissem vobis totum regnum acquirere, libentissime fecissem, sed quia illud facere non valeo, pro salute vestra filiorumque vestrorum Dominum exorabo.*

23. P. 110 Sackur: *Inde ergo dicit Paulus apostolus, Antichristum non antea in mundum venturum, nisi venerit discessio primum, id est, nisi prius discesserint omnia regna a Romano imperio, que pridem subdita erant.* On this tradition, see Bousset, *Antichrist*, pp. 77–83.

24. P. 110 Sackur: *Hoc autem tempus nondum evenit, quia, licet videamus Romanorum regnum ex maxima parte destructum, tamen, quamdiu reges Francorum duraverint, qui Romanum imperium tenere debent, Romani regni dignitas ex toto non peribit, quia in regibus suis stabit.*

men." This source, according to Adso, predicted that "one among the kings of the Franks would possess the Roman Empire in its entirety." Adso's wish in the prologue—that he could obtain for King Louis "the entire kingdom" (*totum regnum*)—thus echoed the prophecy of a Frankish king governing *Romanum imperium ex integro*. The prophecy then went on to say that the Frankish king would be the greatest and last of all kings. At the end of his reign he would journey to Jerusalem and lay down scepter and crown on the Mount of Olives.[25]

It was pointed out long ago by Zezschwitz that this prophecy as cited by Adso was derived ultimately from a Byzantine source, the *Revelation of Pseudo-Methodius*.[26] This conclusion was undoubtedly correct, for the designation of the ruler in question as "the last of all kings" and the deposition of the symbols of power at Jerusalem point clearly to the Pseudo-Methodian tradition of the Last Roman Emperor. It proved difficult, however, in the years after Zezschwitz's discovery, to define more precisely the process of borrowing and particularly to name Adso's immediate source. It is not too much to say that the occurrence of the passage in Adso's letter became in the late nineteenth century the starting point for a vigorous investigation of the Byzantine traditions underlying the German imperial legends of the Middle Ages.[27] Sackur suggested that it must have been a scholar at the court of Charlemagne or of Louis the Pious who transformed the prophecy about a Roman (Byzantine) ruler into one about a Frankish king; for only as long as the Frankish empire was intact in its integrity could it be considered as the continuation of the Roman Empire.[28] This last conclusion, however, did not follow. It is true that the prophecy of Adso's source was inconceivable before Charlemagne had been crowned emperor and had ruled a large

---

25. P. 110 Sackur *Quidam vero doctores nostri dicunt, quod unus ex regibus Francorum Romanum imperium ex integro tenebit, qui in novissimo tempore erit. Et ipse erit maximus et omnium regum ultimus. Qui postquam regnum feliciter gubernaverit, ad ultimum Ierosolimam veniet et in monte Oliveti sceptrum et coronam suam deponet. Hic erit finis et consummatio Romanorum christianorumque imperii.*

26. This important discovery was made by G. von Zezschwitz, *Vom römischen Kaisertum deutscher Nation: Ein mittelalterliches Drama* (Leipzig, 1877), pp. 43–84. More recently, Percy E. Schramm, *Herrschaftszeichen und Stattssymbolik*, Schriften der Monumenta Germaniae Historica 13, parts 1–3 (Stuttgart, 1954–1956), esp. part 3, p. 917, mentioned that the motif of a Last Roman Emperor taking off his crown derives from a pagan Roman tradition. R. W. Southern, *Western Views of Islam in the Middle Ages* (Cambridge, Mass., 1962), p. 26n.23, connects Adso's general eschatology, rather than the specific passage in question, with Spanish apocalyptic thought of the ninth century.

27. See my "Byzantium and the Migration of Literary Works and Motifs: The Legend of the Last Roman Emperor" ("Introduction," n. 16, above).

28. Sackur, *Sibyllinische Texte*, pp. 168f.

realm. It could, however, have been composed as long as the memory of Charlemagne's empire survived and a hope for its restoration existed. The period of Charlemagne and Louis the Pious, therefore, can serve only as a *terminus post quem* for Adso's source.

This source does, however, prove that at some time prior to the death of King Louis IV d'Outremer of France in 954 its author had prophesied that power over the Roman Empire would be surrendered to God at Jerusalem by a Frankish ruler. It now becomes clear that this notion of Adso's source resembles closely the prophecy of Pseudo-Hippolytus as analyzed above on the strength of Liudprand's summary. There it is shown that in Pseudo-Hippolytus' tract a Western ruler was fated to defeat the Arabs, and we inferred that after his victory that ruler or one of his successors would journey to Jerusalem and surrender his diadem. It is difficult to believe that the two authors, Adso's source and Pseudo-Hippolytus, could have arrived at these highly similar prophecies independently.[29] Both Pseudo-Hippolytus and Adso's source stood in the Pseudo-Methodian tradition.[30] Both prophesied that the principal task assigned in this tradition to a Byzantine emperor would be performed by a Western ruler. It is true that Liudprand mentions in his summary of Pseudo-Hippolytus only a victory over the Arabs, while Adso cited his source for the prediction of the ruler's journey to Jerusalem. As pointed out above, the two features belong so closely together that both must have appeared in the two works.[31] I therefore feel justified in concluding that the text of Pseudo-Hippolytus shown to Liudprand at Constantinople in the summer of 968 was at some time translated from Greek into

---

29. There are two differences between Adso's source and the Pseudo-Methodian tradition. First, according to that source, the last ruler will surrender *sceptrum et coronam*. In the Pseudo-Methodian tradition, on the other hand, beginning with the Syriac original and throughout the Greek and Latin translations and the parts excerpted in the *Visions of Daniel*, the ruler surrenders his diadem (*tāgā*, στέμμα, *diadema*; the Latin translation of Pseudo-Methodius, p. 186 Sackur, adds *omnis habitus regalis*). Second, throughout this Pseudo-Methodian tradition, the place of surrender is Golgotha, the place of the Crucifixion, and the Holy Cross plays a key role in the act of surrender. In Adso's source, however, the Frankish king surrenders his power *in monte Oliveti*, on the Mount of Olives. The question, then, to which I shall return (see n. 67 below), is whether these deviations from the Byzantine apocalyptic tradition appeared in the Greek text of Pseudo-Hippolytus or whether they were added by the Latin translator or a later redactor.

30. For Pseudo-Hippolytus that follows from the fact that his tract was a *Visio Danielis* (see p. 96 above). So far as Adso's source was concerned the point was proved by Zezschwitz, *Römischen Kaisertum*.

31. So far as Adso's source is concerned, it is obvious that after the Arab conquest of Palestine, a Western ruler could hardly journey to Jerusalem unless he had first defeated their armed forces.

Latin and thus came to the attention of the monk Adso in Gaul.[32] The phrase *quidam . . . doctores nostri* of Adso referred, therefore, to a Latin translation of Pseudo-Hippolytus' *Vision of Daniel*.

Adso's citation makes it certain that Pseudo-Hippolytus' tract cannot have been composed after 954. This conclusion in turn guarantees that Pseudo-Hippolytus must have written his prophecies prior to Otto's reign, for by 954 not even the most farsighted observer could have foreseen that this German king would exert a powerful influence on Italy. If, then, Pseudo-Hippolytus wrote prior to Otto's reign, what earlier period in history satisfies the two requirements stated above: unlikelihood of the Byzantine emperor fighting the Arabs in Sicily, and a probability that a Western ruler might do so?

During the late ninth and early tenth centuries, there were indeed many occasions when a Sicilian Christian must have lost whatever hope of help from Byzantium he had retained, especially after the fall of Syracuse (878) and Taormina (902) to the Moslems. It is difficult, also, to imagine that he could have felt more positively concerning the ephemeral masters of Italy, even those who bore the imperial title, rulers like Charles the Bald, Charles the Fat, Arnulf of Carinthia, or Berengar I. Their energies were altogether consumed in attempts to maintain themselves in northern or, at best, central Italy. The south of the peninsula and Sicily lay altogether beyond their ken.

To answer the question concerning Pseudo-Hippolytus' date one must, therefore, go back further in time, to the reign of the Carolingian king and emperor of Italy Louis II (†875).[33] It is true that this great-grandson of Charlemagne has struck many historians as a dwarfish fig-

---

32. There is no reason for believing that Adso knew Greek. Indeed, the fact that he speaks of his source as *quidam . . . doctores nostri* indicates that he had before him a Latin text. There survives a catalogue of Adso's personal library as he left it when departing for the Holy Land in 922; see H. Omont, "Catalogue de la bibliothèque de l'abbé Adson de Montier-en-Der (992)," **Bibliothèque de l'Ecole des Chartes** 42 (1881), pp. 157–60. It contained twenty-three volumes; the only one of interest in the present context is an *Expositio Haimonis super epistolam Pauli ad Romanos*—interesting because in his letter Adso relied so heavily on the commentary on II Thessalonians attributed to Haimo of Halberstadt.

33. On Louis II I have found the following publications particularly helpful: Amari, *Storia*, I, pp. 510–530; Gay, *Italie Méridionale*, pp. 61–108; Hartmann, *Geschichte* III, part 1, pp. 194–309; Vasiliev, *Byzance et les Arabes*, II, pp. 14–19; Werner Ohnsorge, *Das Zweikaiserproblem im Mittelalter* (Hildesheim, 1947), pp. 39–43 (and other publications by the same author; see nn. 34–36 below); Louis Halphen, *Charlemagne et l'empire carolingien*, Evolution de l'Humanité 33 (Paris, 1949), pp. 397–417; Heinz Löwe, "Die Karolinger vom Vertrag von Verdun bis zum Herrschaftsantritt," in W. Wattenbach and W. Levison, eds., *Deutschlands Geschichtsquellen im Mittelalter. Vorzeit und Karolinger* (Weimar, 1963), pp. 387–96.

ure whom it is difficult to take seriously, but this impression may be exaggerated or even unjustified. From the vantage point of the later historian it seems pathetically clear that Louis II's power in Italy was built on shaky foundations and that his far-reaching ideological and political claims had little basis in fact.[34] The historian also knows that southern Italy was eventually to be freed from the Moslems not by a Western ruler but by the revived Byzantine Empire under the founder of the Macedonian dynasty, Basil I, whose troops occupied Bari in 876 and then, especially under the command of the Byzantine general Nicephorus Phocas the Elder, were to reconquer Calabria. On a contemporary observer, however, especially on one stationed in Sicily or southern Italy, the figure of this late Carolingian prince must have made a very different and much more powerful impression.

In Italy the reign of Louis II was reckoned to have begun in 840, when the prince was at most eighteen years old.[35] In peace-time his normal residence was Pavia, and he left Italy only on three occasions during the more than three decades of his reign. Much of his time was spent away from his court, in warfare against rebellious Lombard princes and against the Saracens. It has been suggested that even Louis's first march on Rome in 844, ostensibly undertaken in reaction to Pope Sergius II's illegal elevation, was meant to be the prelude to a campaign against the Saracens in southern Italy.[36] However that may be, there can be no doubt that at the latest the Moslem sack of Rome in 846 committed the emperor Lothar I (†855) and his son Louis II to an active policy against the Arabs in southern Italy.[37] In October 846 the emperor and the king evolved an elaborate plan for a campaign to be undertaken under the leadership of Louis. This plan and this campaign mark a change in the

---

34. Amari, for example, that good Italian patriot and spokesman for the *risorgimento*, saw in Louis II the foreign ruler determined to enslave the Lombards and considered the emperor's struggles against the Arabs to have been a pretext (*Storia*, I, pp. 517, 522). Later he expressed the opinion that at no time between the reigns of Charlemagne and of Frederick of Swabia were the prospects of uniting Italy from the Alps to the Straits of Messina as favorable as during the period of Louis II, but that in spite of his personal bravery Louis was "a man without great vices or conspicuous virtues and of average talent in all respects" (ibid., p. 530). Halphen, *Charlemagne*, p. 410, considers that the capture of Bari in 871 went to Louis's head. Werner Ohnsorge, "Byzanz und das Abendland im 9. und 10. Jahrhundert," *Abendland und Byzanz*, p. 29, speaks of "das politisch macht— und bedeutungslos gewordene Zwergkaisertum" of Louis II.

35. Werner Ohnsorge, "Das Kaiserbündnis von 842–844 gegen die Sarazenen," *Abendland und Byzanz*, pp. 131–83, esp. 145. The date of Louis II's birth is uncertain: see Halphen, *Charlemagne*, p. 397.

36. Ohnsorge, "Kaiserbündnis," p. 178; also "Die Entwicklung der Kaiseridee im 9. Jahrhundert und Süditalien," *Abendland und Byzanz*, pp. 206–218; "Sachsen und Byzanz," ibid., pp. 518–21.

37. See p. 77 above.

Carolingian attitude toward southern Italy: for the first time, a Frankish ruler was attempting to exercise the sovereign rights claimed over the Lombard duchy of Beneventum.[38] The most tangible result of this campaign was the expulsion of the Saracens from the city of Beneventum (847). Partly because of this military success, Louis II was made co-emperor in 850 and emerged as sole emperor after Lothar I's death (855).

The victory over the Arabs at Beneventum was, however, only a beginning; the task remained of forcing them out of Apulia and its principal city, Bari. Until 866, Apulia and much of southern Italy remained in Arab hands or were at least exposed to periodic incursions and depredations. In 852, Louis II conducted an unsuccessful siege of Bari, and in 858 his army was once again defeated by the Saracens. Finally, in 866, the emperor decided to make an all-out effort against Bari. At the head of a large army he first secured the allegiance of the Lombard princes and then turned against his Moslem enemies. Toward the end of 867 he captured the Apulian fortresses of Matera, Venosa, Canosa, and Oria. The siege of Bari itself, for a while conducted in desultory fashion, took a long time. In 870, while the siege was in progress, envoys from Calabria arrived in the emperor's camp to ask for aid against Moslem raiders and promised in turn to take an oath of allegiance and to pay tribute to Louis. These emissaries came from cities in the valley of the river Crati—Cosenza, Bisignano, Cassano—that belonged to the prince of Salerno but had submitted to the emir of a city which the Moslems had taken from the Byzantines, Amantea.[39] A small Frankish army commanded by Count Otto of Bergamo defeated the emir of Amantea and returned to the siege of Bari. This was a military success; more important, it demonstrated that Louis was not averse to intervening in territories formally claimed by the Byzantine emperor. Finally, in 871, Louis II succeeded in capturing Bari from the Moslems.

Louis's capture of Bari was both the high point of his reign and the beginning of the end. Much of Apulia and Calabria still remained to be cleared of the Moslem occupants. After some warfare against the Moslems of Tarentum, Louis and his Frankish army withdrew to Beneventum. There the Frankish warriors lorded it over the Lombard population and thus provoked a combined Lombard revolt against the emperor. He was captured and held prisoner for several months, then released. The shocking reversal of his circumstances after his capture of

---

38. Gay, *Italie Méridionale*, p. 61.
39. Ibid., pp. 96f.

Bari profited the Arabs, who immediately sent a large new force to Italy and laid siege to Salerno. Louis II was called upon once again to wage war against the Arabs, especially against the besiegers of Salerno, as well as against the Lombards. Finally, he withdrew to the north and died near Brescia on 12 August 875.

Louis's capture of Bari had been a great triumph and it is not surprising that, in Louis Halphen's words, it went to his head.[40] His reign had been dedicated to an attempt to place the entire Apennine Peninsula under his direct authority and for him the implications of his imperial title had had precedence over all other considerations.[41] These ambitions of Louis's were later to be recorded in the *Libellus de imperatoria potestate in urbe Roma*, a piece of political propaganda perhaps composed during the first decade of the tenth century and well informed on Louis II's reign.[42] Here it was claimed specifically that Louis II had entered "the territory of all of Calabria"—that is, including its Byzantine parts—because, first, he considered it a part (*provincia*) of Italy and because, second, the emirate of Bari had expanded to the boundaries of Calabria.[43] It is not difficult to imagine what the Byzantine reaction to these justifications must have been if they ever reached the eyes or ears of Byzantine officials. The second reason advanced by Louis, in particular, could easily have been used as the pretext for a Frankish invasion of Byzantine Sicily.

Louis's claims found partial political and military implementation in his interventions in Calabria in the year prior to the fall of Bari and again in Salerno after his release from Lombard captivity. The emperor's ambitions and projects were even more pointedly formulated in a letter that he addressed to the Byzantine emperor Basil in 871, shortly after his capture of Bari. Here, as happens not infrequently, the ideology of a historical movement—in this case, of Louis II's concept of the imperial office—found its most eloquent and most ambitious expression at the moment when the institution itself, which it was to define and

---

40. Halphen, *Charlemagne*, p. 410.
41. Gay, *Italie Méridionale*, p. 64.
42. Ed. G. Zucchetti, in *Fonti per la Storia d'Italia* 55 (Rome, 1920), pp. 191–210. There has been a great deal of controversy about the date of this pamphlet and related problems. It has been dated variously from the end of the ninth to the mid tenth century. See Heinz Löwe in Wattenbach and Levison, *Geschichtsquellen*, pp. 425f.
43. Ed. Zucchetti, p. 200.7: *hic etiam princeps* (Louis II) *Beneventi fines ingressus est et totius Calabriae duobus modis: uno, quod provincia esset Italiae, volens totius regni fines suae vendicare ditioni; altero eo quod immanissima gens Aggarenorum illa iam tangebat confinia, capientes quandam urbem quae vocatur Bari, quam munientes, et multis victualibus implentes, pro refugio habebant. et ideo a comprovincialibus terrae illius benigne susceptus est.*

justify, was on the point of disappearance. The document was, in all probability, drafted by the famous papal secretary Anastasius Bibliothecarius, who was also a fervent supporter of Louis II.[44]

In the heading of the letter, Louis II calls himself *imperator augustus Romanorum* and addresses Basil as *imperator Novae Romae*. As the title of Roman Emperor was guarded at Byzantium with special jealousy, Louis's assumption of that title constituted an affront of the first order, an affront Charlemagne had carefully avoided perpetrating. Much of the letter is then taken up with Louis's attempt to justify his use of the title. Essentially, this is that Louis had received at Rome the anointment from the hands of the pope, a view of the imperial office that reflects the views of the papal curia and of Anastasius Bibliothecarius, but there is no reason to assume that it was not also fully approved by the emperor.[45]

Otherwise Louis in his letter rejects Basil's claim that an expeditionary force sent from Byzantium had brought about the surrender of Bari and emphasizes instead that Bari had fallen to the Franks. He reminds Basil that even prior to the capture of the city his forces had defeated three Arab emirs and a great multitude of Saracens who were then sacking Calabria. This is undoubtedly a reference to the Frankish victory over the emir of Amantea (870) already mentioned (p. 111 above). Finally, at the end of his letter, Louis gives a clear hint of his plans: to subdue the Moslems of Tarentum and of Calabria and finally to free Sicily. He even urges Basil to send a fleet promptly so that these objectives may be achieved.[46]

It is not difficult to imagine the effect the activities, claims, and plans

---

44. The most recent edition is found in Ulla Westerbergh's text of the *Chronicon Salernitanum: A Critical Edition with Studies on Literary and Historical Sources and on Language*, Acta Univ. Stockholmiensis, Studia Latina Stockholmiensia, 3 (Stockholm, 1956). I shall cite it after the older edition by W. Henze, *MGH, Epistolae Karolini Aevi* V (Berlin, 1928), pp. 385–94, primarily because I found Henze's historical annotation helpful. Recent bibliography on the letter is given by Heinz Löwe, "Die Karolinger," p. 394n.31.

45. Ed. Henze, p. 387.25: *unctionem et sacrationem, qua per summi pontificis manus impositione et oratione divinitus ad hoc sumus culmen provecti*; p. 389.8: *Nam Francorum principes primo reges, deinde vero imperatores dicti sunt, hii dumtaxat qui a Romano pontifice ad hoc oleo sancto perfusi sunt*. On this curial concept of the imperial title see, for example, Halphen, *Charlemagne*, p. 413; Ohnsorge, *Zweikaiserproblem*, p. 42; "Byzanz und das Abendland," pp. 28f.

46. Ed. Henze, p. 393.34: *De cetero, frater carissime, noveris cum virtute summi opificis exercitum nostrum ordine praenotato Bari triumphis nostris summissa Saracenos Tarenti pariter et Calabriae mox mirabiliter humiliasse simul et comminuisse hos celerius duce Deo penitus contriturum. . . . Nos enim Calabria Deo auctore purgata Siciliam pristinae disponimus secundum commune placitum restituere libertati*. Here is the claim, later incorporated into the *Libellus de imperatoria potestate* (n. 42 above), that Louis arrogated to himself the right of entering any part of Italy threatened by the Arabs, except that here the claim is specifically extended to Sicily.

of Louis II must have had on the Greek-speaking Christian population of southern Italy and Sicily. His military exploits were undoubtedly acclaimed in these circles with mounting enthusiasm. Such acclaim may have greeted him as early as 852 during his first siege of Bari, but the admiration for the Frankish emperor must have intensified significantly when in 866 it became clear that he was determined to wage all-out warfare against the Moslem occupants. Undoubtedly, this admiration reached its zenith during the period when the letter to Basil was written, in the months between the capture of Bari (February 871) and Louis's surrender to the Lombard rebels (August 871). It may even have survived the Lombard rebellion, for, as was mentioned, the new Arab invasion and the siege of Salerno made it impossible for the Christian princes of Lombard Italy to dispense with the emperor's military leadership. On the other hand, during the entire reign of Louis II the Byzantine rulers had achieved very little in their attempts to defend Sicily and southern Italy against the Arabs. The Byzantine chronicles complain that prior to the reign of Basil the Byzantine government had been unable to prevent the devastation of Sicily, Calabria, and Longobardia by the Arabs.[47] In 859 the Arabs had even captured the great rock-fortress of Enna in the center of the island. Clearly, to a contemporary observer the energy, good fortune, and military successes of Louis II must have appeared impressive as compared to the paltry Byzantine record in the West. Undoubtedly, it was also known to many people in the West that, as we know from Louis's letter to Basil and from the *Libellus de imperatoria potestate*, Louis would not permit his warfare against the Moslems to be hampered by considerations of diplomatic or legal niceties. He had treated Naples and Amalfi, which prior to the Arab invasion had owed allegiance to Byzantium, as if they were his own vassals. He had not hesitated, in 870, even before the capture of Bari, to come to the aid of the population of Calabria. He had continued to fight for the liberation of Calabria after the capture of Bari.

It is against this international constellation that the extraordinary step taken by Pseudo-Hippolytus must now be reconsidered. As has been shown, this anonymous Sicilian author broke with tradition by proclaiming in a *Vision of Daniel* that Sicily would be liberated from her Moslem conquerors not by a Byzantine $\beta\alpha\sigma\iota\lambda\varepsilon\acute{u}\varsigma$ but by a Western ruler and his Frankish people. The reign of Louis satisfies the two conditions mentioned before: the inefficacy of the Byzantine Empire during

---

47. Theophanes Continuatus, *CSHB*, 2.83, 5.52; Cedrenus II, *CSHB*, p. 218. See Gay, *Italie Méridionale*, p. 75.

the reign of Michael III (842–867) and the early years of Basil I in protecting Sicily and southern Italy from the Arabs, and the astonishing energy and success with which Louis II pursued this fight. In the forties of the ninth century the Byzantines had lost the Sicilian towns of Messina, Modica, Leontini, and Ragusa to the Arabs. In the fifties the Moslems had captured Gagliano, Cefalù, and the mighty fortress of Enna. In the sixties it was the turn of Noto, Scicli, and Traina. It is true that the Byzantine government had on several occasions sent armies to the island to help the threatened cities—for example, between 843 and 845 and again in 859 or 860—but they had given a very poor account of themselves.

The seventies of the ninth century promised to produce the great crisis in Byzantine-Arab relations so far as Sicily was concerned. Already when in 859 or 860 a Byzantine army had been sent to Sicily, the Christian inhabitants of certain fortresses—Platani, Caltabellotta, Caltavuturo, and others, which had already been paying tribute to the Moslems—had risen to cooperate with the forces from overseas, but both overseas troops and local militias had been beaten near Cefalù. This rising by the local populations had alarmed the emir of Palermo so much that he had given orders for the repair of Enna's fortifications and had sent a strong garrison there.[48] In 869 the Christian population of Sicily successfully defended Taormina, Randazzo, and Syracuse against Arab attacks.[49] There existed in those years, among the Moslems of Sicily and between them and the Aghlabid rulers of North Africa, a great deal of disunity. Between 871 and 873 six or seven emirs succeeded each other in rapid succession in Sicily and achieved very little, one among many signs that with the invasion of Sicily and southern Italy the Moslems in North Africa found it difficult to maintain both internal unity and their military impetus.[50]

Again, the later historian knows that in the end the Arabs overcame these difficulties and in 878 succeeded at long last in capturing the most important Byzantine city on the island, Syracuse, which for half a century had been the goal of their military activities. But for a Sicilian observer in the sixties or early seventies of the ninth century, it must indeed have looked as if the time were ripe for a general uprising of the Sicilian Christians against their Arab masters, yet it was highly unlikely that the Byzantine government, occupied as it was with its warfare

---

48. Amari, *Storia*, I, pp. 471f.
49. Ibid., pp. 487f.
50. Ibid., pp. 531–34.

against its Eastern enemies, would make a major effort for the defense or reconquest of its westernmost possessions. The Carolingian emperor Louis II, whose efforts at least since 847 had been concentrated on warfare against the Arabs of southern Italy, Sicily, and North Africa, must have looked like a much better candidate for the leadership of a campaign to liberate Sicily. Louis's campaign in Calabria in 870 and his purpose, clearly expressed after the capture of Bari in 871, of freeing Calabria and Sicily from the Moslems made it clear that he would not allow himself to be stopped in his campaigns against the Arabs by Byzantine claims to these Western provinces.

True, the letter to Basil provided that Sicily would be freed *secundum commune placitum*, in accordance with a project agreed upon by Basil and himself. After all, in 871, Byzantium was still in effective control of much of the east coast of the island, especially of Syracuse, Catania, and Taormina. But Louis II left no doubt that he would be in charge of the campaigns in Calabria and Sicily and that the Byzantine forces would play second fiddle. In the same vein, Pseudo-Hippolytus seems to have interpreted the old Lion-Whelp oracle of the Byzantine tradition to mean that in the warfare against the Arabs the lion's share would be Louis's and that Basil would have to be satisfied with the role of a junior partner. Undoubtedly, Louis's arrogation of the title *imperator augustus Romanorum*, which appears in the heading of his letter to Basil, facilitated the shift of the role of principal from the Byzantine to the Western emperor. Just as Louis II in his letter claimed to be the true *imperator augustus Romanorum* and allowed for his Byzantine contemporary merely the rank of *imperator Novae Romae*, so Pseudo-Hippolytus asserted that the task of "crushing" the Saracens behooved the Franks and not the Greeks.[51] The same polemical tendency to assert the Roman basis of Louis's power over the traditional claims of Byzantium appears in Louis II's letter to Basil and in Pseudo-Hippolytus' tract.[52]

In fact, the relationship between the two documents is so close that one cannot help wondering whether the Sicilian Pseudo-Hippolytus composed his tract in the entourage of Louis II or of Anastasius Bibliothecarius. And indeed, in the ninth century both the Byzantine Empire

---

51. Compare Liudprand's (p. 198.16 Becker) summary of Pseudo-Hippolytus, *Saracenos . . . conterere*, with Louis's expectation that after his army's exploits at Bari and against the Saracens of Tarentum and Calabria it would soon *hos celerius . . . penitus contriturum*, etc. (p. 393.37 Henze).

52. [For Pseudo-Hippolytus' insistence on the relationship between Frankish kingship and Roman Empire see Adso as cited in n. 25 above.]

and Italy were full of Sicilian refugees who had left the island because of the Arab invasion.[53]

It is difficult to suggest an exact date for the composition of Pseudo-Hippolytus' tract. The few months from the capture of Bari in February 871 to the Lombard rebellion in August of the same year are the most plausible period for the high-flowing ambitions expressed in the tract, but later or earlier dates during Louis II's reign cannot be excluded. At the latest, from 866 onward it must have become very clear that Louis II was preparing a major and promising campaign against the Arabs in Sicily and even after the emperor's release from Lombard captivity he was still a power to be reckoned with in the warfare against the Arabs, as is proved by his role in the fight against the Arab besiegers of Salerno.

It now becomes possible to solve a problem that was postponed earlier in this chapter: the question of exactly how Pseudo-Hippolytus designated the ruler who would defeat the Arabs. Pseudo-Hippolytus' reference (*imperium vestrum*) seems to have allowed no doubt whatsoever that he meant a Western rather than a Byzantine ruler, for both Liudprand and his Byzantine informants interpreted it to refer to the two Ottos. It has also become clear that Pseudo-Hippolytus wrote at the time of the Frankish emperor Louis II and specifically referred to the Franks as conquerors of the Arabs. Normally, Louis II's chancery and that of the other Frankish rulers referred to Louis II as *imperator augustus* or simply *augustus*.[54] In the letter to Basil, Louis referred to himself as *imperator augustus Romanorum*, but this titulature was exceptional and was due to the controversy with Basil I over the imperial title. It is impossible that Pseudo-Hippolytus should have used this exceptional title, since any formula such as βασιλεὺς 'Ρωμαίων would have been interpreted by any Greek-speaking reader as a reference to the Byzantine emperor rather than to Louis II. On the other hand, Pseudo-Hippolytus, who, as we have seen (p. 113 above), demonstrated a keen awareness of the ideology of Louis II's court, cannot have possibly referred to the Western emperor by an unattested formula such as βασιλεὺς Φράγγων.

53. In 870 the bishops *in partibus* of Cefalù, Alesa, Messina, and Catania signed the acts of the Council of Constantinople (Amari, *Storia*, II, p. 462). Noteworthy also is the career of St. Elijah of Enna in Sicily, who fled his native island at the time of the Arab invasion and became a great founder of monasteries in Calabria at the end of the ninth century (*BHG*³ 580; Amari, *Storia*, I, pp. 654–61; Gay, *Italie Méridionale*, pp. 255–60).

54. Percy E. Schramm, "Die Titel der Karolinger," in *Kaiser, Könige und Päpste* (Stuttgart, 1968), II, pp. 80–82.

In this impasse the previous conclusion proves useful—that Pseudo-Hippolytus' prophecy was cited not only by Liudprand but also by Adso: *Unus ex regibus Francorum Romanum imperium ex integro tenebit.*[55] If *unus ex regibus Francorum* or, rather, its Greek equivalent, εἶς (ἐκ) τῶν βασιλέων τῶν Φράγγων, was Pseudo-Hippolytus' formula for designating Louis II, it is easy to see why in 968 it was interpreted at Constantinople to refer to Otto I: he ruled over the Franks as their king, as he ruled over many other German tribes; he had been crowned emperor by the pope; and his imperial authority was generally recognized in Western Europe. Otto did indeed fulfill Pseudo-Hippolytus' prophecy that the Roman Empire would be united as it had been under the Frank Charlemagne. But, as we have seen, the prophecy had actually been devised not for Otto I, but half a century earlier for Louis II. The words εἶς (ἐκ) τῶν βασιλέων τῶν Φράγγων made it clear that the author was not so much using a formal title as describing in apocalyptic language the position of the ruler. The term βασιλεύς was suitably ambiguous—it could designate both (Frankish) emperors, and kings; and the word εἶς gave the impression that as a prophet the author did not wish to commit himself too closely. However, any reader contemporary with Louis II would know that of the three Frankish βασιλεῖς then reigning—Charles the Bald, Louis the German, and Louis II—only the last was interested in warfare against the Arabs.

The formula εἶς (ἐκ) τῶν βασιλέων τῶν Φράγγων followed by the prophecy that he would rule over the entire Roman Empire suited Louis II admirably, because in his entourage there was indeed a good deal of daydreaming about the unity of the Carolingian Empire. This is shown once again by Louis's letter to Basil. In a (lost) letter Basil had insisted that the four patriarchal sees—Alexandria, Antioch, Jerusalem,

---

55. It is true that Adso is citing here a part of the prophecy in which it is predicted that the emperor will journey to Jerusalem, while Liudprand is paraphrasing a part dealing with the emperor's victory over the Arabs. Still, it is certain that Pseudo-Hippolytus on the two occasions referred to the emperor in identical or similar terms, for in the Byzantine tradition, from which he is borrowing, it is always the same emperor, or at least one of his successors, who goes to Jerusalem. Pseudo-Methodius assigned both the victory over the Arabs and the journey to Jerusalem to the same emperor (chs. XI f., pp. 40ff. Istrin). In *BHG*³ 1872 (pp. 40ff. Vasiliev) they are both performed by a βασιλεύς Ῥωμαίων, but the emperor who goes to Jerusalem is a later ruler. The same is true of the *Slavonic Daniel*. Pseudo-Hippolytus changed this tradition by substituting a Western ruler for the Byzantine emperor, but it is highly probable that, like his Byzantine models, he either made the same emperor defeat the Arabs and visit Jerusalem or assigned the latter event to a successor of the first emperor. If, therefore, Adso is our authority that the emperor who journeyed to Jerusalem was referred to by his source, i.e., Pseudo-Hippolytus, as *unus ex regibus Francorum*, it stands to reason that earlier in the prophecy he must have spoken of the emperor who will defeat the Arabs in identical or at least similar terms.

and Constantinople—following apostolic tradition, were commemorating in the liturgy only one empire and had asked Louis to discourage the use of *imperator*.⁵⁶ Louis proudly replied that even his two royal uncles, Louis the German of the Eastern Frankish realm and Charles the Bald of the Western Franks, were calling him *imperator*.⁵⁷ There is indeed, he continued, only one empire, that of the Holy Trinity, of which the Church as constituted on earth was a part. This Church might be governed by more than one ruler, and the patriarchs were therefore right in commemorating one sole empire in the liturgy.⁵⁸ At the same time Louis reacted sharply against a claim of Basil that he, Louis, did not effectively govern the entire Frankish realm. Louis replied that he was indeed the ruler of the entire realm because he and his two uncles were related by blood.⁵⁹ Louis's doctrine thus was clear: one empire and one Church, though governed by more than one *imperator*; and one Frankish realm with one *imperator* at its head who exercised his imperial authority with the help of the other Carolingian princes. It is true that the reality looked very different from this ideal: since the days of the Treaty of Verdun (843) the several Frankish realms had increasingly gone their separate ways and had quite often resorted to warfare against one another. Yet Louis II never surrendered the notion that hegemony over all the Frankish realms belonged to him as the bearer of the *nomen imperatoris*.

His successor in the imperial dignity, Charles the Bald (875–877), not only united his Western Frankish realm with Italy but in 876 even attempted to conquer the Eastern Frankish realm by the force of arms. If he had succeeded, Pseudo-Hippolytus' prophecy would have been largely fulfilled by the first successor of Louis II.⁶⁰ As it was, Charles the

---

56. Ed. Henze, p. 387: *Dicis autem, quod quatuor patriarchales sedes unum imperium inter sacra misteria a deiferis apostolis usque nunc traditum habeant.* . . . The number four is interesting. Basil must have omitted Rome, either because he was uncertain of Roman practice in this matter or because he knew or suspected that the popes commemorated the Western emperors in the liturgy.

57. Ibid.: *Invenimus praesertim, cum et ipsi patrui nostri, gloriosi reges, absque invidia imperatorem nos vocitant et imperatorem esse procul dubio fatentur.*

58. Ibid.: *Porro si unum imperium patriarchae inter sancta sacrificia memorant, laudandi sunt utique inconvenienter agentes; unum est enim imperium Patris et Filii et Spiritus Sancti, cuius pars est ecclesia constituta in terris, quam tamen Deus nec per te solum nec per me tantum gubernari disposuit.*

59. Ibid., pp. 388f.: *Porro de eo, quod dicis, non in tota nos Francia imperare, accipe, frater, breve responsum. In tota nempe imperamus Francia, quia nos procul dubio retinemus, quod illi retinent, cum quibus una caro et sanguis sumus.*

60. Walter Schlesinger, "Die Auflösung des Karlsreiches," in Wolfgang Braunfels, *Karl der Grosse* I (2nd ed., Düsseldorf, 1966), 792–857, esp. 799 (on Louis II): "Seit 850 auch Kaiser, hat er zwar den Anspruch auf Oberherrschaft über das ganze Frankenreich nie aufgegeben." On Louis's acquisitions in Provence and Lorraine, see ibid., p. 848; and on Charles the Bald's attempt of reuniting the empire of Charlemagne, ibid., p. 847.

Bald was defeated in the battle of Andernach, and the fulfillment of Pseudo-Hippolytus' prophecy about the reunification of the Roman Empire was delayed until the reign of Otto I in the next century. But Pseudo-Hippolytus' prediction, summarized by Liudprand and Adso, that one of the rulers ($\beta\alpha\sigma\iota\lambda\epsilon\hat{\iota}\varsigma$) of the Franks would reunite the Roman (i.e., Carolingian) Empire, would free southern Italy and Sicily from the Arab invaders, and would finally abdicate in the holy city of Jerusalem—this prophecy was inspired by the achievements and ambitions of Charlemagne's great-grandson, the Carolingian emperor Louis II.

Liudprand's acquaintance with Pseudo-Hippolytus' prophecy raises a last question. He writes that he discussed this text, especially the Lion-Whelp oracle, at length with Greeks who were experts in this type of writing.[61] It is at first sight puzzling that a document that contained so serious a break with Byzantine tradition—the transfer of the future victory over the Arabs from a Byzantine to a Western ruler—and that was therefore so pessimistic as to Byzantine prospects of conquering the Western Arabs should have been shown to a Western envoy by his Byzantine contacts. What objectives may they have pursued with this action? Here an observation made by Martin Lintzel a generation ago provides the answer. This scholar pointed out that at Constantinople Liudprand established, or reestablished, relationships with a group or groups that opposed the usurpation of power by Nicephorus Phocas and worked for a restoration of direct rule by the legitimate heirs to the Macedonian house, the child-emperors Basil and Constantine, heirs of their father Romanos II.[62] This opposition party not only considered Nicephorus Phocas a usurper, it favored a foreign policy that in several ways disagreed with his. Lintzel pointed out that while Liudprand was in Constantinople, Nicephorus Phocas sent a naval force to southern Italy. There, a few months later, warfare between Germans and Byzantines again erupted. At the same time the opposition, which in 969 succeeded in bringing to the throne John Tzimisces, favored an alliance with the German emperor Otto I.[63]

To this observation a further consideration may be added. As we have

---

61. See n. 9 above. Liudprand later repeatedly refers to an *interpretatio secundum Grecos* of the Lion-Whelp oracle.

62. Martin Lintzel; *Studien über Liudprand von Cremona*, Historische Studien 233 (Berlin, 1933), now most conveniently accessible in his *Ausgewählte Schriften*, 2 vols. (Berlin, 1961), II, pp. 351–98, esp. 377–79.

63. Lintzel, *Studien*, pp. 372f., 378.

seen above, in 967, the year prior to Liudprand's embassy, Nicephorus Phocas and the Fāṭimid khalif of North Africa, al-Muʿizz (952–975), had made peace because both of them were on the point of seizing territories, in Syria and Egypt respectively, belonging to the Ikhshīdid rulers of Egypt.[64] On both fronts the murder of Nicephorus Phocas in 969 and the accession of John Tzimisces brought a significant change: the new emperor came to a peaceful understanding with Otto, and the peace established by his predecessor with the Fāṭimid ruler was not renewed.[65] Liudprand, therefore, visited Constantinople at a time when a momentous reversal of alliances was in the making. Now there is clear evidence in Liudprand's *Legatio* that the persons at Byzantium with whom he discussed the text of Pseudo-Hippolytus and who, presumably, had called this text to his attention were connected with the group or groups advocating this reversal. He writes that the Byzantines with whom he was debating the interpretation of the Lion-Whelp oracle thought that by the Lion, Pseudo-Hippolytus had meant the emperor of the Romans or Greeks; by the Whelp, the king of the Franks; and by the Wild Ass, the African king of the Saracens—in other words, al-Muʿizz.[66] Liudprand's Byzantine contacts, therefore, were dissatisfied with the foreign policy espoused by Nicephorus Phocas, of warfare against the Christian Otto I and peace with the Moslem al-Muʿizz. They advocated instead a joint military enterprise of Germany and Byzantium against the Fāṭimid ruler. It was undoubtedly with the purpose of furthering this policy that in the summer of 968 they showed Liudprand the prophecy of Pseudo-Hippolytus.

In conclusion, it may be said that Pseudo-Hippolytus composed his *Vision of Daniel*, as summarized by Liudprand and cited by Adso, in the Greek language. The Greek original was shown to and discussed with Liudprand of Cremona at Constantinople in the summer of 968 by members of the legitimist opposition to Nicephorus Phocas interested in a rapprochement with the emperor Otto I and hostile to the peace treaty recently concluded by the Byzantine emperor with the Fāṭimid khalif, and a Latin translation of Pseudo-Hippolytus' work reached

---

64. Amari, *Storia*, II, pp. 318f.; Gay, *Italie Méridionale*, p. 301; F. Dölger, *Regesten der Kaiserurkunden des oströmischen Reiches vom 565–1453* (Munich-Berlin, 1924–) vol. 1, no. 708; Canard, *CMH* IV, part 1, p. 731.
65. Amari, *Storia*, II, pp. 365f.
66. Liudprand, *Legatio*, ch. 40, p. 196.21 Becker: *Cuius* [the Lion-Whelp oracle] *interpretatio secundum Grecos: Leo, id est Romanorum sive Grecorum imperator, et catulus, Francorum scilicet rex, simul his praesentibus temporibus exterminabunt onagrum, id est Saracenorum regem Africanum.*

Adso, who cited it sometime prior to 954 in his letter *De ortu et tempore Antichristi*.[67] Pseudo-Hippolytus was a Sicilian and wrote either in Sicily or as a refugee from Sicily in southern Italy, and his tract contains some historical material relating to the Arab conquest of Sicily. Its main significance lies, however, in the fact that, unlike all earlier and most later *Visions of Daniel*, Pseudo-Hippolytus' prophecies assign the primary role in defeating the Arabs and the surrender of imperial power at Jerusalem to a Western rather than to a Byzantine emperor—although the two acts were not necessarily performed by the same Western ruler. Pseudo-Hippolytus' tract therefore has a polemical purpose and is in this respect comparable to the Syriac original of Pseudo-Methodius' *Revelation*. He probably allowed for some degree of cooperation on the part of the Byzantine emperor, as is suggested by the retention of the Lion-Whelp oracle. His prophecy of a Western emperor conquering the Arabs and thus freeing Sicily was inspired by the achievements and plans of the Carolingian emperor Louis II. As date for the composition of the tract the months from February to August 871 would be most appropriate, for Louis II was then at the height of his power and ambition, but a date between 866 and 871, when Louis was conducting successful warfare against the Arabs in southern Italy, or even a date between October 871 and 875, when he was again fighting the Arabs, is not impossible.

67. Above, n. 29, I left open the question of whether two features distinguishing the citation in Adso from all other *Visions of Daniel* were part of Pseudo-Hippolytus' original Greek text or were due to the Latin translator. The first of them was the surrender of scepter and crown by the Last Emperor, in lieu of the imperial diadem mentioned in the Syriac and Greek texts of Pseudo-Methodius and in the tradition of the *Visions of Daniel*. The change was certainly a modernization prompted by the realization that, at the time when the change was made, scepter and crown rather than a diadem had become the most important insignia of imperial office. Now the *sceptrum* or short staff, as distinct from the *baculus* or long staff, first appeared in Carolingian royal portraiture with Charles the Bald in the sixties and seventies of the ninth century (Schramm, *Herrschaftszeichen*, part 1, pp. 16, 264, 373). Schramm (p. 373) called attention to the funeral inscription in S. Ambrozio at Milan honoring Louis II, in which it is said that already Louis the Pious (*avus*) had left to Louis II on the day of his birth "the scepters of Italy" (*nam ne prima dies regno solioque vacaret / Hesperie genito sceptra reliquit avus*). He had thus suggested that the *sceptra* might be the long and short staves; if this is true, use of the *sceptrum* could be dated back to the twenties of the ninth century. In a footnote (p. 373n.5) Schramm himself seems to have hesitated about this oversharp interpretation, quite apart from the fact that this line of the poem is difficult to interpret (see the text of the inscription in Percy E. Schramm and Florentine Mütherich, *Denkmale der deutschen Könige und Kaiser* [Munich, 1961], p. 128 and pl. 38). It is, therefore, uncertain whether the *sceptrum* as symbol of the imperial office was in use as early as the reign of Louis II and, consequently, whether the change from diadem to scepter in the text of Pseudo-Hippolytus was part of the Greek original. Nor can I offer an explanation for the second change in the text quoted by Adso—the surrender of power *in monte Oliveti*, rather than on Golgotha as in the rest of the Pseudo-Methodian tradition. The Mount of Olives does play a role in the tradition of the Tiburtine Sibyl (see my *Oracle of Baalbek*, lines 67–69, 116n.68), but the surrender scene is never connected with the Mount of Olives except by Pseudo-Hippolytus.

# V.
# Three Conglomerate Texts

## 1. THE *APOCALYPSE OF ST. ANDREW THE FOOL*

An elaborate apocalypse was attributed by a Constantinopolitan priest and hagiographer, Nicephorus, to St. Andrew the Fool, whose biography he composed.[1] For a long time there had been a great deal of controversy concerning the date of this biography, but there now seems to be general agreement that it was composed early in the tenth century.[2] However, the date of the *Life* furnishes no more than the *terminus ante quem* for the apocalypse that it contains, and that date could in fact be earlier than the early tenth century, especially as scholars have discovered in it references to much earlier periods.[3]

---

1. *BHG*³ 117 = *PG* 111.625–888. The apocalypse is found in chs. 25f. (852–874) and has also been edited separately (*BHG*³ 117d) by Vasiliev, *Anecdota Graeco-Byzantina*, pp. 50–58. On the *Vita Andreae Sali* see Sara C. Murray, *A Study of the Life of Andreas the Fool for the Sake of Christ* (Munich dissertation, Borna-Leipzig, 1910), and the important review by Paul Maas, *BZ* 21 (1912), pp. 317–19. [See now the edition by Lennart Rydén with translation and full commentary, "The Andreas Salos Apocalypse," *Dumbarton Oaks Papers* 28 (1974), pp. 197–261.]

2. Murray, *Study*, pp. 17–33; G. da Costa-Louillet, "Saints de Constantinople," *Byzantion* 24 (1954), pp. 179–214; John Wortley, "A Note on the Date of the *Vita Sancti Andreae Sali*," *Byzantion* 39 (1969), pp. 204–208 ("between ca. 910 and ca. 920"). The text cannot be much later than the date proposed by Wortley, since a Munich uncial manuscript of the tenth to eleventh century, no. 443, contains the text.

3. Bousset, "Beiträge," pp. 103–131, 261–90, esp. 274–80, discovered allusions to the eighth century. A. A. Vasiliev, "The Emperor Michael III in Apocryphal Literature," *Byzantina Metabyzantina* 1 (1946), pp. 237–48 (repeated in *The Russian Attack on Constantinople* [Cambridge, England, 1946], pp. 161ff.) thought that the first emperor mentioned in the apocalypse was Michael III (842–867). This theory has been questioned by Lennart Rydén, "Zum Aufbau der Andreas Salos-Apokalypse," *Eranos* 66 (1968), pp. 101–117, esp. 108f., and convincingly refuted by John Wortley, "The Warrior-Emperor of

The structure of this apocalypse has recently been studied by Lennart Rydén,[4] who is preparing a critical edition of this difficult and important text. In spite of criticisms that have been levelled against Rydén's analysis, it seems to me that his study marks a significant advance over earlier work; my discussion here is heavily indebted to Rydén.[5] Rydén has discovered eleven "moments" in the apocalyptic sequence, of which four are historical or at least incorporate historical elements, while the other seven are traditional products of eschatological fantasy. He has shown, in my opinion convincingly, that by the first three rulers the apocalyptist meant the emperors Constantine the Great, Constantius II, and Julian, although even here features of the seventh or eighth century were merged with the earlier materials. There followed, parenthetically, a fourth ruler, patterned after Alexander the Great, and then a highly legendary description of Jovian's reign. As Rydén has emphasized, the general correctness of his analysis is confirmed particularly by the fact that this fifth emperor, Jovian, was said to have surrendered his diadem to God, a function ever since Pseudo-Methodius reserved for the Last Roman Emperor. All later events mentioned in the text are, therefore, traditional and have no relation to actual history.

Rydén's conclusion is that nothing in St. Andrew's apocalypse referred to a date later than the eighth century, that it did not originate, as

---

the *Andreas Salos Apocalypse," Analecta Bollandiana* 88 (1970), pp. 43–59, esp. 56–58. Wortley pointed out, correctly, that the characterization of the warrior-emperor awakening from sleep, as found in the *Apocalypse*, long antedated Michael III, appearing already in the seventh century in the First Greek Redaction of Pseudo-Methodius. On Wortley's attempt to identify the warrior-emperor with Basil I, see n. 5 below.

4. See n. 3 above.

5. Rydén holds that the first of the rulers "prophesied" in the apocalypse combines features of Constantine the Great and Leo III ("Zum Aufbau," pp. 106–109). Against this view, Wortley, "Warrior-Emperor," pp. 43–59, argues that it was the author's intent that "the reader should identify the warrior-emperor as Basil I." He attempts to prove his point by comparing eleven features mentioned by the apocalyptist with other source materials concerning Basil I. This is not the place for a detailed refutation of Wortley's thesis: it must suffice to point out that most of Wortley's comparisons require a great deal of "manipulation" to make them fit and that they therefore fail to carry conviction. St. Andrew prophesies, for example, that the warrior-emperor will destroy the Moslems by fire. Wortley suggests that this is a confusion with the Paulicians who under Basil I fought on the Arab side. The apocalyptist further prophesies that Egypt will pay tribute to the Byzantine Empire, a prophecy that Wortley sees as fulfilled by a very uncertain tradition according to which Crete, conquered by Andalusian Arabs setting out from Egypt, paid tribute to Basil. These two examples must suffice here to demonstrate the shakiness of Wortley's comparisons and thesis. While his paper has the merit of disproving Vasiliev's identification of the warrior-emperor with Michael III (n. 3 above), Wortley's own identification of this emperor with Basil I is untenable. Rydén's thesis that he is a traditional figure combining features of Constantine the Great and Leo III comes much closer to the truth. One is reminded in this respect of Bousset's advice that the cautious scholar will adopt a *zeitgeschichtliche* interpretation of apocalyptic materials only where it can be done without forcing the issue (*Antichrist*, p. 7).

do genuine apocalypses, in a period of crisis, and that it was therefore less a genuine apocalypse than an apocalyptic romance. The author of the *Life of St. Andrew the Fool* felt prompted to incorporate into his work answers to a variety of spiritual or scriptural problems, invariably of a simple or vulgar kind, which presumably interested the circles in which he moved. He attributed to St. Andrew homilies on many topics, by the simple device of having Epiphanius, St. Andrew's disciple, bring up the topic in the form of a question. Thus St. Andrew discourses, for example, on the nature of the human soul (801B), the order of creation (804B), the number of heavens (809C), the meaning of John the Evangelist's designation as "Son of Thunder" (813C) and of a large number of scriptural passages (e.g., 824–832), and the nature of lightning and thunder (816A). It is to be hoped that Rydén will soon publish his critical and annotated edition of the text and discuss, among other things, the sources of St. Andrew's views on these subjects. Meanwhile, one has the impression that St. Andrew's answers to Epiphanius' questions usually represent an uncritical and vulgarized potpourri of opinions held by the Church Fathers. The hagiographer must have felt that the encyclopedic character of his work would suffer if it did not contain a discussion of eschatological problems. So he had Epiphanius raise the question of the end of time (852Dff.) in the same way in which he brought up all the other questions. It is to be supposed that, as in all the other cases, St. Andrew's answers to Epiphanius' eschatological questions are uncritical compilations from earlier materials. For this reason, I am inclined to call the apocalypse of St. Andrew encyclopedic, rather than having the character of a romance as Rydén suggested. It is comparable in this respect to the anonymous paraphrase of the *Oracles of Leo the Wise*, perhaps of the fourteenth or early fifteenth century, where apocalyptic materials of the sixth century are found side by side with later materials.[6]

It is striking that the hagiographer Nicephorus, writing in the early tenth century, failed to incorporate into his apocalypse materials referring to periods later than the eighth century, as Bousset and Rydén have shown. A parallel observation may be made concerning the literary sources used by the hagiographer in the entire *Life of St. Andrew*, including the apocalypse. Nicephorus named Hippolytus (865C), Athanasius

---

6. On this paraphrase, see Bousset, "Beiträge," pp. 283–85; Cyril Mango, "The Legend of Leo the Wise," *Zbornik Radova Vizantoloshkogo Instituta* 6 (1960), pp. 59–93, esp. 61. I have shown (*Oracle of Baalbek*, p. 37) that the author of the paraphrase cited the *Oracle of Baalbek*, of the early sixth century. (See "The *Cento of the True Emperor*," Section 2 below.).

(684C), and Basil (873B), but no author later than the fourth century. There is clear evidence that he knew, directly or indirectly, the Greek apocalypse of Pseudo-Methodius, for he summarized the abdication of the Last Roman Emperor at Jerusalem (860C), a motif that, as we have seen (p. 22), was introduced into Byzantine literature through this seventh- or eighth-century text. Undoubtedly, Nicephorus believed that this work had in fact been written by the Church Father Methodius in the third century. But there is no trace, in St. Andrew's apocalypse or elsewhere in the *Life of St. Andrew*, of any features derived from the *Visions of Daniel*, a tradition that began in the ninth century and was extremely popular in the author's own tenth century. The author relied instead on a form of the Pseudo-Methodian tradition that had been reached by the eighth century. He also cited traditions about St. Symeon the Fool, undoubtedly as described by Leontius of Neapolis (*BHG*³ 1677) in the seventh century, but here again he seems to have believed that he was an early saint, for he called him ὁ πάλαι Συμεὼν ἐκεῖνος ὁ θαυμαστός (that ancient Symeon the Miraculous) (648A).[7]

A possible explanation for this striking avoidance of later materials, both in the *Life of St. Andrew* and in his apocalypse, suggests itself. There has been so much controversy over the date of the text because its author, Nicephorus, posed as a contemporary of the fifth-century saint (e.g., 648B, 881B). To support this pretense, the author took considerable precautions. It has just been pointed out that he named no literary source that he believed to have been written after the lifetime of his hero. In other words, he pretended to write against the literary background of the fifth century. Similarly, he avoided mentioning Constantinopolitan buildings that he believed to have been erected after the supposed period of the saint—so successfully that modern scholarship has only recently and with considerable effort been able to prove the existence of certain anachronisms with respect to the architectural development of the capital.[8]

---

7. [Rydén believes that the apocalypse includes similarities to a later revision of the second *Vision of Daniel* (Bousset's version D II) and the *Vision of Methodius of Patara* printed by Istrin (pp. 145–50) and that Nicephorus consequently must have known some versions of the *Vision of Daniel*. "In the case of Nicephorus, his polemics against different τινες who say certain things indicate that he was familiar with several apocalyptic documents. It seems to me that one of these was the second *Vision of Daniel* in a form not yet fully developed in the ninth century" (p. 237). An important correspondence is the prediction of four emperors in D II and the *Andreas Salos Apocalypse*. Rydén agrees with the author that the work is best characterized as encyclopedic in nature (p. 238).]

8. The first scholar to use the architectural data of the *Life* to ascertain its date was Paul Maas, in the review mentioned in n. 1 above. Murray, *Study*, pp. 27–30, felt that the architectural evidence was inconclusive. More recently it has been applied by John Wortley, "Note," pp. 204–208.

Three Conglomerate Texts [ 127

It may be instructive to consider one instance in which the hagiographer went to considerable lengths to camouflage his date but left a rather clear clue. In chapter XIII he reported that once, during a dark night, St. Andrew fell into a muddy hole and was on the point of death when he was saved by the miraculous appearance of a cross borne through the air by the apostles Peter and Paul, whose chapel (εὐκτήριον) was nearby. It had been built, so Nicephorus claimed, following "the ancients of the city," by Constantine the Great (740B ff.). After the two apostles had conveyed the saint to the safety of a portico, he had a vision in which he saw the chapel of the apostles Peter and Paul transformed on divine orders into "a cruciform church with five domes, very beautiful in size and inimitable in form."[9] St. Andrew then prophesied that "a pious emperor" would rebuild this church, strong, beautiful, large, and in the form in which he had seen it.[10]

This passage has caused a great deal of difficulty for students of the ecclesiastical architecture of Constantinople. R. Janin, for example, listed four Constantinopolitan churches dedicated to the apostles Peter and Paul, but none of them filled the specifications given in the *Life of St. Andrew the Fool*. In particular, a Church of Sts. Peter and Paul, which Justinian I combined with a Church of Sts. Sergius and Bacchus, had one rather than five domes. Janin therefore declared himself nonplussed by the data in the *Life of St. Andrew the Fool*.[11] There is, however, a possible solution, considered but rejected by Janin. The hagiographer made St. Andrew predict that the Church of the Apostles Peter and Paul would be rebuilt with five domes on a cruciform plan. The suspicion arises that this may be a prophecy *ex eventu*. The Church of the Holy Apostles had been built (or at least begun) by Constantine the Great in basilical shape with a wooden roof. It had been rebuilt under Justinian I in the form of a Greek cross with five cupolas and was once again restored by Basil I. Certainly, the Church of the Holy Apostles was not specifically dedicated to Peter and Paul, but the hagiographer's remarks about the great size of the church, its five cupolas, and its cruciform plan make it highly probable that he was under the mistaken impression that this was so.[12] If this assumption is correct, we have here a

9. PG 111.741A πεντακόρυφος ναὸς σταυροειδῶς ἐγεγόνει, καὶ περικαλλὴς τῷ μεγέθει καὶ τῷ εἴδει ἀμίμητος.
10. Ibid., 741B Καιρῷ . . . προβαίνοντι ἀναστήσει αὐτὸν εὐσεβὴς βασιλεὺς καθ' ὃν τρόπον ἐθεασάμην αὐτόν, εὐσθενῆ καὶ περικαλλῆ τῷ μεγέθει. οἷον δὴ καὶ σχήματι ἐθεασάμην αὐτόν.
11. R. Janin, *La Géographie ecclésiastique de l'empire byzantin*, part I: *Le Siège de Constantinople*, vol. 3, *Les Eglises et les monastères* (Paris, 1953), p. 415.
12. Janin, *Eglises*, p. 46; Krautheimer, *Early Christian and Byzantine Architecture*, pp. 174ff. and frontispiece as well as pl. 86. J. Grosdidier des Matons, "Les Thèmes d' édifica-

remarkable demonstration of the hagiographer's concern to hide his knowledge of tenth-century Constantinople and to recreate for his hero the urban environment of the fifth century. It is only his desire to glorify St. Andrew's prophetic qualities that makes it possible to unravel this case of antiquarianism. Nicephorus represented his hero as visiting the small Constantinian chapel of the apostles Peter and Paul as it existed in the fifth century, but attributed to him a prophecy that "a pious emperor," either Justinian I or Basil I, would rebuild it in the form known to Nicephorus' own tenth century—a large church with five domes in the form of a cross. In doing so he blundered, for the chapel of Sts. Peter and Paul, which his tradition seems to have connected with St. Andrew, had nothing to do either with the Constantinian Church of the Holy Apostles or with its Justinianic successor.

My suggestion, then, is that Nicephorus was an antiquarian hagiographer and apocalyptist, just as he was an architectural antiquarian. He avoided as best he could bringing his fifth-century saint into contact not only with buildings erected after his lifetime but also with literary works that a man living in the fifth century could not have known. This would explain why, in the *Life of St. Andrew the Fool* as a whole and particularly in its apocalypse, he referred by name only to authors who wrote prior to the fifth century. It is true that without naming them he availed himself occasionally of sources later than that period, but in all such cases he seems to have considered them ancient and not to have been aware of their true origin.

So far as the date of St. Andrew's apocalypse is concerned, it seems that it was given its final form by the author of the saint's *Life*. In fact, a number of features connect the *Life* with the apocalypse. For example, in the apocalypse St. Andrew adduces an opinion according to which the restored tribes of Israel will rule after the end of the Gentile kingship for what is left of the seventh age of the world.[13] This notion of the

---

tion dans la *Vie d'André Salos*," *Travaux et Mémoires* 4 (1970), pp. 277–328, esp. 307n.104, also believes that the Church of the Holy Apostles was meant and that in popular usage it was called the Church of Sts. Peter and Paul.

13. PG 111.865B Τινές φασιν ὅτι μετὰ τὸ πλήρωμα τῆς τῶν ἐθνῶν βασιλείας μελλήσεται ὁ θεὸς τὰ θεόσκηπτρα Ἰσραὴλ ἀναστῆσαι πρὸς τὸ βασιλεῦσαι τὸ λοιπὸν πρὸς ἀναπλήρωσιν τοῦ ἑβδόμου αἰῶνος κτλ. [Some say that after the fulfillment of the kingdom of the Gentiles God will establish the divine tribes of Israel to rule the remaining time until the fulfillment of the seventh age.] This passage was part of a curious and highly original section of the apocalypse which has not, to my knowledge, received the attention it deserves. It refers in polemical fashion to a tradition that assigned to Israel an important role in eschatology. In a highly corrupt passage, St. Andrew argues against the view that after the end of the Gentile empires God will reestablish Israel to last for the balance of the seventh age and until the resurrection. The proponents of this view apparently justified their contention by references to a suitably interpolated text of Isaiah

Three Conglomerate Texts [ 129

seven ages of the world figures prominently in an earlier passage of the *Life* where St. Andrew discusses the problem of the order of creation and of the nature of the ages: at present the seven ages are still incomplete.[14] Furthermore, the apocalyptist cites Hippolytus to the effect that "the Jews will be the first to be deceived when the Antichrist arrives," a notion earlier expressed when St. Andrew interprets various biblical passages.[15] Furthermore, several favorite expressions of the hagiographer recur in the apocalypse.[16] Thus, although the author of the saint's *Life* undoubtedly used earlier materials for the composition of his apocalypse, as he did in all other parts of the *Life*, it seems that

---

11:12–16 and to Romans 11:26. Neither the notion of a Jewish role at the end of time nor that of a sequence of seven ages is unusual, but to the best of my knowledge the combination is unattested elsewhere. The refutation of this view is very much on St. Andrew's mind, and Epiphanius has great difficulty in steering St. Andrew back to his apocalypse. It is therefore probable that the problem of the role of the Jews at the end of time was or had been a subject of a real debate within the Eastern Church and that the *Life of St. Andrew* is here preserving vestiges of that debate.

There is one other piece of evidence of two divergent traditions in the apocalypse. St. Andrew predicts that three youths will wage war upon each other (860C ff.). The second youth will journey "to the navel of the earth" (Jerusalem?), "but some say to Alexandria" (861B). Since Jerusalem seems to play a role both here and in the prophecy of the restoration of the tribes of Israel, it is possible that there is a connection between the two points of divergence. It would be interesting to date the debate on the eschatological function of the Jews in the Byzantine Church. [Rydén, "*Andreas Salos Apocalypse*," pp. 248 and 252–53, provides further commentary on the passages. He also was unable to identify the source of these views on Israel in the eschatological drama.]

14. PG 111.804D–805A Ἡ δὲ οὐσία αὐτῶν [sc. τῶν αἰώνων] πνεῦμα ἕν . . . ἑπτὰ σημείοις σταδιοδρομούμενον . . . ἕως νῦν γὰρ οἱ ἑπτὰ αἰῶνες τοῦ κόσμου τούτου οἱ χρόνοις μετρούμενοι οὐ συνετελέσθησαν. [The substance (of the ages) is one spirit . . . running the course in seven signs . . . for up to the present the seven ages of this world, measured out in year-weeks, have not been completed.]

15. PG 111.865C Ἱππόλυτος δὲ ὁ μάρτυς ἔφησεν ὅτι ἐν τῇ ἐπιδημίᾳ τοῦ Ἀντιχρίστου πρῶτοι Ἰουδαῖοι πλανηθήσονται [Hippolytos the martyr said that at the arrival of the Antichrist the Jews first will be deceived]. (Migne printed μακάριος instead of μάρτυς but Professor L. Rydén kindly informed me that the latter is the correct reading.) Cf. 821B ἔτι γὰρ πάσῃ τῇ γῇ σκορπισθέντες [the Jews] πίνουσιν ἐν τῇ τρυγίᾳ τὴν πλάνην προσδοκῶντες τὸν Ἀντίχριστον. [For even scattered over the whole earth they (the Jews) drink, in the sediment of the wine, their error awaiting the Antichrist.]

16. The hagiographer is fond of compounds with θεο-, e.g., 632C θεόφοροι; 769A, C, 821B θεόπνευστοι; 821B θεοφόρητος. Compare in the apocalypse 865B τὰ θεόσκηπτρα Ἰσραὴλ (n. 13 above), which Professor L. Rydén explains (personal communication) as "God's tribes." The hagiographer frequently uses the adjective βλοσυρός [grim] of a person with a disapproving or sinister mien, e.g., 745A βλοσυρὸς (-ῶς) ἀπιδών; 757B βλοσυρὸν; and at least four times (656B, 680D, 697D, 760D9 βλοσυρῷ τῷ ὄμματι [grim-eyed]. Undoubtedly this is also what is meant in a corrupt passage of the apocalypse, 856C Μετὰ δὲ ταῦτα ἐγερθήσεται βασιλεία ἑτέρα ἐπὶ τὴν πόλιν ταύτην, καὶ αὐτὸς βλοσυρὸς ὄνος καὶ ἔξαρνος Ἰησοῦ Χριστοῦ κτλ. [After this another empire will arise against this city, and that ruler will be a grim ass and denier of Jesus Christ, etc.] Here Vasiliev, *Anecdota Graeca-Byzantina*, p. 52, recorded a variant, βλοσυρὸς ὄνομα [grim in name] in lieu of the meaningless καὶ αὐτὸς βλοσυρὸς ὄνος [and that grim ass] in Migne. Probably the author wrote βλοσυρὸς ὄμματι or βλοσυρῷ τῷ ὄμματι. Another example: in a wrestling match with the Devil, St. Andrew is γυροβολούμενος [turned around in a circle, 636C] and in the apocalypse it is prophesied that Constantinople will be lifted up ὡς μύλον γυροβολούμενον [as a millstone turned in a circle].

the apocalypse, too, received its present shape from him in the early tenth century.

## 2. THE *CENTO OF THE TRUE EMPEROR* ("ANONYMOUS PARAPHRASE OF THE *ORACLES OF LEO*")

A few words are indicated concerning a short tract entitled by its first editor, Petrus Lambecius, Ἀνωνύμου παράφρασις τῶν τοῦ βασιλέως Λέοντος χρησμῶν, but henceforth to be cited as the *Cento of the True Emperor*.[1] The edition is based on a single manuscript of the sixteenth century.[2] In the printed edition the title is followed by a subtitle that corresponds somewhat better to the content:

Concerning the much-discussed beggar and chosen emperor, known and unknown, residing on the first citadel of Byzantium.[3]

The text itself begins with the words Ὁ ἀληθινὸς βασιλεύς (The True Emperor).[4]

Both the content and structure of the work are frequently obscure, but it may be helpful to present a brief analysis, at least to the extent that I was able to understand its meaning. It begins with observations about the time when the True Emperor will be revealed (ἀποκαλυφθήσεται): at the end of the Ismaelite domination, in the days τοῦ λιβός (see below), at the third hour of a Friday. There follows information on means used by the Lord (Κύριος) to reveal the Anointed (ὁ ἠλειμμένος), namely, "(rain-)bows and signs" (τόξα καὶ σημεῖα). Three times the True Emperor will receive instructions from an angel, twice orally and the last time by means of stone tablets handed to him by the angel.[5] The signs identifying him are then set forth at great

---

1. *Georgii Codini Excerpta* (Paris, 1655), pp. 275–78. I shall cite the reprint in *PG* 107.1141–50.
2. See Lambecius' remarks, *PG* 107.1122, 1139. The manuscript is Cod. VI E 8, Universiteits Bibliotheek Amsterdam, of the sixteenth century. It is described by H. Omont, "Catalogue des manuscrits des bibliothèques publiques des Pays-Bas (Leyde exceptée)," *Centralblatt für Bibliothekswesen* 41 (1887), pp. 185–214, esp. 197f., and by M. B. Mendes da Costa, *Bibliotheek der Universiteit van Amsterdam, Catalogus der Handschriften* II (Amsterdam, 1902), p. 15. According to a scribal note at the end of the manuscript, it was copied "from a very ancient manuscript the script of which, it is said, was four hundred years or more old," i.e., of the twelfth century at the latest.
3. *PG* 107.1141 Περὶ τοῦ θρυλλουμένου πτωχοῦ καὶ ἐκλεκτοῦ βασιλέως, τοῦ γνωστοῦ καὶ ἀγνώστου, τοῦ κατοικοῦντος ἐν τῇ πρώτῃ ἄκρᾳ τῆς Βυζαντίδος.
4. The same designation occurs twice later in the treatise, at 1148B10 and B13.
5. *PG* 107.1141 line 30 πλάκας λιθίνας; that is, the True Emperor is here imagined as a Moses *redivivus*. On this concept in Late Judaism, cf. Wilhelm Bousset and Hugo Gressmann, *Die Religion des Judentums im späthellenistischen Zeitalter* (3rd ed. Tübingen, 1926), pp. 232f., and Paul Volz, *Die Eschatologie der jüdischen Gemeinde im neutestamentlichen Zeitalter* (Tübingen, 1934), p. 195.

length: physical characteristics, costume, moral and mental qualities partially expressed by means of pairs of paradoxes, as well as cryptic allusions to his name.[6] In this section there occurs a brief interruption referring to the anointment and activities of the True Emperor, notably his victory over the Ismaelites and their harassment of the population.[7] The rest is taken up largely with data on the True Emperor's place of residence at the time of his revelation, as well as its circumstances: a star will shine for three days, and in heaven will be seen a body of clouds, as large as the sun, from which are suspended a heavenly host ($\sigma\tau\rho\alpha\tau\acute{o}s$) clad in purple, and the rainbow set as a permanent covenant at the time of the Flood.[8] The rainbow will stand over the True Emperor's place of residence and the people will conduct the scion of the palace ($\dot{\alpha}\nu\alpha\kappa\tau o\rho\acute{\iota}\delta\eta s$) solemnly to the great Sion ($\dot{\eta}$ $\mu\varepsilon\gamma\acute{\alpha}\lambda\eta$ $\Sigma\iota\acute{\omega}\nu$). The star and a herald will also announce him, and once again the people will lead him to the great Sion. Its doors will be opened for him. Two angels will instruct him in his duties, and many persons will lament the fact that they had failed to listen to the Lord's kindness.[9] Everyone will then be at rest. The piece ends with a particularly obscure reference to another illustrious person from the East resembling the beggar (i.e., the True Emperor).

It will be important to define clearly the nature and purpose of the *Cento of the True Emperor*, for its usefulness as a source will largely depend on this definition. Here it is important to note that its designation as a paraphrase of the *Oracles of Leo* printed in Lambecius' first edition and in Migne's reprint is not based on manuscript evidence.[10] Apparently invented by Lambecius, it represents his conception of the nature of the text. He supported his view by citing, in the footnotes to his edition of the "paraphrase," the lines of the *Oracles of Leo* that he supposed certain passages to restate. Many of these alleged parallels belong to the standard repertoire of apocalyptic speculation and do not prove any dependence of the *Cento* on the *Oracles of Leo*.[11] There re-

---

6. PG 107.1141 line 36–1145B3. Pairs of paradoxes, e.g., servile descent and imperial ancestry: 1144C.

7. PG 107.1144B5–13.

8. PG 107.1148B τόξον οἷον διέθετο [i.e., ὁ θεός] τοῖς πράγμασιν ἡμῶν εἰς διαθήκην αἰώνιον [a (rain)bow which He (God) set as an eternal covenant for our affairs].

9. PG 107.1148D οὐ ἠκούομεν χρηστὸν Κυρίου [we did not listen to the Lord's kindness].

10. This point was confirmed, upon my inquiry, by Carla M. Faas, Keeper of the Department of Manuscripts at the Universiteits-Bibliotheek, Amsterdam. I wish to thank her here for her kindness.

11. For example, the characterization of the Emperor as πολιός [gray-haired] (1143 n. 52), πραΰς [mild] (n. 54), πτωχός [poor] (n. 56); cf. *Slavonic Daniel* #6: (the inhabitants of the Rebel City) "find there someone by divine revelation carrying two coins in

main four passages where a connection between the two texts is beyond doubt, but their relation is not that of original and paraphrase. In two of them the same topic is mentioned in similar language, in one case a mysterious figure called Lips(?) and in the other the residence of the True Emperor in a western quarter of Constantinople.[12] In a third case the *Cento* quotes verbatim from one of the *Oracles of Leo* (but omitting a key phrase),[13] yet a literal citation hardly qualifies as a paraphrase. The fourth passage is partially also a direct quotation, and partly may represent a paraphrase, but it presents special problems and is at any rate not a sufficient basis for characterizing the entire work as a paraphrase.[14] It is not even certain, though it is probable, that the author of the *Cento* knew the *Oracles of Leo*, for in the two instances where he seems to cite them (n. 12 above), he may be quoting from a source of the *Oracles* rather than from the *Oracles* themselves.[15]

---

order to receive crumbs"; *Apocalypse of Andrew the Fool*, PG 111.853B βασιλέα ἀπὸ πενίας [Emperor from poverty]. The ξανθὰ ἔθνη [Blond Peoples] (1145 n. 60) are a standard feature of the *Visions of Daniel*; cf. the ξανθὰ ἔθνη of Pseudo-Chrysostom (p. 36.32 Vasiliev) and of Daniel Καὶ ἔσται (p. 39.32 Vasiliev).

12. Compare 1141.13 ἐν ταῖς ἡμέραις τοῦ λιβὸς [in the days of Lips] with Oracle 8 (1136B) Δράκοντα συρίξουσιν τὸν λιβοκτόνον [they will hiss at the serpent who kills Lips (?)] and 1144C κατοικῶν . . . ἀπὸ τῆς δυτικῆς πόλεως πύλης [living by the western gate of the city] with Oracle 13 (1137C) Ἄπιτε σπουδῇ πρὸς τὰς δυσμὰς ἑπταλόφου [go in haste to the western parts of the seven-hilled (city, Constantinople)]. The words τοῦ λιβός remind us of *Oracle of Baalbek* (my ed., line 186) ἀναστήσεται ἄλλος βασιλεὺς ἀπὸ Ἀνατολῆς, οὗτινος τὸ ὄνομά ἐστι †Ὀλιβός [another emperor will arise from the East, whose name is *Olibos*]; see my remarks pp. 112f., n. 50.

13. Compare 1141 line 19 καὶ ἀποκαλυφθήσεται ὁ ἠλειμμένος [and the Anointed will be revealed] with Oracle 11 (1137A) Καὶ ἀποκαλυφθήσεται ὁ ἠλειμμένος ἐπώνυμος Μεναχείμ [and the Anointed, called Menachem, shall be revealed].

14. At 1141, line 18, the *Cento* reads καὶ τριῶν ταραττομένων ὁ τρίτος πρῶτος [and of the three woes arising, the third is first]. Lambecius compared Oracle 9 (1136C) τῶν δύο δερνόντων [sic] ὁ τρίτος πρῶτος [of the two flayings (?) the third is first]. This line is missing in the *editio princeps* of the *Oracles* by Ianus Rutgersius, *Variarum Lectionum Libri Sex* (Leiden, 1618), p. 476, and therefore presumably was also missing in the manuscript(s) used by him. In two Vatican manuscripts I consulted, Vat. Gr. 1188, fol. 16 recto, and 1713, fol. 65 recto, they are not part of the text but serve as legend for a miniature. Whatever their place in the tradition and their meaning, the words ὁ τρίτος πρῶτος [the third first] are again a literal quotation rather than a paraphrase, while the mysterious remainder of the phrase may conceivably be paraphrased by τριῶν ταραττομένων [three scourges].

15. The *Oracles of Leo* is similar to the *Cento* in a number of passages not noted by Lambecius. *Oraculum* 13.2 Οἴδασι πολλοὶ κἂν μηδεὶς τοῦτον βλέπῃ [many know him even if no one sees him] partly agrees and partly contradicts *Cento* 1144C παρ' οὐδενὸς βλεπόμενον καὶ παρὰ μηδενὸς γνωριζόμενον [seen by no one and recognized by no one]. *Oraculum* 13.6 Κῆρυξ ἀφανὴς τρὶς ἀνακράξει [an unseen herald will cry out three times] shares with *Cento* 1148A7 Καὶ κῆρυξ βοῶν τρανῶς ἐν ταῖς τρισὶν ἡμέραις ἀνακαλῶν κτλ. [and a herald shouting clearly will summon in those three days, etc.] the notion of the triple call, but conflicts with the *Cento* because the latter says clearly that the people see the herald (Τότε ὁ δῆμος ὁρῶν κτλ.) [then the people see, etc.]. Later, however, the *Cento*, citing from another source, returns to the herald and introduces him as speaking unseen to the people (1148C4). Finally, when in *Oracle* 15.10 the apocalyptist urges

Three Conglomerate Texts							[ 133

The conclusion that the author is citing his sources verbatim is confirmed if one considers his use of apocalyptic texts earlier than the *Oracles of Leo*. Repeatedly, he refers to the Emperor as of "no utility," in words reminiscent of Pseudo-Methodius and of the *Visions of Daniel* derived from Pseudo-Methodius.[16] Two further passages are taken, with minor variations and corruptions, from the Greek text of the Tiburtine Sibyl,[17] and the statement about the Lord laying his hand on the Emperor's head derives from *Daniel Καὶ ἔσται*.

The most interesting borrowing is the first set of instructions given by an angel to the True Emperor. The passage looks at first glance like a citation of Ephesians 5:14. This is, however, unlikely, on a priori grounds, as it would be the only biblical quotation in the *Cento*. It reads: "Awake, O sleeper and arise from the grave, and Christ will give

---

the True Emperor to leave τὴν φυτοῦ κατοικίαν [the dwelling of the plant] he is clearly thinking of the fir tree planted at his birth near his residence according to the *Cento* (1145C13); however, the much fuller detail given shows that the author of the *Cento* cannot possibly have derived his information from *Oracle* 15 but must have consulted its source.

16. Compare 1144B1 ὃν ἐδόκουν οἱ ἄνθρωποι ὡς οὐδὲν ὄντα καὶ εἰς οὐδὲν χρησιμεύοντα. ἐπιθήσει Κύριος τὴν χεῖρα αὐτοῦ ἐπὶ τὴν κορυφὴν αὐτοῦ [whom men thought of as being nothing and useful for nothing. The Lord will place his hand on his head]; 1144C εἰς οὐδὲν χρησιμεύων [useful for nothing]; 1145D7 εἰς οὐδὲν χρησιμεύσας, ὃν ἐξουδένουν οἱ ἄνθρωποι ὡς νεκρὸν ὄντα καὶ μηδὲν χρησιμεύοντα [useful for nothing, whom men scorned as being a dead man and useful for nothing]; with Greek Pseudo-Methodius, p. 40.3 Istrin (= p. 122.4 Lolos) ὃν ἐλογίζοντο οἱ ἄνθρωποι ὡσεὶ νεκρὸν καὶ εἰς οὐδὲν χρησιμεύοντα [whom men reckoned as a dead man and useful for nothing]; *Slavonic Daniel* #6: "whom people considered as a dead man"; Pseudo-Chrysostom, p. 36.22 Vasiliev ὃν εἶχον οἱ ἄνθρωποι ὡσεὶ νεκρὸν καὶ οὐδὲν χρησιμεύοντα; *Daniel Καὶ ἔσται* p. 39.21 Vasiliev ὃν ἐδόκουν οἱ ἄνθρωποι ὡς νεκρὸν εἶναι καὶ εἰς οὐδὲν χρησιμεύειν. καὶ ἐπιθήσει κύριος ὁ θεὸς τὴν χεῖρα αὐτοῦ ἐπὶ τὴν κορυφὴν αὐτοῦ [whom men reckoned as being dead and useful for nothing. And the Lord God will place his hand on his head]. Elements of the physical description of the True Emperor also are derived from that of the Last Emperor in *Daniel Καὶ ἔσται*, e.g., 1141 line 40 ἡ λαλία αὐτοῦ ἡδεῖα [his sweet speech] and p. 39.17 Vasiliev; and 1144A2 ἡ ῥὶς αὐτοῦ ἐπικεκυφυῖα [his crooked nose] and p. 39.17 Vasiliev (ἐπίκυφος) [crooked]. The passages immediately preceding in both texts, concerning a τήλωμα or τίτλωμα [tattoo-mark] upon big toe or finger (1141 line 39 and p. 39.16 Vasiliev) also agree.

17. Cf. 1144 A 11 τὸ δὲ ὄνομα τοῦ βασιλέως κεκρυμμένον ἐν τοῖς ἔθνεσι. Ὁμοιοῖ δὲ τῇ ἐσχάτῃ ἡμέρᾳ τῇ ἑβδόμῃ. Γράφεται δὲ καὶ ἀπὸ τοῦ πρώτου γράμματος ἐν τῷ ὀκτωκαιδεκάτῳ ἤτοι ἐν τῷ τριακοσιοστῷ πρώτῳ. Φυλάττων θεοσέβειαν καὶ προφητείαν [The name of the emperor is hidden from the Gentiles. It is similar to the last day of the week. It begins with the 18th or the 301st letter (of the alphabet). Guarding reverence and prophecy.] with my edition of the *Oracle of Baalbek*, Dumbarton Oaks Studies 10 [1967], lines 163–65, τὸ δὲ ὄνομα τοῦ βασιλέως κεκρυμμένον ἐστὶ τοῖς ἔθνεσιν, ὁμοιοῖ δὲ τὸ ὄνομα αὐτοῦ τῇ ἡμέρᾳ τῇ ἐσχάτῃ, γράφεται δὲ ἀπὸ τοῦ γράμματος τοῦ ὀκτωκαιδεκάτου and 169f. καὶ καθελεῖ τοὺς τηροῦντας θεοσέβειαν [The name of the king is hidden from the Gentiles, but his name resembles the last day (i.e., the day of the resurrection or *anastasis*) and begins with the eighteenth letter (and 169f.) and will depose those who observe godliness.] (Two manuscripts read πλησίον or πλὴν φυλάττον θεοσέβειαν καὶ προφήτας or προφητείαν.)

you light, for he summons you to tend his peculiar people."[18] Moreover, in the *Cento* the apparently Pauline verses are followed by a phrase that does not occur in the Bible, yet resembles in vocabulary and syntax the Greek Old and New Testaments.[19] Now Eph. 5 : 14 is specifically introduced in the Bible as a citation (διὸ λέγει) and it has been held from ancient to modern times that it derives from a Jewish or Christian extracanonical source. This derivation may or may not be true, but a number of Church Fathers certainly read the passage in an Old Testament pseudepigraphon variously attributed to Elijah, Jeremiah, or an unnamed prophet.[20] It is therefore at least worth considering the possibility that the author of the *Cento* may have borrowed the passage from the Old Testament pseudepigraphon and that the additional phrase not known from the New Testament or anywhere else may be part of the quotation.[21]

This composite character of the *Cento* explains its structural defects, its repetitions and inconsistencies.[22] In particular, the style vacillates between extreme bathos, rhetorical polish, and hymnic enthusiasm,[23] and the author refers to the expected Emperor by a bewildering variety of terms. In addition to the term King or Emperor, he speaks of the Holy

---

18. 1141 line 25: Ἔγειραι, ὁ καθεύδων, καὶ ἀνάστα ἐκ τοῦ μνημείου· καὶ ἐπιφαύσει σοι ὁ Χριστός· προσκαλεῖται γάρ σε τοῦ ποιμαίνειν λαὸν περιούσιον. The text of the New Testament differs on two points: it reads τῶν νεκρῶν (the dead) in place of τοῦ μνημείου, and it lacks the last phrase (προσκαλεῖται . . . περιούσιον).

19. Note the reference to the "peculiar people" (Exod. 19:5, etc.) and the construction of προσκαλέομαι with the genitive of the articular infinitive, a construction frequent in the Septuagint but rare in the New Testament except in Paul and Luke; cf. H. B. Swete, *An Introduction to the Old Testament in Greek* (Cambridge, England, 1900), p. 306, and F. Blass and A. Debrunner, *A Greek Grammar of the New Testament*, trans. R. W. Funk (Chicago, 1961), pp. 206f.

20. Theodor Zahn, *Geschichte des neutestamentlichen Kanons*, vol. II, I (Erlangen and Leipzig, 1890), p. 804; Emil Schürer, *Geschichte des jüdischen Volkes im Zeitalter Jesu Christi*, 3, 4th ed. (Leipzig, 1909), pp. 365f. (who gives all the patristic material); Albert-Marie Denis, *Introduction aux pseudépigraphes grecs d'Ancien Testament* (Leiden, 1970), pp. 165f., 284.

21. The possibility should not even be excluded that all or part of the angel's second summons and the injunctions on the "stone tablets" are part of the pseudepigraphon.

22. On structure, see the analysis on p. 130 above. For repetitions, see, for example, note 16 above; also the twofold citation of the words φυλάττων θεοσέβειαν καὶ προφητείαν [observing godliness and prophecy] in 1144A15 and 1145D6 (with slight variants); and the double reference to the people escorting the True Emperor to "the Great Zion," 1148B12 and C12.

23. Compare, for example, the prosaic descriptions of the True Emperor (1141 line 36ff.; 1145A8) with the polished paradoxes of 1144C τὸν χρηστὸν καὶ ἄχρηστον, τὸν πτωχὸν καὶ μὴ ὑστερούμενον . . . τὸν γυμνὸν καὶ βύσσινα ἠμφιεσμένον κτλ. [useful and useless, poor and not inferior, naked and clothed in linen, etc.] and with the panegyrical νικητής, τροπαιοῦχος, ἄναξ ἀνάκτων ἄριστος (1145B) [the victor, trophy-bearer, great lord of lords].

One of the Lord,[24] the Chosen King (or Emperor),[25] the Hoped-For,[26] and the Anointed (ὁ ἠλειμμένος). The last designation was a Late Jewish term introduced by Aquila, a translator of the Old Testament into Greek, to avoid the word χριστός, then appropriated by Christianity.[27] The author of the *Cento* had access to a variety of sources that he related, rightly or wrongly, to the True Emperor and which, in his opinion, referred to that figure in different ways. Some of them, such as the Greek text of the Tiburtine Sibyl (early sixth century) and the texts belonging to the Pseudo-Methodian tradition (beginning in the seventh century), were written long before his time. Most ancient are his borrowings from Judaism: the designation of the Messiah by the term ὁ ἠλειμμένος and a reference to the God of Heaven and Earth,[28] the possible reference to an Old Testament pseudepigraphon underlying or paralleling Eph. 5:14, and the notion that the Messiah would reside on Mount Zion.[29] About the date of the *Cento* it is unfortunately impossible to say more than this: if the author cited the *Oracles of Leo*, as seems probable, he must have written between the twelfth century and the sixteenth, the date of the Amsterdam manuscript.[30]

What was the purpose of his compilation? The prominence given to the term the True Emperor, the exclusive emphasis on the time of his "revelation," his circumstances, and his appearance, the fact that his function (victory over the Ismaelites) is presupposed or mentioned only incidentally rather than developed fully, and the omission of any reference to his surrender of imperial power, to his death, or to the role of the Antichrist—all these factors make it plain that the author designed his *Cento* for readers expecting the coming of a Messianic ruler yet aware of the Gospels' warning against "false Christs" (Matt. 24:23ff.) and therefore anxious to obtain guidance as to how to distinguish the genuine Emperor from pretenders. To provide such guidance, the author collected citations from earlier literature. Some of the fragments collected by him are precious because they can be shown to be excerpts from early texts (Pseudo-Methodius, Tiburtine Sibyl, perhaps an Old

24. 1144B14 τὸν ἅγιον αὐτοῦ [= Κυρίου]; cf. 1145A 11 ἅγιος τῷ Κυρίῳ.
25. 1141 line 4 ἐκλεκτοῦ βασιλέως; 1145B14, 1148B5 (ὁ ἐκλεκτός); 1150A10 (ἐκλεκτός).
26. 1148A12 τὸν ἐλπιζόμενον; cf. B8.
27. 1141 line 19; 1144B5, B15; 1148A2. Cf. Schürer, *Geschichte*, II, p. 615 and n. 12; Bousset-Gressmann, *Religion des Judentums*, (above), p. 227.
28. 1141 line 35: τοῦ θεοῦ τοῦ οὐρανοῦ καὶ τῆς γῆς; also 1144B9. Cf. Bousset-Gressmann, *Religion des Judentums*, pp. 312f.
29. On this last point see Volz, *Eschatologie*, p. 225.
30. It may be unwise to attach much importance to the scribal note (n. 2 above) according to which the model of the Amsterdam manuscript dated from the twelfth century at the latest.

Testament pseudepigraphon). In other cases, content and style make it probable that they are taken from lost Jewish sources. It is likely, therefore, that the remainder also reproduces passages from earlier apocalyptic and other writings now lost. The *Cento* thus emerges as a valuable repository of Jewish, early Christian, and Byzantine fragments on an expected Messianic ruler.

It is a precious document, but it should be used with great caution. The citations from the Pseudo-Methodian tradition show that the author identified the Last Roman Emperor of that tradition with the True Emperor who is the subject of the *Cento*. But it is equally clear that other fragments originally had an entirely different meaning and that the author, in citing passages of a vaguely Messianic character, with little discrimination conflated materials of very different meaning. The quotations from the *Oracle of Baalbek* (n. 17 above), for example, originally characterized an historical Late Roman emperor, Anastasius I (496–518), and any Messianic flavor that they may possess is due merely to the fact that the sixth-century author of that text described Anastasius' rule in Messianic language. Yet this earlier writer by no means thought of Anastasius as the Last Roman Emperor; he expected a long series of further eschatological rulers.[31] It is also highly doubtful that the injunction to "the sleeper," in the Old Testament pseudepigraphon resembling Eph. 5:14, "to tend the peculiar people" (n. 18 above) could have anything to do with the expectation of a Last Roman Emperor. The content of the "stone tablets," finally—that is the order for a moral, religious, and ecclesiastical purge of laity and clergy—is nowhere else attested among the functions of a Last Roman Emperor and must in the original context have referred to a figure of an entirely different kind. In exploiting the *Cento of the True Emperor*, therefore, for the study of the expectation of a Last Roman Emperor, one should bear in mind that the incorporated passages, valuable as they may be, are due to the arbitrary judgment of the author and in many cases have no relevance whatsoever to the notion of the Last Roman Emperor.

## 3. PSEUDO-EPHRAEM

One of the most interesting apocalyptic texts of the early Middle Ages is a sermon *On the Last Times, the Antichrist, and the End of the World* preserved in Latin in four manuscripts and ascribed in them either to St. Ephraem or to St. Isidore. The four manuscripts are listed

---

31. See my edition of *Oracle of Baalbek*, lines 180ff.

by Albert Siegmund, *Der Überlieferung der griechischen christlichen Literatur in der lateinischen Kirche bis zum zwölften Jahrhundert*, Abhandlungen der Bayerischen Benediktiner-Akademie 5 (München-Passing, 1949), p. 69.[1] The Sangallensis is the only manuscript to ascribe the piece to St. Isidore. The piece was edited, with a valuable discussion and commentary, by C. P. Caspari.[2] While the editor's commentary exhibits wide learning and is still valuable, the Latin text deserves and needs a new critical edition, not only because Caspari did not use two of the manuscripts (the Parisinus and the Augiensis), but also because the collations of the Barberini and St. Gallen manuscripts on which he relied are faulty.[3]

The homily combines parenetic and apocalyptic materials. The author begins with a warning that the end of the world is at hand. Crime and immorality are rampant in all classes of mankind. Wars against Persians are already raging, against "various nations" warfare is impending, the Evil One (*malus*: Antichrist? Devil?) is coming. The end of the Roman Empire will of necessity bring about the consummation of (this) age. "In those days" (i.e., at the time of the end of the Roman Empire) "two brothers will come to the Roman Empire." They will be of one mind, but one brother will precede the other and there will be conflict between them.[4] The Adversary (Devil?) will then be released and will stir up hatred between the realms of Persians and Romans. In those days many will arise against the Roman rule and the Roman people will be its enemies. There will be stirrings of peoples, pestilence, famine, earthquakes; prisoners will be distributed over all nations, then will be "wars and rumors of wars" (Matt. 24:6) (ch. 1).

---

1. Vat. Barb. Lat. 671, second half of eighth century, Italy, fols. 167–71 (palaeographic description in E. A. Lowe, *Codices Latini Antiquiores* I [Oxford 1934], no. 64); Paris. 13348, mid eighth century, fols. 89–93 (palaeographic description in Lowe, V [Oxford, 1950], no. 656: France, provenance Corbie); St. Gallen 108, eighth to ninth century, western Switzerland or north Italy(?), pp. 2–10 (palaeographic description in Lowe, VII [Oxford, 1956], no. 905); Karlsruhe, Augiensis CXCVI, fols. 24–29.

2. C. P. Caspari, *Briefe, Abhandlungen und Predigten aus den letzten zwei Jahrhunderten des kirchliche Alterthums und dem Anfang des Mittelalters* (Christiana, 1890), pp. 208–220 (text), 429–72 (discussion).

3. This was noted by A. Wilmart, "Le Discours de Saint Basile sur l'ascèse en Latin," *Revue Bénédictine* 27 (1910), p. 226n.5, for the Barberini ms. bibliography: Bousset, Sackur, Johannes Dräsche, "Zu der eschat Predigt Pseudo-Ephräms," *Zeitschrift für Wissenshaftliche Theologie* 35 (1892), pp. 177–84; E. Dekkers and Ae. Gaar, *Clavis Patrum Latinorum* (2nd ed. Steenbruge, 1961), no. 1144; D. Hemmerdinger-Iliadou, "Ephrem (Les Versions)," *Dictionnaire de Spiritualité* 4, 1 (Paris, 1960), pp. 800–819, esp. 817; Maurice Geerard, *Clavis Patrum Graecorum* II (Brepols, 1974), no. 3944–3946. There are apparently no recent studies, except from a palaeographical point of view.

4. Caspari 209.9: *uno quidem animo praesunt* [mss.: *praefiunt*] *sed quoniam unus praecedit alium fiet inter eos scidium.*

Pseudo-Ephraem continues his admonitions by observing that all the "signs" (of the end) predicted by the Lord (Matt. 24:6f.) have already been fulfilled and that nothing remains except the advent of the Evil One at the end of the Roman Empire. Therefore there is (no?) sense in busying oneself with worldly concerns; rather, men should prepare themselves to meet (*in occursum*) with the Lord Christ. His advent is near, so the preacher warns emphatically. It is foolish on the part of the audience to refuse to heed this advice just because they have not yet witnessed anything of the sort with their own eyes. Such persons draw upon themselves the condemnation expressed by the prophet (Amos 5:18): "Woe to those who wish to see the day of the Lord."[5] For God's saints and elect will be gathered to him prior to the coming tribulation precisely so that they may not witness the confusion that will then overwhelm the entire world. It is now the eleventh hour; the end of this world has reached the point of the harvest (*ad metendum peruenit*), and the angels already hold the scythes in their hands. The parenetic part (chs. 1–2) ends with another call to repentance (*poenitentia*).

The preacher now describes the disasters of the final period of the world, as before: there is disaster in nature and disorder in human society (ch. 3). The world will be shaken by warlike nations (*gentes bellicae*) and men will hide in mountains, caves, and tombs. In their panic men will flee from East to West and West to East and will find no peace, for the world will be covered with iniquitous nations (*nequissimae gentes*) who resemble wild beasts rather than men. These nations will be exceedingly horrifying: they will not spare the living; they will devour carcasses; they will drink the blood of beasts of burden; and they will defile the earth. Nobody will be buried, neither Christian nor heretic nor Jew nor pagan, for men will be too afraid and in their flight will not know themselves (ch. 4).

The days of "those nations" will come to an end and the earth will be in repose. Then the Roman Empire will be taken "out of the way" (II Thess. 2:7) and the Christian Empire (*Christianorum imperium*) will be "delivered to God and the Father" (I Cor. 15:24). The end (of the world) will come when the Roman Empire begins to end and all principalities and powers have been completed. Then the Antichrist, "that most foul and abominable dragon," will appear as predicted in Moses' Blessing on Dan and he will, like the partridge in Jeremiah (17:11) who summons the brood which she "did not hatch," call men

---

5. Caspari 211.3: *Uae his qui concupiscunt uidere diem domini*.

who are not his children, but God's. But at the end of time they will abandon the Antichrist (ch. 5).

The Antichrist will be born from the (Jewish) tribe of Dan when the end of the world comes. He will be conceived by a man (a human being) and a most foul maiden, by the intervention of an evil and foul spirit. While he is growing up and before he assumes his royal power (*dumque adulescens . . . antequam sumat imperium*) he will pretend to be gentle, incorruptible, unselfish, kindly to all. Men will therefore praise him and say he is a just man; but in reality a wolf hides underneath the skin of a lamb (ch. 6).

Yet when the time of "the desolating sacrilege" (Dan. 9:27; cf. Matt. 24:15) has come, he will come of age (*factus legitimus*)[6] and will assume his royal power (*sumet imperium*); and, in accordance with Psalm 83:9, Moabites and "Ammanites" will be the first to recognize him as their king. He will have the (Jewish) Temple at Jerusalem rebuilt for himself, will sit in it as if he were God, and will give orders that he be worshipped by all the nations. This will be the fulfillment of Dan. 11:37. He will also issue an edict that men should be circumcised "according to the rite of the ancient law." Then the Jews will congratulate him because he has "restored to them the use of the Old Testament." All men will converge on him in Jerusalem, and the holy city "will be trampled over" by the nations during forty-two months, as is said in Revelation (11:6), or three and a half years or 1,260 days (ch. 7).

During those three and a half years there will be drought and famine, "great tribulation such as had not been" (Matt. 24:21) since the creation of man. Children and women will die from starvation. Only those who have (tattooed) on their forehead or hand the (Antichrist's) sign of the snake (*serpentinum signum*) will be able to sell or buy some of the *frumentum caducitatis*, the uncultivated grain of the second year.[7] Gold, silver, precious clothes and stones, and all kinds of pearls will lie unclaimed in the streets of the cities. The pious, however, will flee from the serpent and wander in the deserts, "awaiting the Lord's salvation" (Gen. 49:18) and praying to God (ch. 8).

As mankind is faltering under the breath of the horrible dragon, God will send them the "comforting preaching" (*consolatoria praedicatio*) by his servants Enoch and Elijah. They have not tasted death but have been spared to announce Christ's Second Coming and to denounce the

---

6. Caspari 435: acknowledged [as king] but adulterous(?).
7. Caspari 435: "das kraftlose Getreide," "das Getreide der Hinfälligkeit."

Enemy (the Antichrist). They will refute him and recall the faithful who have been led astray by him to God (ch. 9; the editor, rightly, assumes a lacuna at the end of the chapter where the author must have spoken of Enoch and Elijah being killed by the Antichrist and later revived).

After the three and a half years, the time of the Antichrist will have come to an end, and after the resurrection of Enoch and Elijah, at an hour unknown to the world and on a day unknown to the Enemy, the sign of the Son of Man (the Cross) will appear. The Lord will come forth with a large host and in great majesty, preceded by the sign of the Cross. An angel will blow his trumpet, which will announce: Arise, ye who sleep, arise, come to meet Christ, because the hour of his judgment has come. Then Christ will come and slay (*interficiet*) the Enemy "with the breath of his mouth" (II Thess. 2:8). The Enemy, together with his father, Satan, will be bound and plunged alive in the abyss of eternal fire (*in abyssum ignis aeterni uiuus*). All his servants will perish with him in eternity. The just, however, will forever inherit eternal life with the Lord (ch. 10).

The first and only editor of the sermon, Caspari, discussed whether the text was composed in Latin or was translated from a Greek original. He concluded that the latter view was much more probable and even briefly considered the possibility that the lost Greek model was itself a translation from a Syriac original.[8] The possibility of a Syriac original, even of a twofold translation, first from Syriac into Greek, then from Greek into Latin, has become much more plausible since Caspari's time. Two of the Latin manuscripts preserving Pseudo-Ephraem's homily contain the Latin Pseudo-Methodius in its immediate vicinity: codd. Vat. Barberini Lat. 671 and Paris. Lat. 13348. The Latin text of Pseudo-Methodius is certainly the product of this type of twofold translation.

One might expect that the question of the language of the original could be settled easily by a study of the biblical quotations. This evidence, however, is not conclusive. A thorough study of the text demonstrates that, where they differ, most of the biblical citations agree with the Latin Bible rather than with the Greek or Syriac text. This is of

---

8. Caspari's principal reasons for assuming a Greek original were the Eastern perspective of the author (he emphasizes Persian wars) and the transitive use of *aridare* (218.4) which is unknown in Latin (458f.). Arguments in favor of a Latin original are, according to Caspari, the greater closeness of the text to a Latin work, *De beatitudine animae*, attributed to St. Ephraem, than to the Greek version, the twentieth of the Μακαρισμοί ἕτεροι; and the use of the *Vetus Latina* where it disagrees with the Septuagint (pp. 456f.). Caspari noted, however, that these features can also be explained differently. Possibility of a Syriac original is mentioned on p. 459.

course what one would expect of a text composed in the West. Yet even if it was composed in Greek or Syriac, it would be natural for a Latin translator to adjust (wherever feasible) the biblical quotations to the Latin Bible, with which his readers would be familiar. The use of the Latin Bible, therefore, is reconcilable not only with a Latin original but with a Syriac or Greek original translated into Latin. For a decision of the problem of the original language it is, therefore, immaterial that the majority of the biblical citations in Pseudo-Ephraem *follow* the Latin Bible. On the other hand, even a few agreements of the biblical texts with the Syriac or Greek and *against* the Latin Bible would be precious links to show that the original must have been composed elsewhere than in the Latin West. Now, among the various biblical passages cited by Pseudo-Ephraem there seems to be only one where this is the case. Where the author discusses the Antichrist's attempts to win adherents he quotes Jeremiah 17:11 in the following way:

*Qui sicut perdix colliget sibi filios confusionis, et multiplicabit agere, et uocat, quos non genuit, sicut dicit Hieremias propheta* (Like a partridge he will gather to himself the sons of confusion and will increase [their number?] and [will] summon whom he did not beget, as the prophet Jeremiah says).

Now both the Septuagint and the Latin form of Jer. 17:11 cited by St. Ambrose make the relative clause *quos non genuit* depend on the partridge "gathering" children not her own.[9] In the Pešitta, on the other hand, the verse reads in literal Latin translation in the London Polyglot:

*Vt perdix quae vocitat quos non peperit* (Like a partridge which summons whom she did not bear).

In other words, Pseudo-Ephraem's citation of Jer. 17:11 agrees with the Pešitta alone in attaching the relative clause *quos non genuit* directly to the "summoning" of the partridge, while both the Septuagint and *Vetus Latina* interpolate after her summons the thought that she "gathered" whom she did not bear. This one agreement of Pseudo-Ephraem with the Syriac Bible certainly is not sufficient to prove that the original was written in Syriac, but it does point in that direction. Any further light on the question will have to come from Pseudo-Ephraem's own words, rather than from his biblical quotations.

9. LXX ἐφώνησεν πέρδιξ, συνήγαγεν ἃ οὐκ ἔτεκεν; *Vetus Latina* (cf. Petrus Sabatier, *Bibliorum Sacrorum Latinae Versiones Antiquae*, II, 2 [Paris, 1751], p. 675): *Clamavit perdix, congregavit quae non peperit*. The Vulgate is quite different: *perdix fovit quae non peperit*; still different is the Hebrew Bible translated literally as follows in Brian Walton, ed., *Biblia Sacra Polyglotta* (London, 1657), III, p. 234: *Perdix collegit et non peperit* (i.e., the "summoning" is not mentioned at all).

APPENDIX: SYRIAC ORIGINAL
OF PSEUDO-EPHRAEM

A number of passages preserved in Latin make little or no sense as they stand but can be explained satisfactorily in terms of an original composed in the Syriac language.

1. On pp. 214f. Caspari, Pseudo-Ephraem cites Deut. 33:22 about the tribe of Dan, from which the Antichrist is expected to come, and he interprets the *Basan* of that text to mean "confusion." This makes him think of another Old Testament passage, Jer. 17:11, that speaks of the partridge calling and gathering (LXX, *Vetus Latina*) or cherishing (Vulgate) children not born from her—"sons of confusion," as Pseudo-Ephraem calls them. Into this prophetic context Pseudo-Ephraem inserts, according to Caspari's edition, the words *et multiplicabit agere*; the entire passage reads as follows:

*Qui sicut perdix colliget sibi filios confusionis, et multiplicabit agere*[10] *et uocat, quos non genuit, sicut dicit Hieremias propheta.*

What do the words *et multiplicabit agere* mean? The editor, citing Amos 4:4, wondered whether *impie* or a similar word had been omitted, but this is obviously a counsel of despair. The Syriac word for *multiplicare* is *asgī* (Aphel of *segā*), which is frequently construed with an infinitive.[11] It is a so-called absolute infinitive and serves to express intensity.[12] The Vat. Barb. Lat. 671, fol. 169 recto, reads *augere* rather than *agere*, and this seems the preferable reading. It would correspond to the Syriac infinitive *masgāyā*, formed from the same root as the Syriac model of *multiplicabit* (*asgī*), and would be an "inner object" again expressing intensity: "he will increase very much and call those whom he did not beget." The translator seems to have imitated slavishly a characteristic Syriac construction.

2. A little later (p. 216.4) Pseudo-Ephraem describes how the Antichrist succeeds in winning adherents by hypocritically laying claim to a number of good qualities: he pretends to be gentle, uninterested in gifts (bribes), lovable, quiet, affable, etc. Among these qualities appear the words *personam non praeponens*. These words, while not impossible, seem vague, but they yield a more precise meaning as soon as the Syriac model is envisaged. The Syriac word for *persona* is *nafshā*, but this word is frequently used, with the appropriate personal suffixes, in the

10. Manuscripts: *aggerem, augere*(?).
11. Cf. Payne Smith, *Thesaurus Syriacus* II, p. 2518.
12. Nöldeke, *Kurzgefasste Syrische Grammatik* [Leipzig, 1880], pp. 206f.

sense of the reflexive pronoun.[13] Pseudo-Ephraem meant to say that the Antichrist pretended to be humble and did not claim preference for himself. The Latin translator, failing to understand the reflexive force of the noun, translated it literally and thus deprived the phrase of its precise meaning.

3. Where Pseudo-Ephraem describes the drought and famine prevailing during the reign of the Antichrist, he mentions that nobody will be able to sell or buy *de frumento caducitatis* unless he has tattooed on his forehead or hand the sign of the serpent (p. 218.10). What is the *frumentum caducitatis*? The Latin word *caducitas* is not recorded in the lexica and was obviously invented by the translator. The sense requires grain related to something that has fallen. Now the Syriac term *kātha̱*, *kā'tha̱* means *frumentum quod crevit e granis, quae in priore messe exciderant*,[14] and Ephraem, one of Pseudo-Ephraem's models,[15] frequently uses the compound *kākātha̱*,[16] meaning "the uncultivated produce of the second year."[17] This is exactly what Pseudo-Ephraem seems to have meant by *frumentum caducitatis*.

4. One effect of the drought and famine prevailing during the reign of the Antichrist is, according to Pseudo-Ephraem, the deaths of children and women (p. 218.7):

*Et tabescent filii in sinu matrum suarum, et coniuges super genua uirorum suorum, non habentibus escas ad comedendum.* (And sons will waste away on their mothers' bosom, and wives on their husbands' knees, from having no food to eat.)

While it is not difficult to see why sons should be expected to perish at their mothers' bosoms, the statement that wives should die on the knees of their husbands is ridiculous. Contrast the parallel passage from Ephraem's genuine works cited by Caspari, p. 450:

Τότε ἐκλίπῃ τὰ νήπια ἐν τοῖς κόλποις τῶν μητέρων, θνῄσκει πάλιν μήτηρ ὑπεράνω τοῦ παιδίου, θνῄσκει πάλιν πατὴρ σὺν γυναικὶ καὶ τέκνοις ἐν ταῖς ἀγοραῖς. (Then infants will die on the bosoms of their mothers, a mother will die over her child, and a father will die with his wife and children in the public squares.)[18]

---

13. Nöldeke, *Syrische Grammatik*, p. 157.
14. Carl Brockelmann, *Lexicon Syriacum* (Halle a.S., 1928), p. 351a.
15. Caspari 445–52.
16. Payne Smith, *Thesaurus Syriacus* I (Oxford, 1849); Brockelmann, *Lexicon Syriacum*, p. 351b.
17. R. Payne Smith, *A Compendious Syriac Dictionary* (Cambridge, England, 1903), p. 230; cf. Isaiah 37:30.
18. Assemani, *S.P.N. Ephraem Syri opera omnia, graeca* (Rome, 1743), II, pp. 227f.

One expects a misunderstanding of the model. The word for *knee* in Syriac is *beru<u>kh</u>, burkā*, plural *burkē*, which can also mean *genuflectio*,[19] while the kindred *burke<u>th</u>a*, plural *burkāh, burka<u>th</u>ā*, and *burā<u>kh</u>ā*, plural *burā<u>kh</u>ē*, mean *blessing*. The word *blessings* thus differs from *knees* only by the consonant *t* or even merely by one vowel, depending on which of the two synonyms for *blessings* is chosen. I suggest, then, that *super genua* is a misunderstanding of a Syriac original meaning that wives died while their husbands blessed (them).[20]

The conclusion that Pseudo-Ephraem composed the homily in the Syriac language does not exclude the possibility that the Latin translation was made from a Greek original (itself a translation from the Syriac). Caspari, p. 459, already pointed to a transitive use of the verb *aridare* (p. 218.4): it is always intransitive in Latin, but ξηραίνειν or ἀναξηραίνειν is transitive. But this could also be explained by the Syriac *ṣaf* = *arefecit*, transitive, attested for Ephraem Syrus.[21]

When was the original of Pseudo-Ephraem composed? All that is certain is, as Caspari pointed out, that it must have been written prior to Heraclius' victories over Sassanid Persia,[22] for the author talks repeatedly of wars between Rome and Persia (pp. 209.4, 210.1) and such discussions do not make sense after Heraclius' victories and the beginning of the Arab invasions. Unfortunately, it is difficult to establish an earlier *terminus ante quem*. Caspari hesitated between a date late in the fourth century and one in the second part of the sixth or early seventh century, but finally decided in favor of the later date. He pointed out that a passage in the first chapter of the homily fitted the joint reign of the brothers Valentinian and Valens (364–375) and no other period. The passage in question as published by Caspari runs as follows:

In those days two brothers come to the Roman Empire. They preside over it with one mind, but because one of them precedes the other a rupture [division?] will occur between them. Therefore the Adversary will be released and will stir up hatred between the kingdoms of the Persians and Romans.[23]

---

19. Payne Smith, *Dictionary*, p. 613.
20. The *super* = ʿal is bothersome. Can it mean "during, while"? Cf. Payne Smith, *Thesaurus Syriacus* II, 2886; closest meaning *pro* in Lev. 7:12.
21. Cf. Brockelmann, *Lexicon Syriacum*, p. 634a. Add: 216.11 (*sicut dicitur in psalmo*). *Dicitur* emendation of Caspari; codd.: *dicit*. Normal λέγει (sc. ἡ γραφή); cf. Greek patristic texts, New Testament. There is not much evidence for this, but it is not an impossible reading.
22. Caspari 626–28.
23. Pseudo-Ephraem, pp. 209.8–210.2: *In illis diebus ueniunt ad regnum Romanum duo fratres, et uno quidem animo praesunt, sed quoniam unus praecedit alium, fiet inter eos scidium. Soluitur itaque aduersarius et excitabit odium inter regna Persarum et Romanorum.*

According to Caspari, these two brothers "come to the Roman Empire in the sense that they become emperors. Valentinian preceded Valens because he was elected by the army on 26 February 364 while the latter was designated co-emperor only on 28 March of the same year. They ruled harmoniously but divided the Empire between them and during their rule the enmity between Rome and Persia that had been dormant since Julian's death erupted once again into warfare around A.D. 373."[24] Caspari, however, did not think that the homily containing this passage was itself composed during the reign of Valentinian and Valens. In that case it would constitute a *vaticinium ex eventu*, but there is no other instance of such a practice in the homily. Caspari therefore concludes, after many hesitations that are not always easy to follow, that Pseudo-Ephraem is here citing an old *vaticinium*. It appealed to him because he lived at a time when Romans and Persians were at war with each other; he considered this a fulfillment of the ancient prediction, and was not disturbed by the fact that the passage about the two brothers, which was part of the *vaticinium*, did not fit the present situation. In conclusion, Caspari argued for a date in the fifth, the sixth, or the final decades of the seventh century.[25]

Bousset, on the other hand, opted for the earlier date (ca. A.D. 373), largely on the grounds that the supposed reference to the brothers Valentinian and Valens and to the outbreak of a war with the Persians occurs precisely in the parenetic, not the apocalyptic, part of the homily and that here the author talks in his own name and of his own time.[26] Other scholars have pronounced in favor of the early or the late date without advancing important new arguments.[27] It will indeed not be easy to decide on the matter.

I begin with a critical remark concerning the passage about the "two brothers" that has played such an important role in the issue.[28] There are several textual variants and difficulties, but the only one that matters for the exegesis concerns the words printed by Caspari, *inter eos scidium*. Here the Vaticanus has *inos discidit*, with a letter, possibly *e*, written over the uncertain letters *-os*. The St. Gallen manuscript has

---

24. Caspari 438f. In reality hostilities with Persia over Armenia began as early as 371: see Stein, *Histoire du Bas-Empire*, I, p. 187.

25. Caspari 438–43, esp. 443n.1 and 472.

26. Bousset, *Antichrist*, pp. 20f.

27. For the early date see, for example, Franz Kampers, *Kaiserprophetien und Kaisersagen im MA* (München, 1895), pp. 218–20. For the later date, see Sackur, *Sibyllinische Texte*, 93n.3; Hemmerdinger-Iliadou, "Ephrem," pp. 800–819, esp. 817; Dekkers-Gaar, *Clavis Patrum Latinorum*, no. 1144.

28. See above at n. 23.

*inter eis scidium*, the Augiensis *inter eis scędium* (with the *e* being uncertain). Caspari noted that *scidium*, which he thought meant rupture or division, did not occur in the lexica. Furthermore, it should be noted that the *eos* in his text is the result of an emendation. A more satisfactory emendation would be *inter e‹os d›iscidium*, based on a combination of all four manuscripts. It has the advantage that *discidium* (an emendation based on the Vaticanus) is a well-known Latin word meaning parting, separation, or dissension.

Second, Pseudo-Ephraem's data on the two brothers are indeed, as Caspari and everybody else has assumed, reconcilable with the joint reign of Valentinian and Valens, but this is by no means the only possibility.[29] Could they not equally well refer to Arcadius and Honorius? At the death of their father, Theodosius, they were aged 18 and 11 respectively. The *discidium* between them might well be a reference to one of the conflicts between Stilicho and the Eastern government; and although no war with Persia was fought during their reign, there was great fear of such a development in 399, at the time of the accession of a new Persian king, Yesdegerd I the Sinner(?).[30] Or could the author, who was certainly writing prior to 630, have been envisaging future conflicts between the sons of Heraclius (†641) from his first and second wives, Constantine III and Heraclonas?[31] None of these alternative explanations of the passage can be proved, but they may serve to show the weakness of previous attempts to date Pseudo-Ephraem's work principally on the basis of this passage.

It will, therefore, be advisable to look elsewhere for evidence on the date of the work. Here the prophecy of an invasion by *gentes bellicae* or *nequissimae* is illuminating (ch. 4). On the one hand, Pseudo-Ephraem, in order to illustrate the panic into which mankind will be thrown by their attack, observes that in those days men will not be buried, neither Christians nor heretics nor Jews nor pagans. This fourfold religious division of mankind cannot have been written long after the end of the fourth century, for after the defeat of Eugenius at the river Frigidus by Theodosius I in 394, paganism ceased to be a significant political factor in the Roman Empire.[32] Yet another passage in the same chapter points

---

29. I have wondered whether the phrase *ueniunt ad regnum Romanum* really means that two brothers will become emperors, especially as the word *praesunt* is again an emendation of Caspari's for the unusual *praefiunt* of the mss. Could it refer instead to a pair of foreigners entering the Roman Empire? This is, however, unlikely, for the parting or dissension of the brothers has public consequences (*itaque*, p. 210.1), i.e., the development of hatred between the Persian and Roman states.

30. Stein, *Histoire du Bas-Empire*, Vol. I, p. 235.

31. G. Ostrogorsky, *History of the Byzantine State* (New Brunswick, 1969), pp. 113–15. Enmity of Jews (210.3) would fit particularly well into the seventh century.

32. Stein, *Histoire du Bas-Empire*, I, pp. 217f.

almost certainly to a much later period. Pseudo-Ephraem calls the invading peoples "most vile" (*nequissimae*), "most wicked" (*profanissimae*), "foul" (*coinquinatae*). He says that they look like wild beasts rather than human beings, that they feed on human carcasses (*caro morticina*), drink the blood of beasts of burden, and in general defile the earth and taint everything. None of these features is derived from the accounts of Gog and Magog in the books of Ezekiel and Revelation. They are, however, familiar from what Arturo Graf called "the epic legend" of Gog and Magog.[33] There the uncleanness of Gog and Magog and the foul practices of those peoples serve as a reason for Alexander the Great's imprisoning them behind powerful gates so as to prevent their ravaging the civilized world prior to the last times. Neither Alexander nor his gate is mentioned by Pseudo-Ephraem, but his insistence on the uncleanness of the invaders can only have the purpose of motivating their imprisonment. It follows that this passage was written at a time when the biblical data on Gog and Magog had merged with the Alexander legend or were on the point of doing so. Now, according to Graf this merger is not attested prior to the seventh century: in the Koran, in Pseudo-Methodius, in recension λ of Pseudo-Callisthenes, and in a Syriac legend of Alexander.[34] But Graf was wrong. The Syriac legend of Alexander published by E. A. W. Budge already has the feature, as does a poem by Jacob of Sarug also published by him.[35] And Jacob died in A.D. 521.[36] The reference to uncleanness is unlikely to have developed prior to the invasion of the Huns in the first half of the fifth century. It appears, therefore, that ch. 4 of Pseudo-Ephraem is a mosaic of fragments of very different date: the fourfold subdivision of mankind still belongs to the fourth century or at least not much later: the uncleanness of the invaders dates from the seventh century or a period not much earlier. The work as a whole must therefore not have received its final form until the late sixth or early seventh century, as Caspari had thought.

---

33. Arturo Graf, *Roma nella memoria e nelle immaginazioni del Medio Evo* II (2nd ed. Torino, 1923), pp. 517–35.

34. Earliest testimony of merger: Koran sura 18 (cf. 21). Other evidence: Pseudo-Methodius, fol. 134 verso–135 recto; see appendix to Chapter I above; Pseudo-Callisthenes, ed. Helmut Van Thiel, *Die Rezension λ des Pseudo-Kallisthenes* (Bonn, 1959), pp. 51.10–55.16.

35. E. A. W. Budge, *The History of Alexander the Great, Being the Syriac Version of Pseudo-Callisthenes* (Cambridge, England, 1889). Jacob of Sarug's poem edited by E. A. W. Budge is in *Zeitschrift für Assyriologie* 6 (1891), pp. 357–404.

36. See Th. Nöldeke, "Beiträge zur Geschichte des Alexanderromans," *Denkschriften der Kaiserlichen Akademie der Wissenschaften, philosophisch-historische Klasse* 38, 5 (1890), pp. 31f.

PART TWO
# Themes

# I.
# The Last Roman Emperor

The expectation of a Last Roman (i.e., Byzantine) Emperor plays a key role in Byzantine (as well as in Western) apocalyptic, but—strangely, in view of the importance of the concept—so far the Byzantine material has neither been collected in systematic fashion nor has its historical development been studied.[1] Preliminarily and for the purposes of this discussion, the concept of a Last Roman Emperor may be defined as the prediction that at the end of time a Roman Emperor would surrender his imperial office and power to God and would thus put an end to the existence of the Roman Empire. The act of surrender invariably follows upon the discharge, by the Emperor, of the principal function assigned to him by tradition, the decisive defeat of a hostile army, and expresses

---

1. The existing discussions of the expectation of a Last Emperor either approach the concept from the point of view of its role in German history and legend or in connection with specific medieval texts. I mention only a few studies because they touch, more or less fully, on Late Roman and Byzantine views (further bibliography for Western notions may be found in Marjorie Reeves, "Joachimist Influences on the Idea of a Last World Emperor," *Traditio* 17 [1961], pp. 323–70, esp. 323n.1): Gerhard von Zezschwitz, *Das Drama vom Ende des römischen Kaisertums deutscher Nation und von der Erscheinung des Antichrist* (Leipzig, 1880); Bousset, *Der Antichrist*; F. Kampers, *Die deutsche Kaiseridee in Prophetie und Sage* (München, 1896); Sackur, *Sibyllinische Texte*; Bousset, "Beiträge zur Geschichte der Eschatologie"; Cyril Mango, "The Legend of Leo the Wise." The most important of these titles are still those of Bousset and Sackur, but it is surprising that Bousset, in his profound and comprehensive study of the legend of the Antichrist, mentioned the latter's counterpart, the Last Emperor, only incidentally (*Antichrist*, pp. 29f., 38, 55, 82f., and "Beiträge," pp. 261–90) and thereby failed to push his inquiry into its origins as far as he might otherwise have done. [Alexander's ideas on the origins of the Last Roman Emperor motif, especially in Pseudo-Methodius, were developed in an article that appeared after his death: "The Medieval Legend of the Last Roman Emperor and Its Messianic Origin."]

the notion that by this defeat all political authority has lost its raison d'être. Because of this essential relationship between military victory and surrender of power, it will be legitimate to speak of a Last Roman Emperor even where in the process of revision of earlier apocalyptic texts only the victory over the national enemy survives in its standard form, while the act of surrender has been replaced by other materials.

The most usual designation of the Last Roman Emperor in the Byzantine sources is simply as Emperor or King (βασιλεύς, rex), either alone or followed by a qualification of the people over whom he rules: Greeks, Romans, or both.[2] The Latin Sibyl is alone in giving him a name, Constans, and the eleventh of the *Oracles of Leo* refers to him as ὁ ἠλειμμένος ἐπώνυμος Μεναχείμ.[3] A metaphor used in the *Visions of Daniel* for the Last Roman Emperor is that of the Lion.[4]

When the Last Roman Emperor is first mentioned in Byzantine apocalyptic texts, the circumstances are always to some extent supernatural. In the Latin version of the Tiburtine Sibyl it is said that "he will arise" (*surget*). In the Syriac Pseudo-Methodius "he will go forth" against the Arabs and "will be awakened [aroused] against them like a man who shakes off his wine, one who plots against them [Arabs] as if they were dead." The first part of this prediction reproduces Psalm 78:65 where the expressed subject is "the Lord." In other words, the Syriac Pseudo-Methodius expected the Last Roman Emperor to fulfill the Psalmist's

---

2. Latin version of the Tiburtine Sibyl: *rex Grecorum* (p. 185.1), *rex Romanorum et Grecorum* (185.2), *rex* (185.8); *rex Romanorum* (186.5). Syriac Pseudo-Methodius: king of the Greeks (throughout); Greek Pseudo-Methodius βασιλεὺς Ἑλλήνων ἤτοι Ῥωμαίων (40.1 = pp. 122.56 Lolos); βασιλεὺς Ῥωμαίων (41.9; 42.1, 12; 45.1, 11, 14 = p. 124.65, 68, 126.79, 130.112, 132.7, 10 Lolos); Slavonic Daniel: emperor (throughout). Pseudo-Chrysostom ὁ βασιλεύς (37.1). Daniel Καὶ ἔσται: βασιλεύς (39.34); ὁ βασιλεὺς τῶν Ῥωμαίων (40.6).

3. Name Constans: p. 185. 1 Sackur. *Oracula Leonis*, PG 107.1137 A. The designation ὁ ἠλειμμένος was introduced by the Jewish translator of the Bible, Aquila, to avoid the synonym ὁ χριστός, which by that time had been monopolized by the Christians. The name Μεναχείμ (= the Comforter) also is of Late Jewish origin; cf. Bousset, "Beiträge," p. 287, and Bousset-Gressmann, *Religion des Judentums*, p. 227. It should be noted that *Oraculum* 11, in which this verse occurs, differs from all the other oracles by the fact that it is prose rather than verse and that the passage about ὁ ἠλειμμένος, without the reference to Μεναχείμ, is cited in the *Cento of the True Emperor* (PG 107.1141.18).

4. In the (lost) Greek model of *Slavonic Daniel* the word λέων (lion) was corrupted into κύων (dog); cf. #7: "And then there will be fulfilled the saying that dog and whelp together will pursue the field" (τὸν ἀγρόν [field], corruption for τὸν ὄναγρον [ass]); Pseudo-Chrysostom, p. 36.34 καὶ τότε πληρωθήσεται ἡ προφητεία ἡ λέγουσα ὅτι κύων καὶ σκύμνος διώξουσιν ἀγρόν (same corruptions, ὁμοῦ omitted); Daniel Καὶ ἔσται p. 39.32 καὶ πληρωθήσεται ὅτι λέων καὶ σκύμνος ὁμοῦ διώξουσιν ἀγρόν (ἀγρόν again a corruption of ὄναγρον; the word is missing in Vasiliev's edition, but it is clearly legible in the only manuscript, Cod. Vat. Barb. Gr. 284, fol. 144 verso); Pseudo-Hippolytus in Liudprand of Cremona *Legatio* 40: *Ait enim nunc complεtum iri scripturam, quae dicit*: λέων καὶ σκίμνος ὁμοδιώξουσιν ὄναγρον.

verse about the Lord.⁵ By changing the verbal form, he transformed the Psalmist's statement of fact into a prophecy and, by interpolating a word ("against them"), clarified the notion clearly expressed in the second half of the verse (which Pseudo-Methodius omitted)—that the Emperor will act against an enemy. He also added an explanatory phrase of his own: "One who will plot against them as if they were dead." The purpose of this addition presumably was to emphasize the Emperor's boldness and his confidence in his mission: although his enemies are still alive—in fact, resisting—his planning is based on the assumption that they are already dead.

The Greek translator of Pseudo-Methodius reproduced the first part of his model (based on Psalm 78:65) more or less faithfully, but chose to interpret the Syriac Pseudo-Methodius' addition in a way that, though syntactically possible, yields little sense. He translated:

There then will suddenly arise against them [Ismaelites] with great fury an emperor of the Greeks or Romans. He will awaken from his sleep like a man who had drunk wine, whom men considered like one dead and utterly useless.⁶

The most important change the translator introduced was that he spoke of the Emperor resembling a dead person, while the Syriac original had characterized his enemies as being "like dead men." This change produced a contrast with the Emperor's "great fury" (he acted with extraordinary vigor in spite of his reputation for uselessness), a phrase the translator added, but it missed the Syriac author's notion that the enemies of the Emperor were as good as dead even before he set out on his campaign, and hence omitted an element of the Emperor's boldness. The Greek translator must himself have felt that his translation was less than satisfactory, for he added the thought that the Emperor was considered utterly useless, apparently an attempt to explain the meaning of his being considered "like one dead." The net effect of the Greek translator's changes was to enhance the aura of miracle that surrounded the Last Emperor: he seemed "like one dead and utterly useless," and yet he inflicted a decisive defeat on Rome's secular enemy, the Arabs.

---

5. Syriac Pseudo-Methodius, p. 22. Walton, ed., *Biblia Sacra Polyglotta*, III, p. 212, translates the Syriac text of the Psalm as follows: *exporrectus est dominus tamquam dormiens et quasi vir qui excussit vinum suum, percussit inimicos suos a tergo suo*. The application of this verse to the Last Roman Emperor is puzzling, as the Syriac word *mariā* ("the Lord") is used exclusively for God and Christ (cf. R. Payne Smith, *Thesaurus Syriacus* II [Oxford, 1901], pp. 2204f.). Cf. also n. 59 below.

6. P. 40.1 Istrin (= p. 122.12 Lolos) Τότε αἰφνιδίως ἐπαναστήσεται ἐπ' αὐτοὺς βασιλεὺς Ἑλλήνων ἤτοι Ῥωμαίων μετὰ μεγάλου θυμοῦ καὶ ἐξυπνισθήσεται καθάπερ ἄνθρωπος ἀπὸ ὕπνου καθὼς πιὼν οἶνον, ὃν ἐλογίζοντο οἱ ἄνθρωποι ὡσεὶ νεκρὸν καὶ εἰς οὐδὲν χρησιμεύοντα.

In the form given to it by the Greek translator, the text of Pseudo-Methodius reached the Latin West.[7] In the *Visions of Daniel* the Psalmist's similes of sleeper and drinker are dropped but that of the dead man (and in some texts that of the useless person) are retained.[8] Here the miraculous character of the Emperor is further enhanced because he is discovered "by divine revelation."[9]

The Last Roman Emperor invariably appears on the scene in immediate response to a period of military defeats often accompanied by foreign domination. In the Latin version of the Tiburtine Sibyl, for example, the text speaks of battles, bloodshed, invasions, greed, and injustice, and twice stresses that there is no resistance to these tribulations. "And then there will arise a king of the Greeks whose name is Constans."[10] The Syriac Pseudo-Methodius establishes what then becomes the standard sequence. The Arab invasions and oppression reach their zenith when the conquerors say blasphemously: There is no redeemer (or savior, *perūqā*) for the Christians.

Then all of a sudden [*men teḥeit šeliā*] there will be awakened perdition and calamity . . . and a King of the Greeks will go forth against them in great wrath.

This sequence—zenith of Arab conquests and oppression/Arab blasphemy/sudden rise of Last Emperor—reappears in the Greek and Latin versions of Pseudo-Methodius and in the *Visions of Daniel*.[11] Its im-

---

7. Latin Pseudo-Methodius, p. 89.21 Sackur: *exiliet . . . et expergiscitur tamquam homo a somno vini, quem extimabunt homines tamquam mortuum esse et in nihilo utilem profecisse.*

8. *Slavonic Daniel* #6: "whom people considered a dead man"; Pseudo-Chrysostom, p. 36.17 ὃν εἶχον οἱ ἄνθρωποι ὡσεὶ νεκρὸν καὶ οὐδὲν χρησιμεύοντα [whom men held as if a dead man and useful for nothing]; *Daniel* Καὶ ἔσται p. 39.21 ὃν ἐδόκουν οἱ ἄνθρωποι ὡς νεκρὸν εἶναι καὶ εἰς οὐδὲν χρησιμεύειν [whom men considered as being a dead man and useful for nothing].

9. *Slavonic Daniel* #6: "they [the inhabitants of a Rebel City] will set forth secretly . . . and find there someone by divine revelation. . . . They will anoint him forthwith emperor"; Pseudo-Chrysostom, p. 36.17 Τότε αἰφνιδίως ἐξέλθωσιν οἱ τῆς πόλεως ἐκείνης . . . καὶ εὑροῦσιν δι' ἀποκαλύψεως θεοῦ . . . ἄνθρωπόν τινα . . . κἀκεῖ χρίσουσιν αὐτὸν εἰς βασιλέα [Then they will secretly go out of that city . . . and through divine revelation will find . . . a man . . . and they will anoint him emperor there]; similarly *Daniel* Καὶ ἔσται p. 39.18.

10. Pp. 184f. Sackur.

11. Syriac Pseudo-Methodius, fol. 133 recto. Greek Pseudo-Methodius, p. 39.4 (= p. 120.33 Lolos): [The Ismaelites] βλασφημήσαντες ἐροῦσιν 'οὐκ ἔχουσιν ἀνάρρυσιν οἱ χριστιανοὶ ἐκ τῶν χειρῶν ἡμῶν.' Τότε αἰφνιδίως ἐπαναστήσεται ἐπ' αὐτοὺς βασιλεὺς Ἑλλήνων ἤτοι Ῥωμαίων μετὰ μεγάλου θυμοῦ [They will say blasphemously "the Christians have no safety from our hands." Then suddenly the king of the Greeks or Romans will arise against them with great anger]; Latin Pseudo-Methodius, p. 89.17 Sackur: *blasphemantes dicunt, quia nequaquam habebunt christiani ereptionem de manibus nostris. Tunc subito insurgent super eos tribulatio et angustia et exiliet super eos rex Gregorum siue Romanorum in furore magna* (the Syriac and Latin texts render it probable that in the Greek tradition the equivalent of *super eos tribulatio et angustia et exiliet*

plication is clear: God will refute the Ismaelite blasphemy, that the Christians have no savior, by sending precisely such a redeemer.

In addition to stating that the Last Roman Emperor will arise suddenly, by divine revelation, that he will be awakened as if from sleep, death, drunkenness, or uselessness, some apocalypses stress his humble origin. The *Slavonic Daniel*, for example, has a somewhat obscure passage according to which he is discovered "carrying two coins in order to receive crumbs." Pseudo-Chrysostom is more explicit: "His name is small in the world."[12] The *Apocalypse of St. Andrew* is clearest, for it knows of an Emperor "from poverty."[13]

The Syriac, Greek, and Latin versions of Pseudo-Methodius mention sons of the Last Emperor assisting him in his war against the Ismaelites.[14] This passage does not appear as such in the *Visions of Daniel*, but a trace of the notion survives in the expectation that in his battle against the Ismaelites the victorious Emperor will fulfill prophecy (to be discussed later, pp. 172ff.) according to which "Lion and Whelp together will pursue the Wild Ass."

One text only, the Latin version of the Tiburtine Sibyl, describes the Last Roman Emperor's physical appearance (just as this text is the only one to name him, Constans):

He will be tall of stature, handsome in appearance, his face bright and the lines of each of his limbs well-ordered in seemly fashion.[15]

Nothing whatsoever is said in any of the apocalypses about the Last Emperor's character and his moral or intellectual qualities, except what can be inferred from his activities. Nameless (except for the Latin Sibyl), without physical characteristics (except again for the Latin Sibyl) or other qualities, he remains a shadowy figure.

Among the functions assigned to him by far the most important is

---

has been inadvertently omitted). *Slavonic Daniel* #5 (blasphemy of Arabs) and #6 ("they will anoint him forthwith emperor"). Pseudo-Chrysostom, p. 36.16; *Daniel* Καὶ ἔσται, p. 39.18 (blasphemy of Arabs omitted, τότε αἰφνίδιον ἐξελεύσονται); also Apocalypse of St. Andrew, PG 111.856A (= p. 202 Rydén).

12. P. 36.19 Vasiliev εὑροῦσιν δι' ἀποκαλύψεως θεοῦ . . . ἄνθρωπόν τινα οὗτινος τὸ ὄνομα ἦν ἔλαττον ἐν τῷ κόσμῳ.

13. PG 111.853B (= p. 202 Rydén) Ἐν ταῖς ἐσχάταις ἡμέραις ἀναστήσει Κύριος ὁ θεὸς βασιλέα ἀπὸ πενίας [In the last days the Lord God will set up an emperor from poverty].

14. Syriac Pseudo-Methodius fol. 133 verso: "And the sons of the king of Greece will seize the places of the desert and will destroy with the sword the remnant that is left of them in the land of promise"; cf. Greek Pseudo-Methodius, p. 41.4 Istrin (= p. 124.4 Lolos); Latin Pseudo-Methodius, p. 90.3 Sackur.

15. P. 185.2 Sackur: *Hic erit statura grandis, aspectu decorus, vultu splendidus atque per singula membrorum liniamenta decenter conpositus.*

warfare against non-Christians. In the Latin version of the Tiburtine Sibyl his acts are said to be inspired by a "scriptural" saying: "Let the king of the Romans claim for himself the entire kingdom [empire] of the Christians."[16] Strangely, although this citation seems to limit the Emperor to Christian territories, it is said immediately afterward that he will destroy islands, cities, and temples of pagans. He will summon all pagans to baptism, and the Cross will be set up in all their temples. All those refusing to worship the Cross will be punished, and after one hundred and twenty years the Jews will be converted. The Emperor's warfare thus carries a definite missionary or crusading stamp. A similar "great zeal" against non-Christians distinguishes the Emperor "from poverty" in the *Apocalypse of St. Andrew*, but here it is coupled with a puritanical attitude against any kind of "immorality": he will pursue the Jews and will banish from Constantinople all Ismaelites (Arabs), all players of the lyre, all actors, and any practitioners of shameful activities.[17] In the Latin version of the Tiburtine Sibyl the Last Emperor is given the task of waging war not only against pagans but also against the hosts of Gog and Magog, a function reserved, in later apocalypses, to an angel.[18]

Beginning with the Syriac Pseudo-Methodius, the pagans disappear as the target of the Last Emperor's warfare, and the Jews are mentioned only rarely in this connection. The Ismaelites (Arabs, later Turks) take the place of the pagans, undoubtedly because paganism was then no longer a problem and because Islam and the Arabs have become the all-important military and religious enemies of the Emperor. The Last Roman Emperor is therefore, as we have seen, cast in the role of the "redeemer" or "savior" of the Empire from the Ismaelites. In all the apocalypses he sets out against them "with great fury" immediately after the apocalyptists have recorded their blasphemous boast: The Christians have no redeemer (savior) from our hands.[19] The Syriac Pseudo-Methodius and its Greek and Latin translations describe in great detail the Last Emperor's military exploits against the Ismaelites. He will set out against them

---

16. P. 185.8 Sackur: *Et ipse rex scripturam habebit ante oculos dicentem: Rex Romanorum omne sibi vindicet regnum Christianorum.* On this citation see p. 172 below.

17. *PG* 111.856B (= p. 203 Rydén) Καὶ ἔσται αὐτῷ ζῆλος μέγας, καὶ τοὺς Ἰουδαίους καταδιώξει, καὶ ἐν τῇ πόλει ταύτῃ Ἰσμαηλίτης οὐχ εὑρεθήσεται· καὶ αὐτὸς φοβήσει μεγάλως τὴν πόλιν, καὶ οὐκ ἔσται ὁ λυρίζων ἢ κιθαρίζων ἢ ὁ τραγῳδῶν, ἤ τις αἰσχρὸν πρᾶγμα ἐργαζόμενος· πάντας γὰρ τοὺς τοιούτους μισήσει καὶ ἐξολοθρεύσει ἐκ πόλεως Κυρίου. [And he will have great zeal, and will pursue the Jews, and no Ismaelite will be found in this city. And he will terrify the city, and there will be no playing the lyre or playing the kithara or acting, or anyone performing a shameful activity. For he will hate all such people, and he will expel them from the city of the Lord].

18. P. 186.4 Sackur.

19. Cf. p. 175 and n. 11 above.

from the "sea of the Cushites" (the Red Sea), will carry the warfare to the Ismaelites' own country, to the desert of Jethrib (Medina), will liberate the "land of promise" (Palestine), will annihilate, capture, or otherwise vanquish and harass them, and will repatriate Christian exiles and prisoners.[20] The conflict with the Ismaelites retains the character of a war against the enemies of the Christian religion that was assigned in the Latin version of the Tiburtine Sibyl, for all three versions of Pseudo-Methodius insist that the Emperor's ire will be directed against those who deny Christ.[21]

The *Visions of Daniel* add rich detail on the decisive victory of Romans over Ismaelites. It will take place at a place called Perton (or Petrinon or Partēnē) and a well or cistern with two openings will play a part in this battle.[22] *Daniel Καὶ ἔσται* speaks in addition of a second victory of the Last Emperor over the Ismaelites at the Well of Jacob in which, curiously, both Ismaelites and Emperor call upon the Lord to grant them victory.[23] The text then continues with a (heavenly) order to the Emperor to summon birds and land animals, to eat the flesh of men, and to drink the blood of the impious. The passage is taken, with some variants, from the Greek Pseudo-Methodius, where it occurs in a different context and goes back ultimately to Ezekiel's prophecy of the de-

---

20. Syriac Pseudo Methodius, fol. 133 recto and verso; Greek Pseudo-Methodius, pp. 40–42 Istrin (= pp. 122–26 Lolos); Latin Pseudo-Methodius, pp. 89f. Sackur.

21. Syriac Pseudo-Methodius, fol. 133 verso: "And all the wrath of the ire of the king of the Greeks will be completed upon those denied"; Greek Pseudo-Methodius, p. 42.12 Istrin (= p. 126.9 Lolos) καὶ πᾶς ὁ θυμὸς τοῦ βασιλέως τῶν Ῥωμαίων καὶ ὀργὴ ἐπὶ τοὺς ἀρνησαμένους τὸν Κύριον ἡμῶν Ἰησοῦν Χριστόν [and all the anger and rage of the Roman emperor [will be] toward those who deny our Lord Jesus Christ]. Latin Pseudo-Methodius, p. 91.4 Sackur.

22. *Slavonic Daniel* #6: "He [Last Emperor] will meet the Ismaelites in a place called Perton and will fight a fierce battle. And there is in that place a well with two mouths so that the blood of Romans and Ismaelites will be mingled"; Pseudo-Chrysostom, p. 36.24 Vasiliev οὗτος ἐξελεύσεται εἰς τοὺς Ἰσμαηλίτας ἐν τόπῳ τινὶ λεγομένῳ Πετρίνῳ καὶ συγκροτήσουσιν πόλεμον ἰσχυρόν. ἐν δὲ τῷ τόπῳ ἐκείνῳ ἐστιν φρέαρ δίστομον κἀκεῖ συγκόψονται ἀλλήλους ὥστε ἐκ τῶν αἱμάτων τῶν Ῥωμαίων καὶ τῶν Ἰσμαηλιτῶν μεστὸν γενέσθαι τὸ φρέαρ· [He will go out against the Ismaelites in a place called Petrinon and they will wage a violent battle. In that place is a cistern with two openings and there they will cut each other down so that the cistern becomes filled with the blood of the Romans and the Ismaelites]. *Daniel Καὶ ἔσται* p. 39.24 Vasiliev ἐξελεύσεται δὲ κατόπισθεν τῶν Ἰσμαηλιτῶν ἐν ὄχλῳ ἐκείνῳ καὶ συνάψωσιν πόλεμον ἐν τόπῳ Παρτηνῆς, οἷος οὐ γέγονεν ἀπὸ καταβολῆς κόσμου, ὥστε ἐκ τῶν αἱμάτων τῶν Ἰσμαηλιτῶν καὶ τῶν Ῥωμαίων ἵππον ἐπιβατούμενον ἀποθανεῖν. [He will go out after the Ismaelites in that great mob and they will join in battle in the place of Partēnē, such as has not taken place from the beginning of the world, so that a mounted horse would die from the blood of the Ismaelites and the Romans]. Similar passages were interpolated into the Greek Pseudo-Methodius. There the battle takes place either in the plain of Gersion or in a place called Gephyra (Bridge); cf. Istrin's edition p. 40n.5 (line 4) of apparatus (= p. 124n.58 Lolos). The material has been collected and arranged in intelligible and convenient form by Bousset, "Beiträge," pp. 261–81.

23. Pp. 39.34–40.10 Vasiliev.

feat of Gog.²⁴ The episode in *Daniel* Καὶ ἔσται thus shows that the Last Emperor's victories over the Ismaelites in the Pseudo-Methodian tradition are a demythologized adaptation of his traditional victory over Gog and Magog, as described, for example, in the Latin version of the Tiburtine Sibyl (p. 156 above).

In Pseudo-Hippolytus, whose (lost) *Vision of Daniel* was composed, as has been shown (Part One, Ch. IV above), in the late ninth century, the task of defeating the Ismaelites is assigned to a Western people and ruler rather than to a Roman (Byzantine) emperor.²⁵ Pseudo-Hippolytus is probably also a source of Adso's statement that a last king of the Franks will go to Jerusalem and lay down scepter and crown on the Mount of Olives.²⁶ The prophecy of the Erythraean Sibyl of "a very strong lion from the West" who will weaken the Beast (Islam) and perhaps partially that of the Cumaean Sibyl, where the victorious emperor will proceed from Byzantium but may be a descendant of Henry IV, express the same notion that the great counterattack upon Islam will come from the West.²⁷

It is not immediately clear whether in origin the role assigned to the Last Roman Emperor in some Byzantine apocalyptic texts, of bringing peace, abundance, and economic prosperity, is related to his military functions. The Latin version of the Tiburtine Sibyl, for example, predicts that during his reign

there will be much wealth and the earth will yield fruit in abundance so that a measure of wheat will be sold for one denarius, a measure of wine for one denarius, and a measure of oil for one denarius.²⁸

A tantalizingly obscure passage in the Greek version of the Sibyl may also express the notion of the Last Emperor's being responsible for the

---

24. P. 26.12 Istrin (= p. 96.8 Lolos). There the Ismaelites defeat the Romans at Gabaon; cf. Ezek. 39:17.

25. Cf. Liudprand of Cremona *Legatio* ch. 43, p. 198.15 Becker: *Scribit etiam praefatus Hippolytus Grecos non debere Saracenos, sed Francos conterere.* Cf. ch. 44, p. 196.11: *Sed Hippolytus . . . eadem scripsit et de imperio vestro et gente nostra etc.*

26. P. 110.10 Sackur: *Quidam vero doctores nostri dicunt, quod unus ex regibus Francorum Romanum imperium ex integro tenebit. . . . Et ipse erit maximus et omnium regum ultimus. Qui postquam regnum feliciter gubernaverit, ad ultimum Ierosolimam veniet et in monte Oliveti sceptrum et coronam suam deponet.*

27. Erythraean Sibyl, p. 163.3 Holder-Egger: *Porro leo fortissimus ab occidente rugiet. . . . Irruet in bestiam et conteret vires eius*; Cumaean Sibyl, p. 398.17 Erdmann: *De illo* [Henry IV] *tunc debet rex procedere de Bizantio . . . qui subiciet filios Ismahel.* Cf. Erdmann's comments, p. 402.

28. P. 185.5 Sackur: *In illis ergo diebus erunt divitiae multe et terra abundanter dabit fructum ita ut tritici modium denario uno venundetur, modium vini denario uno, modium olei denario uno.* This passage is clearly related to Rev. 6:6, where at the opening of the third seal a heavenly voice announces that the price of a quart (χοῖνιξ) of wheat has reached a denarius, as has the price for three quarts of barley, but that oil and wine are not (should not be?) affected by this inflation.

well-being of his subjects. The author mentions, immediately preceding the rise of the Antichrist, an emperor from the East called Olibos who "will grant an exemption from the payment of public taxes and will renew all the peoples of the entire East and of Palestine."[29] In the later texts, peace, economic prosperity, and popular rejoicing are represented as consequences of the Last Roman Emperor's victories over the Ismaelites. The Syriac Pseudo-Methodius, for example, predicts that after the victory but prior to the onslaught of Gog and Magog

> the earth will be at peace ... and men will multiply like locusts ... and there will be peace on earth the like of which never existed because it is the last peace of the perfection of the world. And there will be joy upon the entire earth, and men will sit down in great peace and the churches will arise anew, and cities will be built and priests will be freed from the tax, and priests and men will rest at that time from labor and tiredness and torture ... and men will sit down in repose and will eat and drink and rejoice in the gladness of their heart.[30]

The passage recurs, with minor variants, in the Greek and Latin versions of Pseudo-Methodius and in two *Visions of Daniel*.[31] The *Apocalypse of St. Andrew the Fool* represents, in this respect as in others, a conflation of earlier traditions, for there prosperity both precedes and follows the victory of the Emperor "from poverty" over the sons of Hagar (Arabs). Prior to the war "he will put an end to all warfare, will enrich the poor, and the years will be as at the time of Noah," while, after his victory, "Illyricum will be restored to the Roman Empire, Egypt will pay its agreed tribute, and in the twelfth year of his rule he [the Emperor "from poverty"] will not take poll tax and gifts."[32]

---

29. *Oracle of Baalbek*, line 186, my edition: καὶ μετὰ ταῦτα ἀναστήσεται ἄλλος βασιλεὺς ἀπὸ 'Ανατολῆς, οὗτινος τὸ ὄνομά ἐστι †'Ολιβός . . . καὶ δώσει ἀτέλειαν τοῦ μὴ παρασχέσθαι δημόσιον τέλος καὶ ἀνανεώσει πάντας τοὺς λαοὺς τῆς 'Ανατολῆς πάσης καὶ τῆς Παλαιστίνης [And after that another emperor will arise from the East, whose name is Olibos(?). . . . And he will grant an exemption from paying a public tax and will restore all the people of the entire East and of Palestine]. Cf. my comments at 112n.50, 126n.15; *Oracles of Leo* 8.13 (1136B) Δράκοντα συρίξουσι τὸν λιβοκτόνον [They will hiss at the serpent that kills Lips(?)] *Cento of the True Emperor* (1141.13) Παρακολουθήσει δὲ οὗτος [the True Emperor] ἐν ταῖς ἡμέραις τοῦ λιβός [He will follow in the days of Lips(?)].
30. Syriac Pseudo-Methodius, fols. 133 verso–134 recto.
31. Greek Pseudo-Methodius, p. 42.5–44.1 Istrin (= pp. 126.73–128.95 Lolos); Latin Pseudo-Methodius p. 91.6–21 Sackur; *Slavonic Daniel* #9 (drastically shortened); *Daniel Καὶ ἔσται* p. 41.12–26 Vasiliev. It is omitted by Pseudo-Chrysostom.
32. PG 111.853B (p. 202 Rydén) πάντα πόλεμον παύσει [the βασιλεὺς ἀπὸ πενίας] . . . καὶ τοὺς πένητας πλουτίσει, καὶ ἔσται ὡς ἐπὶ τοῦ Νῶε τὰ ἔτη . . . ; 856A καὶ ἀποκαταστήσεται πάλιν τὸ Ἰλλύρικον τῇ βασιλείᾳ 'Ρωμαίων, κομίσει δὲ καὶ ἡ Αἴγυπτος τὰ πάκτα αὐτῆς . . . τῷ δωδεκάτῳ ἔτει τῆς βασιλείας αὐτοῦ κῆνσον καὶ δόματα οὐ λήψεται. It is plausible that a Byzantine victory over the Arabs might restore tribute payments from Egypt, but the return of Illyricum depended on Byzantium's relations with the Slavic world rather than with the Arabs. Did the author of the *Apocalypse of St. Andrew* connect the Emperor ἀπὸ πενίας with the victories over the Slavs in the Balkan Penin-

In this connection it is worth noting that several other Byzantine apocalypses, beginning with the Greek Pseudo-Methodius, refer to Matt. 24:37f.:

As were the days of Noah, so will be the coming of the Son of Man. For as in those days before the Flood they were eating and drinking, marrying and giving in marriage, until the day when Noah entered the Ark. . . . So will be the coming of the Son of Man

and related texts and thus represent this Last Roman Emperor as the restorer of human prosperity at the time of Noah and prior to the Flood.[33]

In one of the *Visions of Daniel*, moreover, several new features follow from this picture of peace, abundance, and economic prosperity after a victorious war. In the first place, there will be a concern for justice. According to *Daniel Καὶ ἔσται*, the Last Emperor "will sell officials for two pieces of silver . . . and there will be none either to do or suffer injustice."[34]

According to the author of the *Apocalypse of St. Andrew the Fool*, under the Emperor "from poverty"

there will no longer be lawsuits, wrongdoers or wronged. . . . And there will then be much joy and exultation; the land and the sea will produce goods and wealth, and men will live in joy and free from worry as they did at the time of Noah prior to the Flood.[35]

Second, according to certain texts, the new wealth will be used by the Last Roman Emperor to rebuild churches and to promote the cause of religion and orthodoxy.[36]

---

sula? [See the discussion of this text ("The *Andreas Salos Apocalypse*"), and Alexander's refutation of Wortley's attempt to associate the passage with the reign of Michael III or Basil I in Ch. V.1 n.5)].

33. No explicit reference to a restoration of the Age of Noah occurs in the Syriac Pseudo-Methodius (fol. 134 recto), although the author describes the prosperity under the Last Emperor in the language of Matt. 24:37f. The verse is cited as a dominical saying in Greek Pseudo-Methodius, p. 43.7 Istrin (= p. 128.5 Lolos) ὁ Κύριος ἐν τῷ εὐαγγελίῳ; Latin Pseudo-Methodius, p. 91.15 Sackur; cf. also *Apocalypse of St. Andrew* 853B (= p. 201 Rydén) under the Emperor ἀπὸ πενίας: ἔσται ὡς ἐπὶ τῷ Νῶε τὰ ἔτη [it will be as in the years of Noah].

34. P. 41.20 Vasiliev πιπράσει δὲ ἄρχοντας ἐν δυσὶν ἀργυρίοις . . . καὶ οὐκ ἔσται ἢ ἀδικῶν ἢ ἀδικούμενος ἐν τοῖς καιροῖς ἐκείνοις.

35. *PG* 111.856B (= p. 203 Rydén) δίκη οὐκέτι ἔσται οὐδὲ ὁ ἀδικῶν οὔτε ὁ ἀδικούμενος. 856C καὶ ἔσται πολλὴ χαρὰ τότε καὶ ἀγαλλίασις. καὶ ἀγαθὰ ἀπὸ τῆς γῆς καὶ ἀπὸ τῆς θαλάσσης ἀνατελεῖ πλούσια, καὶ ἔσται [lege ἔσονται?] ὃν τρόπον ἦσαν ἐπὶ τοῦ Νῶε ἐν ἀμεριμνίᾳ εὐφραινόμενοι μέχρις οὗ ἦλθεν ὁ κατακλυσμός.

36. *Slavonic Daniel* #9: "And they will assemble pious men who fear God and seek retaliation for innocent blood and for the scoffing of the Church. And there will be talking

Finally, while in the various versions of Pseudo-Methodius' apocalypse the Last Roman Emperor is assisted by his sons in his warfare against the Ismaelites, the *Visions of Daniel* substitute for this intradynastic military aid an expedition of the Emperor to Rome which is described as having both a military and an economic aspect: he gains by it both allies and treasure. The *Slavonic Daniel* predicts that immediately after his victory over the Ismaelites the Last Roman Emperor will send his forces against the "Blond Peoples," will subdue them and, with their aid, will pursue the Arabs (into their own country?). He will then attack "Longobardia"—either those parts of southern Italy that had escaped Lombard domination (Otranto, Gaeta, Sorrento, and Amalfi), which were already threatened by the Arabs from North Africa and were late in the ninth century set up as a Byzantine theme by the emperor Leo VI, or southern Italy in general.[37] There he will discover a treasure of gold in a vessel hidden within a bronze idol and will distribute the gold to his troops. He will then march overland to the City of the Seven Hills, i.e., Constantinople, and enter it from the west.[38]

The story is told almost in the same words by Pseudo-Chrysostom, and is further embellished in *Daniel Καὶ ἔσται*.[39] There the military exploits of the Last Roman Emperor in Longobardia are omitted altogether. The idol (τὸ ζόδον, i.e., ζῳδίον) at Rome is shattered by his whip "like the dust on[?] a threshing floor in summertime." Nothing emerges from it but an evil spirit that escapes to the top of the Capitoline Hill, looks down on the city of Rome ([?]τὴν πόλιν Ῥωμανοῦ) and addresses her: Your daughter Byza has committed adultery. Although the incident of the treasure find is omitted, the Emperor is able to distribute gold, for

---

among the many [people] assembled. And the emperor will sit with them and they will discuss together. And the churches of the saints will be restored even in their images. And they will build the destroyed altars." Cf. *Daniel Καὶ ἔσται*, p. 41.19–21; *Apocalypse of St. Andrew the Fool*, PG 111.856B (= p. 203 Rydén). This feature, too, is missing in Pseudo-Chrysostom.

37. A. Pertusi, *Costantino Porfirogenito De Thematibus*, Studi e Testi 160 (Citta del Vaticano, 1952), pp. 180f.; Arnold Toynbee, *Constantine Porphyrogenitus and His World* (Oxford, 1973), pp. 267–69, 472.

38. *Slavonic Daniel* #7 and #8. *The Apocalypse of St. Andrew the Fool* reproduces only two elements of the campaign in the West: it speaks of the "taming" of the "Blond Peoples" by the Emperor "from poverty" (*PG* 111.856B); and later it attributes an expedition to Rome to the first of three "impudent, stupid, and useless" rulers (861A). The author also predicts that during the reign of the Emperor "from poverty" all gold hidden anywhere will be revealed to him on God's order and that he will distribute it to his state with a winnowing fan (856B), but here the distribution of treasure is not specifically connected with the expedition to Italy.

39. Pseudo-Chrysostom, pp. 36.29–37.9 Vasiliev; *Daniel Καὶ ἔσται*, pp. 39.31–34; 40.16–26; 41.1–4 Vasiliev.

ten thousand pieces of gold are brought to him by ten thousand officials. *Daniel Καὶ ἔσται* also shows how the Last Roman Emperor's Italian expedition might have paved the way for the notion, already discussed, that he was of Western origin: for in that text he enters Constantinople after his overland march from Italy and solemnly addresses the city: "Receive, O Babylon of the Seven Hills, him who arises and shines from the West."[40]

Byzantine apocalypses are inconsistent in predicting the length of the Last Roman Emperor's reign. The Latin text of the Tiburtine Sibyl mentions one hundred and twelve years; a little later, however, it speaks of the conversion of the Jews at the end of one hundred and twenty years, and it seems from the context that the starting point for this interval is the Last Emperor's accession.[41] The length of the reign is not indicated in the various versions of Pseudo-Methodius or in Pseudo-Chrysostom, but the *Slavonic Daniel* and *Daniel Καὶ ἔσται* allow thirty-two years.[42]

Wherever the circumstances of the Last Roman Emperor's death are mentioned, they follow directly upon his surrender of imperial power to God at Jerusalem. This act in turn is invariably related to his victory over the infidels and thus expresses the notion that by it the Last Roman Emperor has discharged the function assigned to him by God, so there is no further need for his offices or his person. Because of this intrinsic connection between the Last Emperor's actions, especially his warfare, and his surrender at Jerusalem, it is methodologically permissible to identify a ruler mentioned in an apocalypse as the Last Roman Emperor even if one of the two elements has, through an accident of the literary tradition, been omitted.[43]

The earliest apocalypse to mention the surrender at Jerusalem by a Last Roman Emperor is the Latin version of the Tiburtine Sibyl. Here,

---

40. P. 41.3 Vasiliev δέξαι, ἑπτάλοφε Βαβυλών, τὸν ἐκ δυσμῶν ἀνατέλλοντα καὶ περιαστράπτοντα.
41. P. 185.4 Sackur: *Et ipsius regnum C et XII annis terminabitur*. Cf. 185.15: . . . *cum completi fuerint centum et viginti anni, Iudei convertentur ad Dominum*.
42. *Slavonic Daniel* #9; p. 41.10 Vasiliev.
43. Thus Adso, p. 110.14 Sackur, speaks of a last king of the Franks laying down scepter and crown at Jerusalem. Nothing is said about the Emperor's victories over the Moslem occupants of Palestine, but because of the consistency of the apocalyptic tradition, not to mention the military, religious, and political situation of Adso's time, one may assume that Adso's source (*quidam vero doctores nostri*—in my opinion, Pseudo-Hippolytus, p. 108 above) had mentioned victories of the Frankish king over the Palestinian Arabs prior to his act of surrender.

too, it follows immediately upon his victory over the hosts of Gog and Magog:[44]

But when the king of the Romans will hear [about the attack of Gog and Magog], he will summon his army, destroy [the enemy] to the point of death, then go to Jerusalem, there lay down the diadem from his head and all his royal attire, and relinquish the kingdom of the Christians to God the Father and to Jesus Christ his Son.[45]

The Latin Sibyl is alone among these apocalypses in assigning the Last Roman Emperor the victory over Gog and Magog. In the other texts, the enemy vanquished by him are the "Ismaelites," that is, the Arabs, later the Turks. In the Syriac, Greek, and Latin versions of Pseudo-Methodius, the Last Emperor first defeats the Arabs; an angel then destroys Gog and Magog. The Last Emperor settles in Jerusalem for one week (of years) and a half (ten and a half years) and finally on Golgotha "will hand over the kingship to God the Father . . . and . . . give up his soul to his creator."[46] In all three versions, too, it is predicted that the Last Roman Emperor will surrender his power by placing his diadem on the Cross, which is imagined as standing there (again), will stretch out his hands to heaven, and thus will bring to fulfillment the word of the Psalm 68:31 ("Ethiopia will stretch out her hand to God").[47] The episode reappears in the *Slavonic Daniel*, except that here the Last Emperor resides at Jerusalem for twelve years, and his death is omitted (as in several Greek manuscripts of Pseudo-Methodius). In Pseudo-Chrysostom it is replaced by the Emperor's journey to Italy and Rome (already discussed), but it is mentioned in *Daniel Καὶ ἔσται*, albeit in corrupt and abbreviated fashion.[48] In the *Apocalypse of St. Andrew the*

---

44. [Note in the author's hand: I no longer believe that the passage on the Last Roman Emperor in the Latin Sibyl is fourth-century. The combination of Gog and Alexander is not attested before the seventh century. So this interpolation, if not derived from Pseudo-Methodius, is contemporary with it, or possibly may have a common source. See below, "Gog and Magog," Part Two, Chapter II; also Nöldeke, "Beiträge," Appendix, pp. 14–15.]

45. P. 186.4 Sackur: *Cum autem audierit rex Romanorum, convocato exercitu debellabit eos atque prosternet usque ad internicionem et postea veniet Ierusalem, et ibi deposito capitis diademate et omni habitu regali relinquet regnum christianorum Deo patri et Iesu Christo filio eius.*

46. Syriac Pseudo-Methodius, fols. 133 recto–134 verso; Greek Pseudo-Methodius, pp. 40–46 Istrin (= pp. 120–132 Lolos) (the death of the Emperor is omitted in all but one manuscript); Latin Pseudo-Methodius, pp. 89.19–94.9 Sackur.

47. Syriac Pseudo-Methodius, fol. 135 recto; Greek Pseudo-Methodius, p. 45.14 Istrin (= p. 132.10 Lolos); Latin Pseudo-Methodius, p. 93.15 Sackur (here the imperial diadem is transformed into a crown).

48. *Slavonic Daniel* #11; Pseudo-Chrysostom, p. 36.29 Vasiliev; *Daniel Καὶ ἔσται*, p. 42.22 Vasiliev κατοικήσει ἐν Ἱερουσαλὴμ ἑβδομάδι χρόνον (after twelve and a half

*Fool* the scene of the surrender is attributed, as are so many other activities of the Last Roman Emperor, to the Emperor "from poverty," and Golgotha is replaced by "the place where the feet of Jesus Christ, our true God, had stood."[49]

A stable feature of the Byzantine apocalypses is the beginning of the Antichrist's domination immediately after the Last Roman Emperor's surrender of imperial power (and his death, where it is mentioned). Thus in the Latin version of the Tiburtine Sibyl, the Antichrist "will be revealed clearly" (*revelabitur manifeste*) after the surrender.[50] In Pseudo-Ephraem—where, it will be remembered, there is a surrender of the "empire of the Christians to God the Father" but no personal agent is mentioned to carry out the surrender—the Antichrist "will appear" (*apparebit*) immediately after it.[51] In the Syriac Pseudo-Methodius, he "will be revealed" immediately after that event, while in the Greek and Latin versions the formulae used are "he will become manifest" and "he will be revealed" respectively, always with a mention that the Antichrist will follow "immediately."[52] In two of the *Visions of Daniel*, also, the Antichrist is mentioned immediately after the act of surrender.[53] The sequence: surrender and death of the Last Roman Emperor/domination of the Antichrist is therefore expressed or implied in all the apocalypses, and in the three versions of Pseudo-Methodius it is specifically stated that the second event will follow immediately upon the first. The variations in the terminology characterizing the Antichrist's seizure of power (revelation, clear revelation, appearance, manifestation) are related to the fact that in this apocalyptic tradition the entry of the Antichrist is mentioned in two separate stages and will therefore also be discussed in Part Two, Chapter III, "The Legend of the Antichrist."

It remains to consider the evidence from Scripture and prophecy cited in Byzantine apocalypses with regard to the expectation of a Last Roman

---

years the Antichrist appears, the Emperor of the Romans "goes up," prays to the Lord, stretches his hands upward—no mention of Psalm 68:31).

49. PG 111.859C ἐν τῷ τόπῳ οὗ ἔστησαν οἱ πόδες Ἰησοῦ Χριστοῦ κτλ.
50. P. 186.9 Sackur.
51. P. 214.4 Caspari.
52. Syriac Pseudo-Methodius, fol. 135 verso; Greek Pseudo-Methodius, p. 46n.5 Istrin (= p. 134.21nn. Lolos) (ἐμφανὴς γένηται; variants φανεὶς γεννήσεται, ἐμφανὴς γεννήσεται); Latin Pseudo-Methodius 94.8 Sackur (*appareat manifestus*).
53. *Slavonic Daniel* #11: he "will begin to do signs and wonders"; *Daniel Καὶ ἔσται*, p. 43.5 Istrin (= p. 128.2 Lolos): "he will appear and do imaginary signs on earth." In Pseudo-Chrysostom the sequence is disturbed by the Last Roman Emperor's Italian expedition, and the surrender in Jerusalem is omitted altogether. In the *Apocalypse of St. Andrew the Fool*, in keeping with its encyclopedic character, the material has been divided between two emperors: the scepter Emperor "from poverty will pass away" and the Antichrist "will then arise" (*PG* 111.856C); a ruler "from Ethiopia" will surrender his diadem and die and three shameless, stupid, and useless youths will arise there (860C).

Emperor. For the genesis of this concept Pseudo-Ephraem is especially revealing. Here there is no Last Roman Emperor yet, but it is said:

Already the kingdom of the Romans is taken out of the way and the empire of the Christians delivered to God and the Father. Then comes the end when the kingdom of the Romans has begun to end and all principalities and powers are finished.[54]

The author is here combining the language of II Thess. 2:7 with that of I Cor. 15:24.[55] In the light of the Last Emperor's principal function, the military conflict with the enemies of the empire, the bond with I Cor. 15:24 is particularly important, for the biblical passage shows clearly the essential relationship, in St. Paul's thought, between the surrender of kingship to God the Father and a victory over an enemy.[56] For St. Paul the enemy was death; Pseudo-Ephraem, while proposing (following?) another interpretation referring to the *nequissimae gentes*, Gog and Magog, as the last enemy, draws the same conclusion as St. Paul—namely, that there will be no further need for any kingship other than God's, for the earthly kingship (of Christ in St. Paul, of the Roman emperors in Pseudo-Ephraem) will have fulfilled its mission and can now give way to the kingdom of God. The use of the passive voice (*tollitur, traditur*) by Pseudo-Ephraem suggests that he was still thinking of a surrender of royal power by Jesus Christ, but from a formulation such as that of Pseudo-Ephraem it was a natural development to assume that the surrender of earthly power could be carried only by its de facto holder, a Roman emperor, who by this act of surrender would become the Last Roman Emperor.

Indeed, all Byzantine apocalyptists except Pseudo-Ephraem assign this episode of the surrender to a Roman emperor. Thus it is said in the Latin version of the Tiburtine Sibyl:

But when the king of the Romans has heard [of the invasion of Gog and Magog], he will summon his army, destroy them and ruin them to the point of death and afterward come to Jerusalem. There he will lay down the diadem from his head and all regal attire and will relinquish the kingship over the Christians to God the Father and Jesus Christ his son.[57]

---

54. Pp. 213.17–214.4 Caspari: *et iam regnum Romanorum tollitur de medio, et Christianorum imperium traditur Deo et Patri; et tunc uenit consummatio, cum coeperit consummari Romanorum regnum et expleti fuerint omnes principatus et potestates.*
55. II Thess. 2:7: *tantum ut qui tenet nunc, teneat donec de medio fiat* and I Cor. 15:24: *cum tradiderit regnum Deo et Patri, cum evacuaverit omnem principatum, et potestatem, et virtutem.*
56. Cf. I Cor. 15:25f.: *Oportet autem illum regnare, donec ponat omnes inimicos sub pedibus eius.*
57. P. 186.4 Sackur. Cf. p. 151 above.

In the Latin Sibyl, therefore, Jesus Christ—who, in St. Paul's thought (as well as, presumably, in Pseudo-Ephraem's) had been the agent of the surrender of earthly power to God—became its co-recipient and thus made way for a different actor in the eschatological drama: a Last Roman Emperor. The Latin Sibyl stands alone, among the apocalypses here to be discussed, in assigning him a victory over God and Magog. In all other texts this victory is the work of an angel, and the Last Roman Emperor is given the task of defeating not a mythological but an historical enemy, the Ismaelites—a process of demythologization not infrequent in the history of apocalyptic thought. The language of these two Pauline texts, however, affected the formulation of the act of surrender in all later texts.

The Latin version of the Tiburtine Sibyl is also the only apocalypse to name the Last Roman Emperor (Constans) and to provide a physical description (p. 155 above). It seems that the author is thinking of him in concrete terms as a figure comparable to the Roman emperors of the past and present, rather than as the shadowy figure known from the other texts. Inasmuch as, in contrast to all other texts, the author has nothing to say on the more or less miraculous way in which this emperor is discovered, he must have assumed that the Last Roman Emperor, Constans, would acquire power in one of the ways in which past Roman emperors had normally done, rather than by any kind of supernatural intervention. There was therefore no need to find biblical warranty for his accession.

It is in the Syriac Pseudo-Methodius, composed not long after the Arab occupation of Mesopotamia, that the emergence of the Last Emperor is for the first time based on a biblical passage: "A king of the Greeks will go forth against them [Ismaelites] in great wrath and he will be aroused against them like a man who shakes off his wine, one who plots[58] against them as [against] dead [men]." In part this is an allusion to Psalm 78:65, where the Syriac Old Testament (Pešitta) reads: "The Lord was aroused like a sleeper and like a man who shakes off his wine."

In transforming the Psalmist's interpretation of a past punishment of Israel's sinfulness by God ("the Lord") into an eschatological prophecy,

58. In the only manuscript of the Syriac text, Cod. Vat. Syr. 58, fol. 133 recto, line 16, a hand, not necessarily that of the original scribe, has placed two dots (i.e., *rebāsā kariā*) below the consonant *šin* of the word *dmtḫšb*, thus interpreting it as a form of the *Etpe'el*. Its meaning would then be "to be numbered [or] counted." The fact that it is followed by the preposition *'l* makes it probable, however, that the participle is of the *Etpa'al* form and means "to plan, plot against." The preposition would be unintelligible if interpreted as an *Etpe'el*.

with the Last Roman Emperor (rather than God) as the actor, the Syriac Pseudo-Methodius established a long apocalyptic tradition.[59] His allusion was taken over by the Greek translator, who also introduced significant changes. The Syriac version of the Psalm had gone on to speak of the Lord attacking his enemies,[60] and the Syriac Pseudo-Methodius had interpolated these enemies into the part of the Psalm quoted; in order to emphasize the Emperor's fury, he had added that he would treat them "as dead [men]" (although in fact they were alive and resisting). The Greek translator understood the phrase "as dead" to refer to the subject (the Emperor) rather than to his enemies, an interpretation that though grammatically possible yields a less satisfactory meaning, and added, probably by way of explanatory gloss on the difficult notion of the Emperor being "as dead," the further statement that he was considered useless.[61] This misunderstanding of the Syriac text served to intensify the aura of paradox and mystery created by the citation of the Psalm: the Emperor will conquer the enemy not only though he resembles a man awakening after a drinking bout but though he will be "considered like one dead and utterly useless." It was in this form that the scriptural allusion and its Pseudo-Methodian context became part of the tradition of the Last Roman Emperor.[62]

While the Byzantine apocalypses cited Psalm 78:65 to characterize the first emergence of the Last Roman Emperor, they referred to another passage as a basis for his later activities. The Latin version of the Tiburtine Sibyl predicted that the Last Roman Emperor, Constans, would call

---

59. More exactly, he followed such a tradition, for the verse had already been cited, also in a Messianic context but without any reference to a Last Emperor, in a sixth-century work of Syriac literature, the *Cave of Treasures* (German translation by C. Bezold, *Die Schatzhöhle* [Leipzig, 1883], esp. pp. 25f.): "Noah aber deutet durch seinen Schlaf im Rausche das Kreuz des Messias an, wie von ihm der fromme David psalmierte und sprach: 'Es erwachte der Herr wie ein Schläfer und wie ein Mann, der seinen Wein gebrochen hat.'" This work was intensively used by Pseudo-Methodius: cf. pp. 10–14 Sackur.

60. In the Pešitta, Psalm 78:65, after the line cited above, continues, "he smote his enemies at his back" (or "backward": the meaning of this word, *lbstrh*, is difficult).

61. The Syriac Pseudo-Methodius used the phrase *ik mit*, where the second word may be either singular or plural. Cf. Greek Pseudo-Methodius, p. 40.1 Istrin (= p. 124.4 Lolos) ἐπαναστήσεται ἐπ' αὐτοὺς βασιλεὺς Ἑλλήνων ἤτοι Ῥωμαίων μετὰ μεγάλου θυμοῦ καὶ ἐξυπνισθήσεται καθάπερ ἄνθρωπος ἀπὸ ὕπνου καθὼς πιὼν οἶνον, ὃν ἐλογίζοντο οἱ ἄνθρωποι ὡσεὶ νεκρὸν καὶ εἰς οὐδὲν χρησιμεύοντα [The emperor of the Greeks or Romans will arise against them with great anger and he will awake like a man from sleep when drinking wine, whom people reckon as if a dead man and utterly useless].

62. Latin Pseudo-Methodius, p. 89.20 Sackur: *expergiscitur tamquam homo a somno vini, quem extimabant homines tamquam mortuum esse et in nihilo profecisse*; Slavonic Daniel #6: "whom people considered like a dead man"; Pseudo-Chrysostom, p. 36.22 Vasiliev ὃν εἶχον οἱ ἄνθρωποι ὡσεὶ νεκρὸν καὶ οὐδὲν χρησιμεύοντα; Daniel Καὶ ἔσται, p. 39.22 Vasiliev ὃν ἐδόκουν οἱ ἄνθρωποι ὡς νεκρὸν εἶναι καὶ εἰς οὐδὲν χρησιμεύειν; *Oracula Leonis* 13.3 (PG 107.1137B) ὡς ἐκ μέθης δὲ φανείς.

upon all pagans to be baptized and would set up Christ's Cross in all their temples. It continued, "For then Egypt and Ethiopia will stretch forth their hand to God."[63] This is an allusion to Psalm 68:31, here cited in a contracted form.[64] In the Sibyl's quotation, Egypt and Ethiopia represent the nations at large and the verse is referred to as evidence for the Last Roman Emperor's expected success in converting the pagan world.

The same verse serves a different purpose in all the other apocalypses that cite it. It plays a central role in the Syriac Pseudo-Methodius, for this author dedicates the entire first half of the work to the proof of the proposition that the "Ethiopia" of the Psalmist was not, as some earlier members of the clergy had believed, the historical and contemporary kingdom of Ethiopia but the Roman (i.e., Byzantine) Empire:

> However, many brethren of the clergy supposed that the blessed David spoke this word [Psalm 68:31] concerning the kingdom of the Cushites [= Ethiopians]. And those who thought so erred. For concerning this kingdom of Greece, which descends from the offspring of [the Ethiopian princess] Cusheth and will possess that thing which is placed in the center which is the Holy Cross—concerning this kingdom, yea, concerning it the blessed David said: Cush will hand over the hand to God.[65]

In fact, the entire "historical" part of the treatise has no other purpose than to show that because of a series of dynastic marriages the Byzantine emperors are heirs to the Ethiopian royalty and therefore will be its legitimate representatives at the end of time. For that reason the Syriac Pseudo-Methodius sees in the surrender of imperial power by the Last Emperor—to be precise, in his gesture on Golgotha of handing over (stretching out) his hand to God—the fulfillment of Psalm 68:31:

> There [on Golgotha] will be fulfilled the saying of the blessed David which he prophesied concerning the end of times: "Cush will hand over the hand to God," because it is the son of Cusheth, daughter of King Pīl of the Cushites, who will hand over the hand to God.[66]

This view of the act of surrender on Golgotha as the fulfillment of this Psalm dominates the tradition dependent on the Syriac Pseudo-Methodius.[67] It remains puzzling why the Latin version of the Tiburtine

---

63. P. 185.13 Sackur: *Tunc namque preveniet Egiptus et Etiopia manus eius dare Dei* (thus).

64. Vulgate: *Venient legati ex Aegypto, Aethiopia praeveniet manus eius Deo*. The *Vetus Latina* omits the word *Deo*.

65. Syriac Pseudo-Methodius, fol. 126 recto.

66. Syriac Pseudo-Methodius, fol. 135 verso.

67. Greek Pseudo-Methodius, p. 46n.5 Istrin (= p. 134.1–3 Lolos); Latin Pseudo-Methodius, p. 94.2 Sackur. The passage is omitted in the *Visions of Daniel*.

Sibyl and the Pseudo-Methodian tradition agreed in connecting this verse with the Last Emperor but disagreed in the activity concerned: the conversion of the pagan nations to the Last Emperor, in the Sibyl; the surrender of earthly power by the Last Emperor, in the three versions of Pseudo-Methodius.

In many of the same apocalypses the act of surrender is also related to two Pauline passages, I Cor. 15:24 and II Thess. 2:7.[68] They underlie the formulation of the surrender in the Latin version of the Tiburtine Sibyl, in Pseudo-Ephraem (where no personal agent of the surrender is indicated), and in all three versions of Pseudo-Methodius.[69] In applying I Cor. 15:24 to the Last Emperor, these apocalypses transfer to him a passage that in St. Paul's thought had referred to Jesus Christ.

The apocalyptists followed the same procedure when they connected the peace, prosperity, and joyfulness brought by the Last Roman Emperor with Jesus' prediction, in Matt. 24:37 and kindred texts, that at the time of his Second Coming, men would live once again as in the days of Noah and before the Flood. This application of the passage from the Gospels to the reign of the Last Emperor occurs in all three versions of Pseudo-Methodius.[70]

This is the entire canonical evidence cited in more than one of the Byzantine apocalypses here under consideration: one verse of Psalms (78:65), where a poetic description of God's punitive wrath against

---

68. I Cor. 15:24f. εἶτα τὸ τέλος ὅταν παραδιδοῖ τὴν βασιλείαν τῷ Θεῷ καὶ πατρί, ὅταν καταργήσῃ πᾶσαν ἀρχὴν καὶ πᾶσαν ἐξουσίαν καὶ δύναμιν· δεῖ γὰρ αὐτὸν βασιλεύειν ἄχρι οὗ θῇ πάντας τοὺς ἐχθροὺς ὑπὸ τοὺς πόδας αὐτοῦ; II Thess. 2:7 μόνον ὁ κατέχων ἄρτι ἕως ἐκ μέσου γένηται [Then comes the end, when he delivers the kingdom to God the Father after destroying every rule and every power and authority; for he must reign until he has put all his enemies under his feet; (II Thess. 2:7) For the mystery of lawlessness is already at work; only he who now restrains it will do so until he is out of the way] [Translations from Revised Standard Version]. For these texts in the Vulgate see n. 55 above.

69. Latin Sibyl, p. 186.7 Sackur: . . . *relinquet regnum Christianorum Deo patri et Iesu Christo filio eius. Et cum cessaverit imperium Romanum* etc.; Pseudo-Ephraem, pp. 213.16–214.4 Caspari (see n. 54 above); Syriac Pseudo-Methodius, fol. 135 recto: "And the king of the Greeks . . . will hand over the kingship to God the Father. . . . And immediately every leader and every authority and all powers will cease," etc.; Greek Pseudo-Methodius, p. 46.1 and n. 5 Istrin (= p. 132.2 Lolos); Latin Pseudo-Methodius, pp. 93.17, 94.7 Sackur. In the *Visions of Daniel* the citation, usually together with the entire scene of the surrender, is replaced by the Last Emperor's expedition to Rome.

70. Matt. 24:37 ὥσπερ γὰρ αἱ ἡμέραι τοῦ Νῶε, οὕτως ἔσται ἡ παρουσία τοῦ υἱοῦ τοῦ ἀνθρώπου. ὡς γὰρ ἦσαν ἐν ταῖς ἡμέραις [ἐκείναις] ταῖς πρὸ τοῦ κατακλυσμοῦ τρώγοντες καὶ πίνοντες, γαμοῦντες καὶ γαμίζοντες, ἄχρι ἧς ἡμέρας εἰσῆλθεν Νῶε εἰς τὴν κιβωτόν . . . οὕτως ἔσται καὶ ἡ παρουσία τοῦ υἱοῦ τοῦ ἀνθρώπου [As were the days of Noah, so will be the coming of the son of man. For as in those days before the flood they were eating and drinking, marrying and giving in marriage, until the day when Noah entered the ark, and they did not know until the flood came and swept them all away, so will be the coming of the son of man: RSV].

Hebrew sinners is used to buttress the Last Roman Emperor's condition prior to his emergence; another verse from the same book (68:31), commemorating the submission of the nations to God, applied to the Last Emperor's role in the conversion of the pagans in the Latin version of the Tiburtine Sibyl, to his surrender on Golgotha in the other texts; the Gospels' (Matt. 24:37) comparison of the peace, prosperity, and rejoicing at the Second Coming with that of the Age of Noah transferred to the reign of the Last Roman Emperor; and finally the Pauline predictions of an end of the Roman Empire (II Thess. 2:7) and of Christ's surrender of earthly kingship to God (I Cor. 15:24) applied to the Last Roman Emperor. It is not much; and moreover, the biblical passages were applied to the notion of a Last Roman Emperor not without some awkwardness and artificiality.

It seems that some of the apocalyptists, dissatisfied with this state of affairs, attempted to remedy it by two devices by no means mutually exclusive: either by the addition of further more or less canonical citations, or by recourse to non-biblical prophecies. Thus *Daniel* Καὶ ἔσται alone described a second victory of the Last Roman Emperor over the "sons of Hagar" at the Well of Jacob and transferred to it a prophecy cited, in slightly different form, by the Syriac and Greek versions of Pseudo-Methodius (as a "saying of Our Lord" in the former; and as a prophecy of Ezekiel in the latter text). In these earlier apocalypses, however, the quotation accompanied not a Roman victory over the Arabs, but a disastrous defeat. In *Daniel* Καὶ ἔσται the citation reads as follows:

Then a word will be spoken to the emperor of the Romans: Son of Man, summon the birds of heaven and the beasts of the land and order them as follows: eat the flesh of men and drink the blood of the Impious [αἷμα ἀσεβῶν] because today I make a great sacrifice [sacrificial meal].[71]

This citation in *Daniel* Καὶ ἔσται resembles most closely the text of Ezekiel 39:17 in the Pešitta and Septuagint, but differs from all the related texts in characterizing the enemies of the Last Roman Emperor as the Impious (ἀσεβεῖς).[72] It is difficult not to relate this change intro-

---

71. Syriac Pseudo-Methodius, fol. 134 recto, specifically names the Gospel: "that is the peace of which he said in his gospel: there will be great peace the like of which never existed, and men will sit down in repose and will eat and drink and rejoice in the joy of their heart, and men will take wives and wives will be given to men"; Greek Pseudo-Methodius, p. 43.7 Istrin (= p. 128.5 Lolos) refers to I Thess. 5:3 and Matt. 24:37; Latin Pseudo-Methodius, p. 91.14 Sackur, does the same; cf. *Apocalypse of St. Andrew the Fool*, PG 111.853B, 856C.

72. P. 40.11 Vasiliev Τότε γενήσεται λόγος πρὸς τὸν βασιλέα 'Ρωμαίων λέγων· υἱὲ ἀνθρώπου, κάλεσαι τὰ πετεινὰ τοῦ οὐρανοῦ καὶ τὰ θηρία τῆς γῆς καὶ πρότρεψαι αὐτοῖς λέγων· φάγετε σάρκας ἀνθρώπων καὶ πίετε αἷμα ἀσεβῶν διότι θυσίαν μεγάλην θύω σήμερον. Compare Syriac Pseudo-Methodius, fol. 127 verso: "And there will be

duced in Ezek. 39:17 by *Daniel Καὶ ἔσται* (or one of his sources) with another prophecy cited by the same text in connection with the Last Emperor's first victory over the Ismaelites: "And the word of the prophet will be fulfilled: he will hand over the sinner into the hands of the Impious, will turn again and require their blood."[73] It will be noted that the "Impious" reappear here in the phrase: "the blood of the Impious." This is hardly a coincidence. The easiest explanation is to assume that either *Daniel Καὶ ἔσται* or one of his sources incorporated into his text two prophecies, one consisting of an interpolated text of Ezek. 39:17, and the other altogether extra-canonical, where the historical Arab victories over the Byzantine armies had been attributed to the sinfulness of the Byzantine population but where a promise had been held out that at a later time God would redress the balance and punish the impious Arabs.

Other non-biblical prophecies are also cited in the material now under consideration. The Latin text of the Tiburtine Sibyl, immediately before predicting that the Last Roman Emperor would sack the islands

---

fulfilled the word of our Lord who said: We [?] are like the beasts of the field and the birds of heaven, and call them [saying]: Assemble and come because today I shall make a great sacrifice for you. Eat the flesh of the fattened [animals] and drink the blood of mighty men"; Greek Pseudo-Methodius, p. 26.11 Istrin (= p. 96.4 Lolos) κἀκεῖ πληρωθήσεται τὸ ῥηθὲν διὰ προφήτου Ἰεζεκιὴλ τό· υἱὲ ἀνθρώπου, κάλεσον τὰ θηρία τοῦ ἀγροῦ καὶ τὰ πετεινὰ τοῦ οὐρανοῦ καὶ πρότρεψαι αὐτὰ λέγων· συναθροίσθητε καὶ δεῦτε, διότι θυσίαν μεγάλην θύσω ὑμῖν. φάγετε σάρκας δυναστῶν καὶ πίετε αἷμα γιγάντων. [And there will be fulfilled the word of the prophet Ezekiel: son of man, call the beasts of the field and the birds of heaven and turn to them saying: Assemble and come hence, because I will make a great sacrifice for you. Eat the flesh of the powerful and drink the blood of giants.] Latin Pseudo-Methodius, p. 80.17 Sackur. Compare Ezek. 39:17 LXX: καὶ σύ, υἱὲ ἀνθρώπου, εἰπόν Τάδε λέγει κύριος Εἰπὸν παντὶ ὀρνέῳ πετεινῷ καὶ πρὸς πάντα τὰ θηρία τοῦ πεδίου Συνάχθητε καὶ ἔρχεσθε, συνάχθητε ἀπὸ πάντων τῶν περικύκλων ἐπὶ τὴν θυσίαν μου, ἣν τέθυκα ὑμῖν, θυσίαν μεγάλην ἐπὶ τὰ ὄρη Ἰσραηλ, καὶ φάγεσθε κρέα καὶ πίεσθε αἷμα· κρέα γιγάντων φάγεσθε καὶ αἷμα ἀρχόντων τῆς γῆς πίεσθε. [As for you, son of man, thus says the Lord God: Speak to the birds of every sort and to all beasts of the field, "Assemble and come, gather from all sides to the sacrificial feast which I am preparing for you, a great sacrificial feast upon the mountains of Israel, and you shall eat flesh and drink blood. You shall eat the flesh of the mighty and drink the blood of the princes of the earth."]

73. P. 39.29 Vasiliev καὶ πληρωθήσεται τὸ ῥηθὲν ὑπὸ τοῦ προφήτου· παραδώσει τὸν ἁμάρτωλον εἰς χεῖρας ἀσεβῶν καὶ στραφεὶς πάλιν ἐκζητήσει τὸ αἷμα αὐτῶν. The editor, by placing a period after ἀσεβῶν and continuing with a capital letter, may have wished to indicate his opinion that the citation ended at that point. It is much more probable, however, that it continued to αἷμα αὐτῶν. In the first place, ἀσεβῶν is the most natural referent for αὐτῶν. More importantly, the citation is *mal à propos* unless the two clauses are taken together. *Daniel Καὶ ἔσται* is here predicting a Roman victory. To say that by this victory the sinner will be handed over to the Impious would imply that God will reward the impious Romans. On the other hand, if the two clauses are taken together as the "prophetic saying," it makes perfect sense: in the past God has handed over the Romans to the Impious (Ismaelites, Moslems) because they (the Romans) were sinful, but in the future he will avenge their past defeat by putting the infidels to death.

and cities of the pagans and destroy all the temples of the idols, writes: "And the same king [the Last Roman Emperor, named Constans] will have a writing [*scripturam*] before his eyes that says: Let the king of the Romans claim the entire kingdom of the Christians."[74] Whatever the original meaning of this prophecy may have been, it was clearly inserted into the Latin text of the Tiburtine Sibyl to justify the Last Roman Emperor's crusade against pagans and Jews.

Finally, all the *Visions of Daniel* cite an earlier prophecy that, freed of corruptions, ran as follows: "Lion and Whelp will jointly pursue the Wild Ass."[75] In these texts, the purpose of the citation is clearly to provide a sanction for the Emperor's alliance with the "Blond Peoples" of the West and their joint expedition against the Ismaelites. The origin of the prophecy is more difficult to ascertain. Wilhelm Bousset traced the apocalyptic metaphor of the Lion's Whelp for the military leader against Byzantium's (Rome's) enemies back to the wars of the Byzantine emperor Heraclius (610–641) with the Persian king Chosroes II (†628).[76] In the final analysis it is a reminiscence of the Blessing of Jacob on Judah (Gen. 49:8f.), who is there compared both to lion and whelp.[77]

Now already August Dillmann and (following him) Bousset showed that during the reigns of the Byzantine emperors Leo III (717–741)

---

74. P. 185.8 Sackur (n. 16 above). The words *omne regnum* could also be translated "every kingdom," but the date of the passage (fourth century) and the mention of the name Constans just above make it probable that it reflected the period of the conflict between the sons of Constantine the Great over their inheritance. Perhaps the prophecy was circulated by an orthodox partisan of the youngest of Constantine the Great's sons, Constans (murdered in 350), and was directed against the Eastern ruler Constantius, who was an Arian.

75. Texts: n. 4 above.

76. Bousset, *Antichrist*, pp. 45–49. The most important text is a Syriac *Apocalypse of Ezra*, ed. and trans. Friedrich Baethgen, "Beschreibung der syrischen Handschrift 'Sachau 131' auf der Königlichen Bibliothek zu Berlin," *Zeitschrift für die alttestamentliche Wissenschaft* 6 (1886), pp. 193–211, esp. 207: "Aber der junge Löwe wird zwischen die Hörner des Stieres springen und beide abbrechen, und das Land wird er verwüsten und plündern und mit Feuer vernichten . . . und der junge Löwe wird mit grosser Macht in das Land der Verheissung ziehen und es dem Tribut unterwerfen" etc. Add to the texts assembled by Bousset the Oriental versions of the Sibyl, ed. and trans. J. Schleifer, "Die Erzählung der Sibylle. Ein Apokryph," *Denkschriften der Kais. Akademie der Wissenschaften in Wien, philosophisch-historische Klasse* 53 (1908), esp. ch. 18 at pp. 66f. (Karshuni version): "Und was das neunte Zeitalter betrifft, so wird in ihm der Löwensohn vom Frankenlande erscheinen und alles, was auf der Oberfläche der Erde zerstört worden war, aufbauen" (follows a forty-year period of prosperity, fertility, and moral purity, then the Antichrist).

77. Gen. 49:8f. αἱ χεῖρές σου ἐπὶ νώτου τῶν ἐχθρῶν σου . . . / σκύμνος λέοντος Ἰούδα· / ἐκ βλαστοῦ, υἱέ μου, ἀνέβης· / ἀναπεσὼν ἐκοιμήθης ὡς λέων / καὶ ὡς σκύμνος· τίς ἐγειρεῖ αὐτόν; [your hand shall be on the neck of your enemies . . . / Judah is a lion's whelp / from the prey, my son, you have gone up / He stooped down, he couched as a lion / and as its whelp; who will arouse him? (RSV)]

and his son Constantine V (741–775), oracles about victories of a Lion's Whelp enjoyed a remarkable vogue.[78] In 740, Leo III and his son Constantine inflicted a decisive defeat on an Arab army led by Malik and Battal at Akroinon in Phrygia; as a result, Asia Minor was saved for the empire.[79] The emperor Constantine V quickly became the hero, or rather, because of his iconoclastic policies, the villain of legend and epic.[80]

It is therefore plausible that around the time of the victory of Akroinon, presumably while Leo III was still alive, a prophecy should have been circulated that these rulers would do more than merely clear Byzantine territory of the Ismaelites: jointly they would pursue the enemy to his own country. After all, Pseudo-Methodius had predicted that the Last Roman Emperor, assisted by his sons, would attack the Arabs from the Red Sea in the desert of Jethrib (Medina) and that his sons would then destroy their garrisons in Palestine.[81] Reference to the Last Emperor's sons does not reappear as such in the *Visions of Daniel*, but in its original context the Lion-Whelp prophecy may have been related to victories won by a son of the Last Emperor. When Leo III and his son

78. See especially the Ethiopic *Apocalypse of St. Peter*, discussed by August Dillmann, *Göttinger gelehrte Nachrichten* (1858), pp. 185f. This work is inaccessible to me, but Bousset, *Antichrist*, p. 47, cites from it the following passage: "ich werde erwecken den Löwensohn und er wird zerschlagen alle Könige, weil ich ihm die Gewalt gegeben habe." Cf. Bousset, "Beiträge," pp. 269f.; Alexander, *The Patriarch Nicephorus of Constantinople* (Oxford, 1958) pp. 11, 234f.; Stephen Gero, *Byzantine Iconoclasm during the Reign of Leo III with Particular Attention to the Oriental Sources*, Corpus Scriptorum Christianorum Orientalium, Subsidia 41 (Louvain, 1973), pp. 13 and n. 3, 71 and n. 42 (with reservations).

79. Theophanes, p. 411.21 de Boor; Julius Wellhausen, "Die Kämpfe der Araber mit den Romäern in der Zeit der Umaijiden," *Nachrichten von der Königliche Gesellschaft der Wissenschaften zu Göttingen, philosophisch-historische Klasse* (1901), pp. 414–47, esp. 444f.

80. A. Lombard, *Constantin V, empereur des Romains* (Paris, 1902), ch. II, "La Légende de Constantin V"; N. Adontz, "Les Légendes de Maurice et de Constantin V, empereurs de Byzance," *Mélanges Bidez* I= *Annuaire de l'Institut de Philologie et d'Histoire Orientales* 2 (1934), pp. 1–12, esp. 10f. (Constantine the killer of lions, his conflict with a dragon).

81. Syriac Pseudo-Methodius, fol. 133 recto: "He will go forth against them from the sea of the Cushites and will lay desolation and ruin in the desert of Jethrib. . . . And the sons of the king of Greece will seize the places of the desert and will destroy with the sword the remnant that is left of them in the land of promise"; Greek Pseudo-Methodius p. 41.1 Istrin (= p. 124.1 Lolos) οὗτος ἐξελεύσεται ἐπ' αὐτοὺς ἐκ τῆς θαλάσσης Αἰθιοπίων καὶ βάλλει ῥομφαίαν καὶ ἐρήμωσιν ἕως Ἐθρίβον . . . ἐπὶ δὲ τοὺς κατοικοῦντας τὴν γῆν τῆς ἐπαγγελίας κατέλθωσιν οἱ υἱοὶ τοῦ βασιλέως ἐν ῥομφαίᾳ καὶ ἐκκόψουσιν αὐτοὺς ἀπὸ τῆς γῆς [He will go out against them from the sea of Ethiopia and cast the sword and desolation as far as Ethribos . . . the sons of the emperor will attack those inhabiting the land of the gospel and with the sword they will cut them down from his land.] Latin Pseudo-Methodius, p. 89.22 Sackur: *Hic exiet super eos a mare Aethiopiae et mittit gladium et desolationem in Ethribum, super habitantes autem terram promissionis discendent filii regis in gladio.* (I have corrected Sackur's punctuation in the light of the Greek text.)

were active against the Arab invaders of Asia Minor, it was a natural step to apply Pseudo-Methodius' prophecy about a mythological Last Emperor and his sons to the contemporary emperor, Leo ("the Lion"), and to predict their joint offensive against Arabia itself. The ninth-century authors of the various *Visions of Daniel*, then, cited this prophecy of the preceding century but made it serve a new idea: the cooperating Lion and Whelp no longer represented senior and junior emperors of Byzantium, but a Byzantine and a Western (Carolingian) emperor. Thus the old prophecy was made to supplement the somewhat meager scriptural evidence for the activities of the expected Last Roman Emperor and to authenticate a new purpose: the notion introduced in Byzantine apocalyptic by the *Visions of Daniel* that the Last Roman Emperor would need, for his warfare against the Ismaelites, the military aid of the West.[82]

The scarcity and nature of the biblical material cited in the Byzantine apocalypses for this expectation suggests that it is not directly biblical in origin: nowhere in canonical Scripture is there a prediction of a Roman emperor defeating a hostile army and surrendering his imperial power at Jerusalem. The question arises: if the notion of a Last Roman Emperor is not of biblical provenance, how is one to account for its genesis and for the extraordinary tenacity of the tradition in both Byzantine and Western apocalyptic literature? To orient one's search for an answer to this question, which, strangely, does not seem to have been asked before, it is desirable to develop, with the aid of a few of the more striking features of the tradition, a hypothesis and then to test it by looking at the material as a whole.

To begin with an external element, it will be remembered that the *Cento of the True Emperor* combines, in a manner which at first seems arbitrary and confusing, material on the Last Roman Emperor with data on the expectation of a Jewish Messiah. Obviously, this process of combination by a late source may have been due to no more than intellectual fuzziness on the part of the author; taken by itself, it has no special significance. But other internal features of the legend of the Last Roman Emperor point in a similar direction. Thus wherever the Last Roman Emperor's surrender of imperial power is mentioned, this action is said to take place at Jerusalem. This is certainly surprising: it would be more natural for the surrender to take place in the center of imperial

---

82. The role of the emperors Leo III and Constantine V in the *Visions of Daniel* and related pieces was discovered and elucidated by Bousset, "Beiträge," pp. 261–81. On the Lion-Whelp oracle in particular, see p. 270.

power, in the imperial capital and residence—that is, at Constantinople or, possibly, at Rome. While it might be argued that Jerusalem was chosen because of the special position of the city in Christian thought, one wonders whether the true explanation does not lie in an essential connection of the expected action of a Last Emperor with that of an earlier ruler whose capital and seat had been at Jerusalem and for whom an abdication at Jerusalem would indeed have been natural—in other words, with the hope of an anointed king of Israel or Judah, a Messiah.

Finally, beginning with the Syriac Pseudo-Methodius and forever after, the Last Emperor is first mentioned immediately following the account of sweeping Moslem conquests which induce the Ismaelites to speak blasphemously: "There is no redeemer [*perūqā*] for the Christians."[83] Inasmuch as, immediately after this blasphemous boast on the part of the Ismaelites, the Last Emperor sets out against them and defeats them decisively in battle, the author's clear implication is that the Last Emperor fulfills precisely the role of the "redeemer" whose existence the Ismaelites had denied. Now the Syriac word *perūqā*, meaning *liberator, servator*, is used in the Syriac Old Testament to render both the Hebrew term *gōel*, "redeemer," and *māshīah*, "anointed," and in the Syriac New Testament as the translation of λυτρωτής, "redeemer," or of σωτήρ, "savior."[84] Once again there seems to be a connection between the Jewish expectation of a "redeemer" or an "anointed king," a Messiah, and the Last Roman Emperor of the Byzantine apocalypses.

The three observations—the identification of Last Roman Emperor and Jewish Messiah in the *Cento of the True Emperor*, Jerusalem as the scene of the surrender of imperial power, and the designation of the Last Roman Emperor as "redeemer" or "savior" in the Byzantine apocalypses —are, I hope, sufficient for proposing, by way of preliminary hypothesis, that the expectation of a Last Roman Emperor derived from the

---

83. Syriac Pseudo-Methodius, fol. 133 recto. For the Greek and Latin texts see n. 11 above. It will be noticed that the Syriac noun *perūqā* is rendered by ἀνάρρυσις in the Greek translation (*ereptio* in Latin). The Greek translator seems to have read *purqanā* in his model, an easy corruption that does not materially affect the meaning.

84. Payne Smith, *Thesaurus Syriacus* II, p. 3295. The blasphemous boast of the enemy seems to have no precedent in Late Jewish Messianic expectations, but many Jewish texts emphasize that the end will come precisely when the situation of the Jews seems hopeless. See, for example, II Baruch 25:4, p. 496 Charles: "And it will come to pass when they say in their thoughts by reason of their much tribulation: 'The Mighty One does no longer remember the earth'—yea, it will come to pass when they abandon hope, that the time will then awake"; a Messianic passage: *Orac. Sib.* V.106 Geffcken ἀλλ' ὅταν ὕψος ἔχῃ κρατερὸν καὶ θάρσος *ἀηδές*, / ἥξει καὶ μακάρων ἐθέλων πόλιν ἐξαλαπάξαι [i.e., the Persian king] / καὶ κέν τις θεόθεν βασιλεὺς πεμφθεὶς ἐπὶ τοῦτον / πάντας ὀλεῖ βασιλεῖς μεγάλους καὶ φῶτας ἀρίστους; further examples in Volz, *Eschatologie*, pp. 158f.

Jewish (post-canonical) national hope for a Messiah, an anointed king of the Jews who would free the Jewish people from the oppression by foreign powers. Indeed, as one compares the details of the Byzantine expectation with the corresponding Jewish material, one finds that so far as the basic features are concerned, the agreements in content, and sometimes also in literary and linguistic form, are so striking that they cannot possibly be accidental.[85]

To begin with, the modes of referring to the Last Emperor used by the Byzantine apocalyptists are all attested for the Jewish Messiah. As the former is called Emperor—in Greek βασιλεύς, in Latin *rex*—so the latter is referred to as the "King Messiah," the "King of Israel," or simply "the King," of which the Messiah or Anointed (ὁ ἠλειμμένος) is a synonym while the Lion is a metaphorical equivalent.[86] The title "redeemer" or "savior" implied by the Syriac Pseudo-Methodius also has Jewish parallels.[87]

The supernatural aura that surrounds the emergence of the Last Roman Emperor is also a characteristic of Jewish apocalyptic predic-

---

85. The standard works on the subject of Late Jewish (post-canonical) Judaism are: Volz, *Eschatologie*, with the fullest collection of material; Emil Schürer, *Geschichte des Jüdischen Volkes im Zeitalter Jesu Christi*, 2 (4th ed. Leipzig, 1907), pp. 579–651; Bousset-Gressmann, *Religion des Judentums*, esp. pp. 202–289. It is obviously impossible to cite all the Jewish parallels cited in these books, and I have long hesitated whether I should limit myself to referring to the three works just mentioned on each individual point. Such a procedure would, however, both inconvenience the reader and deprive the argument presented here of much of its force. I have therefore chosen to compromise: to cite, often in translation, a few of the most effective parallels and to refer in addition to the three modern works. I am keenly aware that the selection of passages cited is arbitrary and that it compares material of different periods in Jewish history. The references to the modern works are meant to correct this distortion. English translations of Jewish apocalypses are cited from R. H. Charles, *The Apocrypha and Pseudepigrapha of the Old Testament in English*, vol. II (Oxford, 1913), unless otherwise indicated. Useful bibliographical indications on Jewish pseudepigrapha will be found in Albert-Marie Denis, *Introduction aux pseudépigraphes grecs de l'Ancien Testament*.

86. Bruno Violet (ed.), *Die Esra-Apokalypse (IV Esra)*, GCS, vol. 18, pt. 1 (Leipzig, 1910), pp. 355–57, Arab. Gild. 12.31f.: "Und der Löwe, den du gesehen hast, er ist der König, den der Höchste dauernd auf immer und ewig bewahren wird" etc. See also nn. 75–77 above. Cf. Volz, *Eschatologie*, pp. 173f.; Schürer, *Jüdischen Volkes*, p. 613; Bousset-Gressmann, *Religion des Judentums*, pp. 227f.

87. The Messiah as "redeemer" (*gōel*) is mentioned in the *Shemone Esre* prayer, Babylonian version, as cited by Schürer, *Jüdischen Volkes*, p. 539: "Gelobt seist du, Herr, unser Gott und Gott unserer Väter . . . der du . . . bringest einen Erlöser ihren Kindeskindern" etc.; cf. Volz, *Eschatologie*, pp. 52, 174, 216. For "savior," see Bousset-Gressmann, *Religion des Judentums*, p. 228. [Note in Alexander's hand: Discussion of *gōel*-redeemer in Martin Hengel, *Die Zeloten* (Leiden, 1961), pp. 120–23, esp. 122n.4: "Im Rabbinat wurde zum *terminus technicus* für die messianische Befreiung Israels von der Wolkerherrschaft," v. Hermann Strack and Paul Billerbeck, *Kommentar zum Neuen Testament aus Talmud und Midrasch* (Munich, 1926), IV, 860ff.; M. Jastrow, *A Dictionary of the Targumim*, (2 vols., New York, 1950), 1, pp. 201f.]

tions.[88] One of the most striking features of the Last Emperor is that he is invariably mentioned at the point when the military and political fortunes of the "Romans" have reached their nadir and when the Ismaelite enemy threatens the very existence of the Roman Empire: then the Last Emperor appears "all of a sudden." This is precisely the way in which the Messiah was envisaged in Late Judaism: as a helper sent suddenly in the hour of direst need.[89]

There is no Jewish Messianic precedent for a personal name, such as that of Constans in the Latin version of the Tiburtine Sibyl for the Last Emperor, or for the physical description of the Last Emperor in the same text. In fact, these two elements are exceptional in Byzantine apocalypses and are examples of a process of demythologization not infrequent in apocalyptic literature: the legendary figure of the Last Emperor was here related to an historical ruler and given both his name and his physical characteristics. In all other Byzantine apocalypses, silence on the personal name and physical attributes of the Last Emperor is complete: even moral or intellectual qualities are not mentioned except insofar as they may be inferred from his actions. He remains a shadowy figure lacking all individualizing characteristics and his personality is swallowed up by his eschatological functions. The same was true of the Jewish Messiah, except that the Jewish sources do speak of the Messiah's moral and intellectual qualities (wisdom, power, fear of God), while the Byzantine apocalypses only mention the Last Emperor's justice.[90]

Among the Last Roman Emperor's functions, the task of saving the faithful against a victorious and infidel enemy by military action is paramount, both in the Byzantine apocalypses and in Late Jewish Messia-

88. II Baruch (Syriac) 29:3, p. 497 Charles: "... the Messiah shall then begin to be revealed"; IV Ezra 7:28, p. 582 Charles: "... my Son the Messiah shall be revealed"; cf. Volz, *Eschatologie*, pp. 6, 204–207; Bousset-Gressmann, *Religion des Judentums*, p. 230.

89. The suddenness of the Messiah's emergence is stated explicitly only in rare instances (Volz, *Eschatologie*, pp. 210f.; Schürer, *Jüdischen Volkes*, p. 620). However, the notion of the warfare of the nations directed against Israel and threatening the very existence of the people and its capital, Jerusalem, is a regular feature of the Jewish Messianic expectation crystallized by the rabbis in the notion of the "birthpangs of the Messiah": see Volz, pp. 147–63 ("Die letzte böse Zeit"), and cf. p. 158 ("Wenn die Not am grössten ist, dann kommt das Ende"; on warfare in particular see p. 157); Schürer, pp. 609f.

90. Volz, *Eschatologie*, pp. 185f. ("wenig Fleisch und Blut"); Bousset-Gressmann, *Religion des Judentums*, pp. 222f. ("ganz nebensächlich und schattenhaft innerhalb des Zukunftsgemäldes"). On the Messiah's moral and intellectual qualities see Volz, pp. 221–23. Compare, however, the "shining face" of the Last Emperor, Constans, in the Latin version of the Tiburtine Sibyl with Enoch 46:1, p. 214 Charles: "And with him was another being whose countenance had the appearance of a man, and his face was full of graciousness, like one of the holy angels."

nism. In the Jewish texts the contemporary Gentile world is the principal enemy of the Messiah, and sometimes also the hosts of Gog and Magog, just as in the Latin version of the Tiburtine Sibyl the Last Emperor wages war against pagans and Gog and Magog. The substitution in the Pseudo-Methodian tradition of the Ismaelites for the earlier enemies is simply an adaptation to the changed religious and political scene. The basic feature, a military conflict with a great power of another faith, remains the same.[91] It is striking that the Syriac Pseudo-Methodius and the tradition derived from it, which never mention Palestine among the regions overrun by the Ismaelites (cf. p. 34 above), nevertheless emphasize that the sons of the Last Emperor free the "land of promise" from its Ismaelite conquerors. This singling out of the Holy Land by the tradition is due to the fact that the Last Emperor himself is a relic of the national expectations of the people of Israel, among whom the liberation of Palestine from foreign rule naturally was of paramount importance.[92]

Like the Last Roman Emperor, the Jewish Messiah was envisaged as bringing about an end to warfare, and creating a period of abundance, prosperity, and joy.[93] The Last Emperor's concern for justice, on the

---

91. Bousset-Gressmann, *Religion des Judentums*, p. 228: "Seine (des Messias) erste Aufgabe ist die Besiegung der Feinde Israels." Cf. II Baruch 72, p. 518 Charles: "the time of my Messiah is come, he shall both summon all the nations. . . . But all those who have ruled over you, or have known you, shall be given up to the sword"; the Septuagint interprets Numb. 24:7 as prophesying a victory of the Messiah (the Man) over Gog; compare the Revised Standard Version, "his [Israel's] seed shall be in many waters, his king shall be higher than Agag, and his kingdom shall be exalted," with LXX ἐξελεύσεται ἄνθρωπος ἐκ τοῦ σπέρματος αὐτοῦ καὶ κυριεύσει ἐθνῶν πολλῶν, καὶ ὑψωθήσεται ἢ Γὼγ βασιλεία αὐτοῦ, καὶ αὐξηθήσεται ἡ βασιλεία αὐτοῦ; Psalm of Solomon 17:22 καὶ ὑπόζωσον αὐτὸν [the Davidic king] ἰσχὺν τοῦ θραῦσαι ἄρχοντας ἀδίκους, καθαρίσαι Ἱερουσαλὴμ ἀπὸ ἐθνῶν καταπατούντων ἐν ἀπωλείᾳ . . . ὀλεθρεῦσαι ἔθνη παράνομα ἐν λόγῳ στόματος αὐτοῦ; cf. Volz, *Eschatologie*, pp. 183, 189. For further examples of the Messiah's victories over nations cf. Volz, pp. 212f., Schürer, *Jüdischen Volkes*, pp. 621–23; Bousset-Gressmann,, pp. 218–220, 228f. The Latin version of the Tiburtine Sibyl predicts the conversion of pagans and Jews at the time of the Last Emperor. A conversion of Gentiles is also sometimes foreseen by Jewish sources; see Bousset-Gressmann, p. 234 and n. 3.

92. See n. 14 above. On the Holy Land as the center of Jewish Messianism, see Volz, *Eschatologie*, pp. 212–14; Schürer, *Jüdischen Volkes*, p. 629.

93. Enoch 52:8, p. 219 Charles: "And there shall be no iron for war, nor shall one clothe oneself with a breastplate . . ."; *Orac. Sib.*, 5.431 Geffcken οὐ φόνος οὐδὲ κυδοιμός . . . ; IV Ezra 8:52, p. 597 Charles: "For you is . . . the future age prepared, plenteousness made ready"; I Henoch 10:18, p. 195 Charles: "And then shall the whole earth be tilled in righteousness, and shall all be planted with trees and be full of blessing"; II Baruch 29:3ff.: ". . . the Messiah shall then begin to be revealed. . . . The earth also shall yield its fruit ten thousandfold and on each vine there shall be a thousand branches and each branch shall produce a thousand clusters. . . . And those who have hungered shall rejoice. . . ." Cf. Volz, *Eschatologie*, pp. 215, 219; Bousset-Gressmann, *Religion des Judentums*, pp. 240, 260 (in the latter passage, discussion of the Messiah as King of Peace and King of Paradise).

other hand, derives from the Messiah's role as a judge over sinners; and the Emperor's zeal for orthodoxy, from the Messiah's hostility to the impious and the Gentile world that fails to recognize the Jewish God.[94] The Emperor's zeal on behalf of religion and orthodoxy and against Ismaelites residing at Constantinople and any kind of immorality in the capital, as expressed most forcefully in the *Apocalypse of St. Andrew*, may be explained by the Messiah's campaign against sin and his purification of Jerusalem and Israel.[95]

The details about the end of the Last Emperor's reign differ from those predicted in Jewish apocalyptic for the Messiah, but certain general features agree: just as some Byzantine apocalypses are silent on the subject and others give various timespans (32, 112, 120 years) for his reign, so several Late Jewish apocalyptic texts also omit the topic, predict an eternal reign, or allow for a reign varying from forty to seven thousand years.[96]

Finally, only one piece of biblical evidence cited in the Byzantine apocalypses, Psalm 68:31, seems to have had a relation to the Messianic period and to have been so understood in most Christian sources; yet, even in this case the Byzantine apocalypses that interpret it as a prophecy of the eternity of the Roman Empire (Pseudo-Methodian tradition) place on it a meaning it did not have in Judaism.[97]

The use made in Byzantine apocalypses of Psalm 68:31 may serve as a warning against attempting to interpret all aspects of the legend of the Last Emperor as a mere survival of Jewish Messianic notions. In fact, a number of features in the Byzantine expectation of a Last Emperor are clearly later elaborations and developments. Thus the references or allusions to the New Testament (Matt. 24:37; I Cor. 15:24; II Thess. 2) are obviously Christian additions. The name Constans given to the Last Roman Emperor in the Latin version of the Tiburtine Sibyl cannot be earlier than the period of rivalry between Constantine the Great's sons, and the description of his physical qualities in the same text seems to belong with it.[98] The Lion-Whelp oracle and the Last Emperor's expedi-

---

94. Volz, *Eschatologie*, pp. 214f.; Schürer, *Jüdischen Volkes*, pp. 622–25; Bousset-Gressmann, *Religion des Judentums*, pp. 236, 241, 257–59.

95. Volz, *Eschatologie*, pp. 177, 212, 215, 217, 219; Schürer, *Jüdischen Volkes*, pp. 632; Bousset-Gressmann, *Religion des Judentums*, pp. 232, 236.

96. Volz, *Eschatologie*, pp. 226–28.

97. On the Messianic interpretation of certain Psalms, see L. Dennefeld, "Messianisme," *Dictionnaire de Théologie Catholique* 10, 2 (Paris, 1928), pp. 1404–1568; on Psalm 68:29ff., p. 1463 (it was interpreted by the rabbis as referring to God rather than to the Messiah; cf. Strack-Billerbeck, *Kommentar*, III, p. 147 (*ad* I Cor. 10:11). [Note in the author's hand: Psalm 78:65 was also given a Messianic interpretation; see Romanos XLIIX, *On the Resurrection*, st. 10, line 7 (= Grosdidier des Matons, ed., IV, p. 468).]

98. N. 74 above.

tion to "Longobardia" and to Rome arose, as was shown above, in the eighth and ninth centuries respectively. For other details it is not possible to ascertain a date, but although it is difficult to discover a specific Jewish precedent they express the spirit of Jewish Messianic expectations and seem to be embellishments of Jewish conceptions. Thus the blasphemous boast of the Ismaelites, in the Pseudo-Methodian tradition, that the Romans have no redeemer or savior dramatizes the Jewish notion that the Messiah will appear at the moment of deepest crisis. The Last Emperor's humble social origin and his discovery as a consequence of divine revelation, details that do not emerge in Byzantine apocalypses prior to the *Visions of Daniel*, reproduce Jewish views about the supernatural aura surrounding the Messiah. No sons are mentioned in the Jewish tradition as aiding the Messiah in his military tasks, but the fact that, in the Pseudo-Methodian tradition, sons of the Last Roman Emperor liberate the Promised Land from Ismaelite domination is best explained as a development of the Messiah's special relationship to Palestine and Jerusalem.[99]

The most important feature of the Last Roman Emperor for which there is no explicit Messianic precedent, the episode of his surrender of imperial power at Jerusalem, may be explained in a similar way. Here, the process of legendary development can be studied in the extant texts. In the earliest mention, that in the Latin version of the Tiburtine Sibyl, his only gesture is the act of laying down diadem and all other royal attire.[100] In the Syriac Pseudo-Methodius, the Last Emperor not only places his diadem on the Cross (restored to Mount Golgotha by the emperor Heraclius in 630, after its captivity in Persia) but also stretches out his hands to heaven, both gestures being symbolic of his abdication of imperial power. While neither scene nor gestures have a Jewish model, the underlying idea—namely, the notion that the reign of the Messiah will be of finite duration and will be followed by a new age of the world—is well attested in Judaism.[101] Into this basic concept, Byzantine apocalyptists introduced modifications and additions: the author-

---

99. P. 155 above; cf. Schürer, *Jüdischen Volkes*, p. 629. [In "The Last Roman Emperor," p. 7, Alexander states that the references to "sons" in the Syriac Pseudo-Methodius should be taken as "counselors": ". . . in Syriac the two meanings are differentiated merely by one vowel sign (if the text indicates vowels at all) (*bar malka* = "son of the king"; *bar melka* = "counselor"). . . . The development of the idea in the Greek and Latin versions must, then, result from a mis-reading (οἱ υἱοὶ τοῦ βασιλέως and *filii regis*) of the Syriac."]

100. [See n. 44 for Alexander's reconsiderations on the date of the Latin Sibyl in the seventh century.]

101. Volz, *Eschatologie*, pp. 63–66, 71–77, 226–28; Schürer, *Jüdischen Volkes*, pp. 635f.

ity surrendered extended no longer just over Israel but over the Roman Empire, presumably on the basis of II Thess. 2:7 ("only he who now restrains it will do so until he is out of the way"), alluded to by Pseudo-Ephraem and Pseudo-Methodius; the dramatic gestures of laying down imperial insignia (first attested in the Latin version of the Tiburtine Sibyl) on the Holy Cross (first in Pseudo-Methodius) and of the hands stretched out to God (first in Pseudo-Methodius), on the basis of Psalm 68:31; and the ceremony of a surrender or transfer of power, on the basis of I Cor. 15:24 (first attested in the Latin Sibyl). The scene of the surrender at Jerusalem, the most important new aspect of the legend of the Last Emperor as compared with Jewish Messianism, is therefore, like other features of the legend, a dramatization of Jewish notions developed from Old and New Testament passages.

Thus the hypothesis, put forward above, that the Byzantine expectation of a Last Roman Emperor is a survival of the Jewish hope for a national liberator, a Messiah, is now confirmed by a detailed comparison of these beliefs. The point made here is not merely that certain features of the Byzantine belief in a Last Roman Emperor are borrowings from Jewish Messianism. The surprising conclusion is that *all* the constituent elements of the Byzantine legend of the Last Roman Emperor are derived from this source: directly, the Emperor's role as redeemer or savior from foreign domination and oppression by non-believers; his function as bringer of prosperity, justice, and joy; his sudden emergence during a desperate military crisis; even the sources' vagueness as to his personality; indirectly, such later embellishments as the blasphemous boast of the enemy; the humble origin and the sons of the Emperor; his discovery by divine revelation; and, above all, the powerful dramatic scene of the surrender at Jerusalem.

How is one to explain this transformation of the expectation of a Jewish Messiah into that of a Last Roman Emperor? It should be noted that it is a highly selective process. Late Judaism developed not one common set of beliefs regarding the coming Messiah but a number of competing, often conflicting views held by different groups within Judaism and scattered over a large variety of writings.[102] Among them one contrast is particularly important. While in some Jewish apocalypses the expectation is of a Messianic king of Israel from the house of David, this is replaced or combined in other texts with a figure of quite different range and character, a transcendent and preexistent Man or Son

---

102. Volz, *Eschatologie*, 201–203 ("Die Vielfältigkeit der eschatologischen Heilsgestalt").

of Man concerned not so much with the Jewish people as with mankind in general, the establishment of universal peace, and the destruction of evil.[103]

This twofold expectation was but part of a more far-reaching development combining an eschatology of national Jewish origin and intent with a set of beliefs concerned with mankind as a whole. The two kinds of eschatology and Messianism fulfilled different kinds of spiritual needs: the former, that of a group bound together by common origin, religion, and vicinity; the other, of groups residing far from their homeland dispersed among populations of different backgrounds. In order to bring some order into these various eschatological expectations, some Late Jewish writings such as IV Ezra and II Baruch conceived of the period of the national Jewish Messiah as a period preparatory to the new age of the world and to the Last Judgment over all mankind.[104]

It is interesting that the features of Jewish Messianism transformed into the Byzantine legend of a Last Roman Emperor referred exclusively to the Messiah as King of the Jews, rather than to the universal concept. They seem to have originated and been cherished less among the rabbis than in limited circles of apocalyptic sectarians and, especially, among the popular masses. This is clear particularly from the records of the Jewish War (68–70) and of the revolt of Bar Kochba (133–135), when the sources mention a series of Messianic figures finding a large following among the people.[105]

---

103. Ibid., pp. 204–208; Schürer, *Jüdischen Volkes*, pp. 586f.; Bousset-Gressmann, *Religion des Judentums*, pp. 259ff., 286f.

104. II Baruch 40:3, p. 501 Charles: "And his [the Messiah's] principate will stand for ever, until the world of corruption is at an end, and until the times aforesaid are fulfilled"; IV Ezra 7:27, p. 582 Charles: "For my son the Messiah shall be revealed, together with those who are with him, and shall rejoice the survivors four hundred years. And it shall be, after these years, that my Son the Messiah shall die, and all in whom there is human breath. Then shall the world be changed into the primaeval silence seven days. . . ." Cf. Volz, *Eschatologie*, pp. 71–77, 203, 227–29; Bousset-Gressmann, *Religion des Judentums*, p. 259. Volz, p. 71, speaks of "die national Heilszeit als Vorperiode" and of the time of the Messiah as a "Zwischenreich."

105. Volz, *Eschatologie*, pp. 9f., 183f.; Bousset-Gressmann, *Religion des Judentums*, p. 268. [In "The Last Roman Emperor," pp. 11–12, Alexander went on to suggest that the Syriac Pseudo-Methodius' channel for this tradition was a Jewish Messianic community in Northern Mesopotamia (attested by Aphrahates in the fourth century): "That Pseudo-Methodius had access to circles linked to Judaism is shown not only by his date on the Last Roman Empire, but also by the sources used in other portions of his tract. For the early history of the world he depended heavily and for a large part literally, on a Syriac source of the sixth century, the *Cave of Treasures*, which in turn was based on pre-Christian Jewish materials. . . . Furthermore, one of the earliest fathers of the northern Mesopotamian Church, Aphrahates, who died shortly after 345, directed several of his Demonstrations against the religion of the local Jews. The magnitude and intensity of his literary effort bears witness to the appeal that Jewish rites and ideas had for members of the Christian congregations in the area. One Jewish claim that Aphrahates specifically

It is not difficult to surmise that the notion of a Messianic age survived in some of the Jewish circles converted to Christianity, the "Jewish Christians," especially in the shape of a period preparatory to the Second Coming and the Last Judgment. In fact, it has been noted that St. Paul's view, expressed in I Cor. 15:23ff., presupposes the concept of the Messiah's rule on earth.[106] St. Paul was of Jewish origin, as was probably the last redactor of the canonical book of Revelation, where the Christian martyrs are expected to rule with Christ for a thousand years prior to the general resurrection and the Last Judgment (20:4).

Thus while the survival of the belief in a national Jewish Messiah into Christian times is documented, the next step in its development can merely be hypothesis. The principal task of the Jewish Messiah had been the military protection of the land and people of Israel against the unbelieving nations: the Hellenistic powers, later Rome. How was the principal defender of Israel against Rome transformed into a Roman emperor? One factor facilitating this development was, it may be suggested, a rapprochement between certain circles within Christianity and the Roman Empire, accompanied by the weakening of the ties with (even hostility toward) Judaism. Beginning with Irenaeus, almost all the Church Fathers see in the Roman Empire the power "restraining" the Antichrist and the end, according to II Thess. 2:7. From this even a Tertullian, normally hostile to Rome, occasionally draws the conclusion that Christians should pray for the Roman "emperors, for the entire order of the empire, and for Roman institutions." A century later Lactantius expressed himself in similar terms.[107] Simultaneously the Antichrist was often expected to be not of Roman but of Jewish origin, and it has been plausibly suggested that this notion is due to the early Christian community's growing hatred of the Jews.[108]

In addition, as memories of the Jewish origins of Christianity, the independent Jewish state, and the Temple receded, as Christians came to

---

refutes is that 'it is still certain for Israel to be gathered together' which makes clear that his Jewish neighbors expected to be recalled from the Dispersion to the Promised Land by an act of divine 'redemption'—a concept which played a key role in Pseudo-Methodius' Christian apocalypse. Thus for the Syriac churches of northern Mesopotamia, Judaeo-Christian and Jewish communities may have been the channels through which Jewish Messianism reached the author of the *Cave of Treasures* in the sixth century and Pseudo-Methodius in the seventh."]

106. Bousset-Gressmann, *Religion des Judentums*, p. 288; W. Bauer, "Chiliasmus," *Reallexikon für Antike und Christentum* 2, pp. 1073–78, esp. 1076.

107. Bousset, *Antichrist*, pp. 16, 77–79 (where the passages from Tertullian and Lactantius are cited).

108. Bousset, *Antichrist*, pp. 85f.; cf. W. H. C. Frend, *Martyrdom and Persecution in the Early Church: A Study of a Conflict from the Maccabees to Donatus* (Oxford, 1965), pp. 258f. and passim.

think of Jews as members of isolated congregations living in the Diaspora within a foreign environment, and as Christianity came to conceive of itself as a missionary religion destined to convert the Roman world, the expectation of a Messianic king of Israel bringing peace, justice, and prosperity to the Christian churches may have seemed more and more incongruous. The conversion of Constantine, in particular, must have served as an incentive for substituting a powerful Roman emperor for the by-now-nebulous Jewish king. An eschatological identification between Roman and Christian Empire occurs in Pseudo-Ephraem, which probably belongs to the fourth century.[109] It is therefore not unreasonable to surmise that during the reign of Constantine the Great at the latest, in Christian eschatology a Last Roman Emperor took the place held in Late Jewish apocalyptic by a Jewish king.

109. P. 213.17 Caspari: *et iam regnum Romanorum tollitur de medio et Christianorum imperium traditur Deo et Patri.*

# II.
# Gog and Magog

All the Byzantine apocalypses here under consideration insert—normally between the victorious campaigns of the Last Roman Emperor and his establishment of peace and prosperity, on the one hand, and the Antichrist's domination, on the other—a terrible onslaught of barbarian peoples. It is the legend of Gog and Magog, although these names are not always mentioned.[1]

In the Latin version of the Tiburtine Sibyl the story makes its appearance during the reign of the Last Roman Emperor, following a description of the prosperity of his reign, his campaigns against pagans, his conversion of Jews, and the first "rise" of the Antichrist, but prior to the Last Roman Emperor's surrender of empire at Jerusalem and the "manifest revelation" of the Antichrist. The invaders from the North are named Gog and Magog; they are designated as "very impure nations" (*spurcissime gentes*) said to have been imprisoned by Alexander the Great. They number twenty-two (variant: twelve) kingdoms and are subdued by an army summoned by the Last Roman Emperor.[2]

1. A convenient summary of the legend of Gog and Magog in Judaism and early Christianity has been provided by Karl Georg Kuhn, "Γὼγ καὶ Μαγώγ," *Theologisches Wörterbuch zum Neuen Testament* I (Stuttgart, 1933), pp. 790–92: Strack and Billerbeck, *Kommentar*, III, pp. 831–40; also the commentaries on Rev. 20:7–10, e.g., by Bousset, *Die Offenbarung Johannis* (repr. Göttingen, 1966), pp. 438–40; on Late Judaism in particular see Volz, *Eschatologie*, pp. 149–52; Bousset-Gressmann, *Religion des Judentums*, pp. 218ff.; on the medieval legend the classic account is that by Graf, *Roma nella memoria e nelle immaginazioni del Medio Evo*, pp. 507–563. See also Bousset, *Antichrist*, pp. 128f. (and passim); "Beiträge," 113–31; Sackur, *Sibyllinische Texte*, pp. 33–39.

2. Pp. '186.1–6. There is no parallel account in the *Oracle of Baalbek*, except that perhaps the description of the reign of the "Emperor with the Changing Shape" (lines 190ff.) may embody certain features elsewhere associated with the legend of Gog and Magog, such as the use of poisoned arrows (see my note on the passage, *Commentary*, pp. 37–40) and the flight of the woman from West to East (line 200).

In Pseudo-Ephraem the invasion of *gentes bellicae* or *nequissimae* appears among the signs of the end. As we have seen (Part One, Chapter V.3) these nations are not named but described: they resemble wild animals rather than men. Although their foul habits are described, Pseudo-Ephraem gives no details of the fate of the invaders except to say that their days "will be completed" and that then the earth (*terra*, land [of Israel?]) will be in repose.³

In the Syriac Pseudo-Methodius, the invaders are mentioned twice, once in the "historical" section in connection with the account of Alexander the Great's reign and again in the eschatological part. The first reference, discussed in Part One, Chapter I, describes in some detail the impurity of the "sons of Japheth"; here the author also recounts Alexander's imprisonment of the invaders behind a bronze gate, held fast with a miraculous substance. This gate stopped the nations but the author prophesies that, in accordance with the prophecy of Ezekiel (38:8, freely quoted) "in the end of times, at the end of the world, the followers of Āgōg and Māgōg will come out upon the land of Israel." This first account of the future invaders ends with a list of the twenty-two kingdoms imprisoned by Alexander, beginning with Āgōg and Māgōg.⁴

The Syriac Pseudo-Methodius returns to Gog and Magog after he has predicted the defeat of the Ismaelites by the Last Roman Emperor and a period of peace and prosperity following upon his victories. During this period of peace, he prophesies, the Gates of the North will be opened and the nations imprisoned behind them will rush forward. He describes, in terms similar to those of Pseudo-Ephraem, the fear and flight of men and the impurity of the invaders: the victims will hide in mountains, caves, and tombs; there will be no one to bury them; and the newcomers will eat human flesh and unclean animals and drink the blood of animals. Pseudo-Methodius knows, however, unlike Pseudo-Ephraem, how they will meet their end. After one week (of years?) they will assemble in the plain of Joppe (now Haifa, in Israel) and there they will be destroyed within one hour by "one of the captains of the host of angels," i.e., an archangel.⁵

With minor variants this twofold account of the legend of Gog and Magog reappears in the Greek and Latin versions of Pseudo-Methodius as well as in some of the *Visions of Daniel*.⁶ In the *Slavonic Daniel* the

3. Pp. 212.13–213.17.
4. Fols. 124 recto–125 recto.
5. Fols. 134 verso–135 recto.
6. Greek Pseudo-Methodius, pp. 18.2–20.16 and 44.1–16 Istrin (= pp. 78.1–82 and 128.95–130.112 Lolos); Latin text, pp. 72.10–75.7 and 91.22–93.1; "historical" past alone in Pseudo-Chrysostom: p. 33.13–34.6; free version of eschatological section only

invasion is predicted to occur not during the reign of the Last Roman Emperor, who will surrender his power at Jerusalem, but during that of his immediate predecessor, of whose rule nothing except this incident is reported: "Afterward another scepter will arise. In his times twelve emperors will arise from the Gates of the Snakes." This predecessor himself will succeed an emperor reigning thirty-two years whose wrath will be directed against apostates, who will bring peace, joy, and prosperity and will protect and strengthen the Church. Clearly the normal functions of the Last Roman Emperor are here distributed over a series of rulers, and the "twelve emperors" arising from the "Gates of the Snakes" are the hordes of Gog and Magog.[7]

This survey of the Byzantine apocalyptic material shows that for the episode of Gog and Magog there existed a uniform tradition exhibiting, however, a number of significant variants. Gog (Syriac: *Āgōg*) and Magog are named in all the texts except Pseudo-Ephraem, who refers to *gentes bellicae* or *nequissimae*. Their wildness, cruelty, or impurity is elaborated in all the texts.[8] Except for Pseudo-Ephraem, all of them mention their northern habitat and their imprisonment by Alexander the Great in greater or lesser detail. The Latin Sibyl knows that the invaders consist of twenty-two (twelve) *regna* and the three versions of Pseudo-Methodius, as well as Pseudo-Chrysostom, name the participating nations. The reactions of their victims, their panic and their flight, are detailed everywhere except in the brief account of the Latin Sibyl. Finally, while according to this latter text the invaders are vanquished by an army summoned by the Last Roman Emperor and while according to Pseudo-Ephraem their time simply comes to an end, the Pseudo-Methodian tradition ascribes their annihilation to divine intervention: after a week (of years?) God will send an archangel who will destroy them "in one hour" in the plain of Joppe.

Thus the Byzantine apocalyptic tradition combines a high degree of uniformity with a certain amount of variation. Pseudo-Ephraem in particular offers a number of variants: he does not name Gog and Magog, does not mention that the *nequissimae gentes* reside in the North, and

---

in *Daniel Καὶ ἔσται*, p. 42.3–10. No mention of Gog and Magog occurs in the text of the Erythraean Sibyl.

7. *Slavonic Daniel*, #9–10. Compare the twenty-two (or twelve) kingdoms in the Latin version of the Tiburtine Sibyl. The Gates of the Snakes (*aspidov' vrat'*) undoubtedly are a corruption of the Caspian Gates, with which Alexander's Gates were frequently identified.

8. In the Latin version of the Tiburtine Sibyl it is indicated by no more than the words *spurcissime gentes*.

does not refer to Alexander the Great. One may hesitate to attach much importance to these omissions; Pseudo-Ephraem's account of Gog and Magog is very brief and it could therefore be argued that he decided to sacrifice these details to the cause of concision. Abbreviation rather than divergence may also explain the fact that while in all the other texts the hosts of Gog and Magog are destroyed by an angel, Pseudo-Ephraem alone simply records that "the days of the times of those nations were completed." In this instance we may take as a warning, however, the fact that the Latin text of the Tiburtine Sibyl also differs from the Pseudo-Methodian tradition in this regard: here the Last Roman Emperor rather than an angel defeats the invaders. Moreover, a desire for concision fails to explain one further peculiarity of Pseudo-Ephraem: unlike the other texts here under consideration, in which the invasion is expected during the reign of the Last Roman Emperor, Pseudo-Ephraem predicts it among the tribulations preceding the end of the world. As Pseudo-Ephraem is also unique in that he does not know the figure of the Last Roman Emperor (Part Two, Chapter I, above), there is not necessarily any conflict here. Conflict does, however, arise from the fact that in all other texts the invasions occur after a period of victory and prosperity of the Roman Empire, presumably because the newcomers envy or covet the wealth of the inhabitants, while in Pseudo-Ephraem the invasions form the climax of a series of natural disasters—epidemics, wars, famine, drought, and persecutions—and tranquility follows rather than precedes the invasion.[9]

How is one to explain the origins of this tradition, including its variants? It has long been recognized that one of its sources is the Romance of Alexander the Great as embodied not only in these Byzantine apocalypses but also in other documents such as a Christian legend concerning Alexander written in Syriac, a metrical homily by the Syriac poet Jacob of Sarug (†521), the Koran (sura 18.89) and a late Greek recension of the Romance of Alexander.[10]

---

9. P. 213.16: *Cumque conpleti fuerint dies temporum gentium illarum, postquam terram conrumperint, requiescet [terra]*. A Syriac homily (probably falsely) attributed to St. Ephraem also predicts the coming of Gog and Magog, here identified with the Huns, among the signs of the end and preceding a period of God-given peace: see *Sancti Ephraem Syri Hymni et Sermones*, ed. Th. J. Lamy (Mechlinae, 1889), III, pp. 193–204, esp. 202f.: *Tunc* [i.e., after the destruction of the invaders by the archangel Michael] *Dominus suscitabit pacem suam e coelo suo glorioso*. Bousset, *Antichrist*, pp. 35–37, and "Beiträge," p. 116, considered this part of the work as of fourth-century origin, while Theodore Nöldeke—"Beiträge zur Geschichte des Alexanderromans," pp. 31f., and in his review of Lamy's edition in *Wiener Zeitschrift für die Kunde des Morgenlandes* 4 (1890), p. 144—as well as Sackur, *Sibyllinische Texte*, p. 34, thought that it was written around 640.

10. The classic account is still Graf, *Roma nella memoria*, II, pp. 517–534. The Christian Syriac legend was edited and translated by Budge, *History of Alexander*, pp. 255–75

Among the features of Byzantine apocalyptic derived from this legend of Alexander are the story of his visit to the place where the sun rises; the discovery and the names of twelve or twenty-two or twenty-four barbarian peoples and their repulsive customs; and, above all, the erection by Alexander of a bronze gate designed to hem in these barbarians and the prophecy that at the end of time they would invade the Roman Empire. Even some of these features may have ultimate Jewish roots, for already Josephus and, later, St. Jerome knew of iron gates built by Alexander to prevent as yet unnamed "wild peoples" from crossing the Caucasus.[11]

It is generally recognized, however, that the legend of Alexander was grafted upon the prophecy in Ezekiel of a combined onslaught, at the end of time, of powerful nations allied with Gog of the land of Magog against the Holy Land and their destruction. In chs. 37–39 (and related texts) the prophet predicts a return of the Jews to the land of Israel, to live there under a king from the house of David (37:21–24). God will then rouse Gog, of the land of Magog (38:2) and according to Gen. 10:2 one of the sons of Japheth, at the head of a large army of peoples "in the latter years against the land that is restored from war," the land of Israel where the returnees live securely under Messianic conditions of cultivation and security (38:8). Gog's purpose will be "to seize spoil and carry off plunder" (38:12), but God will destroy him and his host in the land of Israel by pestilence, bloodshed, rain and hailstones, and fire and brimstone (38:22). Gog will perish upon the mountains of Israel, and God will send fire upon the land of Magog. For seven years the people of Israel will burn the weapons of the invaders (39:9).

---

(text), 144–61 (translation). Nöldeke, "Beiträge," p. 31, showed that it was composed in 514–15, and Bousset, "Beiträge," p. 114, added that in its published form it shows traces of a revision around 640. On Jacob of Sarug's homily see Nöldeke, p. 30. The latest studies of the Greek text of Pseudo-Callisthenes arrive at the opinion that the relevant sections are derived from Pseudo-Methodius; see the edition and discussion by van Thiel, *Rezension* λ, pp. 51ff.; Reinhold Merkelbach, *Die Quellen des griechischen Alexanderromans*, Zetemata 9 (Munich, 1954), p. 108; and J. Trumpf, "Alexander, die Bersiler und die Brüste des Nordens," *Byzantinische Zeitschrift* 64 (1971), pp. 326–28, esp. 327f. In the Syriac Pseudo-Methodius' "prophecy" of the Ismaelite invasions it is said (fol. 129 recto) that Ismael "will seize the entrances of the North"; cf. also Greek Pseudo-Methodius, p. 30.1 Istrin (= p. 104.4 Lolos); Latin text, p. 83.18 Sackur. This is presumably a motif of the prophecy of an invasion according to the Alexander legend, here transferred to an historical enemy.

11. Josephus *Bellum Judaicum* 7.7.4: The Alans negotiate with the king of the Hyrcani because they wish to raid Media, τῆς παρόδου γὰρ οὗτος δεσπότης ἐστίν, ἣν ὁ βασιλεὺς Ἀλέξανδρος πύλαις σιδηραῖς κλείστην ἐποίησε [for he is the lord of the passage, which King Alexander made fast with iron gates]; Jerome, *Ep.* 77.8 (*ad Oceanum de morte Fabiolae*): . . . *Caucasi rupibus feras gentes Alexandri claustra cohibent.* Cf. Graf, *Roma nella memoria*, pp. 518–20; Bousset, "Beiträge," pp. 115f. Nöldeke, "Beiträge," p. 26, points out, however, that the rabbinic sources know nothing of Alexander's erection of a gate against the "wild peoples."

Thus the Byzantine apocalypses derive from Ezekiel (and related texts such as Gen. 10:2) the notion of an onslaught of the nations and their destruction by the will of God. It is true that in the Byzantine apocalypses it is not stated clearly, as it is in Ezekiel, that the Holy Land will be the target of the attack; yet, there are traces of this view. Thus it is significant that in the Pseudo-Methodian tradition the plain of Joppe in Palestine is mentioned as the place of convergence and destruction of the invading peoples. Another trace of Ezekiel's prophecy of an attack on Israel may be the (inexact) citation of Ezekiel 38:8 in the Syriac Pseudo-Methodius: "In the end of times, at the end of the world, the followers of Āgōg and of Māgōg will come out upon the land of Israel."[12] The names of Gog and Magog, and their relation to Japheth in the Pseudo-Methodian tradition, also derive from Ezekiel and Genesis. So does their northern starting point in the Latin version of the Tiburtine Sibyl and in the Pseudo-Methodian tradition (cf. Ezek. 38:6). Finally, the timing of Gog and Magog's attack during a period of peace and prosperity in the entire Byzantine tradition (except in Pseudo-Ephraem) is reminiscent of Ezek. chs. 37–39, where the attack of Gog not only follows the reestablishment of the Jews to Palestine under a Messianic king (37:24ff.) but it is repeatedly stressed (38:8, 10, 13, 14) that Gog's invasion of Israel will take place at a time when Israel is at peace and the population lives in security.

Byzantine indebtedness to Jewish tradition appears even greater if one includes Jewish materials outside the Old Testament that refer to the legend of Gog and Magog. While in Ezekiel the name Gog had been a personal name—namely, that of the prince of Magog—those Byzantine apocalypses that contain that name agree with the Revelation of John 20:8 (the work of a Jewish Christian), and with most of the rabbinic sources, in seeing in it the name of a people paralleling Magog.[13] As to the place of Gog and Magog's attack in the eschatological time schedule, there is, as shown above, no agreement in the Byzantine apocalypses. An even greater hesitation as to the timing of Gog's invasion prevails in the rabbinic sources: they place it prior to the days of

---

12. Fol. 124 verso. Another verse of Ezekiel (39:17) is also cited freely but as a saying of the Lord, fol. 128 recto: "We are like[?] the animals of the field and the birds of heaven, and call them [saying]: Assemble and come because today I shall make a great sacrifice for you. Eat the flesh of the fattened [animals] and drink the blood of the mighty men." Here a biblical prophecy concerning the destruction of Gog and Magog is applied to an historical Arab victory over the Romans (Byzantines) at Gaba'ōt the Great (the battle on the river Jarmuk, A.D. 636).

13. Strack and Billerbeck, *Kommentar*, III, pp. 831f.

the Messiah, during the time of the Messiah, or after it.[14] Just as many Jewish teachers felt that an invasion of Gog after the reign of the Messiah would cast doubt on his efficacy, so the authors of Byzantine apocalypses were unwilling to allow for this new outbreak of evil after the Last Roman Emperor, the medieval counterpart of the Jewish Messiah, had surrendered his power to God on Golgotha. But the vacillation among Byzantine apocalyptists in assigning the time of the attack as either prior to or during the period of Messianic repose and prosperity is a survival of differences in Late Judaism.

Furthermore, if Pseudo-Ephraem remarks laconically that the earth (or the land [of Israel?]) will be at rest when the time of the *nequissimae gentes* is completed, this notion of a definite time-limit allowed to the invaders may be either a reference to Ezek. 39:9 (the Israelites will burn the invaders' arms during seven years) or an echo of the ambiguous opinion, expressed by certain rabbis of the third and fourth centuries, that "the years of Gog" will amount to seven.[15] Probably this is also the source of the prediction, in the Pseudo-Methodian tradition, that the hosts of Gog and Magog will assemble and be defeated in the plain of Joppe "after one week [of years] of calamity."[16] The plain of Joppe does not seem to be attested, in Jewish rabbinical literature, as the place of the destruction of Gog and Magog, but the plain of Jericho is.[17] Perhaps it is legitimate to infer from the fact that a plain is mentioned with regard to their annihilation in both traditions, combined with St. Peter's vision of unclean animals at Joppe (Acts 10:9), that Christian circles shifted the end of the unclean hordes of Gog and Magog from the plain of Jericho to that of Joppe. Finally, just as according to the Latin version of the Tiburtine Sibyl the Last Roman Emperor is the agent of the destruction and in the Pseudo-Methodian tradition an archangel, so according to the Jewish sources both the Messiah and the archangel Michael are mentioned as alternative destroyers of Gog.[18]

In the Byzantine apocalypses the legend of Gog and Magog invariably appears in close relationship with the career of the Last Roman Emperor or, where he is not mentioned, as in Pseudo-Ephraem, with the emergence of a period of repose and prosperity elsewhere associated with this figure. It may serve as a confirmation of the conclusions

---

14. Ibid., pp. 832–34, where the texts are translated or summarized. See also Volz, *Eschatologie*, p. 151; Kuhn, "Γὼγ," p. 791.

15. Strack and Billerbeck, *Kommentar* I, pp. 517f.; III, p. 835.

16. Syriac Pseudo-Methodius, fol. 134 verso.

17. Strack and Billerbeck, *Kommentar* III, p. 837.

18. Ibid.; for Michael see also pp. 832f. On the Messianic role of Michael in Late Judaism, see Bousset, *Antichrist*, pp. 151–53.

reached in Part Two, Chapter I, "The Last Roman Emperor," that the legend of Gog and Magog, too, has strong roots in Old Testament prophecy and in the teachings of the rabbis. Just as in the case of the Last Roman Emperor, however, these Jewish roots alone do not suffice to explain the Byzantine development: in all Byzantine apocalypses the Jewish legend of Gog and Magog appears combined with the story of Alexander and his bronze gate, which was unknown to the rabbis until it reached them by way of Pseudo-Callisthenes.[19] Even this source does not explain all the details of the Byzantine development of the legend of Gog and Magog. Just as the figure of the Last Roman Emperor became elaborated in Christian quarters, so the legend of Gog and Magog acquired improvements and embellishments among Christians. The substitution of the plain of Joppe for that of Jericho as the place of annihilation, just mentioned, may be a case in point. Another may be the vivid description of the flight and the hiding-places chosen by the victims of Gog and Magog, in Pseudo-Ephraem as well as in the Pseudo-Methodian tradition, and the intensification of the impurity of the invaders in the various descriptions.[20]

19. Nöldeke, "Beiträge," p. 26.
20. Flight of victims: Pseudo-Ephraem, Caspari, pp. 212.13–213.3; Syriac Pseudo-Methodius, fol. 134 verso; Greek Pseudo-Methodius, p. 44.4 Istrin (= p. 128.97 Lolos). Latin Pseudo-Methodius, p. 92.1 Sackur. On the impurity of Gog and Magog, compare Latin Sibyl 186.2 (the only pertinent remark: *spurcissime gentes*) with Syriac Pseudo-Methodius, fols. 124 verso and 134 recto (filthy and ugly, eat vermin, mice, dogs, cats, reptiles, do not bury dead, eat aborted human fetuses, force mothers to eat corpses of children, eat human flesh and drink blood of animals); cf. Greek Pseudo-Methodius, pp. 18.5 and 44.7 Istrin (= p. 78.23 Lolos); Latin Pseudo-Methodius, pp. 72.13 and 92.1 Sackur.

# III.
# The Legend of the Antichrist

While for the expectation of a Last Roman Emperor there exists no previous study of a comprehensive kind, for the Antichrist there exist a number of important studies, above all the classic and profound monograph by Wilhelm Bousset, who collected and analyzed the material pertaining to the early Church.[1] Furthermore, Bousset established sound principles for the interpretation of apocalyptic materials, gave precious hints on the prehistory of the idea of the Antichrist in biblical and extra-canonical texts, and included much information on its development during the Middle Ages in East and West. In spite of the existence of this and other studies, I hope that a concentration on Byzantine materials here will lead to new results.

Whatever opinion one may hold on the thorny question of the pre-Christian origins of the notion of the Antichrist, it is clear that by the beginning of the Byzantine period the word Antichrist (ὁ 'Αντίχριστος, Antichristus) was well established. In fact, as early as the beginning of the third century, Hippolytus of Rome had composed a monograph entitled *Demonstration from Holy Scriptures Concerning Christ and the Antichrist*.[2] In Byzantine apocalypses the term is current, but it is worth noting that while at the time of Hippolytus the word χριστός, as is indicated by the lack of the definite article in the title of Hippolytus' work, had already become and was felt to be a proper name, no similar devel-

---

1. See the bibliography in the short but informative article of E. Lohmeyer, "Antichrist," *Reallexikon für Antike und Christentum* I (Stuttgart, 1950), pp. 450–57, esp. 456f.
2. 'Απόδειξις ἐκ τῶν 'Αγίων Γραφῶν περὶ Χριστοῦ καὶ περὶ τοῦ 'Αντιχρίστου: ed. Hans Achelis, *GCS*, vol. I, pt. 2 (Leipzig, 1897), p. 3. In canonical scripture the term *Antichrist* appears only in the Epistles of John, e.g., I John 2:18 and II John 7.

opment took place with regard to his counterpart. The latter was characterized not by a personal name but by an activity: opposition to Christ.[3] It is also noteworthy that in several Byzantine apocalypses there appears a marked reluctance to use the term Antichrist; the authors prefer a series of circumlocutions. Thus in Pseudo-Ephraem's homily the word *Antichristus* occurs only once, in the last section; functional paraphrases are used elsewhere.[4] Similarly, the *Oracle of Baalbek* refers to him by his ability to change his shape (from young to old man, etc.).[5] Syriac or Greek equivalents of such terms occur in several other apocalypses.[6] Other phrases are occasionally added to the repertoire. Thus the Latin text of the Tiburtine Sibyl calls the Antichrist the "prince of iniquity, son of perdition, head of pride, master of error, fullness of wickedness."[7] Pseudo-Ephraem speaks in similar terms of the Antichrist's moral qualities, his wrath, iniquity, cleverness, his tendency to lie, and, especially, his hypocrisy, which enables him to win many adherents:

But the accursed destroyer of souls rather than of bodies, a crafty serpent while he grows up, appears in the cloak of justice before he assumes power. For to all men he will be cunningly gentle, unwilling to accept gifts or to place [his own] person first, lovable to everybody, peaceful to all, not striving after gifts of

---

3. Bousset, *Antichrist*, pp. 86, 99–101, holds, with some hesitation ("scheint"), that already in II Cor. 6:15 Belial was used as a name of Antichrist. Other scholars—e.g., Werner Foerster, "Βελιάρ," *Theologisches Wörterbuch zum Neuen Testament*, I (Stuttgart, 1950), p. 606—think that Belial is, rather, a name of the Devil.

4. Designations of Antichrist in Pseudo-Ephraem, ed. Caspari: *malus* (elsewhere often used for Devil), pp. 209.7, 210.15; *draco* (elsewhere frequently the Devil), pp. 214.5, 216.2, 219.9; *ille nefandus, mendax et homicida*, p. 215.7 (cf. p. 216.1: *nefandus ille corruptor*); *abominatio desolationis* (Dan. 9:27), p. 216.10; *nequissimus serpens* (elsewhere often Devil), p. 217.6; *inimicus*, pp. 219.12, 220.8; *aduersarius serpens*, p. 219.14; *Antichristus* (I John 2:18; II John 7), p. 219.18; *inimicus uel perditionis filius* (II Thess. 2:3), p. 220.1. On the frequent identification of the Antichrist with the Devil, see Bousset, *Antichrist*, pp. 88f.

5. *Oracle of Baalbek*, my edition, line 191 βασιλεὺς μορφὴν ἔχων ἠλλοιωμένην [a king who has a changed shape]; line 209 ὁ ἠλλοιωμένος [he who is changed]; see Bousset, *Antichrist*, pp. 94f.; and my comments in the edition, pp. 113f. and n. 54.

6. Thus *inimicus* in the Latin Pseudo-Methodius (p. 95.16 Sackur) renders ὁ ἀντικείμενος of the Greek text (p. 48.8 Istrin; = p. 138.50 Lolos); cf. Pseudo-Chrysostom, p. 38.6 Vasiliev; there is a lacuna in the Syriac original at this point. *Aduersarius* in Pseudo-Ephraem (n. 4 above) may serve as a translation of Syriac *be'eldebabā* (Beelzebub). The *abominatio desolationis* (n. 4 above) reappears as βδέλυγμα τῆς ἐρημώσεως in Pseudo-Chrysostom, p. 38.6. Some of these circumlocutions were applicable both to Devil and Antichrist (cf. G. W. H. Lampe, *Patristic Greek Lexicon* [Oxford, 1961], s.v. ἀντίκειμαι, p. 154), an ambiguity due to the fact that from early times there was doubt whether these two figures should be distinguished or identified; cf. n. 4 above and, for example, *Apocalypse of St. Andrew* 869B ὁ Σατανᾶς ὁ Ἀντίχριστος. The same text, at 856C, speaks of the Antichrist as ὁ υἱὸς τῆς ἀνομίας, which is an abbreviation of II Thess. 2:3 ὁ ἄνθρωπος τῆς ἀνομίας, ὁ υἱὸς τῆς ἀπολείας.

7. P. 185.19. On *princeps iniquitatis* compare *Oracle of Baalbek*, line 208 ὁ ἄρχων τῆς ἀπωλείας.

friendship, seemingly courteous among his entourage, so that men will bless him and say he is a just man—they do not realize that a wolf is hidden beneath the appearance of a lamb and that he is inwardly rapacious under the hide of a sheep.[8]

On the other hand, descriptions of the Antichrist's physical features as a monster in human shape—such as are found in various Oriental works, a Pseudo-Johannine apocalypse, and Late Jewish writings—do not occur in the major Byzantine apocalypses.[9]

About his origin there exists a number of traditions. From the fifth century onward, Church Fathers, both in the East and in the West, insist that the Antichrist is not to be identified with the Devil but is a human being. Some texts, however, combine this notion of a human Antichrist in various ways with concessions to an older view according to which he is the Devil himself or an even earlier personification of Evil—a serpent or a dragon. Vestiges of this view are found in the Byzantine apocalypses in some of the designations of the Antichrist.[10]

A second tradition has to do with the geographic origin of the Antichrist. All the major Byzantine apocalypses agree that he will be born from the tribe of Dan, i.e., that he will be of Jewish descent.[11] This view occurs in Christian authors as early as Irenaeus and may be older. Related to it is the expectation of an Antichrist from Babylon, for it was assumed that the tribe of Dan had been deported to Babylonia and that it continued to reside there.[12]

The birth of the Antichrist from the tribe of Dan or from Babylon

---

8. Pseudo-Ephraem, Caspari pp. 215.1 (*ira*), 215.2 (*iniquitas*), 215.7 (*mendax*), 219.14 (*calliditas*); the passage translated in the text occurs on p. 216.1–9.

9. On physical descriptions of the Antichrist, see Bousset, *Antichrist*, pp. 101f.; for bibliography see Denis, *Introduction aux pseudépigraphes grecs d'Ancien Testament*, p. 165.

10. Bousset, *Antichrist*, pp. 88–99 and passim, following earlier scholars such as Hermann Gunkel, drew from these divergences important conclusions on the origins of the expectation of the Antichrist in an ancient myth of a marine monster that had fought against God at the time of creation and would challenge him again at the end of time. For vestiges in the Byzantine apocalypses, see n. 4 above.

11. The notion of a Gentile Antichrist and especially of a *Nero redivivus*, so frequent in the early Church, has disappeared from the major Byzantine texts to be discussed here. On his descent from Dan: Latin Sibyl (p. 185.19 Sackur); Pseudo-Ephraem (p. 215.8 Caspari); Syriac Pseudo-Methodius, fol. 135 verso: "And immediately the Son of Perdition will be revealed, who is from the tribe of Dan"; fol. 136 verso: "[the Son of Perdition] is a man of sin clothed in a body from the seed of man and he will be born from a married woman from the tribe of Dan." These passages recur in the Greek (pp. 46.6, 48.3 Istrin; = pp. 134.22, 138.46 Lolos) and Latin (pp. 94.9, 95.10 Sackur) versions (where in the second text it is said that he will be born "from the seed of a man and the *womb* of a woman from the tribe of Dan." The additional word seems genuine as a parallel to the seed of the man and has probably been inadvertently omitted in the Syriac manuscript); in Pseudo-Chrysostom, p. 37.14 Vasiliev; *Daniel* Καὶ ἔσται, pp. 42.30, 43.9 Vasiliev (adding that the Antichrist's mother will be a whore); *Apocalypse of St. Andrew* 869B (p. 212 Rydén).

12. Bousset, *Antichrist*, pp. 112f.

appears combined in some Byzantine apocalypses with the view connecting him with three towns in Galilee—Chorazin, Beth-saida, and Capernaum—mentioned in the Gospels of Matthew (11:21–24) and Luke (10:13–15). Thus the Syriac Pseudo-Methodius predicted:

[The Son of Perdition] will be conceived in Chorazin, will be born in Ṣaidan [i.e., Beth-saida] and will rule [or: begin to rule] in Capernaum. And Chorazin will glory in him that he was born there, and Beth-saida that he was raised there and Capernaum that he ruled [or: began to rule] there. And because of this Our Lord pronounced the *Woes* over the three of them in his gospel when he said: Woe to thee, Chorazin; and woe to thee, Beth-saida; and thou, Capernaum, that hast exalted thyself unto heaven, thou wilt descend to Hell.[13]

The evangelists explicitly explained Jesus' Three Woes by saying that the three towns mentioned had not repented although they had witnessed a very large number of his miracles ($\delta v v \acute{\alpha} \mu \varepsilon \iota \varsigma$, Matt. 11:20). It is perhaps not difficult to imagine that a Christian commentator reflecting on their obstinacy had related it to the presence of an anti-Christian force in the three localities. Once the Antichrist was conceived of as a human being, it was natural to assign his conception, birth, and growth to two of these towns. His kingship also was recognized at least as early as Hippolytus to follow from the general parallelism of the Antichrist with Christ and from the former's Messianic claims.[14] Furthermore, the Antichrist's connection with the three towns does not necessarily conflict with the tradition of his birth from Dan, for the northern shore of Lake Gennesaret, where they were located, had once belonged to the tribal territory of Dan. Still, this interpretation of the Three Woes goes far beyond the scriptural evidence; the notion of the Antichrist's royal rule at Capernaum is particularly surprising. It would be interesting to learn in what quarters and under what circumstances it developed, and whether it represents the same tradition as the view of his descent from Dan or whether it had a different origin.[15]

A similar problem occurs in connection with the advent of the Anti-

---

13. Syriac Pseudo-Methodius, fol. 135 recto. It is not clear why the author first makes Chorazin the place of the Antichrist's conception, then of his birth, and Beth-saida first the place of his birth and then of his adolescence.

14. Hippolytus, p. 8.3, ed. Achelis $\beta\alpha\sigma\iota\lambda\varepsilon\grave{\upsilon}\varsigma\ \acute{o}\ X\rho\iota\sigma\tau\grave{o}\varsigma\ \kappa\alpha\grave{\iota}\ \beta\alpha\sigma\iota\lambda\varepsilon\grave{\upsilon}\varsigma\ \grave{\varepsilon}\pi\acute{\iota}\gamma\varepsilon\iota\sigma\varsigma\ \acute{o}$ Ἀντίχριστος [Christ the ruler and the Antichrist the earthly ruler].

15. Bousset, *Antichrist*, pp. 113f., seems to imply that the passages from the Gospels are a sufficient explanation of Pseudo-Methodius' interpretation. I doubt it. Quite exceptional is the statement of the *Oracle of Baalbek*, line 198 $\kappa\alpha\grave{\iota}\ \sigma\tau\alpha\vartheta\acute{\eta}\sigma\varepsilon\tau\alpha\iota\ \grave{\alpha}\pi\grave{o}\ [\grave{\upsilon}\pi\acute{o}?]\ \tau o\hat{\upsilon}$ $\mu\iota\alpha\rho o\hat{\upsilon}\ \acute{\varepsilon}\vartheta\nu o\upsilon\varsigma\ \tau\hat{\omega}\nu\ K\alpha\pi\pi\alpha\delta\acute{o}\kappa\omega\nu$ [and he will be established by the foul nation of the Cappadocians], which, if I understand it correctly, means that the Antichrist "will be established by the foul nation of the Cappadocians." Or does $\sigma\tau\alpha\vartheta\acute{\eta}\sigma\varepsilon\tau\alpha\iota$ signify that the Antichrist will be stopped by the Cappadocians?

christ. In all the major Byzantine apocalypses, with the exception of the *Oracle of Baalbek*, the Antichrist emerges in two stages or on two occasions. The matter is relatively simple in Pseudo-Ephraem. The author, it will be remembered, mentions a surrender of the *Christianorum imperium* to God but not yet a Last Roman Emperor to carry out the surrender. This surrender is followed immediately by the "appearance" of the Antichrist.[16] Pseudo-Ephraem then reports his birth from Dan, his hypocritical activities designed to win over adherents while he is growing up and before he assumes imperial power, his coming of age and assumption of imperial power, and, finally, his acceptance by Moabites and "Ammanites."[17] His career, here, is divided into two stages—adolescence and maturity, preimperial and imperial—but all this is natural; in particular, the mention of his birth (*nascitur*) after his "apparition" (*apparebit*) can easily be explained by the fact that the author is here returning to his narrative after an excursus on biblical evidence concerning the Antichrist.[18]

A harmonizing explanation of this type becomes more and more difficult, however, as one considers other apocalypses. In the Latin version of the Tiburtine Sibyl, for example, it is said that the Antichrist "will rise" (*surget*) during the reign of the Last Roman Emperor. He will do miracles during this reign and by such practices will win many adherents. The divisions of time (years, months, weeks, days, and hours) will be shortened, a feature that in other texts distinguishes the reign of the Antichrist.[19] After the surrender of imperial power by the Last Roman Emperor, however, and the end of the Roman Empire, "then Antichrist will be revealed manifestly [*revelabitur manifeste*] and will sit in the house of the Lord in Jerusalem."[20] One may feel inclined to argue, as in the case of Pseudo-Ephraem, that between the "rise" of the Antichrist and his "manifest revelation" he grew from child to manhood, but unlike in the text of Pseudo-Ephraem, his adolescence is not men-

---

16. Pseudo-Ephraem, p. 214.4 Caspari: *Tunc apparebit ille nequissimus et abominabilis draco.*
17. Pseudo-Ephraem, p. 215.8 Caspari: *de tribu nascitur Dan*; p. 216.2: *dumque adulescens, subdolus draco sub specie iustitiae uidetur uersari antequam sumat imperium*; p. 216.11: *factus legitimus sumet imperium*; p. 216.12: *occurrent ei primi Moabitae et Ammanitae tamquam suo regi.* Caspari, p. 435, understood the words *factus legitimus* to refer to the recognition of the Antichrist among men. The contrast with his *adulescentia* (p. 216.2), however, makes it likely that his reaching the legal age (*legitima aetas*) is meant.
18. Pseudo-Ephraem, Caspari, pp. 214.5–215.6 (he cites Deut. 33:22, combined with Gen. 49:9; Jer. 17:11).
19. Latin version of the Tiburtine Sibyl, Sackur pp. 185.19–186.1. On the shortening of time cf. Bousset, *Antichrist*, p. 144.
20. Latin version of the Tiburtine Sibyl, Sackur p. 186.9.

tioned in any way. The suspicion grows that two separate traditions have been awkwardly fused, one according to which the Antichrist makes his first appearance during the reign of the Last Roman Emperor and another where this takes place after the surrender. This suspicion gains momentum from the observation of another double feature: the shortening of time intervals also takes place both before and after the surrender.[21] Perhaps it is even worthwhile to consider whether the twofold tradition of the Antichrist's birth (from Dan and from Chorazin–Beth-saida) may not be after all another indication of the combination of two alternative traditions.

The conflict about the timing of the Antichrist's emergence within the eschatological schedule is even clearer in the Pseudo-Methodian tradition. In its fountainhead, the Syriac text, the Antichrist is first mentioned after the "king of the Greeks" (the Last Roman Emperor) has taken up residence in Jerusalem: "And then the Son of Perdition will be revealed [*metgelē'*]." The author then mentions his interpretation of the Three Woes as referring to the Antichrist's conception, birth, and kingship, and continues:

And immediately when the Son of Perdition is revealed [*metgelē'*], then the king of the Greeks will go up and stand on Golgotha [follows a lengthy account of the surrender of his imperial power and his death]. And immediately the Son of Perdition will be revealed [*metgelē'*], who is from the tribe of Dan.[22]

In other words, according to this Syriac author the "revelation" of the Antichrist will occur twice, once prior to the Last Emperor's surrender and death and preceding the narrative of his (the Antichrist's) birth, growth, and accession, and again after the surrender.

The translators seem to have been disturbed by this duplication. The Greek translator decided to tone down the conflict by using a word for the "second" revelation slightly different from that for the "first." While before the Last Emperor's surrender he writes twice of an appearance ($\varphi\alpha\nu\acute{\eta}\sigma\epsilon\tau\alpha\iota$; variant: $\varphi\alpha\nu\hat{\eta}$), he chooses the term $\grave{\epsilon}\mu\varphi\alpha\nu\grave{\eta}\varsigma\ \gamma\acute{\epsilon}\nu\eta\tau\alpha\iota$ (variants: $\varphi\alpha\nu\epsilon\grave{\iota}\varsigma\ \gamma\epsilon\nu\acute{\eta}\sigma\epsilon\tau\alpha\iota$, $\grave{\epsilon}\mu\varphi\alpha\nu\grave{\eta}\varsigma\ \gamma\epsilon\nu\nu\acute{\eta}\sigma\epsilon\tau\alpha\iota$) for the event mentioned after the surrender.[23] Strictly speaking, the difference between the terms is not great (perhaps the second formula lays somewhat greater stress on the Antichrist's visibility than does the first), but the mere variation of the vocabulary served (and was undoubtedly meant) to disguise the duplication, at least for the casual reader. The Latin

21. Compare Latin version of the Tiburtine Sibyl p. 185.24 Sackur with p. 186.15.
22. Syriac Pseudo-Methodius, fol. 135 recto.
23. Greek Pseudo-Methodius, pp. 45.3, 45.10, 46n.5, line 10 Istrin (= pp. 130.113, 132.7, 134.20 Lolos).

translator went a step further, using the verb *apparere* on both occasions but adding the adjective *manifestus* for the Antichrist's "second" appearance as a substitute for the ἐμφανὴς γένηται of the Greek text.[24]

The *Visions of Daniel*, in this as in many other respects, follow the Greek Pseudo-Methodius, at least to the extent that they preserve the relevant portions of that text. In the *Slavonic Daniel* the Antichrist ("the Son of Perdition") is expected to "appear" after the Last Emperor has resided twelve years at Jerusalem. The author then tells of his birth in connection with the Three Woes and of the Last Emperor's surrender: "And after that the Son of Perdition will begin to do signs and wonders."[25] The effect of the duplication is here mitigated because the translator does not use the same term as in the earlier passage, but the arrangement of the material suggests that he found the double advent in his Greek source. In Pseudo-Chrysostom the traces of the Antichrist's twofold emergence are faint. It will be remembered that in that text the Last Emperor's activities at Jerusalem are omitted altogether. The author also dispenses with the first appearance of the Antichrist prior to the surrender. He does refer to his emergence after the surrender, but he replaces Pseudo-Methodius' ἐμφανὴς γένηται by ἀναστήσεται, "he will arise."[26] In *Daniel Καὶ ἔσται* the Last Emperor's surrender recurs and with it the double appearance of the Antichrist, before and after the Last Emperor's surrender, both times expressed by the word φανήσεται, "he will appear."[27]

It seems clear, then, that the twofold emergence of the Antichrist in many Byzantine apocalypses is evidence for the existence of two somewhat different traditions, one of which produced him prior to the Last Emperor's surrender, the other of which made him enter the eschatological scene after that event. There are other indications of this double tradition. One has already been mentioned: the repetition of the shortening of time in the Latin version of the Tiburtine Sibyl. Another is Pseudo-Ephraem's reference to the end of the Antichrist. He first predicts that "the Lord will slay him with the breath of his mouth." He is here following literally II Thess. 2:8. In the next sentence, however, he continues: "He will be bound and plunged alive into the abyss of eternal fire together with his father Satan."[28] Now the second prediction clearly

---

24. Latin Pseudo-Methodius, Sackur pp. 93.5 (*apparebit*), 93.13 (*apparuerit*), 94.8 (*appareat manifestus*).
25. *Slavonic Daniel* #11.
26. Pseudo-Chrysostom, Vasiliev p. 37.13.
27. *Daniel Καὶ ἔσται*, pp. 42.29, 43.5.
28. Pseudo-Ephraem, Caspari, p. 220.8: . . . *interficiet eum Dominus spiritu oris sui. alligabitur et demergetur in abyssum ignis aeterni uiuus cum patre suo Satan.*

is irreconcilable with the first.[29] The notion of an Antichrist thrown alive into the fire evidently expects that he will be subjected to eternal torture and punishment, while the first sentence predicts his immediate execution.

This last duplication serves to explain the nature of the two traditions. It seems no accident that the passage predicting the Antichrist's eternal punishment makes him share this punishment with his father, Satan. The concept of the Antichrist as the son of Satan conflicts sharply with the notion normally expressed in the Byzantine apocalypses, i.e., that he is a human being. The Antichrist as son of Satan is, however, attested as early as Hippolytus and is itself but a variant of another view identifying the Antichrist with the Devil.[30] Eternal punishment befits an immortal being such as Satan or his son and is thus appropriate for the ancient monster whose challenge to God Gunkel and Bousset have shown to have been the source of the Antichrist legend. It was, therefore, natural to assume that the Antichrist as the monstrous son of Satan (or Satan himself), the dragon, could enter the eschatological scene as he does in Pseudo-Ephraem—as soon as Christ himself had returned the power over Christians to God, all political authority on earth had disappeared, and only the primeval conflict between God and the Antichrist remained to be fought.[31] When this older concept of the Antichrist as an immortal diabolical monster came to confront the view of an Antichrist born from human parents, as represented by the New Testament and the most important Fathers of the Church both East and West, the consequence was not merely that the end of the Antichrist had

---

29. It is curious that the conflict between these two traditions was not recognized by Caspari. Even Bousset, who in his ch. 17 (pp. 48–154) collected the material on the end of the Antichrist, emphasized instead the question of whether God (or Christ) deals with the Antichrist alone or is assisted by Michael. Yet several of the passages collected by Bousset (e.g., pp. 150, 152) demonstrate the second prediction.

30. Cf. Bousset, *Antichrist*, pp. 89ff. The *Apocalypse of St. Andrew* says (869B [p. 212 Rydén]) Τότε ἐγερθήσεται ὁ Σατανᾶς ὁ 'Αντίχριστος ἐκ φυλῆς τοῦ Δὰν κτλ. [Then Satan the Antichrist will arise from the tribe of Dan, etc.] Hippolytus, *De Antichristo*, cap. 14f., p. 11.15 Achelis ὄφις οὖν τίς ἄρα ἢ ὁ ἀπ' ἀρχῆς πλάνος, ὁ ἐν τῇ γενέσει (49.16) εἰρημένος, ὁ πλανήσας τὴν Εὐαν καὶ πτερνίσας τὸν 'Αδάμ; . . . ὅτι μὲν γὰρ ὄντως ἐκ τῆς φυλῆς Δὰν, μέλλει γεννᾶσθαι καὶ ἀνίστασθαι τύραννος, βασιλεύς, κριτὴς δεινός, υἱὸς τοῦ διαβόλου κτλ. [Who then is this serpent or deceiver from the beginning, the one known from Genesis (49:16) who deceived Eve and tripped up Adam? . . . Because truly he will be born from the tribe of Dan and set up as tyrant, emperor, terrible judge, son of the devil, etc.]

31. Pseudo-Ephraem, pp. 213.17–214.5 Caspari. In the *Oracle of Baalbek*, line 191, also, the designation of the Antichrist as the King with the Changing Shape (cf. n. 4) characterizes him as a superhuman being, and he is introduced at the end of a long line of historical and eschatological rulers (the passage on the war between the king of the East and the king from Heliopolis in lines 205–208 is an interpolation: see my edition, pp. 57f.).

to be transformed from an eternity of torture for an essentially indestructible being into the sudden death by execution of a human person. It became necessary, also, to assign him a more or less ordinary human birth and adolescence before he could be supposed to embark upon his eschatological career. Thus it came about that in many Byzantine apocalypses he is first mentioned long before he begins to play an active part in the eschatological events—to be precise, during the reign of the Last Roman Emperor. In this way apocalyptic speculation prepared the way for his decisive entry upon the eschatological stage after the consummation of all terrestrial authority, and only a few awkward formulae remain to show that the Byzantine apocalyptic account of the Antichrist combines two heterogeneous notions of his essence and mission.

Among the Antichrist's actions all Byzantine apocalypses, with the exception of Pseudo-Ephraem, mention his miracles.[32] In the Latin version of the Tiburtine Sibyl, they are apparent and false miracles which occur during the reign of the Last Roman Emperor (i.e., before the surrender), and their expressed purpose is to win converts. The only specific miracle to be mentioned is the apparent descent of fire from heaven.[33] In the Greek version, the *Oracle of Baalbek*, the designation of the Antichrist as the "King with the Changing Shape" presumably indicates such miracles as flying or assuming the alternative appearance of child, youth, or adult.[34] In addition, the Greek text mentions specifically that "he will do signs and wonders on earth," as Jesus had warned in the Gospels (Mark 13:22; John 4:48), among them the transformation of the sun into darkness and of the moon into blood, the drying up of springs and rivers, and the change of the Nile into a river of blood.[35] The purpose of these miracles is not stated, but presumably they were performed, as in the Latin text, with the purpose of winning souls.[36] Inasmuch as the Antichrist's reign in the *Oracle of Baalbek* immediately

---

32. In Pseudo-Ephraem, the Antichrist's hypocrisy before he seizes his imperial power (p. 216.1–9 Caspari) and the disorder in nature that he produces during his reign of three and a half years (pp. 217.14–219.2) may serve as substitutes, for they fulfill the function, elsewhere assigned to his miracles, of bringing about his recognition and acceptance.

33. Latin version of the Tiburtine Sibyl, p. 185.22 Sackur: *Deludet autem per artem magicam multos ita ut ignem de caelo descendere videatur.*

34. *Oracle of Baalbek*, line 191 (n. 5 above). Cf. Bousset, *Antichrist*, pp. 94ff. and my edition of *Oracle of Baalbek*, line 113 and n. 54.

35. *Oracle of Baalbek*, line 210.

36. This is clearly the direct purpose of the miracles implied by the designation of the Antichrist as "the King of the Changing Shape" (n. 5 above). But probably it was also the indirect purpose of the Antichrist's miracles with regard to springs and rivers, for the ensuing drought was bound to produce famine and thus enable the Antichrist to pose as the dispenser of food for his flock, as he does in fact in Pseudo-Ephraem (p. 218.10 Caspari) and the Pseudo-Methodian tradition (see p. 202 below).

precedes the Second Coming, the author probably thought of the Antichrist's miracles as occurring after the end of earthly authority.

Indeed, in all later Byzantine apocalypses the Antichrist's miracles are mentioned after the Last Roman Emperor's act of surrender on Golgotha. In the Syriac Pseudo-Methodius, they appear in the context of the author's detailed exegesis of Jacob's Blessing on Dan (Gen. 49:17f.; see p. 223 below). This text, following the Church Father Hippolytus, interprets the verse as a prophecy of the Antichrist to be born from the tribe of Dan. In the biblical passage Jacob compares Dan with a serpent "that biteth the horse's heel" and the means of the "biting" are, according to Pseudo-Ephraem, "the signs of fantasy of his acts of deception," i.e., the Antichrist's false miracles: lepers are cleansed, the blind made to see, paralytics to walk, demons are cast out, the sun darkened, the moon changed into blood, etc.[37] There is emphasis on the deceptiveness of these miracles, as well as on their purpose of leading men astray (Matt. 24:24).

These features, including their context in the interpretation of the Blessing of Jacob on Dan, are reproduced with minor variants in the translations of Pseudo-Methodius and in the *Visions of Daniel*. Some manuscripts of the Greek Pseudo-Methodius add that the miracles of the Antichrist are impotent and evanescent (ἀδρανῆ καὶ ἐξίτηλα).[38] The Latin translation faithfully renders the Greek text.[39] Because the *Visions of Daniel* are partially excerpts from the Greek Pseudo-Methodius, context and miracles are here subject to the process of selection. The context of Gen. 49:17 reappears in the *Slavonic Daniel* and Pseudo-Chrysostom, but is missing in *Daniel* Καὶ ἔσται. In the *Slavonic Daniel* the transformations of sun and moon are conflated: the Egyptian sun is turned into blood (in the Greek Pseudo-Methodius the sun is turned into darkness and the moon into blood).[40] Pseudo-Chrysostom reproduces a long list of miracles: those of the blind, the lame, the deaf, the

---

37. Syriac Pseudo-Methodius, fol. 136 recto. Other miracles not mentioned above are not clear in the Syriac text. They seem to refer to fruit, plants, and springs and may indicate that, as in Pseudo-Ephraem, the Antichrist produces famine and drought to force men into his camp.

38. Greek Pseudo-Methodius, p. 47.6 Istrin (= p. 136.30 Lolos) (but see Istrin, *apparatus criticus*). The Greek text furthermore omits the cure of the lepers, as well as the miracles concerning fruit, plants, and rivers. Several manuscripts add a miracle: the deaf will hear (p. 47, *apparatus criticus* on line 7).

39. Latin Pseudo-Methodius, Sackur p. 94.18. It mentions the cure of the deaf and omits that of the lepers and the miracles of fruit, plants, and springs.

40. *Slavonic Daniel* #11. Or is this an echo of *Oracle of Baalbek*, line 212, where the Nile of Egypt is turned into blood? One manuscript of the *Oracle of Baalbek* even reads ἥλιος in lieu of Νεῖλος.

possessed, the sun, and the moon.⁴¹ *Daniel* Καὶ ἔσται mentions, in addition to the miracles of the blind and the lame, the healing of the lepers, which had appeared in the Syriac text but not in the Greek (and Latin) translation. According to the Erythraean Sibyl, heaven, fire, and the elements will bear testimony to the Antichrist (*abhominatio*). He will do miracles, in particular "blacken" the stars and weaken (lead astray?) the man of perfection.⁴²

All Byzantine apocalypses state or imply that the Antichrist will rule as king or emperor (βασιλεύς): he is a pseudo-Messiah and, as such, an anointed king. The Latin version of the Tiburtine Sibyl speaks of his royal power immediately after mentioning the surrender of the Last Roman Emperor, the end of the Roman Empire, and the Antichrist sitting in the Jewish Temple: "And while he will be king, two very famous men step forth, Elijah and Enoch, to announce the advent of the Lord."⁴³ The Greek *Oracle of Baalbek* predicts that "there will arise another emperor with a changing shape; and he will rule thirty years."⁴⁴ Pseudo-Ephraem warns his audience that the end is near and that all the signs have been fulfilled except for the *adventus mali*—the coming of the Evil One, the Antichrist.⁴⁵ The term *adventus* suggests that he expects him to come with royal power, and this point is made a certainty later in his homily where he distinguishes two stages in the Antichrist's career: his adolescence, before he assumes imperial power, and a later period in his life, when he will have become *legitimus* (have come of age, *legitima aetas*) and have assumed imperial power.⁴⁶ He continues: Moabites and "Ammanites" will be the first to meet (*occurrere*) the Antichrist as their king, and after receiving the kingship he will order the Jewish Temple at Jerusalem to be rebuilt for himself.⁴⁷

---

41. Pseudo-Chrysostom, p. 37.18.
42. Erythraean Sibyl, ed. O. Holder-Egger, "Italienische Prophetieen des 13. Jahrhunderts" *Neues Archiv der Gesellschaft für ältere deutsche Geschichtskunde* 15 (1890), p. 172.1.
43. Latin version of the Tiburtine Sibyl, p. 186.11 Sackur: *Regnante autem eo, egredientur duo clarissimi viri Helias et Enoch ad annuntiandum Domini adventum*. . . .
44. *Oracle of Baalbek*, line 191 . . . ἀναστήσεται ἄλλος βασιλεὺς μορφὴν ἔχων ἠλλοιωμένην καὶ βασιλεύσει ἔτη τριάκοντα.
45. Pseudo-Ephraem, p. 210.4 Caspari, and cf. 209.7.
46. Pseudo-Ephraem, p. 216.2 Caspari: *dumque adulescens, subdolus draco sub specie iustitiae uidetur uersari antequam sumat imperium*; p. 216.11: *factus legitimus sumet imperium*.
47. Pseudo-Ephraem, p. 216.10 Caspari: *Occurrent ei primi Moabitae et Ammanitae tamquam suo regi. Cum ergo regnum acceperit, iubet sibi reaedificari templum Dei quod est in Hierusalem*. The terminology of *aduentus* and *occursus* borrowed from the visits of Roman rulers to the cities of their empire is ubiquitous in Pseudo-Ephraem's remarks on the Antichrist.

The three texts of Pseudo-Methodius and the *Slavonic Daniel* agree in predicting that the Antichrist will rule (or begin to rule) at Capernaum,[48] while *Daniel* Καὶ ἔσται, probably aware that Jesus had been active at Capernaum (cf., for example, Luke 4:23, 31; Mark 2:1; John 6:59), connects the Antichrist's royal rule at Capernaum with his supposed residence there.[49]

The Erythraean Sibyl mentions a division of the world into "ten scepters" and continues to say that the Antichrist, called in this text *abhominatio*, will be their head.[50] Finally, the *Apocalypse of St. Andrew* expressly mentions the Antichrist's royal rule following his birth (incarnation) and growth.[51] This is the scheme known from the Pseudo-Methodian tradition and based on the Three Woes (see. p. 196 above), except that neither Jesus' pronouncements nor the names of the three Galilean towns against which they were directed are mentioned.

One of the characteristic features of the reign of the Antichrist, according to the Byzantine apocalypses, is his (largely successful) attempt to win adherents. It motivates, at least in part, his hypocritical practices and the miracles he performs, as well as the measures of persecution to be discussed presently, for one of their purposes is to force his victims to accept him.[52]

In this connection, one of the most dramatic episodes is his sitting in the Jewish Temple at Jerusalem and demanding to be worshipped as God. This feature, mentioned in II Thess. 2:4 and found in many texts of the early Church Fathers, reappears in most Byzantine apocalypses.[53] Thus the Latin version of the Tiburtine Sibyl predicts his sitting "in the house of the Lord at Jerusalem" after the Last Roman Emperor's sur-

---

48. Syriac Pseudo-Methodius, fol. 135 verso; Greek Pseudo-Methodius, Istrin p. 45.5 (= p. 132.2 Lolos); Latin Pseudo-Methodius, Sackur p. 93.7; *Slavonic Daniel* #11.
49. *Daniel* Καὶ ἔσται, p. 42.31 κατοικήσει εἰς Καπερναοὺμ διότι ἐβασίλευσεν ἐν ἑαυτῇ [He will reside at Capernaum because he ruled there].
50. Erythraean Sibyl, p. 171.19 Holder-Egger: *Post hec fiet multarum gentium bestialiter viventium congregatio, orbe in X sceptra divisio* [variant: *diviso*]; *precedent turpissimi concubitus conceptus, abhominatio capud ipsorum. Tunc reges plurimos morte afficiet, quosdam sub iugo submittet.* (I take the phrase *precedent . . . conceptus* as a parenthesis).
51. *Apocalypse of St. Andrew*, PG 111.869B (p. 212 Rydén) καὶ γεννηθέντος αὐτοῦ ἀνθρώπου καὶ ἀνδρυνθέντος καὶ βασιλεύσαντος τότε ἄρξεται ἐπιδεικνύειν τὴν πλάνην αὐτοῦ καθά φησι περὶ αὐτοῦ Ἰωάννης ὁ θεολόγος [and when he has been born as a man and become a man and is ruling then he will begin to display his deception as John the Theologian said about him]. (I have been unable to identify this Johannine passage).
52. Cf., for example, the Latin version of the Tiburtine Sibyl, Sackur p. 185.21: *subvertet orbem et faciet prodigia et signa magna per falsas simulationes. Deludet autem per artem magicam multos.*
53. Bousset, *Antichrist*, pp. 104–108.

render. The episode is missing in the *Oracle of Baalbek*, and it may be that the Antichrist's (re-?)building of the "altars of Egypt" has taken its place.[54]

It does, however, play a very important role in Pseudo-Ephraem. This author applies to the Antichrist Jeremiah 17:11 (ἐφώνησε πέρδιξ, συνήγαγεν ἃ οὐκ ἔτεκε, "the partridge called, it gathered a brood which it did not hatch") as had been done by, for example, Hippolytus and Origen before him. In Pseudo-Ephraem's citation of the prophetic text, the Antichrist will call men whom he did not beget (that is, those who were the children of God). Apparently, he will temporarily be successful in seducing them but at the end of time they will abandon him "as one confused."[55] While he grows up and before he assumes his royal power, he will deceive men by his pretense of justice so that they will say: This is a just man.[56] After he has come of age, he will be joined first (*occurrent ei primi*) by Moabites and "Ammanites" as if he were their king.[57] Pseudo-Ephraem interprets the Antichrist's friendly reception (*occursus*) by the "sons of Lot" as his accession to royal status, for he immediately summarizes this event by the clause "therefore when he has received royal power." He then will give orders that the Temple of the Lord

---

54. Latin version of the Tiburtine Sibyl, Sackur p. 186.9: *tunc revelabitur manifeste Antichristus et sedebit in domo Domini in Jerusalem.* Oracle of Baalbek, line 190 καὶ ἀναστήσεται ἄλλος βασιλεὺς μορφὴν ἔχων ἠλλοιωμένην . . . καὶ ἀνοικοδομήσει τοὺς βωμοὺς τῆς Αἰγύπτου κτλ. [And after that there will arise another king who has a changed shape . . . and he will rebuild the altars of Egypt].

55. Pseudo-Ephraem, p. 215.3 Caspari: *Qui sicut perdix colliget sibi filios confusionis . . . et uocat quos non genuit, sicut dicit Hieremias propheta. Etiam in nouissimo die relinquent illum uelut confusum.* Cf. p. 219.15: *eius seductione*, and Hippolytus *De Antichristo* 56, p. 28.24 Achelis.

56. Pseudo-Ephraem, p. 216.1–9 Caspari.

57. Pseudo-Ephraem, p. 216.12 Caspari: *et, sicut dicitur in psalmo: Facti sunt in susceptionem filiis Loth. Occurrent ei primi Moabitae et Ammanitae tamquam suo regi.* The author here expressly bases his prediction on Psalm 83:8 (Vulgate: *facti sunt in adiutorium filiis Loth*) because according to Gen. 19:30–38 Lot was the ancestor of Moabites and Ammonites. Actually, Pseudo-Ephraem relies here, as elsewhere, on the text of the *Vetus Latina*, which reads *susceptionem* in lieu of the *adiutorium* of the Vulgate; cf. Sabatier, *Bibliorum Sacrorum Latinae Versiones Antiquae* II, p. 168. The subject of *facti sunt* seems to be Assur and its coalition, the enemies of Israel mentioned earlier, including Moab and Amman [*sic*]. In fact, only the *in susceptionem* of the *Vetus Latina* fits the argument of Pseudo-Ephraem. He cites the verse to justify his prediction that Moabites and "Ammanites" will join the Antichrist as if he were their king. *Susceptio* can mean acknowledgment or acceptance, but neither the "strong arm" of the Hebrew original nor the "aid" of the Pešitta (*'udranā*) or Septuagint (ἀντίλημψις) or Vulgate (*adiutorium*) have that meaning. Whoever cited Psalm 83:8 in this context thought in terms of the *Vetus Latina*. It is true that the subject of the Psalmist's *facti sunt* is in all versions Assyria or, rather, the collective noun "the Assyrians," but perhaps because it was thought that the Antichrist would come from Babylonia (p. 195 above), the verse could without much difficulty be applied to him.

at Jerusalem be rebuilt. He will sit in it like God and give orders that he be worshipped by all the nations.⁵⁸

It then becomes clear that the activities of the Antichrist have a two-fold purpose. On the one hand, he will demand to be worshipped by the Gentiles and will make himself the object of all worship.⁵⁹ On the other hand, his rebuilding of the Jewish Temple and his edict imposing universal circumcision "according to the rite of the ancient law" (i.e., the Old Testament) result in his acceptance by the Jews.⁶⁰ A consequence of the Antichrist's efforts will be that everyone will gather at Jerusalem from all sides and Jesus' prophecy will be fulfilled, according to which "Jerusalem will be trodden down by the Gentiles [Luke 21:24], for forty-two months [or three and a half years] as the holy apostle [John] says in Revelation [11:2]."⁶¹

The Syriac Pseudo-Methodius and the tradition dependent upon it are brief on the subject of the Antichrist's relation to the Jews.⁶² Another tradition, known also to Lactantius, is represented by *Daniel Καὶ ἔσται*. According to him the Antichrist will trample the Temple of God under foot.⁶³ It differs from most other apocalyptic texts in that the Antichrist is here conceived of as hostile to Judaism.

The close bond of the Antichrist to Judaism and the Old Testament recurs in the oldest stratum of the Erythraean Sibyl. It is true that here the Antichrist is regularly designated by the term *abhominatio*, in accordance with Daniel 11:31 ("the abomination that makes desolate,"

---

58. Pseudo-Ephraem, p. 216.13 Caspari: *Cum ergo regnum acceperit, iubet sibi reaedificari templum Dei, quod est in Hierusalem; qui ingressus in eo sedebit ut Deus et iubet se adorari ab omnibus gentibus.* A comparison with II Thess. 2:4 shows that the new feature in Pseudo-Ephraem is the rebuilding of the Jewish Temple by the Antichrist, a trait that must have originated after its destruction in the Jewish War (A.D. 70), for if the Antichrist was to sit in the Temple it had to be rebuilt first; cf. Bousset, *Antichrist*, p. 105. The emperor Julian had planned to rebuild it: Ernest Stein, *Histoire du Bas-Empire* I, p. 164.

59. Pseudo-Ephraem, p. 217.6 Caspari: *Omnem enim cultum ad se conuertet nequissimus serpens.*

60. Pseudo-Ephraem, p. 217.6 Caspari: *Proponet enim edictum ut circumcidantur homines secundum ritum legis antiquae. Tunc gratulabuntur ei Iudaei eo quod eis reddiderit usum prioris testamenti.*

61. Pseudo-Ephraem, p. 217.13 Caspari: *tunc confluent ad eum in ciuitatem Hierusalem undique omnes et calcabitur a gentibus urbs sancta menses quadraginta duo, sicut sanctus apostolus in Apocalypsi dicit.*

62. Syriac Pseudo-Methodius, fol. 136 verso: "this Son of Perdition will enter Jerusalem and will sit in the Temple of God and will pretend to be like God"; cf. Greek Pseudo-Methodius 48.1 (= p. 136.42 Lolos); Latin Pseudo-Methodius, p. 95.8; Pseudo-Chrysostom, p. 37.27 Vasiliev. The passage is omitted in the *Slavonic Daniel*.

63. *Daniel Καὶ ἔσται*, p. 43.8 Vasiliev ἐξελεύσεται [δὲ] εἰς Ἱερουσαλὴμ καὶ καταπατήσει τὸν ναὸν τοῦ θεοῦ [He will go to Jerusalem and trample the temple of God under foot]; cf. Lactantius *Divinae Institutiones* 7.16: *eruere templum Dei conabitur.* Cf. Bousset, *Antichrist*, pp. 105f.

cited in Matt. 24:15), a stenographic allusion, as it were, to the Antichrist's profanation of the Jewish Temple, and the Jews are called *Apellae* (cf. Horace *Sat.* 1.5.100). But it is also said that the Antichrist will recall the Jews and thus "renew what is old and reject what is new."⁶⁴ This is reminiscent of Pseudo-Ephraem's predictions that the Antichrist will order all men to be circumcised "according to the rite of the ancient law" and that he will restore to the Jews the use of the Old Testament.⁶⁵ Indeed, the Erythraean Sibyl's next sentence proves that the "old" and the "new" refer to the two Testaments: "And [still] more and innumerable [persons] abandon the Lamb and will shout: he is the person announced in [the Old] Testament."⁶⁶ The Antichrist will extend his "lips and palate" to the heavens and will stretch out his hands to take hold of (God) the Highest. Under the impact of this blasphemous challenge "the earthborn" will say: Is this not he whom the prophets had announced? And the Antichrist's servants will say: Where are now those who had magnified the Lamb to [the rank of] a Lion? Is this one [the Antichrist] not the Son of [God] the Highest?⁶⁷ Thus the Erythraean Sibyl expects first the Jews and then a large number of Christians to abandon Christ in favor of the Antichrist and to worship the latter as the true Messiah promised by the prophets of the Old Testament. Her prophecy also expresses, most forcefully of all the apocalypses under consideration here, the notice that the Antichrist will challenge, even

---

64. Erythraean Sibyl, p. 172.3 Holder-Egger: [*abhominatio*] *Apellas revocet, ut vetera renovet et renovata repellat.*

65. The Antichrist's special appeal to the Jews is also attested in a corrupt and difficult passage of the *Apocalypse of St. Andrew* (n. 69 below).

66. Erythraean Sibyl, p. 172.5 Holder-Egger: *Et clamabunt plures et innumeri qui delebuntur* [variant: *delabuntur*] *ab agno: Hic est testamentarius.* If one prefers the reading *delabuntur*, one must assume that the author here means Christians led astray by the Antichrist; see also the exclamation of the "earthborn" when they witness the ruin (*excidium*, apostasy?) of the Saints: Is he not the one whom the prophets announced? (p. 172.9: *nonne hic est, quem prescii nunciaverant?*). If one accepts, as did the editor Holder-Egger, the reading *delebuntur*, one must interpret it to mean that the apostates will be destroyed by Christ (the Lamb) at the Last Judgment. The word *testamentarius* is difficult and rare and does not occur in the Vulgate. Medieval Latin dictionaries such as that of Leopold Favre, *Glossarium Mediae et Infimae Latinitatis*, vol. 8 (Niort, 1887), p. 84, record the meanings: *executor testamenti, scriptor testamenti, heres testamento institutus.* I understand it to be synonymous with the Sibyl's phrase *hic est, quem prescii nunciaverant* (p. 172.9), i.e., the Antichrist's partisans call him *testamentarius* because the prophets of the Old Testament supposedly had announced his coming in the Messianic passages misunderstood by these "earthborns" and apostates.

67. Erythraean Sibyl, p. 172.5–14 Holder-Egger: *Os et palatum eius ad celos, et manus suas extendet ut apprehendat altissimum. Et cum viderint terrigene sanctorum excidium . . . clamabunt et dicent: Ve, ve, diutina derisio, et nonne hic est, quem prescii nunciaverant? Et dicent latera eius: Ubi sunt qui agnum exaltaverant in leonem? Nonne hic est filius altissimi? Et aperiet abhominatio os suum in contumeliam agni ut nomen eius deleat et sibi primevam superbiam applicabit.*

attempt to capture, God in his heaven and to destroy the name of Christ the Lamb. The passage is one of the clearest medieval relics of that ancient myth of a cosmic struggle between a primeval monster and God which Gunkel and Bousset showed to be the source of the legend of the Antichrist.[68]

This struggle is described in similar yet somewhat more stereotyped fashion in the *Apocalypse of St. Andrew*:

> Then there will occur a terrible war between him [the Antichrist] and the Lord Christ. When he [the Antichrist] realizes that prior to the end he is possessed with fearful fury, he will oppose heaven by hurling lightning and thunder and rumblings so that the noise of his clamoring will shake the earth and disturb[?] it in frightening fashion.[69]

The reign of the Antichrist will be marked not only by his attempts to win adherents and his conflicts with Christ and God, but also by the harassment and persecution of mankind. The Latin version of the Tiburtine Sibyl speaks of a great persecution never equalled either before or subsequently.[70] The *Oracle of Baalbek* gives a moving description of the disappearance of cities, depopulation, and drought during the reign of the Antichrist.[71] According to Pseudo-Ephraem, there will then be the greatest tribulation since the creation of man.[72] It will last the three and a half years mentioned in Revelation (11:2, 13:5), to which reference is here made specifically, and will be marked by drought, famine, and death from starvation.[73] No one who does not have the Antichrist's symbol, the snake, tattooed on forehead or hand will be able to purchase even the grain growing spontaneously from an uncultivated crop, and precious objects will be lying unwanted in the streets.[74] The human race will fal-

---

68. The prophecy of the Erythraean Sibyl was not utilized in Bousset's book. Presumably he was not aware of the antiquity of its nucleus, which was discovered only by the researches summarized by Evelyn Jamison, *Admiral Eugenius of Sicily* (London, 1957), pp. 21–32.

69. *Apocalypse of St. Andrew* 869C–871A (= p. 213 Rydén). This text, in an interesting but corrupt passage (865B–D), also speaks of a gathering of the Jewish Diaspora in Jerusalem and cites Hippolytus to the effect that at the time of the Antichrist's visitation the Jews will be the first to be led astray.

70. Latin version of the Tiburtine Sibyl, p. 186.14 Sackur: *Tunc erit persecutio magna qualis non fuit antea nec postea subsequetur*.

71. *Oracle of Baalbek*, lines 199–204, 213f.

72. Pseudo-Ephraem, p. 218.5 Caspari: *erit tribulatio magna qualis non fuit ex quo homines coeperunt esse super terram*.

73. Pseudo-Ephraem, p. 218.7 Caspari: *et erit fames et sitis inportabilis. Et tabescent filii in sinu matrum suarum, et coniuges super genua uirorum suorum, non habentibus escas ad comedendum*.

74. Pseudo-Ephraem, pp. 217.14–219.2 Caspari. On the *frumentum caducitatis* see p. 143 above.

ter under the breath of the horrible dragon, the Antichrist.[75] The Greek and Latin texts of Pseudo-Methodius follow Matt. 24:29 in referring laconically to "the tribulation of those days," while the *Slavonic Daniel* merely records that the springs will dry up.[76] The Erythraean Sibyl includes an elaborate description of disorder in the world of nature and of men: the majority of animals die, birds are afraid to fly, humans will flee terrified into caves and will reject money, hills will collapse and mountains shake, and the moon will be changed into blackness.[77] The *Apocalypse of St. Andrew* briefly remarks that the Antichrist "will bitterly humiliate the Christians then living until their last breath and will much harass and destroy them."[78]

Most Byzantine apocalypses mention certain measures taken by God in order to mitigate the effects of the Antichrist's persecution. One of them is the shortening of the time intervals. As already mentioned, the Latin version of the Tiburtine Sibyl refers to it, once after the first "rise" of the Antichrist and his miracles and again during his persecution, presumably because the author is here combining, awkwardly, two alternative traditions. In the *Oracle of Baalbek*, too, it is said that during the ninth and last generation of the world, "the years will be shortened [to be] like months and the months like weeks and the weeks like days and the days like hours."[79]

This shortening of the time intervals based on Jesus' prophecy about the signs of the end (Mark 13:20; Matt. 24:22) is not mentioned in the same way in the other Byzantine apocalypses. However, Bousset realized that this feature presupposed the notion of a time-limit for the persecution of the Antichrist and that this limit was, if I understand him correctly, the "time, two times and a half a time" of the Fourth Beast in Daniel (7:25, 12:7), or the "half of the week" of the cessation of sacrifices under "the prince who is to come" in the same book (9:27), or the forty-two months or one thousand two hundred and sixty days of the "trampling over the holy city" according to Revelation (11:2f.), or fi-

---

75. Pseudo-Ephraem, p. 219.9 Caspari: *humanum genus periclitantes et afflatu draconis horribilis fluctuantes.*
76. Greek Pseudo-Methodius, p. 48.4 Istrin (= p. 138.46 Lolos) ἡ θλῖψις τῶν ἡμερῶν ἐκείνων; Latin Pseudo-Methodius, p. 95.12 Sackur; *Slavonic Daniel* #11; Pseudo-Chrysostom, p. 37.32 Vasiliev. The passage is missing in the single manuscript of the Syriac Pseudo-Methodius and in *Daniel Καὶ ἔσται*.
77. Erythraean Sibyl, p. 173.9–13 Holder-Egger. The timing of these events is not clear. They are mentioned after the universal repudiation of the Antichrist (p. 172.17) but prior to his appearance before the Lamb's judgment seat (p. 173.13).
78. *Apocalypse of St. Andrew* 869C (= p. 212 Rydén).
79. *Oracle of Baalbek*, lines 178–80.

nally, the forty-two months of the Beast from the Sea (Rev. 13:5).[80] Indeed, as already indicated, Pseudo-Ephraem specifically cites the two passages from Revelation for the trampling of Jerusalem by the nations and for the persecution of the Antichrist, and a reign of three and a half years is also attributed to the Son of Perdition in the *Apocalypse of St. Andrew*.[81] The Pseudo-Methodian tradition seems to refer to this temporal limitation of the Antichrist's rule—but only in the vaguest terms—when it speaks of "the affliction of those days."[82] Finally, the prophecy of the Erythraean Sibyl confirms Bousset's hint that the shortening of the time intervals during the Antichrist's reign presupposed its limitation to three and a half years for it restricts his crimes and blasphemies to three shortened "feet" and a half.[83]

Pseudo-Ephraem does not refer to the shortening of time.[84] This author, however, mentions another measure taken by God in order to alleviate the period of tribulation for his saints and for the Elect:

For all the saints and Elect of God are gathered, prior to the tribulation that is to come, and are taken to the Lord lest they see the confusion that is to overwhelm the world because of our sins.[85]

It is probably no accident that Pseudo-Ephraem does not mention the shortening of the time intervals for the Antichrist's persecution, for if prior to it the Elect are "taken to the Lord," i.e., participate at least in some measure in beatitude, there is no need for further mitigating ac-

---

80. Bousset, *Antichrist*, p. 144: "Bei der 'Verkürzung der Tage' muss es sich doch um eine bestimmte Zeitfrist handeln. In der Parallelüberlieferung wird diese angegeben. Es ist die Zeit der 3½ Jahre, der Herrschaft des Antichrist, um die es sich hier handelt."

81. *Apocalypse of St. Andrew* 856D (= p. 202 Rydén).

82. The passage is missing in the Syriac original; Greek Pseudo-Methodius, p. 48.4 (= p. 138.46 Lolos) (ἡ θλῖψις τῶν ἡμερῶν ἐκείνων); Latin Pseudo-Methodius, p. 95.12 Sackur; Pseudo-Chrysostom, p. 37.12 Vasiliev; missing in *Slavonic Daniel* and in *Daniel Καὶ ἔσται*.

83. Erythraean Sibyl, p. 172.14 Holder-Egger: *conscribetur undique sceleribus et nominibus blasphemie, donec tres pedes semique abbreviati discurrant.* In this text the word *pes* normally stands for *annus*.

84. Unless a reference to it was made in the lacuna assumed by Caspari after p. 219.15.

85. Pseudo-Ephraem, p. 211.4 Caspari: *Omnes enim sancti et electi Dei ante tribulationem quae uentura est colliguntur et ad Dominum adsumuntur, ne quando uideant confusionem quae uniuersum propter peccata nostra obruet mundum.* For the sake of this view Pseudo-Ephraem even interpolates the word *uidere* into his citation of Amos 5:18: *Uae his qui concupiscunt uidere diem Domini.* The word *uidere* is attested neither for the Hebrew nor for the Greek, Latin, and Syriac texts of this biblical verse. The editor, Caspari (p. 447), noted close parallels to Pseudo-Ephraem's data on this point in the works of the Greek Ephraem, most closely in a passage from a Latin translation of the Μακαρισμοὶ ἕτεροι entitled in one manuscript *De beatitudine animae*. It runs as follows: *omnes sancti et electi ante tribulationem, quae uentura est, colliguntur et a Domino assumuntur, ut non uideant confusionem illam magnam, quae uniuersum obruet* [variant: *obruit*] *mundum*. Bousset, *Antichrist*, p. 25, observes that Pseudo-Ephraem normally does not depend on Ephraem but that both use the same apocalyptic material.

tion on their behalf. The Gathering of the Elect according to Pseudo-Ephraem is an alternative to the shortening of the time intervals.

Another measure undertaken by God, according to most Byzantine apocalypses, to relieve mankind during the reign of the Antichrist is the dispatch of Enoch and Elijah. The Latin version of the Tiburtine Sibyl mentions them during the reign of the Antichrist, immediately after his sitting in the Jewish Temple at Jerusalem and prior to the great persecution:

> While the Antichrist rules, two most famous men will come forth, Elijah and Enoch, to announce the coming of the Lord. And the Antichrist will slay them and they will be revived by the Lord after three days. Then there will be a great persecution such as there never was before nor will ever be thereafter.[86]

The Greek version, the *Oracle of Baalbek*, further explains some aspects of Enoch and Elijah's mission. "Two men" make their appearance after the "Emperor with the Changing Shape," the Antichrist, has performed his miracles and has produced a terrible drought. It is said that they have not experienced death and that they will wage war against the "ruler of Perdition." He will say: My time has drawn near (ἤγγικεν ὁ καιρός μου), as Jesus had warned that the pseudo-Messiah would say, and slay them, but the Crucified Jesus will come from heaven like a great and shining luminary and will revive them and destroy the Antichrist and his entire host.[87]

This prediction differs from the Latin version in several respects. First, Enoch is here mentioned before Elijah (an order that will prevail in the later texts). Second, it is stated that the "two men" never died. This remark elucidates the prophecy of the Latin Sibyl that they will "come forth" (*egredientur*), obviously from some place to which they had been transported at the end of their earthly career as recorded in the Old Testament. Third, it is here said expressly that they will fight the Antichrist; and the words placed in the mouth of the Antichrist ("my time has drawn near"), because they echo Luke 21:8, show that the author considered the Antichrist a pseudo-Messiah. The reasons for the two men's attack on the Antichrist, however, are not yet clear.

Further clarifications emerge from the text of Pseudo-Ephraem. Here

---

86. Latin version of the Tiburtine Sibyl, p. 186.11 Sackur: *Regnante autem eo egredientur duo clarissimi viri Helias et Enoch ad annuntiandum Domini adventum et Antichristus occidet eos, et post tres dies a Domino resuscitabuntur. Tunc erit persecutio magna qualis non fuit antea nec postea subsequetur.*
87. *Oracle of Baalbek*, lines 214–21 (cf. Luke 21:8 πολλοὶ γὰρ ἐλεύσονται ἐπὶ τῷ ὀνόματί μου λέγοντες· ἐγώ εἰμι, καί· ὁ καιρὸς ἤγγικεν κτλ. [For many will come in my name saying: "I am he," and "the time is at hand."])

the prediction concerning the "prophets" Enoch and Elijah follows upon the Antichrist's activities at Jerusalem and the *tribulatio magna* of three and a half years. As God will see mankind, so Pseudo-Ephraem predicts,

> endangered and wavering under the blast of the horrible dragon [the Antichrist], he sends them [mankind] a preaching of comfort through his servants Enoch and Elijah who have not yet tasted death and have been preserved so that they may announce Christ's Second Coming and may denounce the Enemy [the Antichrist].[88]

They will recall men who have been led astray by the Antichrist to their divine allegiance, will be slain by him, and will revive prior to the Second Coming.[89]

Here the mission of Enoch and Elijah is expressed quite clearly: they have been spared from death in order that they may comfort men during the reign of the Antichrist, by their preaching may recall to divine allegiance those who have succumbed to the Antichrist's seductive practices, and may announce the Second Coming and with it the end of the Antichrist's domination.[90] Obviously, it is these activities that prompt the "warfare" of the "two men" against the "ruler of Perdition" and their death in the *Oracle of Baalbek*.

In the Syriac Pseudo-Methodius the passage on Enoch and Elijah is not preserved.[91] Its content can, however, be recovered from the Greek

---

88. Pseudo-Ephraem, p. 219.8 Caspari: *aspiciens Deus humanum genus periclitantes et afflatu draconis horribilis fluctuantes mittit eis consolatoriam praedicationem per famulos suos, prophetos Enoch et Heliam qui necdum mortem gustantes ad pronuntiandum secundum adventum Christi et ut arguant inimicum seruati sunt.*

89. Pseudo-Ephraem, pp. 219.13–220.2 Caspari. Details on the Antichrist's leading astray of mankind and of their death at the hands of Antichrist are lost due to a lacuna in the only manuscript, but the data on his *seductio* (p. 219.15 and 18) and their *resurrectio* (219.18) guarantee their mention. On Enoch as prophet, see *Iudae Epistola* 14; Rev. 11:3; Ethiopic Enoch.

90. On the "two witnesses" as preachers of repentance, cf. Rev. 11:3: προφητεύσουσιν ἡμέρας χιλίας διακοσίας ἑξήκοντα περιβεβλημένοι σάκκους [they will prophesy one thousand two hundred and sixty days, clothed in sackcloth].

91. Solomon of Basra (thirteenth century), in the *Book of the Bee* (ed. and trans. E. A. W. Budge, *Anecdota Oxoniensia*, Semitic Series, vol. I, part II [Oxford, 1886]) excerpted the Syriac Pseudo-Methodius, much of the time literally. According to these excerpts it is said (pp. 130f. of English translation) that after the Antichrist's sitting in the Jewish Temple and other activities, Jews, devils, Indians, and others will believe in him—for two and a half years, according to one opinion; three and a half, according to another. "And when everyone is standing in despair, then will Elijah [Elias] come from Paradise, and convict the Deceiver, and turn the heart of the fathers to the children and the heart of the children to the fathers; and he will encourage and strengthen the hearts of the believers" (p. 131). The hesitation as to the length of the Antichrist's reign as well as the mention of Elijah alone without Enoch show that Solomon is here following other sources, perhaps in addition to Pseudo-Methodius. The Greek and Latin translations of Pseudo-Methodius discussed in the text prove that little or nothing of Solomon's data on Elijah derives from the Syriac Pseudo-Methodius.

and Latin translations. Here, too, God's servants Enoch and Elijah are sent by God in his mercy to the human race during the reign of the Antichrist after the latter has entered the Jewish Temple and when "the affliction of those days" (Matt. 24:29) has been intensified. They denounce the Enemy (the Antichrist) and his deceit publicly and show him to be a liar and of no account (ψεύστην . . . καὶ οὐδὲν ὄντα). In fact, under the impact of their activity, the Gentiles will abandon him and make common cause with "those just men" (Enoch and Elijah). The Antichrist will then slay them. Their revival is not explicitly mentioned, but it is predicted that after the destruction of the Antichrist "the Righteous," either Enoch and Elijah or all the Just including them, will shine forth like luminaries.[92]

Pseudo-Methodius here expresses or implies a great deal that had not been said in the apocalypses so far considered. If Enoch and Elijah, in the course of their public refutation of the Antichrist, denounce him as "a liar and of no account," this implies the notion known, for example, from a Greek homily *In Adventum Domini*, attributed to Ephraem, that the Antichrist will be unable to protect from starvation even those who accept his "seal" (the serpent) and thus acknowledge his domination.[93] Furthermore, the statement that the Gentiles will abandon him seems to imply by contrast the notion, already expressed by Pseudo-Ephraem, of a special relationship between the Jews and the Antichrist that is not shaken by the denunciation of Enoch and Elijah.[94]

A few further details may be gleaned from the *Visions of Daniel*. According to the *Slavonic Daniel* Enoch and Elijah will be slain by the Antichrist "on the cross [on which] was crucified our God Jesus, and he will receive their souls from their mouth."[95] Pseudo-Chrysostom reproduces, almost literally, the material of the Greek Pseudo-Methodius but expressly identifies the Antichrist with Daniel's "abomination that makes desolate."[96] *Daniel Καὶ ἔσται* also excerpts the Greek Pseudo-

---

92. Greek Pseudo-Methodius, p. 49.4 Istrin (= p. 140.61 Lolos) τότε ἐκλάμψουσιν οἱ δίκαιοι ὡς φωστῆρες; cf. 48.11 (= p. 138.53 Lolos) τὰ οὖν ἔθνη . . . προσκολληθήσονται τοῖς δικαίοις ἐκείνοις; Latin Pseudo-Methodius p. 95.15 Sackur. See also Dan. 12:3 καὶ οἱ συνιέντες ἐκλάμψουσιν ὡς ἡ λαμπρότης τοῦ στερεώματος καὶ ἀπὸ τῶν δικαίων τῶν πολλῶν ὡς οἱ ἀστέρες [and those who are wise shall shine like the brightness of the firmament; and those who turn many to righteousness like the stars . . .] and Matt. 13:43 τότε οἱ δίκαιοι ἐκλάμψουσιν ὡς ὁ ἥλιος [then the righteous will shine like the sun].

93. Ephraem Graecus, ed. J. Assemani, *Opera Graeca*, vol. III (Rome, 1746), 141 C. Cf. Caspari and Bousset, pp. 133f. The passage is reproduced, almost literally, by Pseudo-Hippolytus, ed. Achelis, GCS vol. I, pt. 2, p. 302.

94. Pseudo-Ephraem, p. 217.6–13 Caspari.

95. *Slavonic Daniel* #11.

96. Pseudo-Chrysostom, p. 38.6 Vasiliev οὗτός ἐστιν ὁ πλάνος, ὁ ἀντικείμενος, τὸ δὲ βδέλυγμα τῆς ἐρημώσεως [this is the deceiver, the adversary, the abomination of desolation]. Cf. Dan. 11:31, 12:11; Matt. 24:15; Mark 13:14.

Methodius and adds that the Antichrist will slay Enoch and Elijah by the sword.[97]

Again very interesting is the prophecy of the Erythraean Sibyl. Enoch and Elijah are not named in it, yet the oldest stratum of this text seems to allude to them in two passages. The author speaks of the rise of a marvellous star (*stella mirabilis*) bearing the image of the four living creatures (Rev. 4:6, etc.: lion, ox, man, eagle) that "will illuminate the Danaans and enlighten the world";[98] St. Paul's mission to the Hellenistic world may be meant. Then a horrible beast will come from the East. Its feet will be six hundred and sixty-three, it will speak against the Lamb, blaspheme against (Christ's New) Testament and increase the waters of the dragon (cf. Rev. 12:15f.). Two stars resembling the first (star) will rise up against the beast but will not be successful until the abomination comes and the will of the Highest is fulfilled "as we shall explain below."[99]

These indications are not altogether clear, but the author seems to be thinking of an anti-Christian force preceding the last Antichrist, the *abhominatio* (Dan. 9:27). The measuring by "feet" normally refers, in this text, to years (of life or rule), but in this case the six hundred and sixty-three feet of the horrible beast are likely to represent the mysterious number of the "beast which rose out of the earth" according to Rev. 13:18.[100]

It is strange that although the author explicitly announces a later discussion (*sicut inferius distinguemus*) of the struggle of the "two stars" against the beast at the time of the *abhominatio*, the "two stars" are never mentioned again in the original kernel of the text.[101] However, when at the end of the text the same author discusses the "signs" preceding the Last Judgment, there occurs the following prediction:

And there will come messengers beyond reproach announcing the ruin of the world and saying: Let there be contrition, let there be penance! Let the trans-

---

97. Daniel Καὶ ἔσται, p. 43.15 Vasiliev.
98. Erythraean Sibyl, p. 162.12 Holder-Egger: *Set surget stella mirabilis quattuor animalium habens ymaginem, eritque in tuba mirabili, Danaos illuminabit, orbem illustrabit.*
99. Erythraean Sibyl, p. 162.22 Holder-Egger: *Stelleque due consimiles prime insurgent contra ipsam* [i.e., *bestiam*] *et non optinebunt usque dum ueniat abhominatio, et voluntas altissimi consumetur, sicut inferius distinguemus.*
100. "Let him who has understanding reckon the number of the beast, for it is a human number, its number is six hundred and sixty-six." A variant reading: 616. The number 663 is not attested as a reading in the biblical text, but is so close to 666 that the suggestion made in the text seems irresistible.
101. The passage (p. 165.8) about the *due stelle lucidissime* belongs to a long thirteenth-century Joachimite interpolation; see Jamison, *Admiral Eugenius of Sicily*, pp. 21–32.

gressors be destroyed so that wrath be averted and men be converted to the Lamb.[102]

This passage must be the discussion of the "two stars" promised earlier by the author, for it alone meets the requirements indicated by him in the former prediction: it deals with the time of the *abhominatio* and of the consummation of God's plan. It thus is permissible to identify the "messengers beyond reproach" with the "two stars." Furthermore, inasmuch as the mission of the "messengers beyond reproach," as described by the Erythraean Sibyl, is at least a call to repentance and as this is the principal eschatological function of Enoch and Elijah in the apocalyptic tradition, the conclusion seems inescapable that it is they who are meant in the two passages about stars and messengers.[103] (It remains unexplained, however, just why the Erythraean Sibyl called Enoch and Elijah the "two stars.")[104]

The *Apocalypse of St. Andrew* adds one other interesting feature. There not only Elijah and Enoch (in this order) but also the "Son of Thunder" are expected to denounce the Antichrist's deceptive activities and announce the Second Coming.[105] The author must mean the apostle John the son of Zebedee and brother of James, "whom he [Jesus] surnamed Boanerges, that is, Sons of Thunder" (Mark 3:17).

It has already been mentioned that according to many Byzantine

---

102. Erythraean Sibyl, p. 173.6 Holder-Egger: *Et nuncii venient inreprehensibiles nunciantes rerum excidium et dicentes: Fiat humiliatio, fiat penitudo! Conterantur qui excesserant ut avertatur furor, convertatur et agnus*. The last two words make no sense in the context and should be emended to read *ad agnum*.

103. On Enoch and Elijah as preachers of repentance see Rev. 11:3 (the two witnesses prophesying "for one thousand two hundred and sixty days, clothed in sackcloth"); Bousset, *Offenbarung Johannis*, p. 317 ("im Bussack, d.h. als Bussprediger"); Joachim Jeremias, "Ἠλ(ε)ίας," *Theologisches Wörterbuch zum Neuen Testament* II (Stuttgart, 1935), pp. 930–43, esp. 935.

104. Is this designation perhaps due to the metaphor of the "two lampstands" (Rev. 11:4 οὗτοί [i.e., οἱ δύο μάρτυρες] εἰσιν αἱ δύο ἐλαῖαι καὶ αἱ δύο λυχνίαι [these (i.e., the two martyrs) are the two olive trees and the two lampstands]) interpreted as constellations? At any rate the passage in the Erythraean Sibyl (n. 99 above) explains a remark made by Berthold Purstinger, *Onus Ecclesiae*, (n.p., 1532), ch. 61: *Sibylla nuncupat eos* (the two witnesses) *duo stellas*, which puzzled Bousset, *Antichrist*, p. 139n.1 ("die rätselhafte Bemerkung"). Purstinger was referring to the Erythraean Sibyl, which had escaped Bousset.

105. *Apocalypse of St. Andrew* 869B (= p. 212 Rydén) Ἠλιοῦ δὲ καὶ Ἐνὼχ καὶ τοῦ υἱοῦ τῆς βροντῆς ἐξελθόντων καὶ προκηρυξάντων τὴν αὐτοῦ ['Ἀντιχρίστου] ἀποπλάνησιν τήν τε τοῦ Κυρίου Ἰησοῦ δευτέραν ἔλευσιν [Elias and Enoch and the Son of Thunder come out and proclaim his (Antichrist's) deception and the Second Coming of Jesus Christ]. Two manuscripts of the Greek Pseudo-Methodius (p. 48.8 Istrin *apparatus criticus* = p. 138.50 Lolos) as well as several Church Fathers (cf. Bousset, *Antichrist*, p. 137) also mention John the Son of Thunder along with Enoch and Elijah; other manuscripts of Pseudo-Methodius mention John "the Theologian." It is not clear to me why Bousset, *Antichrist*, p. 137, speaks of John the Baptist.

apocalypses Enoch and Elijah will eventually be successful, through their preaching, in detaching from the Antichrist all or some of his adherents.[106] Their achievement will then produce a conflict with the Antichrist in the course of which Enoch and Elijah will be slain by the Antichrist, though they will later be revived. Finally the Antichrist will be punished. Where the duration of the Antichrist's domination is mentioned, it is normally given as three and a half years.[107] According to the *Oracle of Baalbek* the Antichrist, presumably in order to win adherents, will grant a tax exemption for three and a half years, but this text is, to the best of my knowledge, unique in allowing him a reign of thirty years.[108]

Concerning the modalities of the Antichrist's final fate there is a great deal of variation in the Byzantine sources. According to the Latin version of the Tiburtine Sibyl he will be slain on the Mount of Olives "through the strength of the Lord by the archangel Michael."[109] In the *Oracle of Baalbek*, on the other hand, it is said merely that the crucified (Christ) will wage war against the Son of Perdition and will kill him and all his host.[110] As already mentioned, Pseudo-Ephraem reproduces one after another two conflicting opinions about the end of the Antichrist: he first follows the view of II Thess. 2:8, according to which Christ will kill the Antichrist "with the breath of his mouth" and then goes on to say that the Antichrist will be plunged alive, together with his father Satan, into the abyss of eternal fire, obviously to be tortured there for eternity.[111] Here Christ alone brings about the discomfiture of the Anti-

---

106. Pseudo-Ephraem, pp. 215.5, 219.14 Caspari; Greek Pseudo-Methodius, p. 48.11 (= p. 138.54 Lolos); Latin Pseudo-Methodius, p. 95.19 Sackur; Pseudo-Chrysostom, p. 38.7 Vasiliev; *Daniel Καὶ ἔσται*, p. 43.13 Vasiliev.

107. Pseudo-Ephraem, p. 217.10–15 Caspari (Jerusalem trodden down by Gentiles for forty-two months or three and a half years, according to Rev. 11:2; drought of three and a half years); Erythraean Sibyl, p. 172.14 Holder-Egger (the Antichrist's crimes and blasphemies last *donec tres pedes semique abbreviati discurrant*; in the language of this text *pedes* normally means years); *Apocalypse of St. Andrew* 856D (= p. 203 Rydén) (the Son of Lawlessness to rule three and a half years at Constantinople).

108. *Oracle of Baalbek*, lines 207, 192.

109. Latin Sibyl, 186.16 Sackur: *occidetur virtute Domini Antichristus a Mihaele arcangelo in monte Oliveti*. It is difficult to decide whether *Dominus* here means God or Christ. A few lines earlier (p. 186.10) the phrase *domus Domini* refers to the Jewish Temple and *Dominus* therefore is God, but in line 12 *Domini adventus* must signify Christ's Second Coming. It is also uncertain whether *virtus Domini* here means "strength" or "host."

110. *Oracle of Baalbek*, line 220 καὶ πολεμήσει ὁ ἐπὶ ξύλου σταυρωθεὶς τὸν υἱὸν τῆς ἀπωλείας καὶ θανατώσει αὐτὸν καὶ πᾶσαν τὴν στρατιὰν αὐτοῦ. [And then he who was hanged on the cross will wage war upon the Son of Perdition and will slay him and all his host.]

111. N. 28 above.

christ; no terrestrial place of execution and no angelic assistance are mentioned.

In the Syriac Pseudo-Methodius it is said that at the Second Coming the Antichrist will be delivered to hellfire together with his adherents.[112] It is the second tradition recorded by Pseudo-Ephraem. However, the Greek and Latin versions of Pseudo-Methodius, and the tradition depending on them, accept Pseudo-Ephraem's first tradition, according to which the Lord will slay the Antichrist "with the breath of his mouth."[113] The Erythraean Sibyl seems to suggest that the Antichrist, the *abhominatio*, will be burned by the Lamb (Christ) together with all creation, prior to the Last Judgment over Good and Wicked.[114] Like the Syriac Pseudo-Methodius, the *Apocalypse of St. Andrew* follows the second of these two traditions: the Son of Perdition will be smitten and placed in unquenchable fire.[115] Later, fuller details about his end are given, apparently within the same tradition: the Antichrist is first smitten, then seized together with his demons, bound and guarded by fiery angels, produced before (Christ's) tribunal, and called to account for the human souls which he has ruined.[116]

The Byzantine apocalypses discussed here frequently disagree on the sequence in which the predictions on the Antichrist are presented. The discussion will begin with the schedule contained in Pseudo-Ephraem, without any claim that in date of composition it is necessarily earlier

---

112. Syriac Pseudo-Methodius, fol. 136 verso: "And at the coming of Our Lord from heaven he [the Antichrist] will be delivered to Hell-fire and outer darkness. And there he will be in weeping and gnashing of teeth, together with all those who believed in him."

113. Greek Pseudo-Methodius, p. 49.4 Istrin (= p. 140.60 Lolos) ἀνελεῖ αὐτὸν Κύριος τῷ πνεύματι τοῦ στόματος αὐτοῦ κατὰ τὴν ἀποστολικὴν ἐκφαντορίαν [the Lord will slay him with the breath of his mouth according to the apostolic revelation]; Latin Pseudo-Methodius, p. 96.4; Pseudo-Chrysostom, p. 38.13. The *Slavonic Daniel* omits the topic, and *Daniel Καὶ ἔσται*, p. 43.15 Vasiliev, predicts that the Lord will exterminate the Antichrist from the face of the earth.

114. Erythraean Sibyl, p. 173.13: *Et venient in conspectu agni abhominatio peccatorum et ultionis appetitus, et descendet ignis terribilis qui universa creata usque ad ethera concremabit.*

115. *Apocalypse of St. Andrew* 857B (= p. 214 Rydén) Παταχθήσεται γὰρ τοῦτο τὸ σκῆπτρον τῆς ἀνομίας καὶ ἐν τῷ ἀσβέστῳ πυρὶ ληφθήσεται [For this scepter of lawlessness will be smitten and thrown into the unquenchable fire].

116. *Apocalypse of St. Andrew* 872D (= p. 214 Rydén) Τοῦ Ἀντιχρίστου [δὲ] ἤδη παταχθέντος καὶ σὺν τοῖς δαιμόσιν αὐτοῦ συλληφθέντος καὶ ὑπὸ πυρίνων ἀγγέλων δεσμευθέντος καὶ φυλασσομένου τῷ κριτηρίῳ παρίστασθαι καὶ ἀπαιτεῖσθαι δίκας περὶ τῶν ψυχῶν ὧν ἀπώλεσεν . . . [When the Antichrist has been struck down and seized with his demons and put in chains by fiery angels and is guarded so he may appear at the court and pay the penalty for the souls he has destroyed]. The text is in disorder (an additional participle or a finite verb seems to be missing) but the recurrence of the verb πατάσσειν (see preceding note) seems to indicate that the two passages represent the same tradition.

than the other texts. It does, however, exhibit a number of features that taken singly show that this text preserves at least some early characteristics. It knows nothing of the Arab invasions; it is concerned instead with warfare between Rome and Persia. It predicts a surrender of the Christian Empire to God but knows nothing of a Last Roman Emperor who will carry out the surrender. It divides mankind into Christians, heretics, Jews, and pagans, a view difficult to imagine as having originated later than the fourth century, by which time paganism had ceased to be a significant force (Part One, Chapter V.3 above).[117] Finally, the account of the *nequissimae gentes* (i.e., Gog and Magog) does not mention Alexander the Great and the imprisonment of the impure peoples—in other words, it is as yet unaffected by the legend of Alexander.

In Pseudo-Ephraem the sequence is as follows. After the attack of the *gentes nequissimae* or *bellicae* (1) there follows the surrender of the Christian Empire (2), the apparition of the Antichrist (3), an allusion to the Blessings of Moses and Jacob on the tribe of Dan (4), then the division of the Antichrist's career into a period of adolescence before his seizure of imperial power and a second period, of maturity, when he will hold imperial power (5). Then comes his challenging God by sitting in the Jewish Temple at Jerusalem (6), the "great tribulation" of three and a half years (drought, famine, etc.: 7) and during it the mission of Enoch and Elijah (8), and, finally, the Second Coming and the punishment of the Antichrist (9). This schedule may be presented schematically as follows:

### Pseudo-Ephraem

| | | |
|---|---|---|
| 1. | Attack of *gentes bellicae* or *nequissimae* | 212.13–213.17 |
| 2. | Surrender of the empire | 214.1 |
| 3. | *apparebit ille nequissimus et abominabilis draco* | 214.4 |
| 4. | Blessings of Moses and Jacob on Dan | 214.6 |
| 5. | *adulescens . . . antequam sumat imperium; factus legitimus sumet imperium* | 216.2, 11 |
| 6. | Sitting in the Jewish Temple | 217.1 |
| 7. | *tribulatio magna* lasting three and a half years | 217.14 |

---

117. Pseudo-Ephraem, p. 213.12f. Caspari.

| 8. | Mission of Enoch and Elijah | 219.10 |
| 9. | Second Coming of Christ and punishment of the Antichrist | 220.2 |

In the Latin version of the Tiburtine Sibyl the attack of Gog and Magog, with which the story begins in Pseudo-Ephraem (1), is preceded by a passage about the Antichrist that has been shown (p. 197 above) partially to duplicate several later items (3, 4, C): the "rise" of the Antichrist from the tribe of Dan, his false miracles, and the shortening of time (A). Then comes the raid of Gog and Magog (1), here previously imprisoned by Alexander, and a further additional feature: their defeat by the Last Roman Emperor (B). There follows the surrender at Jerusalem (2), here carried out by the Last Emperor; the "manifest revelation" of the Antichrist (3); his sitting in the Jewish Temple (6); the mission of Elijah and Enoch (8); the "great persecution" (7); the shortening of time (C) (another new feature), and the punishment of the Antichrist (9). It will be noted that in comparison with Pseudo-Ephraem the Latin version of the Tiburtine Sibyl adds features (A, B, C), omits others (4, 5), and reverses the order of 7 and 8. With regard to the omission of 5, however, it may be observed that the two texts agree in conceiving of the career of the Antichrist as proceeding in two stages: adolescence and private status versus maturity and imperial power in the case of Pseudo-Ephraem, "rise" versus "manifest revelation" in the Latin Sibyl. A graphic presentation of the scheme is given below:

Latin Version of the Tiburtine Sibyl

| A. | *Surget . . . de tribu Dan*, false miracles, shortening of time | 185.9–186.1 |
| 1. | Attack of Gog and Magog | 186.1 |
| B. | Their defeat by the Last Roman Emperor | 186.4 |
| 2. | Surrender of the empire by the Last Roman Emperor | 186.7 |
| 3. | *Revelabitur manifeste Antichristus* | 186.9 |
| 6. | Sitting in the Jewish Temple | 186.10 |
| 8. | Mission of Elijah and Enoch | 186.11 |
| 7. | *Persecutio magna* | 186.14 |
| C. | Shortening of time (cf. A) | 186.15 |
| 9. | Punishment of the Antichrist | 186.16 |

In the Syriac, Greek, and Latin versions of Pseudo-Methodius, the sequence followed by Pseudo-Ephraem reappears relatively undisturbed, with two notable exceptions. The text begins with a long addition on the Arab invasions (D), and after the first "appearance" of the Son of Perdition (see A in the Latin version of the Tiburtine Sibyl) there is inserted a section interpreting the Three Woes pronounced by Jesus on Chorazin, Beth-saida, and Capernaum (Matt. 11:21; Luke 10:13) as referring to the career of the Antichrist (E). The distinction between his adolescence and his maturity is missing here, as it is in the Latin version of the Tiburtine Sibyl, but here again his twofold "apparition" (A and 3) conveys a similar notion. In the only surviving manuscript of the Syriac Pseudo-Methodius the references to the Antichrist's persecution (7) and to the mission of Enoch and Elijah (8) are missing, but the Greek and Latin translations show that this omission is due to an accident of the literary transmission. Here is the graphic scheme according to Pseudo-Methodius:

Pseudo-Methodius

| | | Syriac (fol.) | Greek (p.) | Latin (p.) |
|---|---|---|---|---|
| D. | Arab invasions | 127 verso–134 verso | 26.3–44.1 | 90.4–91.22 |
| 1. | Invading hosts from the North | 134 verso–135 recto | 44.1–16 | 91.24–93.1 |
| A. | Son of Perdition "revealed" (φανήσεται, apparebit) | 135 recto | 45.1 | 93.5 |
| E. | Three Woes | 135 recto | 45.4 | 93.6 |
| 2. | Surrender of the empire by the Last Roman Emperor | 135 recto | 45.10 | 93.14 |
| 3. | Son of Perdition "revealed" (ἐμφανὴς γένηται, appareat manifestus) | 135 verso | 46n.5, line 10 | 94.8 |

| | | | | |
|---|---|---|---|---|
| 4. | Blessing of Jacob on Dan (incl. false miracles; cf. Latin Sibyl A) | 135 verso | 46.7 | 94.9 |
| 6. | Sitting in the Jewish Temple | 136 verso | 48.1 | 95.12 |
| 7. | *tribulatio* | – | 48.4 | 95.12 |
| 8. | Mission of Enoch and Elijah | – | 48.6 | 95.13 |
| 9. | Second Coming of Christ and punishment of the Antichrist | 136 verso | 49.1 | 96.3 |

There is little to be gained from an analysis of the sequence in the other Byzantine apocalypses. The *Oracle of Baalbek* shares the end of the sequence with Pseudo-Ephraem and Pseudo-Methodius, but prior to this point it uses its elements eclectically.[118] The *Visions of Daniel* all contain excerpts from the Greek Pseudo-Methodius, and so parts of the Pseudo-Methodian sequence reappear there.[119] Elements of the legend also occur in the prophecy of the Erythraean Sibyl and in the *Apocalypse of St. Andrew*, but there, too, the sequence appears in highly fragmented condition and intermingled with other materials.[120]

If one reconsiders the three basic patterns in Pseudo-Ephraem, the Latin version of the Tiburtine Sibyl, and the three versions of Pseudo-Methodius, the conclusion emerges that the sequence established for

---

118. *Oracle of Baalbek*, lines 211–21 (nos. 7–9). Other elements used are the shortening of time (line 178; cf. A and C in Latin version of the Tiburtine Sibyl) and the Antichrist's miracles (line 210; cf. A in Latin version of the Tiburtine Sibyl).

119. By way of illustration, Pseudo-Chrysostom reproduces nos. 4 (= Gen. 49:17) (p. 37.13 Vasiliev), 6 (p. 37.27), 7 (p. 37.32), 8 (p. 38.4), and 9 (p. 38.12).

120. Among features of the Erythraean Sibyl not attested in the apocalypses cited so far I mention *exempli gratia*: the division of the world into ten *sceptra*, with the Antichrist (*abhominatio*) at their head (cf. Lactantius *Divinae Institutiones*, ed. Brandt, *Corpus scriptorum ecclesiasticorum Latinorum*, vol. 19, pt. 1 [Vienna, 1890] 635.1 and *Epitome* 756.22). From the *Apocalypse of St. Andrew*: first the listing of the Antichrist's human birth (γεννηθέντος αὐτοῦ ἀνθρώπου), his maturing (ἀνδρύνεσθαι), and his accession to imperial power (βασιλεύειν)—cf. PG 111.869D (= p. 213 Rydén), reminiscent of Pseudo-Ephraem's distinction of two stages in his career (p. 197 above) and of Pseudo-Methodius' interpretation of the Three Woes (p. 196 above)—and second, the notion of "terrible warfare" (872A: πόλεμος φοβερός) between Christ and the Antichrist (see *Oracle of Baalbek*, line 219 πολεμήσει, a remote echo of the four battles fought among them according to Lactantius *Divinae Institutiones* 645.6 and *Epitome* 759.2 Brandt).

Pseudo-Ephraem remains stable and that the variants which at first seem significant either are concessions to changing historical circumstances or are due to disturbances of a literary kind. A notable instance of the first kind of variant is the insertion of the long "prophecy" of the Arab invasions (D) in the Pseudo-Methodian tradition immediately preceding its mythological prototype, the invasion of Gog and Magog. Examples of literary changes are the insertion of an alternative tradition (A) on the Antichrist in the Latin version of the Tiburtine Sibyl and in the Pseudo-Methodian tradition and on the shortening of time (C) in the Latin version of the Tiburtine Sibyl alone; the insertion of the Last Roman Emperor (B) in the Latin version of the Tiburtine Sibyl and Pseudo-Methodius and of the application of the Three Woes to the Antichrist (E) in Pseudo-Methodius; the omission of the Blessing on Dan (4) in the Latin version of the Tiburtine Sibyl; and the reversal of the order of persecution (7) and the mission of Enoch and Elijah (8) in the same text.[121]

There is a further, primarily literary observation to be made concerning the schedule of events relating to the Antichrist. It concerns a flashback technique employed in several Byzantine apocalypses referring to his career. In Pseudo-Ephraem, for example, his "appearance" is first predicted to occur after the surrender of the empire of the Christians, and this mention is followed by the exegesis of several biblical passages supposedly referring to him (Deut. 33:22 combined with Gen. 49:9; Jer. 17:11) and the prediction that "on the last day" he will be abandoned by his adherents.[122] Thereupon the author returns to the Antichrist's birth[123] and then continues to prophesy his career in chronological sequence. This flashback technique is again noticeable in the three versions of Pseudo-Methodius, where it is first said that the Antichrist "will be revealed" and where the texts later mention the Three Woes

---

121. Their mission of comfort and repentance is better motivated if it occurs during (rather than prior to) the persecution; the original order is therefore probably that of Pseudo-Ephraem and Pseudo-Methodius, rather than that of the Latin Sibyl.

122. Pseudo-Ephraem, pp. 214.4–215.6 Caspari.

123. Pseudo-Ephraem, p. 215.8 Caspari. It is doubtful whether this flashback technique is present in the Latin version of the Tiburtine Sibyl. There (p. 185.19) the author mentions the Antichrist's "rise" from the tribe of Dan and continues in the next sentence to say that he will be "the Son of Perdition, the prince of pride, the master of error, the fullness of wickedness." These words are probably no more than characterizations, but it may possibly be significant that the first of them (*filius perditionis*) marks a return to the Antichrist's birth. If the word σταθήσεται in line 198 of the *Oracle of Baalbek* (καὶ σταθήσεται ἀπὸ τοῦ μιαροῦ ἔθνους τῶν Καππαδόκων) means that the "King with a Changing Shape" (the Antichrist) "will be established," as I translated it (p. 28), his accession would be mentioned by a flashback late in his reign. Could the word mean here "he will be stopped"?

(Matt. 11:21; Luke 10:13) signifying, according to Pseudo-Methodius, that the Antichrist will be conceived (born) at Chorazin, be born (raised) in Beth-saida, and rule at Capernaum.[124]

The scriptural evidence cited in the Byzantine apocalypses for the career of the Antichrist is more copious than that for the Last Roman Emperor; it is in fact so abundant that it will not be possible here to present the complete picture. Writers of apocalypses were particularly apt to exploit the short apocalypse attributed by the evangelists to Jesus (Matt. 24:3–31; Luke 17:22–27), the warning about the Second Coming contained in II Thess. 2:1–8, and to some degree at least the canonical Revelation of St. John. From these biblical sources the Byzantine apocalypses partially derived, for example, the Antichrist's sitting in the Jewish Temple at Jerusalem (II Thess. 2:4);[125] his false miracles (Matt. 24:24); the shortening of time during his persecution (Matt. 24:22); much of the eschatological episode of Enoch and Elijah, especially their death and resurrection (Rev. 11:7ff.) and the Antichrist's death by the breath of Jesus' mouth (II Thess. 2:8).

The descent of the Antichrist from the Jewish tribe of Dan is regularly connected, in the Byzantine apocalypses, with an interpretation of Jacob's blessing on that tribe (Gen. 49:17: "Dan shall be a serpent in the way, a viper by the path, that bites the horse's heel, so that his rider falls backward"); in Pseudo-Ephraem, primarily with Moses' Blessing on Dan (Deut. 33:22). These biblical passages were cited in this respect as early as the Church Fathers Irenaeus and Hippolytus—in fact, their application was anticipated by rabbinical interpretation.[126] As time went on, the bond of the Antichrist with Jacob's Blessing on Dan became more complex, and every word of this text was given an eschatological meaning. In the Syriac Pseudo-Methodius, Dan signifies the Antichrist, the path obstructed by the viper is the one leading to the kingdom of heaven, the viper's "bite" is the Antichrist's seemingly (i.e., hypocritically) just pronouncements, and its means are the false miracles he performs. The "horse's heel" stands for the last days; the "rider"

---

124. Syriac Pseudo-Methodius, fol. 135 recto; Greek Pseudo-Methodius, p. 45.3 Istrin (= p. 130.112 Lolos); Latin Pseudo-Methodius, p. 93.5 Sackur; *Slavonic Daniel* #11; *Daniel Καὶ ἔσται*, p. 42.29 Vasiliev. The passage is not reproduced in Pseudo-Chrysostom. An echo of this tradition is preserved in the *Apocalypse of St. Andrew* (n. 51 above).

125. See also the Old Testament sources of II Thess. 2:4, such as Ezek. 28:2; Dan. 11:36.

126. Bousset, *Antichrist*, pp. 112f. Add Hippolytus, *On the Benedictions of Isaac, Jacob and Moses*, edd. M. Brière, L. Mariès and B.-Ch. Mercier, *Patrologia Orientalis* 27 (Paris, 1954), p. 90: the "horse's heel" in Gen. 49:17 means those who travel the straight road and who preach truth and salvation.

is the saints led astray by the Antichrist according to Matt. 24:24; the "horse" is their vehicle, holiness; and the "backward" direction of the fall means sin.[127]

In the Pseudo-Methodian tradition there also appears, for the first time in Byzantine apocalypses, the connection of the Antichrist's conception (birth), birth (adolescence), and royal status with the Three Woes pronounced by Jesus on Chorazin, Beth-saida, and Capernaum (Matt. 11:21; Luke 10:13).[128]

These are only a few gleanings from the rich scriptural evidence used by the Byzantine apocalypses to support their predictions concerning the Antichrist. However, just as in the case of the Last Roman Emperor, there are many data of the Byzantine apocalypses on the Antichrist for which there is no or little biblical foundation. Indeed, it is the principal thesis of Bousset's book on the Antichrist that Church Fathers and apocalyptic writers rely largely on an extra-canonical tradition about the Antichrist that sometimes supplements, and in other cases conflicts with, canonical Scripture. So far as Byzantine apocalypses are concerned, there are many features for which no biblical evidence could be quoted. This is true, for example, of the data on the Antichrist's hypocrisy, on his relations to the Jews, on the sign of the snake imposed upon his partisans, on his ability to assume different shapes, on the gathering of the saints to God during his rule, and on the association of the Son of Thunder with Enoch and Elijah in their conflict with the Antichrist. Other aspects of the Antichrist legend are only tenuously and artificially supported by canonical Scripture. In this respect, the relationship of the Byzantine apocalyptic data on the Antichrist to the Bible is not very different from that of the prophecies concerning the Last Roman Emperor in the same texts. The one significant difference in the attitude of Byzantine apocalyptists to Scripture in their statements on the Antichrist and on the Last Roman Emperor is that on the former

---

127. Syriac Pseudo-Methodius, fol. 135 recto–verso. The Greek and Latin translations distort this exegesis to some degree: the "rider" here is the truthfulness and piety of the Just, and the "horse" is the true faith (Greek Pseudo-Methodius, p. 47.1 Istrin (= p. 134.25 Lolos); Latin Pseudo-Methodius, p. 94.12 Sackur). Contrast the "political" interpretation of Gen. 49:17 offered by a Syriac catena compiled by the monk Severus of Edessa (ninth century) and printed among the Syriac works of Ephraem, vol. I (Rome, 1737), p. 192F: here "horse" and "rider" signify power—to be precise, the Roman people and empire. The Syriac Pseudo-Methodius shows no trace of this political interpretation.

128. Curiously, this matter is not discussed in Bousset, *Antichrist*. He is also misleading in stating (p. 114) that the notion of the Antichrist's birth from Dan does not occur in sources directly dependent on Ephraem. Both Pseudo-Ephraem (p. 215.7 Caspari) and Pseudo-Methodius (Syriac text, fol. 135 verso; Greek Pseudo-Methodius, p. 46.6 Istrin [= p. 134.20 Lolos]; Latin Pseudo-Methodius, p. 95.10 Sackur) have this detail.

topic they fail to cite non-biblical (post-biblical) prophecy, as they frequently do on the Last Emperor. The reason for this differential treatment must be that they felt canonical Scripture and the extra-canonical tradition (established by Bousset) to be sufficient for their purposes, and they saw no need to rely on less authoritative sources, as they were forced to do in the case of the Last Roman Emperor.

# Index

*Abhominatio*/abomination, Antichrist as, 206, 213, 214, 215, 217
Acradina, 68n31, 73. *See also* Akrodunion
Adana, 35, 48
Adramelech, 39
Adroigan (Azerbaijan), 17, 38
Adso, 4; *De ortu et tempore Antichristi* of, 2, 105–107, 122; differs from sources, 108; on Frankish king as last emperor, 106–107, 158; sources of, 7–8, 106, 107, 108–109, 118, 120, 121, 122, 158, 162n43; on II Thess. 2:3, 106
*Adventus mali*, 203. *See also* Antichrist
Āfnasōliōs, 18, 39
Africa/Africans, 21, 35, 49, 77, 104–105
Agag/Agog, 19, 41, 186. *See also* Gog and Magog
Ainqat, 39
Akra, 87, 88, 90, 91, 93
Akrodunion, 63, 68, 69, 73
Akroinon, 92, 173
Alani, 41
Alexander, Paul, 3, 5–7, 8
Alexander the Great, 18–19, 40–41, 42, 124; Greek Pseudo-Methodius on, 56, 57–58, 60; imprisons unclean nations (Gog and Magog), 4, 89, 147, 185, 186, 187, 189, 192, 219; Latin Tiburtine Sibyl on, 185, 219; origins of legend of, 147, 188–89; Pseudo-Ephraem lacks legend of, 188, 218; romance of, 188; succession after, 57–58; Syriac Pseudo-Methodius on, 56, 57–58, 147, 186; titles of, 56

Alexandria, 19, 40, 42, 118
Amalfi, 114, 161
Amantea, 111, 113
"Ammanites," 139, 197, 203, 205
Ammonites, 39
Amorium, 74, 75–76
Anastasius Bibliothecarius, 113, 116
Anastasius I, 3, 82, 136
Anastasius of Sinai, 30n51, 55, 60
Ancyra, 74, 75
Angel: destroys Antichrist, 216; destroys Gog and Magog/unclean nations, 63, 163, 186, 187, 188, 191; Gabriel, 63, 65–67, 69; instructs last emperor, 130, 133–34; Michael, 191, 216
Antichrist, 59, 97, 135, 159, 193–225; as abomination, 206, 213, 214, 215, 217; advent of, 4, 22, 43, 46, 50, 129, 139, 164, 185, 196, 200, 202, 205, 211; (double) advent of, 197–99, 201, 203, 218, 219, 222; "Ammanites" and Moabites accept, 139, 197, 203, 205; angel destroys, 216; *Apocalypse of St. Andrew the Fool* on, 204, 208, 209, 210, 215, 217, 220; in apocalypses, 2, 4, 5, 193, 208, 222; at Beth-saida, 71, 196, 198, 220–21, 223, 224; biblical evidence for, 4, 106, 193, 222, 223–24; birth of, 71, 198, 224; at Capernaum, 71–72, 196, 204, 220–21, 223, 224; challenges God, 207–208, 218; changes shape, 5, 194, 201, 203, 211, 224; at Chorazin, 71, 196, 198, 220–21, 223, 224; circumcision imposed by, 139, 206, 207; con-

[ 227

Antichrist (*continued*)
verts souls, 201–202, 204, 205, 208; *Daniel Καὶ ἔσται* on, 89, 199, 202, 203, 204, 206, 213–14; described, 88, 195; elect led astray by, 51; Erythraean Sibyl on, 203, 204, 206–207, 209, 210, 214–15, 217, 219, 220; as Evil One, 137, 138, 203; fate of, 22, 89, 216–17, 218, 219, 223; fights/kills Enoch and Elijah, 5, 63, 72, 73, 140, 211, 212, 213–14, 215, 216, 224; flashbacks in legends of, 222–23; geographic origin on, 195–96; God destroys, 22; God's response to, 22, 139–40, 209, 210, 211–16; Hippolytus of Rome on, 100, 193, 196, 200; as human, 195, 200–201; as Jewish, 139, 142, 183, 195, 196, 197, 198, 202, 219, 223; and Jews, 5, 206–207, 213, 224; Judaism on, 6, 193, 195, 224; as king/emperor, 203–204; and last Roman emperor, 164, 197, 199; Latin Tiburtine Sibyl on, 164, 185, 197, 199, 201, 203, 204–205, 208, 209, 211, 216, 219, 220, 221–22; length of reign of, 203, 210, 216; miracles of, 197, 201–203, 204; named, 193–94; *Oracle of Baalbek* on, 194, 197, 201–202, 203, 205, 208, 209, 211, 212, 216, 220; persecution by, 143, 199–200, 204, 208–10, 218, 219, 220, 221; Pseudo-Chrysostom on, 73, 199, 202–203, 213; Pseudo-Ephraem on, 137, 138, 139–40, 141, 142–43, 164, 194–95, 199, 200, 202, 203, 205–206, 207, 210, 213, 216, 217–19, 220, 221–22; as pseudo-Messiah, 203, 207, 211; Pseudo-Methodius texts on, 164, 196, 198–99, 202, 204, 206, 209, 210, 217, 220–21, 222–23, 224; qualities of, 142–43, 194–95, 205; and shortening of time, 197, 198, 199, 209–10, 211, 219, 222, 223; *Slavonic Daniel* on, 63, 64, 71–72, 199, 202, 204, 209; snake as sign of, 139, 143, 208, 213, 224; as Son of Perdition, 22, 43, 46, 50, 51, 71–72, 217; as son of Satan, 199, 200, 216; in Temple of Jerusalem, 51, 139, 197, 203, 204, 205–206, 211, 213, 218, 219, 220, 223; two traditions of, 198–201; *Visions of Daniel* on, 164, 199, 202, 220
Antiochus IV Epiphanes, 56, 60, 90, 91, 93, 94

Aphrahates, 182–83 n105
Apocalypse, 1–4; adjustments to, 103, 104; on Antichrist, 2, 4, 5, 193, 208, 222; Byzantine, 5–7, 8; Christian, 1; described, 3; functions of, 8; German historians on, 2; as historical, 3; Jewish, 1, 5–6, 176–77; medieval, 1–2; paraphrasing in, 97; as prophecy, 1, 3, 4; Sicilian, 36 (see also *Visions of Daniel*); as symbolic, 1; tenth-century studies of, 7–8 (*see also* Liudprand of Cremona)
*Apocalypse of St. Andrew the Fool*, 123, 124–25, 126, 159, 179; on Antichrist, 204, 208, 209, 210, 215, 217; on Enoch and Elijah, 215; on last emperor, 155, 156, 160, 163–64; on restored tribes of Israel, 128; on seven ages of world, 128–29. See also *Life of St. Andrew the Fool*
Apodinar, 75, 76
Apostasy, 21. See also Christianity, denied; Jesus Christ, denied
Apulia, 111
Arabia, 21, 49
Arabs, 18, 121, 154, 155; armada of, 75–76, 77; v. Byzantines, 32, 74–75, 104, 105, 114, 115, 116; capture keys of St. Peter, 77, 78; in Constantinople, 25, 72, 74, 75–76, 77; *Daniel Καὶ ἔσται* on, 77–78, 79, 84–86, 87, 94; in Italy, 77–78, 79, 110, 111, 112, 113, 117, 161; last emperor defeats, 34, 69–70, 73, 87, 88, 99, 101–102, 103–104, 108, 117, 118, 122, 131, 135, 157, 158, 163, 170, 173, 178, 186; Leo III against, 173–74; Liudprand on, 96; Louis II against, 110, 113, 116, 117, 122; Mesopotamia conquered by, 7, 27; v. Persians, 218; Pseudo-Chrysostom on, 7, 72–73; Pseudo-Ephraem on, 218; Pseudo-Hippolytus on, 99, 101–102, 103–104, 108, 117, 118, 122; Pseudo-Methodius texts on, 17, 20–21, 24–25, 27, 32, 33, 34–36, 44–49, 52–53, 57, 61–62, 163, 173, 220, 222; in Sicily, 6, 7, 64, 72–73, 74, 75, 77, 84–86, 87, 104, 105, 109, 114, 115; *Slavonic Daniel* on, 63–64, 68–69; as sons of Hagar, 159; in Spain, 79, 94. See also Ismaelites; Moslems; Saracens
Arcadius, 146
Armalāos, 19, 42, 57, 58, 59, 72
Armalāos the Younger, 19, 42

# Index [ 229

Armenia/Armenians, 20, 21, 34, 43, 48, 49, 52, 54
Ashkenazu, 41
Assyrians, 96, 97
Attalia, 7, 74, 75, 76, 77
Auvergne, 79, 94
Avars, 20, 23n28, 25, 44
Azerbaijan. *See* Adroigan
'Azri, 38

Bābek, 74
Babylon/Babylonians, 18, 39, 40, 43; Antichrist from, 195; history of, 26, 27; kings of, 37–38, 53; Medes over, 57; Pseudo-Methodius on, 26, 27, 57
Bari, 77, 110; Louis II captures, 111, 112, 113, 114, 116, 117
Basil I, 80–83, 86, 115, 124n5, 127, 128; corresponds with Louis II, 112–13, 114, 116, 117, 118, 119; *Daniel Καὶ ἔσται* on, 7, 80–81; founds Macedonian dynasty, 110, 120; fulfills lion-whelp oracle, 116; and Iron Gates, 81; in Italy, 110, 113; as king, 80–81; murders Michael III, 7, 83, 87, 94; as new Phinehas, 7, 83, 87, 95; on patriarchal sees, 118–19; Pseudo-Hippolytus on, 116
Beast, 209, 210
Beneventum, 77, 79, 111
Beth-saida, 50, 71, 196, 198, 220–21, 223, 224
Bible, 1; Antichrist in, 4, 106, 193, 222, 223–24; *Cento* quotes, 133–34; in Greek Pseudo-Methodius, 59–60, 160, 167; on last emperor, 164–65, 166–70, 179; Latin, 140–41; Pseudo-Ephraem quotes, 137, 138, 139, 140–41, 142, 169, 205, 210. *See also* Pešitta; Septuagint
Biblical references: Acts 10:9, 191; Amos 4:4, 142; Amos 5:18, 138; I Cor. 15:23, 183; I Cor. 15:24, 32n57, 138, 165, 169, 170, 179, 181; Dan. 7:2, 18n18, 65, 67; Dan. 9:26, 43; Dan. 9:27, 139, 214; Dan. 11:31, 139, 206; Deut. 33:22, 142, 222, 223; Ephesians 5:14, 133–34, 135, 136; Ezek. 38:1, 19; Ezek. 38:8, 186, 190; Ezek. 38:16, 41; Ezek. 39:17, 20, 44, 170–71; Gen. 10–2, 189, 190; Gen. 49:8, 172; Gen. 49:9, 222; Gen. 49:17, 22, 50, 59, 202, 223; Gen. 49:18, 50, 139; Hebr. 12:7, 48; Jer. 17:11, 138, 141, 142, 205, 222; John 4:5, 90; John 4:48, 201; Luke 10:13, 196, 220, 223, 224; Luke 17:22–27, 223; Luke 18:8, 47; Luke 21:8, 211; Luke 21:24, 206; Mark 3:17, 215; Mark 13:20, 209; Mark 13:22, 201; Matt. 5:12, 48; Matt. 10:22, 48; Matt. 11:20–24, 50, 71–72, 196, 220, 223, 224; Matt. 24:3–31, 137, 138, 139, 202, 209, 213, 223, 224; Matt. 24:37, 160, 169, 170, 179; Matt. 24:38, 49; Rev. 11:2, 206, 208; Rev. 11:7, 223; Rev. 12:15, 214; Rev. 13:5, 208, 210; Rev. 13:18, 214; Rev. 20:4, 183; Rev. 20:8, 190; Rom. 1:26, 44, 59; Rom. 9:6, 46; Psalms, *see* Psalm 68:31, Psalm 78:65; II Thess. 2, 106, 109n32, 179; II Thess. 2:1–8, 59, 223; II Thess. 2:2, 43; II Thess. 2:3, 21, 32–33, 46, 106; II Thess. 2:4, 204, 223; II Thess. 2:7, 20, 138, 165, 169, 181, 183; II Thess. 2:8, 199, 216; II Thess. 2:17, 170; I Tim. 4:1, 47, 60; II Tim. 3:1–5, 60
Biblical references, extra-canonical: II Baruch 40:3, 182; IV Ezra 7:27, 182; IV Maccabees, 56, 60
Blond Peoples, 63, 70, 161, 172. *See also* Gog and Magog; Unclean nations
*Book of the Bee*, 15, 21–22n7
Bousset, Wilhelm, 2, 91, 125, 200, 208, 209, 210, 224, 225; on Antichrist, 193; on lion-whelp oracle, 172; on Pseudo-Ephraem, 145
Brazen House, 80, 81
Budge, E. A. W., 147
Büyük Çekmece, 82
Byza, 161
Byzantia (princess), 19, 42, 57, 58, 59, 72
Byzantium/Byzantine Empire, 19, 41, 42, 168; v. Arabs, 32, 73–75, 104, 105, 114, 115, 116; v. Bulgarians, 66n21, 67n22; emperor as last emperor, 2, 7, 22, 23, 103, 107, 114, 152; emperors of, 53, 63, 65–67, 114; founded, 23; in Italy, 114, 115, 116; literature of, 2–3, 8, 13, 14, 52, 61, 107, 190–91; permanence of, 21, 23, 25, 57, 58, 61; Pseudo-Methodius on, 23, 57, 58, 61, 103; *Slavonic Daniel* on, 65–67
Byzas, 19, 23, 41, 42, 57, 72

Calabria, 69, 105, 111; Basil in, 110; invaded, 73n5; Louis II in, 113, 114, 116
Capernaum, 50, 71, 72, 196, 204, 220–21, 223, 224

Cappadocians, 21, 34, 48, 49
Carolingians, 109–12, 118, 120. *See also* Louis II
Caspari, C. P., 137, 140, 142, 143, 144–45, 146, 147
Caspian Gates, 89
Catania, 85, 116
Caucasus Mountains, 189
*Cave of Treasures*, 26, 33n61, 167n59, 182–83n105
*Cento of the True Emperor*, 7, 130–36; astrology in, 131; author of, 135; biblical quotations in, 133–34; date of, 130, 135; on Flood, 131; on Ismaelites, 130, 131, 135; on Lips, 132; on Messiah, 135, 136; and *Oracles of Leo*, 131–32, 135; sources of, 132, 133, 135, 136; on true emperor, 130–31, 132, 133, 134–35, 136, 174, 175
Chalcedon, 97; sea of, 41
Charlemagne, 107–108, 109, 113, 118, 120
Charles the Bald, 109, 118, 119–20
Chelidonian Isles, 75, 76
Chorazin, 50, 71, 196, 198, 220–21, 223, 224
Chosroes II, 28, 172
Christ. *See* Jesus Christ
Christians/Christianity, 28; v. Arabs, 20–21, 103, 114–16, 117; denied, 21, 22, 47, 48, 49, 57; in Ethiopia, 29; in Italy, 114–16, 117; Jewish, 183; on Jews, 183–84; kingdom of, 19–20, 42–43, 53; on Messiah, 154–55, 183, 184; sins/vices of, 20–21, 33, 44–49, 69, 83–86; Syriac, 14, 16, 26, 27, 28, 29; talismans of, 20, 43, 56
Chrysostom. *See* John Chrysostom; Pseudo-Chrysostom
Church of St. Paul (Rome), 77, 78
Church of St. Peter (Rome), 77, 78
Church of Sts. Peter and Paul, 127, 128
Church of Sts. Sergius and Bacchus, 127
Church of the Holy Apostle, 127, 128
Cibyrrhaeot Promontory, 74, 75
Cilicians, 21, 34, 48, 49
Circumcision, 139, 206, 207
City of Seven Hills. *See* Constantinople
City of the Rebel. *See* Syracuse
Claudius, 19, 42
Constans (last emperor), 152, 154, 155, 166, 167–68, 172, 177, 179
Constantine I (the Great), 124, 127, 179, 184
Constantine III, 146

Constantine V, 65n16, 65n17, 67n24, 173
Constantine VI, 66n19
Constantine VIII, 120
Constantinople, 21, 73, 119, 156, 175; Arabs invade, 25, 72, 74, 75–76, 77; architecture of, 126, 127; Avars besiege, 23n28, 25; Brazen House in, 81; churches in, 127, 128; as City of Seven Hills, 63, 67, 70, 71, 72, 161; earthquake in, 86, 87, 94; Golden Horn in, 80, 81; Imperial Palace of, 80; as Iron City, 80; Iron Gates of, 80, 81, 87; last emperor in, 132, 161, 162; Liudprand in, 4, 120, 121; Port of Julian in, 80; Port of Sophia in, 80, 81
Constantius II, 124
Corduenians, 39
Cosmas Indicopleustes, 23n28
Crete, 75, 77
Cross, 47, 140; as Christian talisman, 20, 43, 56; emperor's crown laid at, 4, 22, 50, 63, 64, 72, 163, 164, 168, 180, 191; power of, 42, 43
Ctesiphon, 39
Cush, 19, 39, 41, 50, 57; as Ethiopia, 18; as Nubia, 27. *See also* Cushites
Cusheth, 18, 19, 22, 23, 40, 41, 42, 50, 57, 72, 168
Cushites, 19, 21, 22, 23, 40, 41, 42, 48, 50, 168; sea of, 157
Cynocephali, 41
Cyrus the Persian, 18, 40

Dan, Jewish tribe of, 222; Antichrist rises from, 139, 142, 183, 195, 196, 197, 198, 202, 219, 223; horse of, 22, 50–51, 59; Jacob blesses, 202, 218, 223; Moses blesses, 138, 218, 223; Pseudo-Ephraem on, 138, 142, 218
Daniel (the prophet), 40, 44, 100, 209; Gabriel talks with, 63, 65–67, 69; prophecy of, 18, 43
*Daniel Kaì ἔσται*, 62, 77–95, 96; additions to, 88; on Antichrist, 89, 199, 202, 203, 204, 206, 213–14; on Arabs, 77–79, 83–87, 94; author of, 94; as Basil's apologetic, 7, 80–81; as *Cento* source, 133; on Christian sins, 83–86; date of, 83, 87, 91, 94; on earthquake in Constantinople, 94; on earthquake in Sicily, 83–84, 85, 86; on Elijah and Enoch, 213–14; eschatological section of, 77, 79, 87–94, 95; on Ezek. 39:17,

170–71; historical section of, 77–87, 91, 94; on king, 79–81; Pseudo-Chrysostom agrees with, 87, 88, 89; on Rhegion, 79; and *Slavonic Daniel*, 84, 88–89; sources of, 82–84, 86–87, 88–89, 95; on three emperors, 88; on unclean peoples, 89; on victorious (last) emperor, 87, 88, 89, 91, 92–93, 94, 157, 158, 160, 161–62, 163, 170; where written, 87, 94
Daqlaie, 41
Darius, 40
Darmetaie, 41
David, 20, 42, 168; house of, 40, 181–82, 189; prophecy of, 19, 22, 50
*Demonstration from Holy Scriptures Concerning Christ and the Antichrist*, 193. *See also* Hippolytus of Rome
Demunitehta, 39
*De ortu et tempore Antichristi*, 2, 105–107, 122. *See also* Adso
Deshie, 41
Desolation/despoiler/destroyer, 20, 34, 44, 45–49
Dillmann, August, 172
Dīpar, 41
*Disputatio adversus Judaeos. See* Anastasius of Sinai
Dog and whelp, 63, 70. *See also* Lion-whelp oracle
*Donatio propter nuptias*, 58, 59

Earthquakes, 83–84, 85, 86, 87, 94
Egypt, 18, 20, 21, 27, 34, 38, 39, 40, 43, 45, 49, 168; v. Babylon, 17; Ikhshīdid rulers of, 105, 121
Elect, 51, 138, 210–11, 224
Elijah, 21, 47, 134. *See also* Enoch and Elijah
Emperor, last/Roman/true/victorious, 43, 151–84, 222, 223, 224; Adso on, 106–107, 158; angel instructs, 130, 133–34; anointed, 63, 69, 73; and Antichrist, 164, 197, 199; *Apocalypse of St. Andrew the Fool* on, 126, 155, 156, 160, 163–64; Arabs defeated by, 34, 69–70, 73, 87, 88, 99, 101–102, 103–104, 108, 117, 118, 122, 131, 135, 157, 158, 163, 170, 173, 178, 186; biblical references to, 164–65, 166–70, 179; and Blond Peoples, 63, 70, 161; as Byzantine, 2, 7, 22, 23, 103, 107, 114, 152; *Cento* on, 130–31, 132, 134–35, 136, 174, 175; Constans as name of, 152, 154, 155, 166, 167–68, 172, 177, 179; in Constantinople, 132, 161, 162; converts Jews, 156, 172, 185; converts pagans, 155–56, 167–68, 170, 172, 178, 185; *Daniel Καὶ ἔσται* on, 87, 88, 89, 91, 92–93, 94, 157, 158, 160, 161–62, 163, 170; as dead, 21, 69, 91, 92, 153, 154; death of, 162, 163; described, 155, 166, 177, 179; in desert of Jethrib, 173; as Ethiopian, 57, 103; finds treasure, 161–62; fulfills prophecy, 63, 103, 152–53, 163, 167, 168, 179; functions of, 155–56, 177–78; Gog and Magog defeated by, 158, 163, 166, 178, 185, 187, 188, 191, 219; Greek Pseudo-Methodius on, 153, 155, 156–57, 163; humble origin of, 131, 155, 164, 180; at Jacob's Well, 87, 88, 157, 158, 170; as king of Greeks, 21–22, 42, 49, 50, 154; Latin Pseudo-Methodius on, 155, 156–57, 163; in Latin Tiburtine Sibyl, 152, 153, 154, 155–56, 157, 158, 162–63, 165–66, 167–68, 170, 172, 177, 178, 179, 180, 185, 188, 191, 219; lays crown on Golgotha, 4, 22, 50, 63, 64, 72, 163, 164, 168, 180, 191; lays crown on Mt. of Olives, 107, 108 n29, 122 n67, 158; Leo III as, 173–74; length of reign of, 162, 179; as lion, 152, 155, 158 (*see also* Lion-whelp oracle); Liudprand on, 96–97, 98, 117, 118; to Longobardia, 161, 179–80; Louis II as, 8, 117, 118, 120, 122; Messiah compared to, 174–75, 176–84; as miraculous, 153, 154, 167; Nero as, 92–93, 94; Nicephorus Phocas as, 98; non-biblical prophecies on, 170–74; *Oracle of Baalbek* on, 158–59; *Oracles of Leo* on, 152; origin of legend of, 2, 174–83; Otto I as, 118; peace and prosperity brought by, 49, 158–60, 169, 170, 178–79, 185, 186, 191–92; Pseudo-Chrysostom on, 72–73, 155, 161, 162, 163; Pseudo-Ephraem on, 165, 188; Pseudo-Hippolytus on, 99, 101–102, 103–104, 105, 108, 114, 117, 118, 120, 122, 158; Pseudo-Methodius on, 91, 92, 103, 161, 162, 173; revealed, 72–73, 130, 131, 154, 155, 177; in Rome, 63, 70, 103, 161; as savior, 7, 154–55,

Emperor (*continued*)
156–57, 175, 176, 180; *Slavonic Daniel* on, 63, 64, 69–72, 155, 161, 162, 163, 187; sons of, 155, 161, 173–74, 178, 180; and supernatural, 152–53, 176–77; surrenders to God, 2, 4, 22, 23, 42, 50, 63, 64, 72, 89, 103, 107, 108, 120, 122, 124, 126, 151, 152, 158, 162, 163, 164, 165, 168, 169, 174–75, 180–81, 185, 191, 198, 219; Syriac Pseudo-Methodius on, 152–53, 154, 155, 156–57, 163, 166–67, 175, 176, 178, 180–81, 186; *Visions of Daniel* on, 152, 154, 155, 157, 160, 161; as Western (Frankish/Roman), 7, 99, 101–102, 103–104, 105, 106–107, 108, 114, 120, 121, 122, 158, 165–66
Emrataie, 41
Enna, 63, 69, 84, 85, 86, 87, 114, 115
Enoch and Elijah, 222, 223; announce Second Coming, 139, 203, 211, 212, 215; v. Antichrist, 5, 63, 72, 73, 140, 211, 212, 213–14, 215, 216, 224; *Apocalypse of St. Andrew* on, 215; *Daniel Καὶ ἔσται* on, 213–14; Erythraean Sibyl alludes to, 214–15; as God's response, 139–40, 211–16; Latin Tiburtine Sibyl on, 203, 219; Pseudo-Chrysostom on, 73; Pseudo-Ephraem on, 139–40, 210–11, 218, 219; Pseudo-Methodius on, 212–13, 220, 221; *Slavonic Daniel* on, 72, 213; and Son of Thunder, 5, 224; as two stars, 214–15
Ephraem, 136, 213. *See also* Pseudo-Ephraem
Ethiopia/Ethiopians, 17, 38, 39, 40, 168; as Cush, 18; as Hendū, 27; and last emperor, 7, 57, 103; Macedon over, 57; as military power, 29; Pseudo-Methodius on, 18, 29, 57, 103; as Roman, 168; rulers of, 53; Syriac Christianity in, 29
Euphemius, 64, 84
Euphrates River, 17, 18, 27, 38, 39, 40, 91, 92
Exakonta, 99
Ezekiel, on Gog and Magog, 19, 41, 147, 157–58, 186, 189–90, 191

Fāṭimid khalifs, 104–105, 121
Fire of the Sun, 17, 18, 19, 27, 37, 39, 40
Flood, 17, 37, 131, 160, 169
Franks, 113; provide last emperor, 7, 99, 101–102, 103–104, 105, 106–107, 108, 114, 120, 121, 122, 158, 165–66

Gabaathamōra, 32
Gabaʿōt Ramtā, 32
Gabaʿōt the Great, 20, 44
Gābiia, 32
Gabriel (angel), 63, 65–67, 69
Garmidmaie, 41
Gate(s): of Alexander, 4, 41, 89, 147, 186, 189, 192; Caspian, 89; Iron, 80, 81, 87; of the North, 4, 22, 41, 49, 186; of Rhegion, 81–82; of the Snakes, 71, 187; in Theodosian Land Walls, 81–82; unclean nations contained by, 4, 19, 22, 41, 49, 89, 147, 186, 187, 189, 192, 219; Yenimevlevihanekapi, 81–82
Gaul, 78–79
Ğebel Sinğar. *See* Šenāgar, mountain of; Singara
*Gens nostra*, 98–99, 101, 102
*Gentes: bellicae*, 138, 146, 186, 187–88, 192; *nequissimae*, 138, 146, 147, 165, 191, 218
Gerberga, 105, 106
Germanicus, 19, 41
Girgashites, 39
God, 51; v. Antichrist, 22, 139–40, 207–208, 209, 210, 211–16, 218; v. Gog and Magog, 189; last emperor surrenders to, 2, 4, 22, 23, 42, 50, 63, 64, 72, 89, 103, 107, 108, 120, 122, 124, 126, 151, 152, 158, 162, 163, 164, 165, 168, 169, 174–75, 180, 181, 185, 191, 198, 219; talks to Moses, 44
Gog and Magog, 5, 156, 185–92, 222; Alexander imprisons, 4, 147, 185, 186, 187, 192; and Alexander legend, 147, 188–89; angel destroys, 63, 163, 186, 187, 188, 191; Ezekiel on, 19, 41, 147, 157–58, 186, 189–90, 191; in Genesis, 189, 190; God destroys, 189; as impure, 185, 187; invade Israel, 190; and Japheth, 189, 190; at Jericho, 191; Judaism on, 6, 190–91, 192; at Joppe, 191, 192; in Koran, 188; last emperor defeats, 158, 163, 166, 178, 185, 187, 188, 191, 219; as last enemy, 165, 178; Latin Tiburtine Sibyl on, 163, 185, 187, 190, 191; Messiah destroys, 191; northern habitat of, 186, 187, 190; origins of tradition of, 2, 188–

# Index

92; Pseudo-Chrysostom on, 187;
Pseudo-Ephraem on, 187, 188, 192;
Pseudo-Methodius on, 159, 186,
187, 188, 190, 191, 192; in Revelation, 147; *Slavonic Daniel* on,
186–87; timing of, 187, 188, 190–
91; as twenty-two nations, 185, 186,
187
Golden Horn, 80, 81
Golgotha, last emperor at, 4, 22, 50, 63,
64, 72, 163, 164, 168, 180, 191
Gopsin, 66
Graf, Arturo, 147
Greek(s), 18, 36, 40, 43, 44, 57, 99;
Bible (*see* Septuagint); king(s) of, 22,
42, 48, 49, 50, 53, 121, 154 (*see also*
Emperor); Pseudo-Ephraem in, 140,
141, 144; Pseudo-Hippolytus in,
121; Pseudo-Methodius in, 16, 30,
31–33 (*see also* Pseudo-Methodius,
Greek redaction of); term for Christ,
193; *Slavonic Daniel* translated
from, 53, 65n16, 67n25, 68n35,
69n42, 98
Greek Redaction. *See* Pseudo-Methodius,
Greek redaction of
Gunkel, Hermann, 200, 208

Hadarzaraq, 39
Hagar, 38, 44; sons of, 159, 170 (*see also*
Arabs)
Haimo of Halberstadt, 106, 109n32
Ham, 17, 37, 38
Hauran, 21–22n27. *See also* Hebron
Hebron, 21, 49
Helinia, 84
Heliopolis, 63, 67
Hellas, 20, 35, 36, 45
Hellenes, 35, 48, 49, 93, 94
Hendū, 27
Heraclius, 28, 144, 146, 172, 180
Hippolytus, 202, 205, 223; on Antichrist, 100, 193, 196, 200; as bishop
of Sicily, 7, 100, 103; identity of,
100. *See also* Pseudo-Hippolytus
Hittites, 39
Hivites, 39
Hormazdu, 40, 57
Hormizd, 38
Horse metaphor, 22, 50, 51, 59, 202,
223
Huns, 41

Iberian Peninsula, 78–79, 87
Ibn al-Faḍl, Abbās, 85

Ibrāhīm, Abū al-Aghlab, 77
Iconoclasts, 65n16, 67n24, 67n25,
78n7
Ikhshīdid rulers, 105, 121
Illyricum, 18, 38, 159
*imperator augustus Romanorum*, 113,
116, 117, 119
Ionṭon, 17, 19, 26n37, 27, 37–38, 39
Irenaeus, 183, 195, 223
Irene, Empress, 65n17, 66n19, 66n20,
67n24
Iron City. *See* Constantinople
Iron Gates, 80, 81, 87
Isaurians, 21, 34, 48, 49, 65
Islam, 97, 103, 158. *See also* Arabs;
Moslems
Islands of the Sea, 20, 21, 34, 45, 48
Ismael/Ismaelites, 24, 32, 86, 93, 156,
166, 172, 175; *Cento* on, 130, 131,
135; in Constantinople, 72; four
leaders of, 20, 34, 44, 45–49; invasions by, 18, 20–21, 38–39, 68–69;
Israelites defeat, 18; last emperor defeats, 69–70, 131, 135, 155, 157,
158, 170, 178, 186; sins of, 83–84;
as wild ass of desert, 20, 44, 66. *See
also* Arabs; Moslems
Israel, 18, 128, 175, 183, 189, 190. *See
also* Jews
Istrin, V. M., 2, 3, 5, 13, 14, 15, 53
Italy: Basil I in, 110; Byzantines in, 114,
115, 116; factions in, 77, 79, 87 (*see
also* Lombards); Iconoclasts in,
78n7; Louis II in, 109, 110, 113,
114–16, 117; Moslems in, 77–78,
79, 110, 111, 112, 113, 114, 117,
161; Otto I claims, 105; Pseudo-
Hippolytus written in, 8. *See also*
Rome/Romans

Jacob, 50, 51; blesses tribe of Dan, 202,
218, 223; blesses Judah, 172
Jacob, Well of, 90, 91, 93; last emperor's
victory at, 87, 88, 157, 158, 170
Jacob of Sarug, 147, 188
Janin, Raymond, 81, 127
Japheth, 37, 38, 40, 186, 189, 190
Jared, 37
Jebusites, 39
Jericho, 191, 192
Jerusalem, 69, 91, 118; Akra quarter of,
87, 88, 90, 91, 93; Antichrist in, 51,
139, 197, 203, 204–206, 211, 213,
218, 219, 220, 223; Jesus on, 206;
last emperor in, 4, 22, 50, 63, 71,
103, 107, 108, 120, 122, 126, 158,

Jerusalem (continued)
162, 163, 164, 165, 168, 174–75, 180, 181, 185, 191; liberated, 180; Temple in, 92, 139; trampled, 210
Jesus Christ, 51, 166, 169; apocalypse of, 206, 223; denied, 47, 154, 156, 157; Greek term for, 193; kills Antichrist, 216–17; on Jerusalem, 206; the Lamb, 207, 208; return of (see Second Coming); three woes of, 50, 71, 196, 198, 199, 204, 220–21, 222, 224
Jethrib, desert of, 18, 20, 21, 38, 39, 44, 46, 48, 157, 173
Jews/Israelites/Hebrews, 39, 40, 43, 44, 46, 47, 48, 50, 54, 82–83, 90, 186; anoint kings, 93; and Antichrist, 5, 206–207, 213, 224; Antichrist as, 139, 142, 183, 195, 196, 197, 198, 202, 219, 223; Christians on, 183–84; conversion of, 156, 162, 172, 185; defeat Ismaelites, 18; defeat Seleucids, 93, 94; enemies of, 178; Messiah of, 1, 135, 136, 177, 178–79, 181, 182, 183; return to Israel, 189; role of, at end of time, 128–29 n13; talismans of, 20, 56; war of, 182. See also Judaism
Joel, 41
John Chrysostom, 62, 72, 100
John Tzimisces, 120, 121
Joppe, plain of, 22, 50, 186, 190, 191, 192
Jovian, 124
Jubal, 37
Judaism: on Alexander, 189; on Antichrist, 193, 195, 224; apocalypses of, 1, 5–6, 176–77; as *Cento* source, 135, 136; on Gog and Magog, 6, 190–91, 192; Late (postcanonical), 1, 5–6, 135, 136, 176, 177–83, 190–91, 193, 195; on Messiah, 1, 135, 136, 181. *See also* Bible; Jews
Julian, 124, 145
Justinian I, 58, 90, 127, 128

Kaukebaie, 41
Kelima, 36
Keys, of St. Peter, 77, 78
King: Alexander as, 56; Antichrist as, 203–204; Byzantine, 53, 98, 102, 114, 117, 118, 120, 152, 176; of Greeks (*see* Emperor, as king of Greeks); as *rex*, 79–81. *See also* Kingship

Kingdoms: Christian, 19–20, 42–43, 53; subdued, 18, 19, 20, 23 n28, 38–40, 43–44, 57
Kingship, 20, 38, 43, 56
Kmosko, Michael, 3, 6, 15–16, 23–24 n29, 26–27, 30, 31–33
Kodros, 38

Lactantius, 183, 206
Lambecius, Petrus, 130, 131
Lamech, 37
*Last Daniel*, 62
Last Judgment, 182, 183, 214, 217
Latin: Bible, Vulgate, 140–41; original of Pseudo-Ephraem, 140, 144; original of Pseudo-Hippolytus, 7, 121. *See also* Pseudo-Methodius, Latin; Sibyl, Tiburtine (Latin)
Lebuda, 36
Leo III, 63, 65 n16, 67 n24, 93, 95, 124 n5, 172; as last emperor, 91–92, 94, 173–74
Leo IV, 65 n17, 66 n19, 91
Leo V, 67 n24, 91
*Libellus de imperatoria potestate in urbe Roma*, 112, 114
*Life of St. Andrew the Fool*, 4, 8, 123–30; architectural data in, 126–27; avoids later material, 124, 125, 126, 128; date of, 123, 124, 125, 126–27, 128, 129–30; as encyclopedic, 125; Nicephorus authors, 123, 125–26, 127–28; sources of, 125–26, 129. *See also Apocalypse of St. Andrew the Fool*
Lion-whelp oracle: Basil fulfills, 116; and last emperor, 152, 155, 158; Liudprand on, 99, 120, 121, 122; origin of, 172–74, 179; in Pseudo-Hippolytus, 101, 102, 116, 121; in *Slavonic Daniel*, 70; *Visions of Daniel* on, 172
Lips, 132
Liudprand of Cremona, 7, 96–122; on Arabs, 96; in Constantinople, 4, 120, 121; documents seen by, 97, 98–104 (see also Pseudo-Hippolytus; *Visions of Daniel*); on *gens nostra*, 98–99, 101, 102; *Legatio* of, 96, 99, 100, 104, 121; on lion-whelp oracle, 99, 120, 121, 122; lists emperors, 97–98; on victorious emperor, 96–97, 98, 117, 118
Lombards, 77, 78, 79, 87, 102, 161; revolt against Louis II, 111–12, 114, 117

Longobardia, 63, 70, 105, 114; last emperor in, 161, 179–80
Louis II, 80; corresponds with Basil I, 112–13, 114, 116, 117, 118, 119; death of, 112; fights Arabs, 110, 113, 116, 117, 122; as *imperator augustus Romanorum*, 113, 116, 117, 119; in Italy, 109, 110, 111, 112, 113, 114–16, 117; as last emperor, 8, 117, 118, 120, 122; as lion in oracle, 116; Lombards revolt against, 111–12, 114, 117
Louis IV d'Outremer, 105, 106, 107, 108
Louis the German, 118, 119
Louis the Pious, 107, 108
Lūzā, 18, 39
Lydians, 40, 41

Macedon/Macedonians, 18, 40, 42, 43, 54, 57, 120. See also Alexander the Great; Basil I; Philip of Macedon
Magog, 41, 189. See also Gog and Magog
Manuel Phocas, 99, 104
Manuscripts: Cod. Athos Chilandar 24, 62n3, 65n14, 65n18, 67n28, 68n31, 68n36, 69n42; Cod. Augiensis CXCVI, 137; Cod. Paris, 13348, 137; Cod. St. Gallen 108, 137; Cod. Vat. Barb. Lat. 671, 137, 140, 142, 145; Cod. Vat. Graec. 1912, 85; Cod. Vat. Reg. Pii II 11, 53n4 (*see also* Pseudo-Methodius, Greek redaction of); Cod. Vat. Syr. 58, 3, 15, 16n7, 36, 39, 52 (*see also* Pseudo-Methodius, Syriac)
Mariana, 63, 84, 85
Maslama, 75, 77
Media/Medes, 18, 20, 40, 43, 53, 54, 57
Men-Eaters, 41
Mesopotamia: Arabs in, 7, 27; missionaries in, 28; Monophysites in, 28–29; Pseudo-Methodius composed in, 13, 15, 16, 26–27, 56; rulers of, 27–28. See also Singara
Messiah: Antichrist as false, 203, 207, 211; brings peace and prosperity, 178–79; *Cento* on, 135, 136; Christianity on, 154–55, 183, 184; Gog and Magog destroyed by, 191; Jewish, 1, 135–36, 177, 178–79, 181, 182, 183; last emperor compared to, 174–75, 176–84; on Mt. Zion, 135; qualities of, 177; reign of, 179; task of, 183
Messina, 85, 115; Straits of, 99

Methodius, 16, 36, 126; as bishop of Olympus, 36, 53; as bishop of Patara, 3, 16n9, 53. See also Pseudo-Methodius (texts); Pseudo-Methodius, Greek redaction of; Pseudo-Methodius, Latin; Pseudo-Methodius, Syriac
Michael (archangel), 191, 216
Michael I Rangabē, 67n23
Michael II, 63, 64, 67n25, 98
Michael III, 80–81, 115, 123–24n3, 124n5; murdered, 7, 83, 87, 94
Michael the Syrian, 66n21, 75
Midianites, 18, 24, 32, 39, 82, 83. See also Ismael/Ismaelites
Moabites, 139, 197, 203, 205
Mohammed, 21, 47. See also Islam
Monophysites, 28–29
Moses, 39, 40; blesses tribe of Dan, 138, 218, 223; God talks to, 44
Moslems, 24, 84, 91, 104; in Italy, 77–78, 79, 87, 110, 111, 113, 114, 161; in Spain, 79, 87, 94. See also Arabs
Mount of Olives, 107, 108n29, 122n67, 158, 216
Mount Zion, 135
Muʿāwiya, 25, 76, 77
al-Muʿizz, 104–105, 121
al-Muʿtasim, 74–75, 76

Nebuchadnezzar, 40
Nero, 92–93, 94
Nestorian Church, 28
Nicephorus (hagiographer), 123, 125–26, 127–28
Nicephorus I, 66n21, 67n22
Nicephorus Phocas, 7, 8, 97, 102; and al-Muʿizz, 104–105, 121; captures Antioch, 96; v. Arabs, 96, 104; opposed, 120, 121; as victorious emperor, 98
Nicephorus Phocas the Elder, 110
Nimrod, 17, 37, 38, 39
Noah, 17, 26n37, 27, 37, 38, 39, 160, 169

Og, 43
Ogug, 41
Olibos, 159
*On the Last Times, the Antichrist, and the End of the World*. See Pseudo-Ephraem
*Oracle of Baalbek*, 14, 97, 98, 133, 135, 136; on Antichrist, 194, 197, 201–202, 203, 205, 208, 209, 211,

*Oracle of Baalbek (continued)*
212, 216, 220; on last emperor, 158–59
*Oracles of Leo the Wise,* 125, 131–32, 135, 152. See also *Cento of the True Emperor*
*Oracula Sibyllina,* 92, 93, 97
Oreb, 39
Otto I, 101, 102, 104, 109, 121; in Italy, 105; as last emperor, 118; reunifies Roman Empire, 120
Otto II, 102, 117, 118

Paganism, 146, 156, 218
Palermo, 77, 85, 115
Palestine, 90, 91, 93, 159, 173, 190; liberated, 178, 180; as promised land, 20, 34, 38, 45, 48, 157
Partēnē, 87, 88, 90–91, 92, 157
Patara, 3, 16n9, 53
Paul (apostle), 20, 21, 33, 43, 44, 165, 166, 169, 214; chapel of, 127, 128; on Messiah, 183
Persia/Persians, 18, 20, 34, 35, 38, 40, 41, 43, 44, 45, 48, 69, 180; v. Arabs, 21, 218; v. Rome, 54, 137, 144, 145; Heraclius defeats, 28, 144; rulers of, 39, 53; in Yemen, 29
Perton, 63, 69–70, 73n3, 157. See also Partēnē
Pešitta, 7, 166, 170; on Dan. 7:2, 18n18; on Jer. 17:11, 141; on Psalms 68:31, 19n19; Pseudo-Methodius uses, 59; v. Septuagint, 18n18, 19n19, 31–32; on II Thess. 2:3, 33
Peter, 127, 128, 191; keys of, 77, 78
Philip of Macedon, 18, 19, 40, 57
Philistines, 39, 43
Phinehas, 82–83; Basil as new, 7, 83, 87, 95
Pīl, 18, 19, 22, 40, 41, 42, 50, 168
Piroz, 18, 39
Pīsīlie, 41
Priesthood, 20, 43, 56
Promised land. See Palestine
Psalm 68:31, 29, 50, 170, 181; as bridge between history and prophecy, 22, 42; interpretations of, 19, 22–23, 54, 57, 72, 167–68, 169; last emperor fulfills, 103, 163, 168, 179; in Messianic tradition, 179; Pseudo-Chrysostom on, 72; Pseudo-Methodius texts on, 22, 103, 168–69

Psalm 78:65, 166, 169–70; last emperor fulfills, 152–53, 167
Pseudo-Callisthenes, 147, 192
Pseudo-Chrysostom, 64, 69n42, 72–77; on Antichrist, 73, 199, 202–203, 213; on Arabs, 7, 72–73, 76; attributed to St. John Chrysostom, 62, 72, 100; on Byzantia, 72; on Cusheth, 72; *Daniel Καὶ ἔσται* agrees with, 87, 88, 89; date of, 7, 73, 76; derives from Pseudo-Methodius, 72, 73; on Enoch and Elijah, 73; excerpted *Slavonic Daniel,* 72–73; on Gog and Magog, 187; on last emperor, 72–73, 155, 161, 162, 163; original sections of, 72, 73–77; on Psalms 68:31, 72; on Second Coming, 73; where composed, 73, 76–77
Pseudo-Ephraem, 7, 136–47, 166, 181, 184, 223; admonitions of, 137–38; on Antichrist, 137, 138, 139–40, 141, 142–43, 164, 194–95, 199, 200, 202, 203, 205–206, 207, 210, 213, 216, 217–19, 220, 221–22; apocalyptic section of, 138–41, 145; on Arabs, 218; ascribed to St. Isidore, 136, 137; biblical quotations in, 137, 138, 139, 140–41, 142, 169, 205, 210; date of, 144–45, 146–47; on end of the world, 137; on Enoch and Elijah, 139–40, 210–11, 218, 219; on foul invaders, 138, 146, 147, 165, 186, 187–88, 191, 192, 218; on gathering of elect, 210–11; in Greek, 140, 141, 144; on Jerusalem, 139, 210; lacks Alexander legend, 188, 218; on last emperor, 165, 188; in Latin, 140, 144; manuscripts of, 136, 137, 145–46; on Moabites and Ammanites, 139; on paganism, 218; parenetic section of, 137–38, 145; on Persian-Roman wars, 137, 144, 145; on Second Coming, 138, 139, 140, 218; Syriac original of, 140, 141, 142–47; on tribe of Dan, 138, 142, 218; on two brothers, 137, 144–45, 146
Pseudo-Hippolytus: as Adso's source, 108–109, 118, 120, 121, 122, 158, 162n43; on Arabs, 99, 101–102, 103–104, 108, 117, 118, 122; author of, 116, 122; on Basil I, 116; composed in Italy, 8; composed in Sicily, 99–100, 122; date of, 104, 105, 109, 117, 122; differs from

other texts, 101, 122; in Greek, 121; in Latin, 7, 121; on lion-whelp oracle, 101, 102, 116, 121; Liudprand on, 98–100, 101–102, 117, 118, 120, 121; political implications of, 103–105, 116, 122; on Roman Empire, 120; on victorious emperor, 99, 101–102, 103–104, 105, 108, 114, 117, 118, 120, 122, 158
Pseudo-Johannine apocalypse, 195
Pseudo-Methodius (texts), 63, 69n42, 124, 147, 181; as Adso's source, 107, 108n29; on Antichrist, 164, 196, 206, 210, 221–23, 224; on Arabs, 163, 173; on Babylon, 57; biblical quotations in, 22, 59, 103, 168–69; on Byzantines, 23, 57, 58, 61, 103; as *Cento* source, 133, 135, 136; on Christian talismans, 20, 56; as *Daniel Καὶ ἔσται* source, 83–84, 89, 95; on dynastic marriages, 57; on emperor, 91, 92, 103, 161, 162, 173; on Gog and Magog, 188, 191, 192; in Greek, 16, 30, 31–33 (see also Pseudo-Methodius, Greek redaction of); in Latin, 108–109 (see also Pseudo-Methodius, Latin); Pseudo-Chrysostom derives from, 72, 73; on Roman Empire, 54–55, 61. See also Pseudo-Methodius, Syriac; *Revelation*
Pseudo-Methodius, Greek redaction of, 13, 14, 15, 16, 26, 31, 52–60, 61, 154, 159, 170; additions to, 54, 56; on Alexander, 56, 57–58, 60; on Antichrist, 198, 202, 204, 209, 217, 220, 221; on Armalāos, 58, 59; author/translator of, 52, 53–54, 55–60; biblical quotations in, 59–60, 160, 167; on Byzantium and Rome, 58; on clergy, 54, 56–57, 60; date of, 60; differs from Syriac text, 54–55, 56, 57–58; on Enoch and Elijah, 212–13, 220, 221; on Gog and Magog, 186; on last emperor, 153, 155, 156–57, 163; Nicephorus knew, 126; omissions in, 16n10, 54, 55; reaches West, 154; revised, 61; on Rome, 58; on royal talismans, 56; *Slavonic Daniel* borrows from, 63–64; uses Greek, not Syriac, traditions, 7, 55–56, 58, 59, 60; as *Visions of Daniel* source, 61
Pseudo-Methodius, Latin, 14–15, 16, 24, 26, 31, 55, 60, 61, 140, 154, 159; on Antichrist, 198–99, 202, 204, 209, 217, 220–21; on Enoch and Elijah, 212–13, 220, 221; on Gog and Magog, 186; on last emperor, 155, 156–57, 163
Pseudo-Methodius, Syriac (Codex Vaticanus Syrus 58), 4, 6, 13–51, 72, 83–84, 100, 122, 170; on Alexander, 56, 57–58, 147, 186; on Antichrist, 164, 196, 198, 202, 204, 206, 217, 220–21, 223; on Arabs, 17, 20–21, 24–25, 27, 32, 33, 34–36, 44–49, 52–53, 57, 61–62, 220, 222; author of, 7, 14, 15, 16, 26, 28, 29, 30n51; on Babylon, 26, 27; as beginning of Middle Ages, 7, 14; on Byzantium, 23; on Christian vices, 20–21, 33; date of, 15, 24–25, 166; on Enoch and Elijah, 212, 220, 221; errors in, 52, 53; on Ethiopia, 18, 29, 57, 103; on Ezek. 38:8, 186, 190; on Gog and Magog, 159, 186, 187, 190; historical sections of, 15, 16–20, 22, 24, 27, 36–42, 186; influence of, 13–14, 15, 61; Iranian influences on, 15, 26; on Ismaelites, 34; on kingdoms subdued, 18, 19, 20, 23n28, 38–40, 43–44, 57; on last emperor, 152–53, 154, 155, 156–57, 163, 166–67, 175, 176, 178, 180–81, 186; Mesopotamian origin of, 13, 15, 16, 26–27, 56; on peace, 159; Pešitta used by, 31–32; political implications of, 22–23, 28; preamble of, 16, 27, 54, 55; prophetic sections of, 17, 18, 19, 20–22, 24, 27, 42–51, 186; on Psalms 68:31, 22, 31–32, 168–69; on Roman Empire, 19–20, 25, 57; scholars study, 14–16; Syriac origin/influences on, 14, 15, 16, 26, 27, 30, 31–33; on three woes, 220–21; translated, 36–51; on unclean peoples, 40–41, 49–50
Pupiēnus, 17, 37
Puțoio, 41

Qadišaiē tribe, 27
Queen of Sheba, 40

Reggio di Calabria, 80, 81
*Revelation*, 72, 83–84, 100, 103, 107. See also Pseudo-Methodius, Syriac
Revelation of John, 1, 4, 147
Rhegion, 79, 81; Gate of, 81–82

*Romance of the Emperor Julian*, 26
Romanos II, 98, 120
Rome/Romans, 18, 21, 34, 38, 39, 40, 43, 44, 45, 48, 53, 69, 120, 175; Arab naval attack on, 77–78; Byzantia given, 19, 42, 58, 59; last emperor in, 63, 70, 103, 161; law, 58; Louis II in, 110; Moslems sack, 87, 110; permanence of, 2, 57; v. Persia, 54, 137, 144, 145; Pseudo-Methodius on, 19–20, 25, 54–55, 57, 61; victories of, 54, 57
Romulus. *See* Armalāos
Rud the Persian, 40
Ruin, 20, 34, 44–49
Rydén, Lennart, 124–25

Sāba, 18, 40
Sackur, Ernst, 2, 3, 5, 14–15, 16, 24, 26, 30, 55, 57, 107
Saidan, 50
St. Andrew the Fool, 123, 125, 126, 127, 128. See also *Apocalypse of St. Andrew the Fool*; *Life of St. Andrew the Fool*
St. Isidore, 136, 137
St. Symeon the Fool, 126
Salerno, 111, 112, 114, 117
Saltraie, 41
Saracens, 96, 99, 110, 111. *See also* Arabs; Moslems
Sarah, 38
Sarchadom, 39, 40
Sasan the Old, 18, 39
Sassanids, 15, 26, 28, 144
Satan, 37, 51; Antichrist as son of, 199, 200, 216
Sbah, 39
Scepter, 122 n 67
Second Coming, 4, 50, 51, 169, 170, 183, 223; Antichrist precedes, 22, 201–202; Enoch and Elijah announce, 139, 203, 211, 212, 215; Pseudo-Chrysostom on, 73; Pseudo-Ephraem on, 138, 139, 140, 218
Seleucians/Seleucia, 21, 34, 35, 39, 48, 49
Sennacherib, 39, 40, 57
Septuagint, 59–60, 141, 170; compared to Pešitta, 18 n 18, 19 n 19, 31–32; on Dan. 7:2, 18 n 18; on Psalms 68:31, 19 n 19; as source of *Daniel Καὶ ἔσται*, 82–83, 88; on II Thess. 2:3, 32–33
Serpent/snake, 139, 143, 208, 213, 224
Seth, 36–37

Šam'i'sar, 17, 38
Sheba, 18, 40
Shem, 17, 37
Šenāgar, mountain of, 16, 27, 28, 36, 54, 55. *See also* Singara
Šerāṣad, 39
Sibyl, Cumaean, 158
Sibyl, Erythraean, 186–87 n 6; on Antichrist, 203, 204, 206–207, 209, 210, 214–15, 217, 219, 220; on two stars, 214–15
Sibyl, Tiburtine, (Greek). See *Oracle of Baalbek*
Sibyl, Tiburtine (Latin), 3, 122 n 67; on Alexander, 185, 219; on Antichrist, 164, 185, 197, 199, 201, 203, 204–205, 208, 209, 211, 216, 219, 220, 221–22; as *Cento* source, 133, 135; on I Cor. 15:24, 169; on Enoch and Elijah, 203, 219; on Gog and Magog, 163, 185, 187, 190, 191; on last emperor, 152, 153, 154, 155–56, 157, 158, 162–63, 165–66, 167–68, 170, 172, 177, 178, 179, 180, 185, 188, 191, 219; on non-biblical texts, 171–72; on Psalms 68:31, 167–68, 169; on II Thess. 2:7, 169
Sicily, 20, 35, 45, 63, 69, 113; Arabs in, 6, 7, 36, 64, 72–73, 74, 75, 77, 84–86, 87, 104, 105, 109, 114, 115; bishop of, 7, 100, 103; cities in, 85, 115; defended, 74, 104, 114–16, 117; liberated, 8, 105; Pseudo-Hippolytus composed in, 99–100, 122; *Visions of Daniel* composed in, 7, 36, 64, 100
Siculo-Arab Chronicle of Cambridge, 85
Siegmund, Albert, 137
Singara, 7, 27, 28, 29, 36
Siphon, 43
*Slavonic Daniel*, 6, 61, 62–72, 96; angel Gabriel in, 63, 65–67, 69; Antichrist in, 63, 64, 71–72, 199, 202, 204, 209; on Arabs, 68–69; on Byzantines, 65–67; Chilandar manuscript of, 24, 62 n 3, 65 n 14, 65 n 18, 67 n 26, 68 n 31, 68 n 36, 69 n 42; on Christian sins, 69; *Daniel Καὶ ἔσται* compared to, 84, 88–89; date of, 73; dog and whelp in, 63, 70; English translation of, 65–72; on Enoch and Elijah, 72, 213; on Gog and Magog, 186–87; Greek original of, 7, 63–64, 65 n 16, 67 n 25, 68 n 35, 69 n 42, 98; Greek pseudo-Methodius as source of, 63–64; historical section of, 65–67; on last emperor, 63,

64, 69–72, 103, 155, 161, 162, 163, 187; preamble of, 63; prophetic section of, 63, 67–72; as Pseudo-Chrysostom source, 72–73; Sicilian origin of, 7, 64; unclean peoples in, 63, 64, 71
Solomon of Basra, 15, 16n9, 21–22n7, 34
Son of Perdition. *See* Antichrist
Son(s) of Thunder, 5, 125, 215, 224
Sons of the North, 41
Syracuse (Rebel City), 64n12, 69, 72, 84, 85, 87, 109, 115, 116
Syria, 20, 34, 45, 52, 59, 75, 76, 105; Christianity in, 14, 16, 26, 27, 28, 29; as origin of Pseudo-Methodius, 14, 16, 26, 27, 30, 31–33
Syriac, Pseudo-Ephraem in, 140, 141, 142–47

Taormina, 109, 115, 116
Tarentum, 77, 111, 113
Tāseqtis, 41
Tebelie, 41
Temanŏn, 17, 26n37, 37
Tertullian, 183
Theophilus, 63, 64, 67n25, 74
Thracians, 18, 40, 41
Tigris River, 18, 27, 29, 38, 39
Time, shortened, 197, 198, 199, 209–10, 211, 219, 222, 223
Titus, 20, 43
Tubal-cain, 37

Unclean nations, 46, 47, 50; Alexander imprisons behind gate, 4, 19, 22, 41, 49, 89, 147, 186, 187, 189, 192, 219; *Daniel Καὶ ἔσται* on, 89; *Slavonic Daniel* on, 63, 64, 71; Syriac Pseudo-Methodius on, 40–41, 49–50. See also *Gentes*; Gog and Magog
Urbanos, 19, 42
ʿUthman, 24

Valentinian and Valens, 144, 145, 146
Vat. Barberini Lat. 671, 140, 142, 145
*Vaticinium ex eventu*, 3, 24, 84, 87, 94, 95, 145
Vespasian, 20, 43
*Vetus Latina*, 141
*Vision of Daniel Concerning the Last Time and Concerning the End of the World*. See *Daniel Καὶ ἔσται*
*Vision of the Prophet Daniel on the Emperors and the Last Days and on the End of the World*. See *Slavonic Daniel*
Visions of Daniel, 4, 7, 61–95, 159, 173; on Antichrist, 164, 199, 202, 220; date of, 158; on Enoch and Elijah, 213; extant texts of, 62–95; on Gog and Magog, 186; on last emperor, 152, 154, 155, 157, 160, 161; on lion-whelp oracle, 172; Liudprand saw, 97, 98, 99, 101, 104; on nonbiblical prophecies, 172; Pseudo-Methodius as source of, 14, 61, 133; as Sicilian, 7, 36, 64, 100. See also *Daniel Καὶ ἔσται*; *Last Daniel*; Pseudo-Chrysostom; *Slavonic Daniel*

Whelp. *See* Lion-whelp oracle
Woes. *See* Jesus Christ, three woes of

Year-week, defined, 86n30
Yenimevlevihanekapi Gate, 81–82
Yesdegerd I the Sinner, 146

Zalmunna, 39
Zapetra, 74
Zeeb, 39
Zezschwitz, Gerhard von, 2, 107
Zimri, 82, 83

| | |
|---|---|
| Compositor: | G&S Typesetters, Inc. |
| Text: | Linotron 202 Sabon |
| Display: | Typositor Garamond Old Style |
| Printer: | Braun-Brumfield, Inc. |
| Binder: | Braun-Brumfield, Inc. |

www.ingramcontent.com/pod-product-compliance
Lightning Source LLC
Chambersburg PA
CBHW021702230426
43668CB00008B/700